EUROPE'S LOST
CIVILIZATION

EUROPE'S LOST CIVILIZATION

Uncovering the Mysteries of the Megaliths

PETER MARSHALL

headline

Map of journey © 2004 Emily Gwynne-Jones
Line drawings © 2004 Valerie Baker

First published in 2004
by HEADLINE BOOK PUBLISHING

Peter Marshall would be happy to hear from readers with their comments
on the book at the following e-mail address: petermarshall7@beeb.net
His website is: www.petermarshall.net

10 9 8 7 6 5 4 3 2 1

Cataloguing in Publication Data is available from the British Library

ISBN 0 7472 4201 1

Typeset in Bembo by Avon DataSet Ltd, Bidford-on-Avon, Warwickshire

Printed and bound in Great Britain by Mackays of Chatham plc, Chatham, Kent

Headline's policy is to use papers that are natural, renewable and recyclable
products and made from wood grown in sustainable forests. The logging
and manufacturing processes are expected to conform to the
environmental regulations of the country of origin.

HEADLINE BOOK PUBLISHING
A division of Hodder Headline
338 Euston Road
London NW1 3BH

www.headline.co.uk
www.hodderheadline.com

For Emily and Dylan

Taking up the past
Steering into the future
Living in the present

CONTENTS

ACKNOWLEDGEMENTS

In a voyage of more than four thousand nautical miles from one end of Europe to another, I was assisted inevitably by countless people. I am particularly indebted to Jean-Claude Le Bretton, Martine and Raymond Burnaby, Geraldine Camilleri, Christine Campbell, Margaret and Ron Curtis, Colette Dubois, Thierry Dubois, Francesco Ferrara, Captain Michael Hadley, Frank Harris, David Lumby, Anton Mifsud, Hamish Miller, Olivier Pitroset and Michele Valverola.

My friends Peter Bernays, Gio Bloor, Graham Hancock, Dei Hughes, Anton Mifsud and Robin Waterfield have generously given me materials and offered me leads. Emily Gwynne-Jones drew the evocative map of my voyage.

The skilled staff of the following boatyards have all helped me sail over the ocean wave: Partingtons, Pwllheli, Wales; Dale Sailing, Milford Haven, Wales; Póvoa de Varzam, Portugal; Pedro's, Mahón, Menorca; and Manoel Island Marina, Malta. Fellow members of the Porthmadog Sailing Club and Weir Quay Sailing Club have kindly followed my maritime travels with interest.

For sections of the voyage, I was joined by Paul Green, David Lea, and my son Dylan; thank you, my shipmates, for being so reliable and obliging. Dylan and my daughter Emily, to whom the book is dedicated, also visited some of the sites with me; they continue to buoy me up with their exuberance and warmth.

I would like to thank my mother Vera and my brother Michael for supporting me in my endeavours. As the years go by, I appreciate their love all the more.

Above all, I would like to thank Elizabeth Ashton Hill who has been with me throughout this long journey both at sea and at home. Her loving and thoughtful presence has beautifully shown that a pleasure shared is a pleasure doubled. She not only took most of the photographs in the book but helped edit the draft version of the text.

Finally, I am greatly indebted to Heather Holden-Brown at Headline for boldly commissioning the book; Barbara Kiser for editing it so well; Valerie Baker for carefully drawing the diagrams; and Celia Kent for seeing it through to publication with such ease. My agent Bill Hamilton of A.M. Heath remains a fount of excellent advice.

Many thanks to you all.

Little Oaks, Devon
Winter solstice 2003

LIST OF ILLUSTRATIONS

Skara Brae settlement, Orkney (Peter Marshall)
Dwelling at Skara Brae (Peter Marshall)
Inner circle of Callanish stones, Isle of Lewis (Elizabeth Ashton Hill)
Entrance to chambered mound at Newgrange, Ireland (Peter Marshall)
Author by the Géant du Manio, Carnac, Brittany (Elizabeth Ashton Hill)
Stone row of the Kermario alignments, Carnac (Peter Marshall)
Chûn Quoit, Cornwall (Elizabeth Ashton Hill)
Dolmen de Axeitos, Oleiros, Galicia (Peter Marshall)
Dolmen de Fontanaccia, Cauria, Corsica (Peter Marshall)
Dolmen in the Bugibba temple, Malta (Peter Marshall)
Taula at Torralba d'en Salord sanctuary, Menorca (Elizabeth Ashton Hill)
La Naveta des Tudons, Menorca (Elizabeth Ashton Hill)
Statue-menhirs surrounding the central monument, Filitosa, Corsica (Elizabeth Ashton Hill)
Giants' tomb, Coddu Vecchiu, Arzachena, Sardinia (Elizabeth Ashton Hill)
Neolithic anchors, Archaeological Museum, Palermo, Sicily (Elizabeth Ashton Hill)
Split stone egg, Monte d'Accoddi, Porto Tórres, Sardinia (Elizabeth Ashton Hill)
Limestone altar from Hagar Qim temples, Malta (Elizabeth Ashton Hill)
'Sleeping Lady' taken from the Hypogeum, now in the Archaeology Museum, Valletta, Malta (Elizabeth Ashton Hill)
Author at the main entrance to the Hagar Qim temples, Malta (Elizabeth Ashton Hill)
Mnajdra temples, Malta (Elizabeth Ashton Hill)

MAPS AND DIAGRAMS

Old folk of Skara Brae,
A cold mist blows in from the sea
And your world fades away.
You listened to the pounding of the sea
And followed the flight of the birds.
You buried your dead under the floor
And talked to them in your dreams.
You built great monuments to the sky
And burrowed deep into the earth.
You slept with the cool moon
And rose with the fiery sun.
You knew how to enjoy life
And prepared calmly for death.
Old folk of Skara Brae,
A cold mist blows in from the sea
And your world fades away.

Peter Marshall

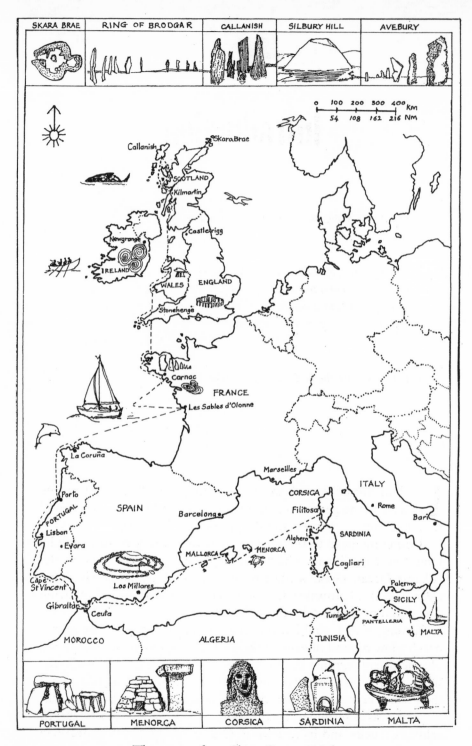

The voyage from Skara Brae to Malta

Introduction

The more we dig, the more the mystery appears to deepen.

WILLIAM HAWLEY

The mysteries of the megaliths will never be solved until they are approached from a more open perspective than the landlubber. They are a problem which will not be resolved until archaeology becomes as efficient on the sea as it is on land.

BOB QUINN

The stones are the bones of a lost world.

PETER MARSHALL

Looking into the rock pool, I watched the tentacles of purple sea anemone gently sway in the incoming tide. A tiny fish darted from a clump of seaweed and disappeared under a ledge.

Raising my head to the west, I could see across a narrow sound a long, low-lying island which was exposed to the full fury of the Atlantic Ocean. Great white blossoms of cloud moved slowly in the clear blue sky. Kittiwakes flew low across the swirling and eddying water, joining a raft of black guillemots.

Turning east, I could make out just beyond the bolder-strewn beach a low mound of stone walls and tufts of grass. Bent double, two old men were scything the grass which had not been cropped by the sheep and rabbits. They were fisher-farmers, their feet on the land and their hands in the sea. Their way of life, hardly changed for thousands of years, was determined by the moods of the sea: its storm and its calm, its cruelty and its generosity. Only recently had they obtained electricity to lighten the long winter months when the windswept and rain-drenched day only lasted for a few hours. They still organized their lives and work on a cooperative basis like their ancient ancestors before them.

I was on Papa Westray, the most northerly inhabited isle of Orkney in Scotland. It lies on the same latitude as Anchorage, Alaska. The pile of grass and stone at the water's edge was known as the Knap of Howar, the oldest standing dwelling in the north of Western Europe. It was built some 6000 years ago, long before the pyramids in Egypt.

When the first settlers came to Orkney – a cluster of sixty or so islands and rocky reefs, or skerries – they would have found a pleasant and fertile land at a time when most of Scotland was darkened by the great Caledonian forest. The skies would have been clearer, the seas calmer and the winters warmer – by at least 2 degrees Centigrade. They would probably have come in boats sewn from skins, crossing the notorious Pentland Firth with its fierce tides and currents from mainland Scotland, laden with livestock and seed.

What's left of their settlement is two interconnected oval houses. Half the site has already been lost to the encroaching sea. The larger house had a floor area of some 50 square metres, divided into four rooms. Large split flagstones were used to make partitions, cupboards, hearths and even a low stone bench. A post hole indicates that the dwelling was probably once covered by a wooden frame topped by turf, held down by weighted ropes made from twisted heather. A beautiful polished quern for grinding shows that the inhabitants grew crops – mainly barley and possibly some wheat – to supplement their diet of fish and meat. Sherds of pottery include those of fine decorated vessels intended for display.[1]

Sitting on the Neolithic stone bench and looking out to sea through one of the two entrances, I felt I could have lived very happily here.

On the beach below the Knap, I came across much driftwood brought by the Gulf Stream from North America, known locally as 'flesh-wood'. There was also the rotting corpse of a small whale being pecked by seagulls. It seems likely that the ancient dwellers would have used such wood and whale bones for fuel and building material. Only hazel, birch and alder grew on the island at the time.

The inhabitants of the Stone Age settlement probably buried their dead on Holm, an islet off the east side of Papa Westray. It has three mysterious cairns. An excavator who broke into the south cairn in 1849 noted that several of the stones in the central chamber were decorated with a variety of symbols – zigzags, inverted Vs, dots and arcs. When excavated by the Irish archaeologist George Petrie five years later, the cairn revealed human and deer bones. One stone, possibly carved by a Pict, still shows a motif of two sets of eyes and eyebrows, forever questioning the disrespect of the archaeologist who dared to disturb the dead.

A more recent excavation in 1984 turned up sherds of undecorated bowls, a few flint tools, and most intriguing of all, a small setting of stones containing a cache of thousands of tiny fish bones. In the end wall of the burial chamber, there was a blocked doorway which gave way to a little cell, about a metre across, with a corbelled stone roof. It was filled with earth and stone in alternating layers, one containing red deer antlers and limpet shells, another skulls of sheep, otters and humans. Clearly used in some elaborate ritual, the sacred objects of the shrine would have provided powerful magic to help the dead in their journey into the next life. Once completed, the entrance of the tomb was carefully blocked up and the whole encased in a cairn of stones. Its secrets had been left hidden for nearly 6000 years.[2]

The people who had landed on this tiny island on the edge of the world were the same people who raised the megaliths, the first stone architecture on this planet and the relics of Europe's lost civilization.

The mystery of the megaliths

Set in some of the wildest and most beautiful places in Europe, the megaliths – Greek for 'big stones' – were built between 5000 and 1000 BC. In recent times, they have become potent symbols of harmony, wisdom and healing for millions. There is something set deep in the modern sensibility which draws us, without knowing exactly why, to visit them each year. Stonehenge in England is as instantly recognizable as the Great Pyramid in Egypt. Yet the origins and meaning of the megaliths remain one of the world's greatest mysteries.

If we care to look, the remnants of this ancient civilization lie all around us. And whenever we pause near a great standing stone, a huge stone circle or a massive chamber, the questions inevitably come tumbling out. Who built them and what are they for? What light do they throw on our origins? What mysteries are encoded in their stones? Do they have any hidden message for our times?

It was with these questions in my mind that I set sail in search of the lost megalithic civilization of Europe. My boat was *Celtic Gold*, a 7-metre sloop that travelled at about 4 knots – the same length and speed of the ancient hide-sewn boats which probably once plied the waters along the Western Atlantic seaboard and into the Mediter-ranean.[3] My intention was to follow in the wake of ancient mariners from Scotland to Malta, gazing at the stars they saw and surveying the horizons they scanned. By travelling in a boat similar to theirs in size and speed, I hoped to demonstrate that the megalith builders were capable of such long-distance navigation.

I had another reason for starting in the north. I wanted to counteract the widespread view, embodied in the phrase *Ex Oriens lux* ('Light comes out of the East'), that civilization originated in the Middle East and gradually spread to the remote corners of northern Europe. I wanted to unveil a peaceful and sophisticated European civilization, mainly connected by the sea, which enjoyed a Golden Age long before the pyramids were raised in Giza. And by sailing from Scotland to Malta, I wanted to recover the lost wisdom of the megalith builders, who not only had a complex religion but were clearly masters of engineering, architecture, astronomy, navigation, science and art.

A map of the megaliths' distribution in Europe shows that their builders mainly settled and built their monuments on islands, along the coasts or up easily navigable rivers. With the interior then thickly wooded and full of ferocious animals, travelling by boat would have been the safest, easiest and quickest form of transport.[4] And with calmer waters and clearer skies during long periods of fine weather in megalithic times, the sea did not separate the scattered communities, as it does today, but united them.

The megaliths went up when humans first settled down. Their building coincided with the momentous shift from nomadic hunter-gathering to farming crops and herding animals. This was not only one of the greatest revolutions in human evolution, but also resulted in a great surge in population. For the first time, there was a surplus of food, and sufficient leisure to enable people to engage in great collective works of building and engineering, art and architecture. It was one of those rare periods in history, as in ancient Egypt and classical Greece, when architectural knowledge, technical engineering, spiritual illumination and the energy of thousands came together in a wonderful explosion of creativity. Far from being the Stone Age savages of popular imagination, the builders of the megaliths were clearly intelligent and resourceful people with a deep vision and a rich social life.

Where did their civilization first emerge? Their prime area of activity ran along the Atlantic seaboard, especially in Britain, Ireland, France, Spain and Portugal, where people first settled. In northwestern France and western Iberia the practice of building houses of wood or stone for the dead, enclosed in an earth mound, began around 4500 BC but soon appeared all along the Atlantic seaboard. Each region went on to develop its own methods, but they tended to be variations on a common theme. And the practice travelled further – into the Mediterranean, and east to the northern Germanic and Baltic regions.

In the Mediterranean the picture was more complex. A local tradition seems to have developed early in Malta, which has the oldest stone temple building in Europe dating from around 4000 BC. In the central Mediterranean, a common culture of stone settlements and communal graves later developed in Sicily, Sardinia, Corsica and the Balearic Islands. By the second millennium this Neolithic culture evolved, no doubt with influences drawn from Egypt and Mesopotamia, into the Bronze Age palace civilizations of Minoan Crete and Mycenaean Greece.

The tradition of megalith building is not, however, unique to Europe. It extends across the globe, from the stone settlements of East Africa, the dolmens of Korea, the mounds of Polynesia and the statues of Easter Island, to the diverse cultures of the Americas, especially the Mayan and Aztec. Although they were built at different times over a period of 5000 years, what is extraordinary is that all these great stone structures share a similar range of forms and techniques. They not only embody a strict sense of geometry, but are aligned also to the movement of celestial bodies. Rooted firmly in the earth, they reach for the heavens.

It would seem that there is something deep within our psyche driving us to build enduring monuments in order to express our universal social and spiritual aspirations. Born to die in an uncertain world, we have all yearned from the earliest times for permanence and immortality. And what better way is there to express this yearning than to raise great stones to the sky?

The megaliths are not just for the dead but for the living. They stand out like enigmatic sculptures on the historical horizon, forever illuminated by the sun and the moon, their meaning waiting to be revealed.

CHAPTER ONE

Orcadian Light

The Orkney imagination is haunted by time.

GEORGE MACKAY BROWN

I left Papa Westray and set sail for Orkney's main island – somewhat confusingly known as 'the Mainland' – intent on exploring a larger and later megalithic settlement at Skara Brae. Nowhere else in the British Isles is there such a wealth of evidence evoking the way of life of our remote ancestors. Built and inhabited from around 3100 to 2500 BC, it is the best preserved prehistoric village in northern Europe and now a World Heritage Site. It is also one of the first examples of 'town planning' that actually worked.

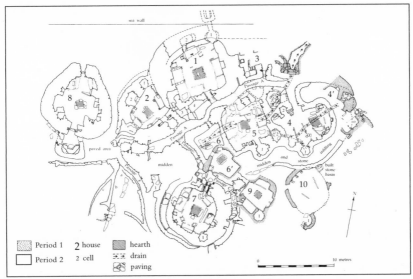

Ground plan of Skara Brae, Orkney

In the winter of 1850 a wild storm stripped the grass from the high dune known as Skara Brae in a sandy bay on the west coast of the Mainland. What was revealed was a huge, ancient refuse heap or midden within which were the ruins of dwellings. When I visited the site on the wild and windswept shore in the luminous light of midsummer, I was astounded to discover a well-excavated site containing a cluster of ten semi-subterranean houses with corbelled roofs, connected by a main passage.[1] While the corridors were covered with stone slabs and material from the midden, the houses themselves probably had turf roofs. The settlement I was able to explore belonged to a second and later phase of development. The inhabitants had used the midden of their ancestors, consisting of ash, shells and broken bones mixed with sand and welded together like clay, to line the stone walls and to cover the corridors of their houses. Having lived among stone walls in Snowdonia, North Wales, for twenty years, I appreciated fully the skilful harmony of hand and eye achieved in their building.

Like the ones I had seen on Papa Westray, the rooms contained cupboards and storage spaces in the walls, large dressers, seats and even box beds made from split stone. In the earlier houses, the beds were set within the walls rather than projecting from them. In one house, I noted by the square hearth a small clay-lined tank probably used to keep fresh shellfish or bait. Thousands of years before the Romans, the dwellers of this Stone Age village built channels for sanitation in one cell of each house.

'It's cosy. You can see how snug they must have been!' an old Texan said to me, pulling up his collar against the freshening onshore wind. I for one would like to have warmed my hands by one of their homely hearths.

Neolithic anarchy

The historian Euan MacKie has suggested that Skara Brae was no peasant village, but a 'palatial structure' housing wise men engaged in astronomical and magical work at the megalithic monuments on the island.[2] To me this seems far-fetched. While there were undoubtedly individuals engaged in such activities, the discovery of similar Neolithic villages at Papa Westray and at other sites in Orkney suggests that Skara Brae was no exception. The fact that the houses do not vary greatly in layout or size implies that it was a community of equals. And while the houses are for family units and offer a degree of privacy, they are all interconnected, suggesting a communal way of life.

Although it is difficult in our own hierarchical society to imagine a society without leaders, according to archaeologists David Clarke and Patrick Maguire, leadership was 'neither hereditary nor all-embracing' at the time.[3] Because of special skills in fishing, farming and navigation, some individuals were probably listened to more than others, but this does not mean that they necessarily 'led' or had coercive power over others. They worked and lived together and probably solved their disputes through discussion and debate rather than appealing to some abstract law. In such a close-knit society, their aim would have been to restore social harmony, not to punish wrongdoers.

The Stone Age inhabitants of Orkney would seem to have lived a life of anarchy. I mean this not in the popular sense of chaos, but in the positive sense of an ordered and self-managing society without leaders. It is a far cry from the image of the savage Stone Age man who hits a woman with his club and drags her into a cave to take his pleasure. The early inhabitants of Orkney were clearly no Flintstones.

While it is difficult to be certain of the exact status of women in this culture, they participated fully in everyday life, lived well and had a sense of beauty. They wore jewellery and probably painted their bodies in red, yellow and blue pigments (dishes with remains of such paints have been found among the ruins). They used a variety of flat-bottomed pots known as Grooved Ware, which ranged from small thumb pots to large storage jars, often decorated with abstract geometric patterns. Similar ware has been found in Ireland, southern England and up the river Tagus in Portugal, implying long-distance trading links.

There is no reason to believe that the people of Skara Brae looked any different from today's Orcadians, except that they were possibly a couple of centimetres shorter and could not expect to live much beyond forty. And even in the Stone Age community, past and present merged. In one house, I was intrigued to discover, the skeletons of two women have been found partly behind one of the stone beds. They clearly believed in sleeping close to their ancestors. By building their houses in the midden of the old folk, they also kept in close touch with their spirits.

Like their descendants, these ancient Orcadians were fisher-farmers. The lochs and sea would have been teeming with fish. With their dug-out canoes and skin boats, they hunted seals and caught ling, cod and saithe. They collected shellfish, especially oysters, limpets, scallops, whelks and razor-shells. Launching the boats which had brought them to the islands in the first place, they could brave the swell of the Atlantic and beach passing whales, as they still do in the Faroes.

Like their nomadic ancestors, they hunted deer, wild boar and birds and gathered wild plants, berries, herbs, fruits and nuts. They kept domestic cattle, a few pigs, sheep or goats. Using a light plough called an ard and a harrow, they grew barley and to a lesser extent, wheat. They brewed beer, apparently flavoured with traces of animal droppings.

They fashioned objects from bone, particularly pins and pendants. Some tools were made from the local chert and a few were fashioned from small flint pebbles thrown up on the beach. Many strange grenade-shaped stones with linear decoration – sometimes called maces – have been found in the houses. These probably had ritual and magical purposes. Some stone slabs in the houses have also abstract carvings with geometrical patterns, mainly of diamonds within squares, which were no doubt thought to have some special power to protect the inhabitants.

The village at Skara Brae consisted of about twenty families who would have been able to satisfy their basic needs. Although virtually self-sufficient, they would inevitably have had relations with other villages to arrange partners and exchange goods as well as to engage in collective rituals and ceremonies. While each village had a collective tomb for their ancestors, it is almost certain that they cooperated with other villages to build the huge stone chambers and circles on the island.

The rebirth of the year

The most amazing chamber in Orkney is at Maes Howe on the Mainland, about 12 kilometres from Skara Brae near the stone circles of Brodgar and Stenness. When I walked over the hills and along the shores of the inland lochs, I watched the cows and sheep grazing in stone-walled fields hard won from the moorland. In prehistoric times, the landscape would have been different only in detail, with perhaps more areas of rough grazing, heather and poorly drained land with stunted willows and alder bushes.

Maes Howe is not only the finest chambered mound in north-western Europe. It is also one of the finest examples of prehistoric architecture anywhere. At first sight it looks like a small circular hill in a flat landscape. But hidden inside this 7-metre-high 'hill' – a man made casing of earth, clay and stone covered in grass – is a stone chamber of stunning workmanship.

As soon as I entered the long, low passage leading to its inner chamber, I was overwhelmed by the precision of the construction. No mortar was used, and some of the slabs fit so well together that it is impossible to insert a knife between them. Built around 3000 BC from local sandstone, some of the slabs weigh up to 30 tonnes. The 9-metre passage slopes gently up to the inner chamber, which is about 4.6 metres square. There are side chambers opposite the entrance and on either side, forming a rough cross. Originally, the whole was covered by a corbelled roof with a huge central capstone.[4]

I noticed on the southern corner pillar of the main chamber an engraving similar to the ones I had seen at Skara Brae. As I was to find out later in my journey, such drawings are not limited to Orkney, but are found all down the Western Atlantic seaboard. They confirmed my thesis that there was at that time a common culture and religion linked by the sea.

I was even more fascinated to discover that the chamber at Maes Howe was exactly orientated to the point where the sun set on the winter solstice. The sun shines directly into the inner chamber for forty days on either side of the shortest day of the year. As I sat in the cool darkness of the chamber, I let my mind wander. Could there be a possible link with the forty days during which the North American Indians exposed their dead in order to lose their flesh and free their spirit? Since partial bones as well as full skeletons have been discovered in megalithic tombs, it would seem that Neolithic people practised 'excarnation', the exposure of the dead to the elements and natural scavengers, before burying selected bones in a second rite.[5] But on second thoughts, it seemed highly unlikely that there was any direct link apart from the fact that forty days was an adequate amount of time for the flesh to rot from a skeleton.

The midwinter solstice marks the death and rebirth of the year, and the event is celebrated throughout the world. I can imagine the people of the island gathered together after a night and day of drumming and dance to witness the last rays of the setting sun penetrate the passage to shine into the womb-like chamber of the inner mound – a cosmic union of Father Sun and Mother Earth. On the shortest day of the year, which lasts for only a few hours in such northerly latitudes, their rites would ensure that the sun would begin its slow return journey northwards to banish the darkness and once again bring fertility to the land.

In 1894 a local schoolmaster, Magnus Spence, made some interest-ing observations about the possible alignments between Maes Howe and other megaliths in the surrounding landscape. He realized that the passageway was orientated in a line running through a tall menhir or standing stone at Barnhouse, which is visible from the entrance. This stone, together with the menhir, the Watchstone, and the centre of the nearby stone circle known as the Ring of Brodgar, were aligned to the axis of the setting sun on the winter solstice.

At the end of the century, fires were still lit on certain hilltops on the island to celebrate the traditional Celtic festivals, especially on the equinoxes and solstices. Spence further observed that some of these features marked the rising and setting of the sun along the alignments between the stones. He concluded that the annual movement of the sun was thus encoded in the landscape.[6]

Maes Howe was clearly more than a tomb for the dead. It seems closer to being a sacred place for the living. The fact that the pivoted stone slab at the entrance to the mound was designed to be closed from the inside confirmed this for me. No human skeletons have been found in the mound, although many archaeologists still insist on calling it a tomb and refuse to speculate about its possible use.[7] When George Petrie broke into the chamber in 1861, he found only tiny fragments of a human skull and some horse bones and teeth. Other tombs in Orkney, as I had seen at Holm by Papa Westray, contained animal bones and pottery which suggest that they were sacred objects offered to the ancestors and gods.

> Mounds of Mother Earth
> Hide the secrets of thy womb darkness.

Before I left Maes Howe, I noted some intriguing runes carved on the stones of the inner chamber. It seems that they were inscribed by Vikings who broke into the mound through the roof in the mid-twelfth century. One reads on the southeastern side: 'These runes were carved by the man most skilled in runes in the Western Ocean.' Others record that gold had been taken earlier from the mound. Incongruously, given the chamber's purpose, a Norse seafarer had written, 'Ingigerth is the most beautiful woman' next to the drawing of a slavering dog. 'Thorni bedded, Helgi carved,' we are also informed. It is a display revealing a serious decline from the high endeavour and spiritual vision of Stone Age times. But the Viking intruders did leave one beautiful emblem on the walls: a lion, a walrus and a knotted serpent, a masterpiece of Nordic art, which is sometimes interpreted to be a dragon.

The Temple of the Moon

The same people who worshipped at Maes Howe and lived at Skara Brae built several other great ceremonial monuments on the island. More then 2 kilometres from Maes Howe you can behold one of the greatest concentrations of big megaliths anywhere in Europe. They are set in a stunningly beautiful landscape between two lochs open to the sea, and are visible from the hills a long way off. The builders knew exactly what they were doing when they chose the site.

When I first approached the great dark slab stones at Stenness, they were looming out of a thick sea mist. All that remains of the original circle are four massive standing stones, the tallest reaching 5 metres. Built between 3100 and 2700 BC, the original twelve stones of the circle are estimated to have taken some 150,000 man hours to raise within their henge, which consists of a rock-cut ditch and outer bank. In Britain, only Stonehenge exceeds their height. The holes made for the stones reveal that the circle originally formed an ellipse, 30 metres in diameter, pointing about 20 degrees west of north. At first a wooden post had been set up in the centre which was later replaced by a roughly 2-metre square setting of stone slabs. The original circle had a single entrance causeway.

The use of the site is broadly contemporary with Skara Brae and shows that the community had sufficient wealth and leisure to engage in monumental works of architecture and engineering. Sherds of the same Grooved Ware pottery used at Skara Brae have been found in the ditch and in the central stone setting. Through their use of Grooved Ware, the Orkney islanders can be linked to the builders of the other great ceremonial monuments of late Neolithic Britain.

According to the eighteenth-century historian Dr Robert Henry, the stones at Stenness were known as the Temple of the Moon and the nearby Ring of Brodgar, the Temple of the Sun. Each New Year's Day, the local people met at Stenness church and danced and feasted for several days. If a man and woman fell in love, they went first to the Temple of the Moon, 'where the woman, in presence of the man, fell down on her knees and prayed to the god Wodden [Woden] . . . that he would enable her to perform all the promises and obligations she had [made] . . . to the young man present, after which they both went to the Temple of the Sun, where the man prayed in like manner before the woman.'[8] They then clasped hands through the hole in the so-called 'Odin Stone', the most dramatic of the Stenness ring, and swore to be true. Woden was the foremost Anglo-Saxon god, the counterpart of the Norse Odin.

Another story tells of a Viking who, for nine months when the moon was full, crawled nine times at midnight on his bare knees around the Odin Stone and then looked through its hole in the hope of glimpsing the future. The number nine is significant, for nine years is roughly half the time it takes for the moon to complete its journey from the north to the south, from its major to minor risings and settings. This knowledge may well have been enacted in ceremonies and dances around the stones.[9] The Odin Stone has since been destroyed, no doubt in an attempt to wipe out pagan ways.

In this picturesque account, we see a dim echo of the original rites which may have taken place on the site, even after the introduction of the Viking gods. The four stones at Stenness certainly look more phallic than the Ring of Brodgar, of which the roundness was much more feminine.

The Temple of the Sun

As I approached the Ring of Brodgar (sometimes called Brogar) the sea mist suddenly lifted and the stones appeared for a second or two like figures slowly dancing in a circle among the heather. They are situated on a slope above a low-lying neck of land between the lochs of Harray and Stenness; I could hear the waves lapping on the shore, where razorbills and oystercatchers paddled in the receding tide.

I walked around the circle in a clockwise direction, with my right side to the stones, following an ancient Indian tradition that you should always walk around a temple with your purest side – the right side – turned towards the sacred monument. In Britain, to move around a circle in the apparent direction of the sun – clockwise – was also considered to be the right way. Circle dances invariably move in this direction and I felt sure that the celebrants going around the Ring of Brodgar would have done the same. To go against the apparent course of the sun – known before the invention of clocks as withershins or widdershins – was long considered to be unlucky and to court disaster.

As I walked slowly around the perfect circle, I noted that it was surrounded by a rock-cut ditch, now partially filled, which had originally been 3 metres deep and 9 metres wide. There were two wide causeways forming entrances in the southeast and northwest, aligned with the rising of the sun on the summer solstice and the setting of the sun on the winter solstice. Two stone pillars about 4 metres tall soared at cardinal points, at the south and the west. The whole circle could have comfortably accommodated some 3000 men and women. The overall impression of this true stone circle set among a ring of low hills under the great arching sky was one of perfect harmony.

I counted and touched twenty-nine megaliths still standing of the original sixty. One had been recently split by lightning. They were covered with beautiful lichens all in different shades of grey, light green and yellow. Having circled the ring, I cut directly to the centre, pacing out just over fifty metres. A small stone rose in the middle which during my midsummer visit was encircled by a curious 'fairy ring' of dead grass in a sea of purple heather.

Built and used in the late Neolithic and early Bronze Ages, the Ring of Brodgar is certainly one of the greatest megalithic sites in Europe. The engineering feat was even greater than at Stenness: the sixty huge stones were raised in an exact circle on uneven ground with astounding accuracy. It has been estimated that 80,000 hours of labour would have been required to move the 12,000 tonnes of rock. The joint energy of at least fifty men would have been necessary to raise the largest stones.

That is not all. Professor Alexander Thom, who more than any other demonstrated the importance of astronomy in understanding the meaning of the megaliths, maintained that the Ring of Brodgar was laid out according to a common unit of measurement which he called a 'megalithic yard' (0.829 metres). He calculated that Brodgar was a true circle with a diameter of 125 megalithic yards. He further concluded that the builders were using subtle geometric forms with 'Pythagorean' right-angled triangles of whole numbers, two millennia before Pythagoras drew them up. Mathematically, the computation has been called 'immaculate'.[10]

The stone circles were undoubtedly sacred enclosures. As temples, they marked out a sacred time and a sacred place – aspects embodied in the meaning of the French word *temps* and the English word 'template'.[11] According to archaeologist Marija Gimbutas, rituals of regeneration probably took place within the Ring of Brodgar through energetic ring dances, drawing on the power of the Great Goddess embodied in the stones.[12]

In addition, the circle almost certainly functioned as an astronomical observatory, recording the movements of the moon as well as the sun. Thom in particular thought the site had been selected because of its natural foresights to provide a perfect platform to watch the setting moon.[13] At this northern latitude, the moon skims barely above the horizon during its major 'standstill' every 18.61 years, when it reaches a certain height in the sky and stays there for three years. An interest in the phases of the moon would come naturally to a seafaring folk aware of the fierce tides around their islands and to farmers who traditionally marked the passage of time by the lunar month. Some local island shepherds still put their rams out to their sheep during the last full moon in November, believing that the ewes at this 'tup' are most fertile.

The ancient Orcadians may well have shared their astronomical knowledge with astronomers in southern England. The site was used until around 1500 BC, when a change in the weather swept in heavy rain and obscured the night skies. As the scientists and celebrants left, the peat moved in.

Circle within a circle

There is an enigmatic outlying stone on a small circular platform to the southeast of the Ring of Brodgar. Called the Comet Stone, it is thought to have been used for tracking heavenly bodies. I found it perfect for leaning against and contemplating the great stone circle which seemed to come and go in the sea mist at the top of the gentle rise. I could hear the waves gently breaking on the loch shore and the cool wind playing in the long grass. It was the end of the day and no one was there. I had taken a sprig of heather from the centre of the ring to take back to the boat. Sitting against the stone, its warm energy seemed to rise up my spine and lighten my head. I wrote in my notebook:

> The circumference and the centre
> The fire at the centre of the hearth
> The sun at the centre of the heavens
> The moon waxing and waning
> The tide flooding and ebbing
> The people living and dying
> The circumference and the centre.

I wondered why the megalith builders had a preference for circles even though they had not invented the wheel. The question has long puzzled historians and archaeologists. I suspect that a stone circle is a symbol of inner harmony, an archetype shared by all nations and cultures. In ancient Egypt, the Ouroboros, the snake swallowing its own tail, is a symbol of rebirth. In the Hermetic tradition of alchemy, a circle with a dot at its centre is a symbol of gold, perfection and eternity.[14] And in the dance of the so-called 'whirling' dervishes, the adept finds a stillness at the centre of the moving circle.

The circle has long been thought to have magical power. In ancient Sumer, priests chanted prayers to create a protective circle around them. Medieval magicians in Europe stood inside a circle inscribed on the ground. Even today, conjurors are elected to be members of the Magic Circle. The circle creates a protected, sacred space.

At a more physical level, the sun always appears as a more or less circular object to the person on earth. Only during eclipses – and no doubt that is why they were so feared – does it appear incomplete for a while. The stars 'turn' in a circle around the pole star. If one stands at the centre of a flat area of land or sits in a boat out at sea, the horizon forms a circle all around. If one drops a pebble into water, it creates widening concentric ripples. The most impressive plants in nature – trees – have inner rings and circular trunks. Glades that occur in forests are naturally round. The circle is to be found everywhere in our minds and in nature, on land and at sea, on earth and in heaven. It is a microcosm of the macrocosm. Small wonder that when early peoples wanted to build a house or a temple, they chose the circle. And when they danced together, they went round in a circle.

I mulled these things over for a long time as I sat by the Comet Stone. Just before I left, the distant stones of Brodgar seemed to glow until I lost them, forever dancing, forever still, in the midsummer twilight. I left with the waves of the loch still quietly lapping on the shore.

The old order and the new

It has recently been suggested that a new order emerged on Orkney at the time the Ring of Brodgar was built, and that emerging leaders exerted growing religious and political power over the rest of the community.[15] But this would seem to be yet another example of archaeologists projecting back into Stone Age society assumptions about hierarchy and domination based on those in their own society. There is no reason to believe that the leaders who helped organize the larger building projects became coercive rulers and lawmakers. Very few finds of pottery of the warlike Beaker people who invaded southern Britain around 2000 BC have been found in Orkney. And so it is likely that the builders of Brodgar were not newcomers, but descendants of those who constructed the circle of Stenness and who disposed of the bones of their dead in special ceremonies at neighbouring Maes Howe.

At the same time, it does seem likely that a group of scholars versed in astronomy and mathematics were supported voluntarily by the wider community. Without written records, they would have had to remember the accumulated history and wisdom of the clan and perhaps act as priests during the rituals and ceremonies. But again it does not mean that they had temporal power over the rest of the community, or crystallized into an elite. Certainly, no warrior class had yet evolved: none of the sites were defended. Any disputes which arose were no doubt resolved peacefully as before.

It was during the Bronze Age (circa 2100–650 BC) that a ruling elite of warlike chieftains emerged on Orkney. It was during that period that the circle of Stenness was abandoned. New developments in the last phase of the nearby Barnhouse settlement may indicate some of the social changes which took place.

The female circle was replaced by the male square. A large, square building with a controlled entrance was erected, and this may suggest that a hierarchy of men had developed into a priestly cult.

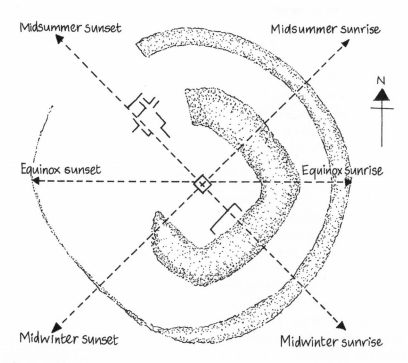

The central hearth at Barnhouse, Orkney, showing its alignment with the solstices and equinoxes

Worship of the sun, associated with a male god, may also have replaced the worship of the moon, associated with a Mother Goddess. The houses at Barnhouse were orientated so that the range between the points of sunrise and sunset at the midwinter and summer solstices was exactly 90 degrees. It would seem more than a coincidence, for the four extremes of the solar cycle intersecting exactly at right angles only occurs at this latitude. The phenomenon was marked by the positions of the hearths in the centre of each house. One house was even aligned so that for one hour on the morning of midwinter, a direct beam of sunlight would enter the doorway and illuminate a stone slab next to the fireplace covering a cist or pit which probably once contained the bones of ancestors.

As the communal bonds began to weaken, the young people of this time moved to live in separate houses. The shift towards individualism was further marked by a move from communal to single burials, sometimes accompanied by rich collections of grave goods, no doubt owned by powerful and wealthy chiefs. During the Iron Age which followed, the increasing social conflict led to the building of huge round stone towers known as brochs on the islands of Orkney and in northern Scotland.

Ex Orkney lux

The sites at Skara Brae and Maes Howe were excavated by Vere Gordon Childe in the 1920s who was so impressed by the life and works of the Neolithic Orcadians that he claimed that they must have migrated from the Middle East via the Iberian peninsula.[16] He shared the predominant world view of an earlier generation of classically minded archaeologists that civilization must have first evolved in the Middle East: in Sumer, Egypt and Greece.

However, the revolutionary technique developed in the 1950s, carbon-dating, showed that the megalithic civilization in northern Europe developed well before the Middle Eastern civilizations – by some 2000 years. There can be little doubt that the megalith builders of Orkney were part of a sophisticated indigenous civilization which had long-distance contacts as far south as the Mediterranean. It is no longer a case of *Ex Oriens lux*, but rather *Ex Orkney lux*: out of Orkney, not the East, comes light.

CHAPTER TWO

The Long Journey

Iron and corn first civilized men, and ruined humanity.

JEAN-JACQUES ROUSSEAU

I left Orkney the way I had come – by ferry, in a cold sea mist on a windy day across the notorious tides of the narrow Pentland Firth. A huge tanker had been caught in the tidal race not long before and ended up on the rocks: how would the first inhabitants with their animals in light skin boats have fared? But they managed it, as otherwise Orkney would never have been settled.

I travelled along the Caledonian canal to Oban, on the north-western coast of Scotland. I had left *Celtic Gold* there because of the gales sweeping in across the Atlantic, which had prevented me from making the crossing to Orkney. It rained and blew all the way, and there was still snow in midsummer on the mountain peaks.

During my return, I mulled over the chronology of the distant past in order to place the sites I had seen in Orkney in the perspective of our known origins. I wanted to come to terms with the broad sweep of prehistory that preceded the megalithic era.

Many years before I had visited Olduvai Gorge in the highlands of Tanzania, where the remains of our remote ancestors had been discovered, dating from more than 2 million years ago. Nearby, in Laetoli, are the first recognizably human footprints: those of a mother and child, set in solidified volcanic ash 3.6 million years old. Since then even older remains have been found in West Africa, confirming that the human race first evolved on the continent and then spread out to populate the world.

During those lost years of evolution, our ancestors, as hunter-gatherers, had little impact on the planet. A great change came when they first began to control their environment by using fire. In Europe our direct ancestors, the Cro-Magnons, replaced or absorbed the fire-using Neanderthals about 40,000 years ago. Fully modern humans (*Homo sapiens sapiens*) emerged about 7000 years later, already using finely crafted tools and jewellery. They buried their dead with ceremony and had a strong sense of the sacred and beautiful. As demonstrated by the delicate cave paintings in France, at Chauvet (dating to more than 30,000 years ago) and Lascaux (dating to about 17,000 years ago), our ancestors had already developed a high level of artistic ability and a rich spiritual life. Their art suggests that they valued animals, especially cattle and deer, as partners in their own right beyond their role as providers of meat, bone and leather.

At Chauvet, there is a drawing in black of a shamanistic figure, half human and half bison, showing how magic and religion had become part of everyday life. A bone found in the Grotte du Taï recording lunar observations from around 9000 BC reflects their scientific knowledge. They studied the world around them and marvelled at what they saw, both in heaven and on earth.

The final retreat of the ice sheets at the end of the Ice Age, around 9000 BC, made it possible for humans to venture into northern Europe. They came principally by sea and explored along the rivers. Conditions for life gradually improved in the Boreal Period (7000–6000 BC), when the weather was dry but still very cold, rather like in the steppes today. Oaks and hazel took root. Around 6500 BC, global warming led to a phenomenal rise in sea level – more than 30 metres – and the land bridge linking Ireland and Britain to the European landmass was broken. The warm waters of the Atlantic flooded into the North Sea.

Meanwhile, in the 'fertile crescent' in the Middle East, cereals such as emmer wheat and barley were brought under cultivation around 7000 BC. After millions of years of nomadic life as hunter-gatherers, people began settling down to become farmers, a momentous event in human evolution which had enormous cultural implications. The agricultural revolution gradually spread out throughout Europe: farming reached Palestine around 6500 BC and appeared in Egypt and Malta about 1500 years later. Brought by boat, it reached northern Europe soon after. With the increased food supply, there was a considerable increase in population: not only was there a low level of fertility among hunter-gatherers (if contemporary groups are anything to go by), but the new settled way of life gave a positive economic value to a large number of children. It has been estimated that in this transitional period, there was a hundredfold increase in population as a result of the increasing birth rate and declining death rate.[1]

This new breed of farmers, who grew crops and reared stock, built the great megaliths. From an ecological point of view, our downfall began when our ancestors first became pastoralists, for it was then that they began to have greater control over nature. But agriculturalists had less impact and developed a different attitude to nature.

These sowers of grain not only cooperated with each other, but also with the forces of nature. They had to be aware of the seasons and the subtle rhythms of nature in order to have a good harvest. They needed to develop rituals and ceremonies to ensure the future fertility of the soil and the continued action of the sun and the rain. A good farmer is a steward who has to coax his seeds into life, just as a hunter needs to husband his prey by watching population levels and understanding their ways. So the first farmers continued a relationship with the land based on respect which their hunting forebears had already developed.

The transition to agriculture was a gradual process. Nomadic hunter-gatherers continued to exist alongside the farmers, while the farmers themselves hunted and gathered. The settlers who came to Orkney in the middle of the fourth millennium BC were both farmers and sailors, hunters and gatherers. Inevitably, some of these settlers periodically went on 'walkabout', keeping the old tracks open and maintaining contact between the scattered communities. Seafarers in particular continued the old roving life. I suspect that after the great settlement they built the megaliths and buried their dead under them partly to ensure the fertility of the land and partly out of a sense of guilt for having forsaken the old nomadic ways which had lasted for millions of years.

The megalith builders were united by shared beliefs and ideals and continued to uphold the values of cooperation and solidarity. They reaffirmed a sense of community through gatherings, gift exchanges and the sharing of food and drink at certain key moments in the year.

When they began to settle down it was in places already made special by tradition and memory. But while there was continuity with the old way of life, there was also a sense of a new beginning. Time, previously seen as cyclical like the seasons, entered their lives as a linear development. Whereas they had lived in a timeless world based on repetition from generation to generation, by occupying one place their sense of passing time inevitably grew stronger. And it was felt necessary to honour the dead to ensure the well-being of the living, to remember the past in order to plan for the future.

This Golden Age of peace, stability and relative plenty lasted until the invasion from the East of warlike people carrying bronze weapons at the end of the third millennium BC. The megaliths could only have been built by a society based on cooperation. The monuments were left undefended and the weapons found in their vicinity could only have been used for hunting and not fighting. The peaceful people who built them were organized into clans and tribes and separated by natural boundaries, such as swamps, mountains, and forests. They lived mainly in these various regions along the coasts and up river valleys, but kept in constant contact with each other via the sea.

It seems likely that men and women lived on fairly equal terms in megalithic times. The earliest cave paintings show how both sexes were considered important. Relationships between them were probably loose and easily dissolved. In the circumstances, the mother was probably the only definite parent and the bloodline would be traced through the females of the clan. The position of women in these matrilineal societies must have been reinforced by the real and symbolic link between women, fertility and the moon.

The sacred was at the centre of the lives of the megalithic builders. They worshipped the Great Goddess, the most widespread form of ancient religion, who, in the form of Mother Earth, was revered as the giver and taker of all life. Their dead ancestors were living presences. Their cave paintings, rock art and stone monuments suggest that they experienced themselves, along with every other living being, as an intricate part of nature's web. They were immersed in a sea of energies like fish in water. And it was undoubtedly their common spiritual beliefs which enabled them to participate in the collective surges of labour that raised the great stones to the sky.

Their thinking was fundamentally cosmological. They studied the movements of planets and stars and felt the need to be in harmony with them. They had a direct comprehension of nature. They were aware of the subtle vibrations and rhythms of the earth and sensitive to the invisible field of energy linking all beings and things. And when they built the megalithic monuments, they no doubt felt that right thoughts were essential to right actions, and that their own energy would remain an integral part of any building as long as it stood.

The great ages of humanity

The great span of prehistory out of which the megalithic age emerged has been classified by archaeologists and historians into three main periods: the Palaeolithic, Mesolithic and Neolithic. The divisions, however, are not rigid: they not only overlap but the chronology is constantly under revision. Traditionally, the Palaeolithic (usually divided in to the African Lower Palaeolithic, Lower, Middle and Upper Palaeolithic) runs from about 2.5 million years ago to about 10,000 BC. It marks the time when humans first emerged as hunter-gatherers using chipped stone tools. The Mesolithic lasted from about 10,000 to 4000 BC and was characterised by the appearance of small flint tools known as microliths.

During the Neolithic, from 4000 to 2400 BC, the first farmers emerged, wielding polished stone and flint tools. This period has also been variously called the age of ancestors, of astronomy and of sacred landscapes.[2]

The times of the principal events in prehistory are given in the table below. All the dates are approximate, however; the periods overlap and are continually being refined.

Date BC	Periods	Date BC	Peoples and events
2.5 m	African Lower Palaeolithic	2.3 m	Homo habilis
		1 m	Homo erectus leaves Africa
800,000	Lower Palaeolithic		
		500,000	Homo sapiens
250,000	Middle Palaeolithic		
		100,000	Neanderthals in Europe
40,000	Upper Palaeolithic	40,000	Cro-Magnons
		17,000	Cave art, Lascaux, France
10,000	Mesolithic		
		9000	Ice Age ends in Europe
		6500	English Channel appears
		4500	Farming reaches Europe Megaliths in France and Iberia
4000	Early Neolithic	4000	Henges in Britain Settlements in Orkney Alignments at Carnac
		3600	Temples in Malta
3400	Middle Neolithic		
		3200	Stonehenge begins
		3000	Minoan culture in Crete
2800	Late Neolithic		

2500	Copper Age	2300	Beaker people in Europe
2100	Bronze Age		
		2000	Statue menhirs in Corsica
		1400	Mycenaean culture in Greece
			Talayots in Menorca
650	Iron Age		
		600	Celts in Europe

The age of the megaliths, which first begins around 4500 BC in western Europe, overlaps the Late Mesolithic, the Neolithic, and the Early Bronze Age. The Copper Age (also known as the Chalcolithic) refers to the period when stone and copper instruments were used, from about 2500 to 2100 BC. Copper metallurgy was probably a local development which took place some time after 3000 BC but it was not until after 2500 BC that it was discovered that tin could be mixed with copper to produce the much harder metal bronze – hard enough to make formidable weapons.[3]

With the discovery of bronze and the invasion of warlike people into Europe from the East at the end of the third millennium, a period of conflict and uncertainty developed. As an emblem of the age, the bronze dagger, symbol of war, replaced the stone axe, symbol of peace.

At this time, northern Europe was invaded by the so-called Beaker people, so named because of the distinctive pottery beakers they buried with their dead. They were stockier and physically more powerful than the earlier Neolithic farmers and their new skill of metal smelting triggered nothing less than an economic and social revolution. They not only used bronze knives and axes but their women decorated themselves with bronze earrings and used long copper pins to hold their hair in place. They buried their dead in single graves under a mound where the bodies were placed in a crouched position. And while they carried on the tradition of the Neolithic megalith builders, they did not build on such a grand scale.

During the Bronze Age the new threat of war probably encouraged men to search for ore and to spend more time in making weapons and artefacts and in organizing defence and attack. During a long period of adjustment, a hierarchical and patriarchal society with chiefs and a warrior class began to emerge, eventually replacing the earlier nurturing, egalitarian, female-orientated community.[4] At first, prestige was no doubt invested in the mother's brothers; but when the role of the father became clearer in more monogamous relationships, the line of descent was traced through the father. By the time the Bronze Age slid into the warring Iron Age around 650 BC, patriarchy was firmly established throughout Europe. Increased trade and material wealth encouraged a sense of private property and the right of inheritance was established: the richer and more powerful warriors passed on their wealth, prestige and power to their sons. And so it remains.

These changes in social organization saw a radical shift in religious ritual from the worship of the Great Goddess, associated with the moon, to male gods associated with the sun. The astronomical alignments of many of the megalithic monuments, including Stonehenge, were reoriented accordingly. The older 'lunar' way of thinking was an intuitive knowledge which grasped things as a whole. It was replaced by what might be called 'solar' thinking – the way of modern civilization – which operates primarily with words and concepts and breaks down the objects of knowledge. One is holistic and organic, the other is analytical and mechanical. But the process was gradual and on the evidence of the monuments they left behind them, the megalith builders were capable of both lunar and solar thinking, reason and intuition, geometry and art.

A changing landscape

Before I set off on my own long journey south, I went out of my way to find out what happened to the landscape of Europe during the Neolithic period. After the ice sheets retreated, it seems that Europe enjoyed a gradual warming. From about 5500 to 4000 BC, the weather became more moist and warmer in northern Europe – a climate now known as 'Atlantic'. The high temperatures and heavy rain fostered the growth of deciduous trees on high ground which is moorland today. Spain, Portugal and southern France were probably at their most fertile during this period. The land along rivers and by the coasts was gradually cleared of forests to make room for crops. The first megaliths began to appear around 4500 BC in western Iberia and France, and from about 3500 BC in the British Isles.

Northwestern Europe enjoyed warm, dry weather from about 4000 to 1400 BC (a period known as the Sub-Boreal). The bleak open moorlands and wild headlands where many megaliths are found today would have been comfortable and productive places to live. The skies were clear, ideal for the stargazer and navigator. With calm seas, travel would have been easy by boat. Pottery and axes as well as ideas and experience were exchanged over long distances.

The earlier half of the Sub-Boreal saw a great deal of megalith building. This was the time when the chambered mounds of Scotland, Ireland and Brittany, the long barrows in England, the rock-cut caves in Iberia and the temples in Malta were built. There was a short break in the fine northern weather around 2900 to 2800 BC, but its ending saw a new surge in building, with the giant stone circles in Orkney and Avebury and the second monument in Stonehenge. The arrival of the belligerent Beaker people in the north led to a major disruption throughout Europe and the end of the Golden Age. Possibly small in number, these powerful invaders may well have established themselves as the new rulers. At the same time, they took over many of the local beliefs and continued to build megaliths. Size gave way to number: 900 small circles have survived from the period in the British Isles alone.

Another dramatic change in the weather occurred after 1500 BC in northern Europe. The dry, warm continental weather gave way to the cool, wet sub-Atlantic weather that persists today. The high, fertile open country where the megaliths were built was abandoned, as peat bogs developed. The thousands of years of clear skies which made astronomical observations and night-time navigation so easy came to an end. As the dark clouds descended in northern Europe, the age of the megaliths was over.

In the clearer and warmer south, the megalithic cultures lingered on in areas not conquered by Greek, Phoenician and Roman invaders. These areas may well have been outlying survivors of a loosely connected megalithic culture.[5] As the rest of Europe moved into the turbulent Bronze Age, the warlike Shardana, who came from the eastern Mediterranean, established themselves in Sardinia and spread to Corsica and the Balearic Islands. This last flowering of megalithic activity ended abruptly with the Roman conquest of Menorca in 23 BC. Five thousand years of raising great stones to the sky came to an unceremonious end.

The march of megaliths

I next considered what kind of megaliths I was likely to encounter during my voyage from northern Europe into the Mediterranean. The great stones did not appear suddenly overnight: there is clear evidence of their Mesolithic origins, and they probably evolved from

earlier wooden structures. Moreover, the megaliths underwent several
different phases of development. At first, burial chambers predomi-
nated, but megaliths were also arranged to form temples, circles and
alignments as well as single standing stones.

The most common megalithic structure is a chamber of upright
stones with one or more flat capstones laid across them to make a
roof. It is usually called a 'dolmen', possibly from the Cornish for
'hole of stone'; confusingly, they are often called 'quoits' in Cornwall.
In Wales it is sometimes called a 'cromlech' from the Welsh for
'crooked stone'. Dolmens were often covered with a mound of
earth (sometimes known as a barrow or tumulus) or a cairn of small
stones. Most today are bare and look like great stone tables or
mushrooms.

The chambers were usually called by earlier archaeologists
'chamber tombs' and were subdivided into 'gallery graves' consisting
of one long rectangular space, and 'passage graves', with a narrow
passage to a central chamber. Some of the chambers have a corbelled
roof, formed by horizontal layers of stone which overlap each other
until closed off at the top by a capstone. It is misleading, however, to
think of the chambers solely as tombs, as they were clearly used for
ritual purposes as well as for burying the dead.

Another widespread phenomenon in Europe is the single standing
stone, often called a 'menhir' after a Breton word meaning 'long
stone'. They are the most simple and the most enigmatic of all
megaliths. Where a chamber suggests a womb, the standing stone
appears to be a phallic symbol. Taken together, they were undoubtedly
key elements in the Great Goddess cult.

Mysterious lines of standing stones are also found throughout
Europe, some standing close together, others extending for long
distances. The largest and most famous alignments are near Carnac in
Brittany. Corsica is also dotted with standing stones known as statue-
menhirs because they have human features.

Stone circles are something of a speciality in the British Isles,
although France, Portugal and Sardinia have a scattering of them. As
we have seen, they seem to have had both ritual and astronomical
purposes. In some places, notably in the Scottish islands and the south
and west of England, stone circles and lines of standing stones occur
close together and clearly form part of a ritual landscape.

During my voyage, I could expect to see huge earthworks like the
ditches and banks of Avebury in southern England and the chambers
of Ireland and Brittany. Sacred enclosures, usually in the form of
stone-kerbed rectangles, are found in Brittany as well as in Malta.

Rock-cut chambers occur throughout Iberia and the Mediterranean islands. A type of drystone walling with large blocks, usually called Cyclopean, was developed in Malta in 3500 BC and flourished 2000 years later in Sardinia, Corsica and the Balearic Islands in the western and central Mediterranean. (The term 'Cyclopean' was first used to describe stone walls in Mycenean Greece.)

It seems extraordinary that the first settled people in Europe should have had the leisure, skill and drive to move and raise so much earth and stone. Yet they did – as their monuments so triumphantly declare some 5000 years later. Why this should be the case was a riddle I hoped to unravel as I sailed south towards the Mediterranean. And in the process, I was determined to try and recreate the lost civilization of megalithic Europe.

CHAPTER THREE

The Great Goddess

The language of poetic myth . . . was a magical language bound up with popular religious ceremonies in honour of the Moon-goddess, or Muse, some of them dating from the Old Stone Age.

ROBERT GRAVES

I set sail in *Celtic Gold* from Oban with my companion Elizabeth on a bright and breezy day in midsummer with white clouds scudding across a deep-blue sky. Our destination: the linked Isles of Harris and Lewis in the Outer Hebrides, where the famous megaliths of Callanish are located. We passed along the sound between the island of Mull and the mainland and anchored off Tobermory, a lovely little town with brightly coloured houses and a distillery making fine malt whisky.

The next day we continued in fine weather to the small island of Canna, passing Muck, Eigg and Rum. They offered none of the latter but plenty of the former two substances, left by the many sea birds – gannets, guillemots and fulmars – nesting on their rocky cliffs. Although we weren't stopping, we knew that at Kinloch on Rum there is the earliest known Mesolithic settlement so far excavated in Scotland, dating from around 7000 to 6800 BC. To the north of the islands hovered the dark, brooding peaks of the Cuillins on Skye.

We anchored overnight in the sheltered bay of Canna and left at first light for the Outer Hebrides. The weather was changing, and I hoped to arrive before the next Atlantic low swept in. We had to cross the stretch of water known as the Minches, notorious to sailors for its uneven sea bed which, coupled with strong winds and currents, can quickly create tumbling seas. I tried to forget that this part of the world has more violent storms than any other in Europe.

In the afternoon, the wind began to pick up and driving rain fell from the low, dark clouds. As I had expected, the sea became lumpy and I was forced to reef down the sails continually. By dusk we still had not reached our destination, the long and protected East Loch Tarbert on Harris. It was almost impossible not to feel edgy at this point, as visibility was beginning to grow poorer by the minute. With Elizabeth below deck feeling sick, I passed several loch entrances which had dangerous rocks and skerries. I thought I might have to press on during the stormy night to Stornoway. Then out of the wind-tossed spray appeared the lighthouse of Loch Tarbert, towering high up on a monstrous, rocky cliff.

With considerable difficulty, I managed to turn into the breaking waves. Sudden gusts of wind funnelling down the surrounding mountains keeled the boat over, even though by now I had virtually no sails. There were many jagged rocks and islets lurking in the gloom. I thought of the ancient mariners in their skin boats and wondered how they would have coped. By the time we reached a quiet little bay off the main loch, it was already dark. As I dropped anchor, I could just make out a few metres away the huge head of an old grey seal, annoyed at our rude intrusion of his domain.

Next morning we woke to find ourselves in a beautiful baylet surrounded by rough fields and stunted trees. I spied a small landing spot where a sparkling stream tumbled into the dark waters of the peaty loch. We scrambled ashore and walked hard across rock-strewn pastures, up and down hills and along craggy streams, until at last we reached a human settlement – Tarbert village.

I thought of the first settlers who may have landed in the same loch some 6500 years ago. Like their neighbours in Orkney, while clearing the ground to grow barley and making pasture for their cattle and sheep, they continued to hunt, fish and gather wild plants. They built permanent houses, made pottery and left behind chambered cairns and standing stones throughout the Western Isles.

Callanish

At Tarbert we found that to visit Callanish – locally called Calanais – we would have to cross the rocky mountain passes to the other end of the wind-swept Isle of Lewis, which is geographically linked to the Isle of Harris. It proved to be a barren, rugged hinterland. The isolated fields won from the bare mountains were scattered with stone outcrops and bogs. It was a rain-drenched land, a windswept land, a bitter land.

We found the Stones of Callanish on a rocky ridge overlooking Loch Roag among rolling hills on the west side of Lewis. At first sight, they looked like a great maze, but gradually they fell into a pattern. Although it was midsummer, a northeasterly wind whistled among the stones and a cold sea mist came and went. We were alone with the ghosts. I wove among the irregular, lichen-graced stones, tracing their weather-rough veins with my fingers. It was difficult to believe that at one time this wild landscape of pasture and heather would have been warmed by the sun and covered in groves of hazel, birch, alder and willow.

Callanish is still a powerful centre of energy. And as we will see, this is unsurprising in a site called the 'Scottish Stonehenge', deemed by some experts to be stunning proof of complex astronomical and geometrical knowledge in ancient Britain.

Apart from the main site, there are a dozen other satellites so far discovered.[1] They include three circles, several arcs, alignments and single stones, many visible from the main site and clearly part of an integrated ritual landscape. Since the land in the area has been sinking over the last 5000 years, there are no doubt many more megaliths submerged under the dark waters of the nearby lochs. By carefully choosing such a dramatic landscape, and by taking full advantage of its symbolic and scientific potential, early Europeans achieved here something equivalent to landing on the moon.

Recent excavations suggest that it was about 6000 years ago when the new settlers first dug a small, roughly circular ditched enclosure. They probably used antlers for picks and made shovels from wood or the shoulder blades of cattle.[2] About 1000 years later, they made long parallel beds in the fertile soil overlaying stiff clay in order to sow bere, a form of ancient barley which is still grown in Orkney. The ring at Callanish was laid out not long after, possibly with its central monolith and southern row of stones.

Built around 3000 BC, the main circle consists of thirteen stones of different heights set unevenly in the ground at the centre of a buckled Celtic cross. Just off centre is the tallest standing stone, shaped like the rudder of a boat. Weighing about 7 tonnes, it is taller than two men.[3] Made from a type of crystalline rock known as Lewisian gneiss, the stones are 3 billion years old, the oldest in Britain – so old that they contain no fossils. About fifty contain greenish hornblende crystals, possibly chosen to be recognizable from afar and for their association with the moon.

The stones were probably brought on sledges and rollers from a quarry about a mile away. It is likely that a wood platform was gradually built under them so that they could be levered into already dug socket holes. With about a quarter of each stone in the ground, their ends were packed with lumps of clay and stones the size of footballs, a method which has enabled them to withstand the fierce gales of the Western Isles for at least 3000 years. About fifty men would have been able to erect the largest central monolith, sometimes called the Callanish Phallus.

In the centre of the circle, there is a small chambered cairn. Residues of cremated bones have been discovered in the chamber. Previously thought to be a later addition, recent excavations have dated it to around 3000 BC.[4] Sherds of Grooved Ware pottery, impressed with cords and dating from 2500 to 1700 BC, have also been found as in Orkney.[5]

Astronomical alignments

Professor Alexander Thom, the man who largely founded the discipline of astro-archaeology, came to Callanish in 1933. He was then young, and travelling by sea. He was fascinated to find that the south row of stones at Callanish was laid out in an accurate north-south line – an experience that proved to be his road to Damascus. He went on to spend the rest of his life measuring more than 900 megalithic sites in the British Isles and Brittany. What he found convinced him that the megalith builders must have been capable of advanced astronomical and geometrical thought.

The ring at Callanish is not a true circle. But according to Thom, there is an underlying geometry to even the most apparently misshapen stone 'circles' in Britain. He identified about 300 true circles, about 100 oval or egg-shaped circles and some 'flattened' circles, with one side pulled in.[6] The main site at Callanish is an example of the latter, with the east side straighter than the rest. Since its builders could easily have built a perfect circle like the Ring of Brodgar, they clearly did what they did for a particular reason. Thom suggested that it was to give the relationship of the circumference to the radius the value of three – a number considered sacred throughout the world.

Single lines of stones span out, probably built at a later date, to the south, ENE and WSW of the main circle. To the NNE a long avenue of two rows run for 83 metres. The southern row lies accurately on a north-south axis. The western row is a few degrees off true west, but the sunset at the spring and autumn equinoxes still occurs close to the

alignment and the sunrise could be visible through the circle. Two stones outside the circle indicate the rising of the moon at its most northerly point.[7] With all these astronomical alignments, the main site at Callanish could therefore have been used as a calendar dividing the solar year into sixteen or thirty-two 'months'.

In many parts of the world, the key moments of the sun's journey from north to south and back again – the shortest day of the winter solstice, the longest day of the summer solstice and the equal days of the spring and autumn equinoxes in between – are still times of celebration, reverence and fear. Farming peoples follow these natural divisions of the year and use them to mark their times of sowing and harvesting as well as their traditional festivals and rites.

The people who raised the stones to the sky at Callanish were clearly preoccupied with the rhythms of the sun and the moon as well as the stars. Living without artificial light, the heavenly bodies would have been much more part of their everyday life. In the clearer skies, the presence of the moon and the stars would have been stronger at night, especially in

The arrangement of the stones at the Callanish main site, Isle of Lewis

the long winter months when the sun retreated to the south. Heaven and earth, like land and sea, were not separate in their lives and imaginations but threads of a subtle and interconnected web of correspondences.

Stargazing

Rear Admiral Boyle Somerville, a naval hydrographer and expert in celestial navigation, was the first to realize how important Callanish was as an observatory to track the northernmost moonrise. He observed that the stone standing alone to the southwest of the circle formed a lunar alignment with a stone to the northeast, which looks like an inverted axehead. He also thought that it could have been a stellar as well as a lunar and solar observatory: the main avenue would have been orientated around 1800 BC towards the bright star Capella, part of the Charioteer constellation on the edge of the Milky Way.[8] About the same time, the eastern row was aligned towards the constellation of the Pleiades, the universally revered group of stars sometimes known as the Seven Sisters. Perhaps it was at this time that the rows were extended from the original circle. Thom later observed that in 1800 BC the eastern row pointed to the rise of the star Altair.

At the time the main site at Callanish was built, Capella was used as the Pole Star. Due to the precession of the equinoxes caused by the slight wobble of the earth on its axis, the astronomical alignments of megalithic sites have changed over the millennia. Nevertheless, the variation is not huge. In the last 4000 years, the inclination of the earth has moved by only 0.5 degrees or less; for practical observations, this means a change of less than one width of the sun as viewed from earth.

More recently, the American astronomer Gerald S. Hawkins has described Callanish as a Scottish Stonehenge in his book, *Stonehenge Decoded* (1966). After a study of both sites, he concluded: 'If Stonehenge and Callanish are related, then the builders may have been aware of some of the fundamental facts which served later as the basis of accurate circumnavigation and led to a knowledge of the curvature of the earth'.[9] The original astonomers of the two sites may well have been in touch with each other and shared their observations. As I was to find out myself, the moon might take three months to travel northwards from Stonehenge to Callanish, but it was only about three weeks away by boat.

Moonrise

Like the Ring of Brodgar, the site at Callanish was particularly well placed in northern latitudes to trace the movements of the moon, a knowledge which would have been useful not only to work out the tides but also to predict eclipses. With the strong tidal streams among the Western Isles, it would be highly prudent to avoid the spring tides when setting sail.

Although the moon, like the sun, rises in the east and sets in the west, it follows a very different course. It waxes and wanes thirteen times every solar year. For an observer on earth, during each lunar month of about twenty-eight days, the moonrise and moonset swing

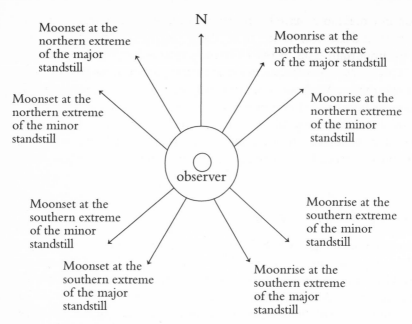

Moonset at the northern extreme of the major standstill

N

Moonrise at the northern extreme of the major standstill

Moonset at the northern extreme of the minor standstill

Moonrise at the northern extreme of the minor standstill

observer

Moonset at the southern extreme of the minor standstill

Moonrise at the southern extreme of the minor standstill

Moonset at the southern extreme of the major standstill

Moonrise at the southern extreme of the major standstill

Lunar alignments for an observer at Callanish, Isle of Lewis. The full cycle between the major standstills takes 18.61 years

from a most northerly point to a most southerly point and back again. Because the moon's orbit is slightly tilted, it also has a much longer and more complicated cycle, taking 18.61 solar years to travel to its most northerly and southerly moonsets, or major standstills, and back again. On its journey, its pauses for a while before moving on, creating the minor standstills.

The moon would have had a special significance for the first settlers of the Western Isles. As seafarers, they would have been aware that its cycle was associated with tides. As farmers, they felt that it influenced the growing of seeds. And women would have observed the link between their menstrual cycle and the lunar month, possibly associating the three phases of the moon – waxing, full, and waning – with the three phases of their life as maiden, mother and old woman.

Then, of course there are the eclipses visible from the area. Sun and moon periodically come together every few years in a lunar eclipse (when the earth's shadow covers the moon) and every few hundred years or so in a total solar eclipse (when the body of the moon covers the visible sun and casts a shadow on earth). Since the sun and moon bring forth life on earth and affect the tides, eclipses for our ancestors were inevitably moments of high anxiety, moments when ritual and magic would be necessary to ensure the deep rhythms of the universe continued. Eclipses have been feared throughout the world as omens of peril and catastrophe and to be able to predict them was one of the most important tasks of the early astronomers.[10]

Obviously it would take many generations to observe the full cycle of the moon. Without a written language, the observations would have to be passed down either orally or in some recorded form – possibly by inscribing tallies on pieces of stone or bone or by placing wooden stakes or stones into the ground. The keeping of this knowledge would have been of key importance.

The Old Woman of the Moors

Just as Stonehenge was built at a latitude particularly suitable for observing the sun, so the northern latitude of Callanish is ideal for tracking the moon. After years of studying the stones and their alignments, Gerald and Margaret Ponting pointed out that for a few days in its cycle of 18.61 years the full moon rises so close to due south of the site that its path skims at less than 2 degrees along the horizon of the Pairc hills, southeast of the circle.[11] Further north in Shetland, the moon cannot be seen at the southern extreme of its major standstill.

The Pairc hills are known locally as the Sleeping Beauty – in Gaelic, Cailleach na Mointeach (meaning 'Old Woman of the Moors') – because they look like a woman lying on her back. After passing along her body for about four hours, the moon sets in the Clisham range to the southwest, where it disappears behind a hill only to reappear in a notch on the horizon known as Glen Langadale. The last time this took place was in June 1987; the next is in 2006.

As it dances over the body of Mother Earth, disappearing for a while and then reappearing, the moon would seem to symbolize the eternal cycle of life, death and rebirth. But there are some even more spectacular views of the moon to be had at Callanish. When viewed from the far northern end of the stone avenue at the main site, the full moon gleams bright against the silhouette of stones and appears to set into the circle. Looking from the north, the stones of the main circle moreover provide a spectacular frame for observing the full moon as it rises and skims over the horizon of the Old Woman of the Moors.[12] I could imagine the outline of a woman standing in the bright circle of moonlight: the Woman – not the Man – in the Moon.

> White Goddess of the night,
> May you dance on the distant hills

> May you help the crops grow
> May you bring in the harvest
> May you keep the tides flowing
> May you ensure the life rhythm
> May you see the traveller home
> May you light the night passage
> White Goddess of the night
> May you dance on the distant hills.

A fascinating reference to the lunar rites which might have taken place at Callanish comes in the work of Diodorus Siculus, the first-century BC Greek author who drew on earlier sources. In a passage describing the Hyperboreans, the people of the North, he observes:

There is also on the island [Hyperborea] . . . a notable temple which is . . . spherical in shape . . . the moon, as viewed from this island, appears to be but a little distance from the earth . . . the god visits the island every nineteen years . . . [and] dances continuously the night through from the vernal equinox until the rising of the Pleiades . . .[13]

Callanish is the only known site containing all three astronomical elements mentioned. Stonehenge is sometimes taken to be Diodorus's temple, but it is 500 miles too far south to witness the dance of the moon.

The Great Goddess

While visiting Callanish, I met Margaret Curtis who, with her husband Ron, was a dedicated guardian of the stones. She knew the site, and every stone, like the back of her hand. As the cold rain swept in from the northeast, she took me to visit some of the outlying satellites to the main site. Many were visible from each other and aligned to the movements of the moon and the sun, so they confirm that the original builders saw their individual works as part of a complex configuration in a ritual landscape.

Crossing the rough moorland, stumbling on the tussocks and sinking into the boggy areas, we eventually ended up at a beautiful group of lichen-covered stones on a small hillock. It was known as Cnoc Fillibhir Bheag. Within a ring, there were four stones of different hues standing about chest high. The largest was embedded with quartz and and looked whitish in appearance.

'It's the phallus', my guide explained, 'upturned in Mother Earth;
its colour symbolizes semen. You can see that the other three are
slightly different colours: red, green and black. They are the three
aspects of the Triple Goddess: the Maiden, the Mother and the Crone.
A crone in Gaelic means wise woman, not an old hag.'

The phallic stone, she pointed out, lined up with the mouth of the
'Sleeping Beauty', formed by the hills on the southern horizon.

The Great Goddess, the principal deity of Old Europe, was a
complex figure: a maternal force directing fertility, a destroyer who
brings about death, and a regenerator responsible for rebirth. So she is
the Great Goddess of life, death and regeneration, waxing and waning
and then waxing again like her emblem the moon.[14] It is for this
reason that the early megalithic monuments, reflecting the Great
Goddess cult, are oriented primarily to tracking the movement of the
moon rather than the sun. As the archaeologist Marija Gimbutas
observed, 'the feminine nature, like the moon, is light and dark'.[15] Her
symbols are the pregnant doe, the chrysalis, caterpillar, butterfly, bee,
toad, turtle and hedgehog, all symbols of embryonic life and regeneration. She clearly reflects the preoccupations of a settled agricultural
people engaged forever in the endless cycle of life and death.

But what about all the erect standings stones, emerging rigidly
from the earth? According to Gimbutas, there is no evidence from
Neolithic times that humanity understood biological conception, so
phallic symbols did not symbolize so much the sowing of seed, but
vital power and spontaneous life energy.[16]

In the Old Europe of the megaliths, the world of myth was not
polarized into male and female. Like the Chinese principles of Yin and
Yang, they were instead interrelated and complementary. The male
principle, in the form of a young man or male animal, appears to affirm
the forces of the creative female. Neither one dominates the other, but
together their power is reinforced. It was only later in the Bronze Age,
after the invasion of patriarchal warriors from the East with their metal
weapons and solar gods, that the Great Goddess of the Stone Age fled
to the caves, wood and mountaintops. In Callanish, on the northern
edge of Europe, she seems to have survived much longer than elsewhere.

False men and fanciful ideas

Local islanders in the Middle Ages said that the stones of Callanish
were *Fir bhreig* – False Men – who had been petrified by some
enchanter. Ever since Martin Martin first published, in 1703, a

description of the 'heathen temple' at Callanish, together with a geometrical plan, speculations have proliferated about its meaning and purpose. He was told by the locals that 'it was a Place appointed for Worship in the time of Heathenisme, and that the Chief Druid or Priest stood near the big Stone in the center, from whence he address'd to the People that surrounded him'.[17] The Deist (or religious rationalist) John Toland declared in 1726 that the 'twelve' stones in the circle stood for the signs of the zodiac, the rows in the four directions symbolized the four winds, and the 'nineteen' stones on each side of the main avenue represented the nineteen-year lunar cycle. And then William Stukeley, the physician and most celebrated antiquary of the eighteenth century, classified it as a type of Druid's temple which he called a *Dracontium*, because it looked like an egg and a serpent.

Since we now know that the Celts only reached northern Britain a few centuries before Christ and normally used oak groves as their sanctuaries, the Druid hypothesis cannot be true.[18] Nevertheless, the Druids undoubtedly took over many sacred sites for their own rituals and absorbed local beliefs – just as the Christians did after them. According to Julius Caesar, the Druids not only studied the heavenly bodies but believed in the migration of the soul after death.

Some of these ancient beliefs undoubtedly lived on in the local community. In the nineteenth century, certain families in Callanish were known to be 'of the Stones', and despite the disapproval of the local ministers they still made visits on the days of the old festivals for 'it would not do to neglect the Stones'.[19]

Another story has it that on his arrival in Lewis, the cuckoo – who comes in April and sings his song in May – was thought to arrive in Callanish and to give his first call from the Stones. It marked the time for the Druids to convene their May festival.[20] Again recalling ancient Druidical rites, it was still remembered at the beginning of the twentieth century that on the festival of Beltane (Mayday), all the fires of the island were put out and new ones were lit. An old 'priest' who lived near the stones took his fire from a tree in a field and then distributed it to the villagers within the stone circle.[21] This rite not only marked the coming of spring but was clearly an act of purification.

The exact purpose of the stones at Callanish will never be known. As we have seen, there are good reasons to believe that they were used for ritual as well as astronomical purposes, for celebrating and marking the key festivals in the year. But it is not simply a question of deciding whether the stones at Callanish were used as an observatory, a calendar, a temple, a burial site, a healing centre, or a focus for the community. They almost certainly embodied all aspects of them. Like many pre-industrial peoples still living close to the earth and sky, the builders of the megaliths did not distinguish between religion and science, medicine and art, ritual and festivity.

Not only was beer drunk on these occasions, but finds of henbane at a site in Fife and fungi found on continental sites suggest that the rituals sometimes involved drug-induced hallucinations and trances. It is a practice that still continues among the thousands of people who gather on the summer solstice at Stonehenge and other sites in Britain.

Many such believers in 'earth energies' have been inspired by the archaeologist and psychic researcher Tom Lethbridge's view that Callanish and other stone circles were landing marks for flying saucers of extra-terrestrials searching for minerals on planet earth. Wild dancing around the rings, he argued, would have charged them with 'bio-electrical potential'.[22] Many believe that rituals involving birth, fertility and death were conducted in the circle in order to awaken the healing and creative powers of the Great Goddess. The psychic Lynne Wood compared the sacred sites of Britain with the Hindu chakra system of energy centres in the human body, with Callanish as the head, Castlerigg in Cumbria as the heart, Avebury as the root and Boscawen-ûn in Cornwall as the foot.[23] This of course can never be proved or disproved. But I for one felt very strong energies among the stones on that wild midsummer day in the driving rain.

The stones and the sea

While the Stones of Callanish remain a delightful riddle which is only beginning to be deciphered, there can be no doubt that the people who raised the megaliths at Callanish had wide maritime connections. The constant presence of the sea was part of the lives of the islanders and part of their rituals. In the interior of the small oval stone ring at nearby Cnoc Ceann a'Gharraidh, southeast of the main circle, at least five small holes lined with pebbles from the seashore have been discovered. The sea, which was 5 metres lower in megalithic times, was inescapably part of the symbolic landscape at Callanish. At Cleitir, for instance, four stones were set in a semicircle on a levelled area at the edge of steep rocky slope overlooking the sea channel separating the island of Great Bernera from Lewis. And the sea brought goods from afar. Not only have mylonite arrowheads from Skye been found in the area but a fine-grained stone axehead made from porcellanite, found near Stornoway and dated to just before 3000 BC, was probably imported from Antrim in Ireland. The sherds of Grooved Ware pottery found at the main site were markedly rare in the Western Isles but common in Orkney and southern Britain, suggesting that Callanish was an important meeting place and ritual centre for peoples travelling up and down the west coast of the British Isles.

A persistent local legend has it that the stones were erected by followers – referred to as 'black men' – of a great priest-king who came to the island with many ships. Dressed in mallard feathers, he was said always to have wrens flying around him. Workers who died while erecting the stones were buried in the circle. When the building was finished, the great priest-king remained with some assistants while the others sailed away.[24]

Many legends contain distorted elements of historical truth, and this one could well refer to dark-haired men from Ireland, or even seafarers from North Africa. It is known that pirates from the Barbary coast in Algeria sailed up to Ireland and Iceland in the seventeenth century in order to seize villagers and their goods. It involved no great navigational skill: after rounding the southwestern tip of Portugal, one can just follow the Pole Star to the northern islands.

The sites at Callanish were used for at least 2000 years, until the weather changed and the peat moss began to close in around 1000 BC. Iron Age people, Druids and Vikings came and went. On its lonely hill by the sea on the edge of the world, weathered by rain and wind for most of the year, Callanish still stands – an enigma with more secrets yet to be uncovered. And the White Goddess, maintaining the daily rhythm of the tides, giving and taking life, returns every nineteen years or so to dance across the distant hills.

CHAPTER FOUR

Mounds and Wheels

Wheel within wheel, in freedom revolve in harmony and peace.

WILLIAM BLAKE

A s storm-battered as Orkney and the Outer Hebrides now are, Mediterranean skies would have shone over them in the time of the megalith builders. And I can imagine it bright with the sails of ancient mariners as they wended their way among the scattered islands up and down the western seaways. There would have been a constant stream of boats to and fro across the Minches between Harris and the mainland.

Like those distant seafarers, I did not leave the Outer Hebrides with empty hands – not a polished stone axe, but a fine coat of Harris tweed made by local crofters. It had within it all the brown, green and blue colours of land and sea. After the ceaseless wind and rain we were fortunate enough to leave Harris on a bright, sunny day with a warm southerly breeze. We sailed across the North Minch north of Skye on a gentle sea with peace in our hearts. That afternoon, we disturbed a raft of some sixty puffins, and as we passed the Old Man of Stoer, a huge natural basalt stack on a bold headland, we were joined by a large dolphin who played in the waves at our bow.

After spending the night in a lonely anchorage in Rona island, hidden behind great rounded rocks, we passed through Khyle Rhea, the notorious channel between Skye and the mainland where a spring tide can reach up to 8 knots. The megalithic seafarers, with their light hide boats, would have had to go with the tide; and so did I. We swirled and swept through the steep-sided narrows, but it was exhilarating rather than terrifying. We stayed well away from the even more impressive Great Race off the Gulf of Corryvreckan at the head of the

Sound of Jura, however. This runs as fast as 12 knots, and if you are caught in such a dangerous tidal stream, you have no choice but to ride it out to sea. When seafarers first arrived in the region they would have had to negotiate some of the most extreme tidal streams in Europe.

Nearly 8000 years ago, someone left an antler harpoon on the shore near Oban. Although people settled in the Western Isles and along the west coast of Scotland around this time and began to break up the earth and sow crops, like the ancients of Orkney they still continued to hunt and fish. Such ritualized activities would enable them to show their prowess, bond with their fellows and still experience the excitement of the chase. The waters would have been teeming with life; on the island of Oronsay near Jura, for instance, the inhabitants of a Neolithic settlement dined on at least thirty species of birds and twenty-three species of fish as well as crab, oysters, whelks, limpets and other types of shellfish. They made ornaments from cowrie shells, and fashioned barbed points, awls and mattocks from antlers and bones which they collected by boat from larger neighbouring islands or the mainland.[1]

If you have rounded Ardnamurchan Point on Skye and made the crossing to the Outer Hebrides, by ancient tradition you should return with a sprig of heather tied to your bow. And as we approached the Sound of Mull, ours proudly withstood the brisk wind. There is a saying on Mull that if you can't see the mainland, it is raining, and if you can, it is going to rain. For a while, the good visibility prevailed and we sighted two minke whales, one in the distance crossing from the mainland. The other swam right alongside us. It had a massive brown head, a small dorsal fin, and stretched about 10 metres – longer than *Celtic Gold*. It stayed with us for some ten minutes, so close that I got a whiff of its strong fishy smell and could have touched its shining back with a boathook.

When I wish to think of something calm, I picture that great whale gently rising and falling in the crystal-clear water. But I also know that in a rage, it could have smashed our boat with its tail or turned it over with its back. I wondered, as I had in Orkney, whether the megalithic seafarers had hunted whales. With such fearful creatures rising regularly from the deep, I could see why Scottish islanders still tell stories of the Stoor Worm, the great sea serpent that can wreak havoc on unwary mariners.

The lure of these waters was such that I could have stayed years island-hopping and exploring the countless lochs, but autumn was approaching and it was time to head south. But I would continue to dream of the selkies, the seal-women who, having discarded their sealskins, dance naked in the evening sun on the strand; or of the lonely mermaid who combs her golden hair and sings for a human lover by a rockpool. When half asleep at the end of a long watch under the moon, had I not seen the Great Goddess herself appear – tall, golden-haired and blue-eyed – rising from the waves? And then there was the oft-felt presence of a dark, female power down in the depths known to the Mesolithic nomads of these northern seas and still called by the Orcadians 'Mither of the Sea'.[2]

A megalithic paradise

As we sailed south into the Sound of Jura, I mulled over the idea put forward by the dowser Tom Graves that megalithic barrows absorb the energy from potential storms. If a site is disturbed or overloads with this energy, he argued, a thunderstorm might break.[3] Jura has one of the highest number of megalithic sites in Britain, and over 1500 pieces of flint have been uncovered at just one of them. It experiences few thunderstorms, but when they come they are particularly violent. Folklore certainly gives accounts of sudden storms breaking out when a barrow is violated or a ring of stones disturbed. There was no obvious way of testing the idea that megalithic sites are a form of weather control; until proven, I would continue to rely on the traditional signs of the weather, such as mares' tails and mackerel skies.

The three standing stones of Ballochroy on the mainland shore look across the Sound of Jura to the west. Their location was carefully chosen, for they have some clear astronomical alignments. From Ballochroy, Cara Island 11 kilometres away acts as a marker for the midwinter sunset, while a line running from the central stone to the mountain of Corra Bheinn on Jura, 30 kilometres away, indicates the position of the midsummer sunset. Moreover, when the mid-summer sets behind the rounded hills known as the Paps (or 'breasts') of Jura, a long ribbon of light plays upon the the sound, linking the phallic stones, the waters of regeneration, the breasts of Mother Earth, and the light of Father Sun in a grand cosmic embrace.

Leaving the Sound of Jura, we decided to cut across the narrow strip of land at the top of the sound which leads to the Firth of Clyde. I imagined that the megalithic seafarers would have carried their light boats overland to avoid the turbulent waters off the Mull of Kintyre.

We left the boat in a basin in the Crinan Canal and along the dead-straight track built across the raised peat bogland known as the Great Moss or Moine Mhor. The weather was muggy and it was a hot and sweaty walk; yet despite all that and the clouds of midges, we were delighted by the wayside reeds, sedges and wildflowers. I thought how much easier it would have been to travel by boat before the sea had retreated here and the land invaded by near-impenetrable bog and thickets of alder and willow.

As I gazed about me I spied, rising out of the flat landscape of the Moine Mhor, the Dunadd hill fortress. This was the seat of the earliest Scottish kings, and first built up in the sixth century AD by the Scotti from Ireland. Dunadd had long been a centre of trade from afar: glass and pottery imported from the continent, as well as coriander and dill, have been found on the site. It was probably near Dunadd that St Columba spoke to Gallic sailors from present-day France, yet another reminder of the maritime connections along the Atlantic seaboard.

It soon became clear that our arduous walk across the midgy bogs was well worth the effort. The green, rock-strewn, tree-scattered pastures of Kilmartin Valley which rose before us contained at least 150 prehistoric sites over 5000 years old, varying from burial cairns to rock carvings, stone circles and standing stones. The area has been rightly called a 'megalithic paradise'.[4]

A string of at least seven cairns meander up the sacred valley of Kilmartin, forming a 'linear cemetery' several kilometres long. Begun around 3000 BC and completed around 1500 years later, they show how the valley was an important ritual site for the large local population. Although not all members of the community were buried in the cairns, they probably provided a focus for everyone. It was a meeting place where the living and the dead could gather, where the strength and wisdom of the ancestors could be drawn upon to ensure prosperity and peace. And in the symbolic language of the Goddess cult, the mound of the monuments was no doubt interpreted as the pregnant belly and the tomb as the womb.[5]

The first cairn we came across, the most southerly survivor, was Ri Cruin, dating from about 2000 BC. It contained three cists or box graves built from stone slabs, one of which had a carving which looked tantalizingly like a boat. Walking up the valley floor, we next visited the Nether Largie South cairn, built around 3000 BC. It is the oldest and the only chambered cairn in the valley. Its rectangular central chamber, measuring about 6 metres by 2, consisted of four compartments separated by massive upright slabs. Like most cairns of its type, the entrance was orientated towards the northeast.

I climbed into the large chamber, which would have been carefully constructed to receive the remains of many generations of the dead. These could have come in the form of ashes from funeral pyres, or as large bones and skulls from corpses previously exposed to the elements.

I noticed a considerable amount of quartz among the stones of the cairn; it is often found in megalithic graves and is considered to have a magical and purifying effect.

From the outside, the Nether Largie North cairn further up the valley looks like a pile of scattered stones. When excavated, it was found to have a large central cist. I entered the cairn and saw the magnificent capstone which had been lavishly incised with images of axeheads and with shallow circular depressions known as cupmarks. Plundered long ago, all that was found in the cist was charcoal, ochre and a human tooth.

Beneath the Glebe cairn, situated towards the head of the valley, excavators made the intriguing discovery of two stone concentric circles, one within the other. They were probably used originally as a sacred space for meeting, praying, celebrating and dancing. The two cists within the cairn clearly received the remains of important people within the community: they contained two finely made and richly ornamented pots, probably imported from Ireland, and a beautiful jet necklace carved lovingly with triangles and lozenges.

The chambers of the cairns are now empty. While their size is impressive, their spirit has gone. Years of turning over the stones in the search for treasure has transformed them into little more than empty shells.

The burial goods found in the cairns not only hint at the comfortable lifestyle of the locals, but also at their wide trading links. Beakers have been found in Nether Largie South – a sign of the Beaker people who introduced the working of copper. The beakers may have contained some intoxicating substances, intended for the souls of the dead or drunk by the mourners.

There is debate over whether the Beaker people brought Beaker pottery, copper and bronze working and the practice of individual burial with them. Some say the skills and traditions were simply passed from community to community. But after much deliberation I believe the sudden and radical appearance of these items and traditions can only indicate a new force on the local scene. Although cultural influence no doubt played its part, a major social revolution took place throughout Europe at the beginning of the Bronze Age. Certainly three beakers found in Nether Largie South are reminiscent of round-based pots discovered in Germany along the Rhine dating from about 2400 BC.

Of twenty-two stone axes found in the area, seven were made of stone from Ireland, and five from Cumbria. Since Kilmartin was not rich in stone suitable for tool making, the axes clearly changed hands as rare and valuable objects.[6] Again, of seventeen food vessels found within 10 kilometres of Kilmartin, eleven are of a type known as Irish Bowls. There were long-established connections between this part of Scotland and Ireland: the North Antrim coast is only 20 nautical miles away. Indeed, Scotland takes its name from the very Scotti tribe who later came from Ireland and settled in the southwest.

Temple Wood

I was delighted to see something I had long read about next – the stone circle of Temple Wood. It appears in W. Daniel's painting of 1818 on an open plain in front of a dramatic backdrop of rugged mountains, but I found it in an intimate space nestling among trees on the edge of the Kilmartin Valley. Sometimes called the Half-Moon Circle, it is slightly flattened on one side like the ring at Callanish. It measures about 13 by 12 metres.

A small northeastern circle has been discovered at the Temple Wood site that began as a timber ring, and was replaced by an ellipse of stones. Oak taken from the hole of one stone has been carbon dated to around 3500 BC, making it one of the earliest known circles in Britain. It is thought that it may have been used as a solar observatory to predict the arrival of midwinter – the earliest evidence of people in southwestern Scotland trying to fix their lives precisely in time by establishing a calendar of the year.[7]

The main circle of Temple Wood started as a free-standing ring of twenty-two stones made from local schist. I noticed that on the outer face of the northern stone are carved two spirals, the eastern one turning anti-clockwise, and the western one, clockwise. A north-south alignment appeared to be significant in the circle as both the North and South stones were made of chlorite schist unlike the other ones. Two of the upright stones show spiral decorations while another has a carving of concentric circles.

It would appear that the main purpose of the site changed from ritual to burial. Two short cists under cairns, built during the Early Bronze Age, contained inhumations; later generations clearly recognized the spiritual power of the place. The cist to the northeast contained a fine beaker, a scraper and three flint arrowheads. The west cist contained the tooth of a child aged between four and six years. At different stages, drystone walls were constructed only to be thrown down. Cairns added inside the circle suggest that it was considered a sacred site to at least the end of the second millennium BC when peat began to form over the site. Although restored, with its shining white stones set among the dappled light of the trees, it still had a very strong presence.

About 250 metres southeast of the Temple Wood circle are the mysterious Nether Largie Stones (as distinct from the cairns), which stand in an open field on the west side of the Kilmartin burn. Erected around 3500 BC, they are the earliest standing megaliths in the valley. I counted five large and eight small stones, as well as two outlying stones; but originally there may have been more. A recent survey suggests that there were once areas nearby enclosed by semi-circular banks and ditches. One stone with slightly bowed sides and an irregular tip was decorated with about forty cup marks, one complete cup and ring mark (depressions circled by incised rings) and two gapped circles, in one case with a radial groove. They added up to a veritable tableau of Neolithic art, the lost symbolism of which suggested to me some obscure metaphysical alphabet of the cosmos. Or taken together, did they offer a map of the night sky at a particularly significant time?

The symmetrical arrangement of the stones in a long rectangular naturally invites astronomical interpretations. Alignments between them have been deduced for the midwinter sunrise and sunrise on the winter quarter days. In conjunction with the Temple Wood circle, the stones may have formed a lunar observatory, tracking the full moon's major northern standstill and the moonrise at minor standstills.[8]

If this is not enough, at Ballymeanoch to the south there are six surviving stones grouped into two parallel lines, each running from the southeast to the northwest. There is also a henge (a circular bank of earth with an internal ditch and two entrances) built about 3000 BC – the only henge so far discovered in the West of Scotland.

It's clear that the megaliths in the Kilmartin valley, taken together, form a complex, interrelated web making up a spectacular ritual landscape. I could imagine the local custodians in those far-away times welcoming travellers to attend the great ceremonies and rituals in the enormous natural amphitheatre formed by the valley.

Cups and rings

It is not only stones at Kilmartin that have been left to beguile the modern walker. In an eastern enclosure slightly above the valley floor, I came across sections of bedrock beautifully decorated with cupmarks. Most had simple cups, while others were contained within single or double rings which uncannily resemble planets circling the sun.

Stones of Kilmartin, cists and cairns,
Robbed, turned over and empty,
Your spirit has fled.
But in rock carvings on the hills
Your spirit still resides
In perpetual peace.

After the recent rain, many of the cupmarks were filled with water, reflecting white clouds in the sky. Like countless little wells, they appeared to hold the sacred water of the life-giving Goddess. Indeed, as Marija Gimbutas has observed: 'Celebration of life is the leading motif in old European art and ideology.' For her, the circles with concentric rings were 'semantic relatives of stone circles and ring dances around a well, which is the concentrated life source of the Goddess'.[9]

Some of the carvings have straight grooves from circumference to centre, called 'extended gutters' by archaeologists. These have been interpreted as the plan of a house or a passage grave.[10] This seems a very literal interpretation, overlooking the fact that all megalithic art was highly symbolic. They reminded me of the great labyrinth I had seen carved on the flagstones of Chartres Cathedral. The devout would walk on their knees along the rings of the circle until they reached the centre. For me, the megalithic cups and rings and the Chartres labyrinth both symbolize the journey of the soul through the labyrinth of this world to the paradise of the heart and the heavenly home. And in both, there is a direct line to the centre, suggesting that, as in alchemy, there is a quick as well as slow path to enlightenment and immortality.[11]

Cup-and-ring marks are scattered all over mid-Argyll – on standing stones, boulders and bedrock – but the most spectacular collection of carvings is to be found at Achnabreck, about 10 kilometres south of Kilmartin and close to the Crinan Canal. To reach them, we walked up a meandering track through open heatherland and pine forests to a hillside looking west to the Sound of Jura and south to the head of the Firth of Clyde. I could just make out the Isle of Arran in the distance. Among the heather and long grass, we came across three outcrops of decorated rock close to each other and covered by moss and lichens. These are said to be the largest and most impressive expanse of prehistoric carvings in the British Isles. How many more, I thought, are there – hidden deep within the forests or under the peat bogs?

The site was clearly a resting spot on a well-trodden pathway linking the two waters, where travellers must have exchanged goods and swapped news and stories. It would not surprise me that it had been a meeting place for nomads long before people settled down. And it still is a very special place, drawing in from all around the elements of being – fire, earth, water and air. No doubt over the millennia it had been a place for rituals and initiation rites, to celebrate life and death, perhaps even to expose the dead. It had become a sacred place where carvers were moved to record their symbols of the infinite on stone which still greets the occasional passer-by 6000 years later. In our more prosaic age, we can only surmise the meaning of their beautiful and enigmatic designs.

The vast majority of the motifs on the outcrops are cup-and-ring marks. But there are also a range of motifs associated with the so-called 'Irish Passage Grave Art', such as spirals, ringed stars, parallel grooves and uncupped rings. A cluster of them appear in the upper group at Achnabreck and were probably the earliest carvings at the site.[12] Moreover, such rock art, as I was to find out, was not only carved in Ireland and Cornwall, but in Brittany, France, and Galicia, Spain. It expressed the cosmology of the megalithic peoples who were in touch with each other all the way into the Mediterranean. It was part of the common language of the Goddess and her life-giving powers.

It is not representative art – there are no figures of humans, animals or plants as in Palaeolithic cave paintings. Yet the abstract power of the symbols make them, if anything, even more compelling. As the light began to fade and the midges renewed their attack, I traced my forefinger along the straight groove which one of my ancestors had made 5000 years ago to the central hollow, and tried to imagine what must have driven him to pick away for hours on the hard rock. As I stood up the circles seemed to turn slowly in the half-light.

What was the meaning of this strange metaphysical 'alphabet'? My earlier interpretation did not exhaust all the possibilities. The cups within the concentric rings not only hold rainwater and reflect the passing clouds, but offer a well of wisdom – if only we could understand it. Was the cup-and-ring motif a fertility symbol – a straight male line entering a female cup? Or was it revealing a black hole at the centre of our universe, a gateway to another world? Did the rings represent a chart of the heavens as understood at the time? Or were they recording the cycles of sun and moon, day and night, life and death – the eternal recurrence of all things? The fact they could inspire so many interpretations, none mutually exclusive, reflects the mythic power of this abstract art.

As I sat marvelling at the circles, I recalled the words of William Blake that unlike the 'cogs tyrannic' in our own age, wheels in Eden 'revolve in harmony and peace.'[13] Then I noticed that on the lowest

Cup-and-ring markings at Achnabreck, Argyll

end of the outcrop, one A. Smith – the modern everyman – had in 1908 carved a rough cross in the rock. His two crossed lines were nowhere near the harmonious symmetry of the neighbouring circles. It was a crude attempt to impose modern beliefs on the old religion. The cross has become a symbol of suffering; the circle remains a symbol of peace, harmony, perfection and eternity. The ancients knew the power of place, the spirit of the landscape; we moderns just lay our grid on the land, cutting through hill and bog, water and wood. We may get to our destinations faster, but we see and understand less on the way.

Southward bound

After leaving Kilmartin, we sailed past the Isle of Arran in the Firth of the Clyde in foul, squally weather – a strong west wind was accompanied by low black clouds and driving rain. The English archaeologist Colin Renfrew has argued that each chambered mound on Arran was the cult centre of an extended family or community working a particular piece of land.[14] He assumes that Neolithic people had a strong sense of exclusive property, but this is by no means clear or proven. Many archaeologists continue to project their own assumptions about human nature and modern society into the past, believing, for instance, that megalithic civilization was driven – as now – by a 'territorial imperative'.[15] The application of this popular kind of sociobiology to ancient peoples distorts the findings of archaeology.

As the wind continued to lash the boat, I heard from the coastguard that a Mayday call had been made and a man was missing off the coast of Arran. I was ready to help, but was soon informed that a lifeboat had arrived on the scene and my assistance was no longer needed. We later learned that a man fishing with his son in a small boat had been dragged overboard by his own nets. His son was not strong enough to pull them back on board and his father had drowned.

It was a tragic reminder of how easily disasters can suddenly happen at sea. Many Scottish and Irish fishermen from remote communities still believe fatalistically that they take life from the sea and occasionally life must be given back. This notion of sacrifice is undoubtedly a very ancient one. I could understand why the ancient seafarers in these regions saw the sea as a demigod, giving and taking life, at one moment raging and ruthless, at another all grace and tranquillity.

I left Scotland having spent five weeks in rain, drizzle, mist and low cloud – all in midsummer! But I had also revelled in the luminous light, the dazzling sea and the billowing clouds. I had memories of bold, rocky headlands, brooding mountains and wild, lonely anchorages. Despite the contrary winds and the lumpy seas, it had been a cleansing voyage which had yet again made me aware of the thin line between life and death. The constant movement of the boat, the ebb and flow of the tides, the rising and setting of the sun and moon, the coming and going of the stars had all entered deep into the well of my being.

As I headed down through the Northern Channel into the Irish Sea, I ruminated on how the megaliths seemed to transcend time in our world of constant change. They will continue to stand as enigmatic question marks on the historical landscape thousand of years after I have gone. I thought of the little pile of thirty-three quartz pebbles, left in a neat cluster, which had been found at a prehistoric site in Brainport Bay on Loch Foyle. The site was directed towards sunrise on the midsummer solstice. What was the purpose of those little stones? Were they used as counters by an astrologer-astronomer to help record the passage of time? Or were they handled like a rosary, jogging the memory of a priest or a storyteller?

My next destination – the great megalithic site up the Boyne Valley in Ireland – would no doubt throw more light on these and other enigmatic remains of Europe's lost civilization.

CHAPTER FIVE

The British Mediterranean

The grey waters of the Irish sea were as bright with Neolithic argonauts as the Western Pacific is today.

VERE GORDON CHILDE

S ailing down the Western seaways heading for Newgrange in Ireland, often out of sight of land, I felt close to the ancient mariners. The Irish Sea, linking what are now four countries, would have been as crisscrossed by seafarers as the Mediterranean in Neolithic times. Like my seafaring ancestors, I sailed the shortest routes between islands and headlands. I suspected that just as there are 'ley lines' linking megalithic sites on land, so there are sea tracks – what I liked to call 'wake lines' – which sailors have been following for thousands of years. It is no coincidence that prominent towers, churches and lighthouses, all essential navigation marks for the mariner at sea, are often built on ancient sacred sites.

Our obsession with roads and admiration for the transport network of the Roman Empire has led us to overlook the fact, as E.G. Bowen pointed out in 1972, that 'the sea has always been the natural highway linking island to island and peninsula to peninsula along the Western Fringes of Europe'.[1] From Mesolithic times when settlers first arrived in Britain to the era of Celtic saints and Vikings, the sea remained the fastest, easiest and safest form of transport.

It has long been assumed that rowing boats and the sail first evolved in the Mediterranean, but the oldest oar, dating from 8000 BC, has been discovered in northern Europe.[2] The feats of navigation and seamanship of the Neolithic voyagers in this part of the world were impressive. Their ships would have to be capable of negotiating tidal races, whirlpools and crosscurrents along the coasts and the fickle waves of the open sea. This would have been impossible in dugouts, although a fine specimen known as the Lurgan longboat, made from an oak about 4500 years ago, has been extracted from a bog in Galway (now lying in Dublin National Museum). The most likely vessels would have been skin boats similar to the sea-going curraghs or currachs of Western Ireland, which are still found in the Aran Islands off that coast.[3] I have seen them at work myself and have visited one of the last boatyards on the Dingle Peninsula in southwestern Ireland still producing such large craft. The same craftsmen made the large curragh for Tim Severin. Author of the *The Brendan Voyage* published in 1978, Severin followed in the wake of St Brendan from Ireland to Greenland. A smaller version of the Irish curragh is still used in the rivers and lakes of Wales, where it is known as a corracle.

Built of wickerwork frames and covered with cowhides sewn together, the ocean-going curraghs are about 8 metres long and 2 metres wide. They are capable of carrying nine or ten people. The Aran islanders consider two cows and twenty sheep a reasonable cargo to take to sea, and their remote ancestors, the first farmers, would undoubtedly have transported their stock in a similar way. The curraghs have a fine, curved sheer and long, rising bows which allow them to rise to a swell and oncoming waves. They are so buoyant they can be turned almost on a coin.

With a sail and a good following wind, these lively boats can travel about 4 knots an hour, 100 nautical miles a day. They had the additional advantage, unlike my yacht *Celtic Gold*, of requiring no moorings or harbours, for they can easily be beached and dragged beyond the tideline. Their main disadvantage is that as light craft they can be easily blown off course; the early navigators would have had to allow for considerable leeway. At the same time, they could always lie at sea-anchor until the wind abated. The ancient mariners probably navigated by dead reckoning (working out their position by direction and speed) and by the position of the sun during the day and the major stars and planets at night. With calmer weather and clearer skies, this would have been easier in megalithic times than at present.

We can be fairly certain that the Neolithic boats were curraghs because there is a depiction of what looks like a skin boat with a wicker framework on the famous Bronze Age bowl from Caergwrle in North Wales (now in the National Museum in Cardiff). On the gold sheet along the gunwale is a series of concentric circles which look like sun discs. It has oculi (decorations resembling eyes) on the bows, still found on fishing boats in Brittany, Spain and Portugal.

Another beautiful representation of a boat, found at Broighter near Limavady in Northern Ireland, can be seen in the National Museum in Dublin. Made in the second century BC, it is a gold ornament fashioned in the form of a ship's hull complete with mast, seven oars on either side and even a grappling hook. At Newgrange there is also the shape of a boat carved on a stone, known as Coffey's Ship, which looks remarkably like a curragh with four oarsmen.[4] Built around 3250 BC, Newgrange is part of the greatest megalithic site in the whole of Ireland and one of the most impressive in Europe.

Newgrange

Newgrange is an immense chambered mound to be found on a spur of a hill by a bend of the River Boyne, which flows into the Irish Sea. It is part of a group which includes two more mounds at Knowth and Dowth. They are older than Stonehenge, older than Mycenae – older even than the pyramids of Egypt. As at Kilmartin, they form part of a larger ritual landscape containing cairns, stone circles and standing stones. More masterpieces of megalithic art are carved on them.

Set in green, rolling farmland, the restored mound at Newgrange looks like a gigantic flying saucer, its white quartz walls sparkling in the sun. I could easily see why some enthusiasts view megalithic sites as landing spots for extraterrestrials. As you approach its entrance, there are three enormous stones lying horizontally on the ground. They are decorated with beautiful double and triple spirals and lozenges.

Decoration is perhaps the wrong word. These stones were carved with great reverence, and for a deep metaphysical purpose. The surfaces would first have been shaped and smoothed and scored with deep marks. These were next rubbed to an even depth using sand and water. The whole surface was then 'pecked' with a pointed stone to produce the required shape.[5] The resulting double and triple spirals on the entrance stone to Newgrange swirl and flow like the starry sky itself. They not only evoke the motion of waves at sea but the serpentine energies of the earth itself.

What are we to make of these double spirals? Could they represent the yearly movement of the sun? The American artist Charles Ross set up an experiment in which he used a lens to focus the sun's rays on to a plank so that it burned a track on the wood. For each day of the year, he put a new plank to burn and then plotted the pattern of the sun's rays on the planks. It turned out to be a perfect double spiral. The track formed a tight clockwise spiral in the summer and a loose anti-clockwise spiral in the winter. At the equinoxes the track began to straighten out. As a result, each spiral represents a quarter of the sun's movement in the heavens.[6]

Walking around the great restored mound, 84 metres in diameter and 13 metres high, I examined the colossal kerb stones. Eleven of the ninety-seven were carved with elaborate and spectacular designs: spirals, chevrons, diamonds, circles, horseshoes, parallel lines, radials, lozenges, zigzags and other enigmatic shapes. The exact meaning of these wondrous illustrations of Neolithic art remains obscure but they might well represent a symbolic alphabet of the various beliefs associated with the cult of the Great Goddess. On a more practical level, they could also have been used to trace the monthly and annual movements of the moon and the sun, possibly with the help of stick which would cast shadows on the ground like the gnomon of a sundial.

To enter the chambered mound of Newgrange is like entering the womb of the Goddess herself. A low and narrow passage – you have to bend down reverentially to pass along – rises slightly for about 18 metres. It then opens about a third of the way to the centre of the monument into a vast central chamber which has a magnificent corbelled vault, the finest of its kind in Europe. There are even grooves cut in the large roof slabs to carry off the rainwater.

On the floor, in three recesses, lie four huge, beautifully propor-tioned stone basins. The bowl-shaped depressions in the surface of the granite bowl in the right hand recess may have held milk or other liquids for religious purposes. Although the remains of two burials and at least three cremated bodies have been found in the central chamber, together with stone beads, small spheres, pendants and bone pins, it seems unlikely that the monument was used only as a tomb. To my mind, it must have been a sacred space for ritual, magic and ceremony.

I lingered on my own in the central chamber. Some 50,000 tonnes of stone arched over my head. It was as dry as a bone. There was an uncanny silence in which I began to hear my own heartbeat. A deep peace fell on me. The only other place in which I have had a similar experience was in the subterranean chamber of the Great Pyramid at Giza.[7]

Within the chamber, I paid particular attention to the upright stone which has an interrelated triple spiral motif – the most famous icon of megalithic art, and instantly recognizable. Its triple spirals evoke not only the three-natured Great Goddess, but anticipates St Patrick's use

Elevation and plans of Newgrange, Ireland

of the shamrock to illustrate the Trinity. Following the spiral with my finger, I realized it was composed of two continuous lines, symbolizing the duality of existence, light and dark, good and bad, life and death. Its creator had thus cunningly woven into a single symbol the mystery of the Three in One.[8]

The design, engineering and orientation of the whole monument at Newgrange was achieved with amazing care. At the entrance of the passage facing southeast, there is a strange, box-like space above the main lintel. As in Maes Howe in Orkney, it is aligned with the midwinter sunrise when rays of light penetrate deep down the dark passage to illuminate the basin stone in the central inner chamber. After a few minutes, the thin beam of light widens dramatically to illuminate the side and end chambers as well as the corbelled roof. The penetration and withdrawal of the light lasts for a total of seventeen minutes – a cosmic union of Father Sun and Mother Earth on the shortest day of the year.[9]

I could imagine a great crowd of worshippers gathered outside at this time of year, watching the first rays of the sun enter the mound after a night's drumming and dancing – only to begin again in a final celebration of new life. Clearly the builders of Newgrange and Maes Howe shared the same beliefs and practised the same rituals to ensure that the sun would roll back from its southernmost position to fertilize the land anew. Life, at its lowest ebb, would grow and blossom once again.

It has also been observed that, on one occasion in its eight-year cycle, the planet Venus shines on the winter solstice through the aperture of the 'light box' at Newgrange to illuminate the inner chamber. This takes place twenty-four minutes before the rays of the sun appear.[10] As the ghostly light of Venus fades, the warm golden light of the sun follows – only to leave the chamber in pitch darkness for another year. The next time this phenomenon will occur will be in 2009.

The chamber at Newgrange may well have been enclosed by a great stone circle; twelve stones remain standing, probably built 1000 years later. Later generations clearly found the place sacred. A double-circle wood henge, enclosing cremation pits of the Beaker people, was built to the southeast. Within a kilometre there are also three other tumuli. And then there is a mysterious 3-metre-high pillar standing 5 metres to the NNE of the monument, possibly as a marker for astronomical alignments.

Dowth and Knowth

Newgrange is not alone. She has two sisters close by in the Boyne Valley. The great mound at Dowth lies about 3 kilometres northeast of Newgrange. It is even older, but it has been plundered and eroded over the millennia and more than half of its original mass has disappeared. In the nineteenth century a summerhouse was even built on top of it. The main passage faces west and is 8 metres long – less than half the length of Newgrange. It leads to a cruciform chamber which contains decorated stones and the remains of another stone basin. A series of small chambers lead off the southwestern corner. A souterrain or underground stone passage was built much later in the Iron Age, when the mound became the foundation of a fortress. The songs of peaceful rituals had given way to the cries of war.

The third great mound in the Boyne Valley, over 3 kilometres northwest of Newgrange, is at Knowth. It is 84 metres in diameter with a height of about 14 metres, with finely decorated kerbstones. It not only has the longest cairn passage in Europe, but its internal structure is intriguing. The layout is like the one in Newgrange with a cruciform shape and corbelled roof. In the inner chamber, there is a beautifully decorated stone basin which was discovered with a ceremonial flint macehead.[11]

The main passage, 36 metres long, leads in from the east. But there is another, shorter passage, which comes in from the west and bends to the right three-quarters along its way before rising to a chamber with a lintel roof. The two passages almost, but not quite, meet in the middle. Its builders clearly understood the complex cycle of the heavens, for they orientated the two passages so that the sun and moon could shine down into the womb of the mound, mingling silver female light with gold masculine light. The passages also face the rising and the setting sun at the equinoxes, when day and night are of equal length.

A stone in one of the recesses in the central chamber deep under the mound at Knowth is incised with a truly remarkable image, pitted into the surface by a piece of quartz. When a transparency with the markings on the stone are placed over a picture of the full moon, they line up exactly.[12] This means that it could be the oldest map of the moon known in the world. It was carved 5000 years before Leonardo da Vinci, who was hitherto thought to be the first person to have made a sketch of the moon around 1505. In a neighbouring recess, there are unmistakeable symbols of the moon and stars carved on the stones.

Even more intriguing is the orientation of the mound to the east. This allows moonlight at certain times to shine down the long passage to the inner chamber to illuminate the ancient map of the moon itself. Other strange circular and spiral patterns in the inner chamber may well be lunar symbols linked to the worship of the Great Goddess. All this suggests that Knowth could have been one of the earliest and most important lunar observatories, the astronomers of which would almost certainly have been in touch with those at Callanish in the Outer Hebrides. The level of detail of the moon map – difficult to achieve with the naked eye alone – further raises the fascinating possibility that the megalith builders may have used crystal lenses thousands of years before the telescope was thought to have been invented.[13]

While guidebooks and gazeteers continue to call the chambers in the bend in the Boyne Valley 'tombs', they were clearly sacred centres of rites and ceremonies in a ritual landscape which extended over several kilometres. All three could be seen from each other's summits.

The site could be easily reached from the sea by boat up the river Boyne, and it was undoubtedly connected to the centres of Stone Age civilization along the Atlantic seaboard from Orkney to North Africa and even beyond. The early Irish myths mention a people from Greece led by one Partholon, who settled in Ireland only to be wiped out by a plague. They were followed by a warrior race called the Fir

Bolg, possible from the Black Sea, who were ousted by the Tuatha Dé Danann, an advanced and civilized people who revered the goddess Danu.[14] While these Irish myths suggest civilization came from the East, they probably refer to seafarers merely visiting from the Mediterranean.

One legend associates Newgrange with Aonghus, the chief of the Tuatha Dé Danann. It is said that they were defeated by the invading Milesians ('the children of Mil') – also known as the Scotti or Gaels – who originated in Egypt and reached Ireland via the Iberian peninsula around 1700 BC (or if it is calculated from the legendary figure of thirty-five generations, around 700 to 800 BC). Tuatha Dé Danann then retreated to a subterranean kingdom beneath the dolmens and earthen ring forts (known as raths), where they became the Fairy Folk, sometimes helping, sometimes hindering humans with their magical lore. The fact that the Tuatha Dé Danann withdrew beneath the dolmens indicates that they came to Ireland long after the megalithic mounds had been denuded of their rock and earth covering.

Mil, the leader of the Milesians, named the new homeland Scotia in honour of his wife Scota, said to be the daughter of an Egyptian pharaoh. This story became so popular during the the Middle Ages that the Irish were referred to as the Egyptians. It is difficult to disentangle the historical truth from the mythic imagination in this account, but it reflects the ancient and long-lasting maritime connections between northern Europe and North Africa.[15]

There is an intriguing reference in Geoffrey of Monmouth's twelfth-century *History of the Kings of Britain* which supports the idea of a link between the megalithic builders in the Mediterranean, Britain and Ireland. Monmouth's 'history' included Arthur in the line of British Kings. He writes that Merlin suggested to King Aurelius, Arthur's uncle, that he raise a lasting monument to heroes – Stonehenge – and send for a Giant's Ring on Mount Killarus in Ireland:'many years ago the Giants transported them from the remotest confines of Africa and set them up in Ireland at a time when they inhabited that country'.[16] And there were indeed giants – in mind if not stature – in those days.

Castlerigg

As I noted earlier, the Irish Sea is the Mediterranean of the British Isles – a huge contrast to the drama and danger of the waters further north. It is sheltered by Ireland, which acts as a breakwater against the full fetch of the Atlantic Ocean. Providentially placed in the middle is the Isle of Man, a convenient one-day sail from any shore. Stone Age argonauts would have crisscrossed the sea as a matter of course, taking from Ireland axes to Scotland and axes and pots to Cumbria. And that was my next destination after the Valley of the Boyne.

Not far inland from the coast is the famed stone circle at Castlerigg in the heart of England's Lake District. Climbing a steep lane from the town, you soon reach the flat plateau of Chestnut Hill, where a wide ring of stones stands in an open field. Made from metamorphic slate, they form a flattened ring of thirty-eight stones with an average diameter of 30 metres; only a few are more than 1.5 metres high. Two tall stones form a broad entrance to the north.

Wherever you turn, you see a spectacular array of rugged mountain peaks and rolling hills which together create a vast natural cauldron. The spirit of the earth here is united with the power of the sky. It is perhaps the most beautiful megalithic site in England and one of the most impressive in the whole of Europe. Castlerigg must have represented a high point in the culture of building stones to the sky: it is designed with an aesthetic sense as much as a scientific one. Its special energy has inspired some highly imaginative speculation. It has not only been called the heart chakra of the energy centres of the body of Britain, but its configuration has also been likened to the Vesica Piscis, the symbolic shape of two interlocking circles which form a 'vulva' in the centre, representing the Goddess.[17]

Be that as it may, Castlerigg is one of the earliest stone circles in Europe, raised around 3200 BC. It was well worth my detour inland. When I visited it, the stones sparkled in the bright light of early morning, darkening dramatically under the shadows of the passing clouds. It was a far cry from Keats's description of it as a 'dismal cirque of Druid stones upon a forlorn moor'.

The ritual landscape at Castlerigg extends for kilometres in all directions, well beyond the stone circle itself. Many of the stones are carefully aligned with distant features such as notches and mounds in the surrounding mountains and fells. Alexander Thom, whose presence I had felt at Callanish, calculated seven key alignments and recognized the site's importance as a lunar observatory.[18] In addition, the tall radial pillar at the southeastern corner lines up with the sunrise on the quarter day at the end of October known as Samhain in the Celtic calendar.

An unpolished stone axe has been found inside the ring itself. Because of its open position, Castlerigg may well have been a marketplace for the stone axe industry in nearby Langdales; the stone was quarried only a few kilometres to the south along a steep pass. Cumbrian axes were transported by sea and have been found as far afield as northern Scotland and southern England. The fact that the sanctuary continued to be valued as a sacred place for many generations is attested by the faint outlines of round cairns, long flattened by the plough, just visible inside the ring.

The Island of the Ocean God

From the shores of Cumbria, the Isle of Man is only a short hop across the Irish Sea. Its highest peak, Snaefell, rises to over 600 metres and can be seen from the mountains of England, Ireland, Wales and Scotland on a clear day. It is a perfect landmark for seafarers.

As I sailed around the the Calf, a rugged islet on the south-westerly tip of the island, I tried to make out the upright stones of Meayll Hill. Local fishermen used to line them up with Calf Sound to indicate one of their fishing grounds. On the hill itself, there is an intriguing ring of stones built of local slate, although they do not form a true circle. The circumference is composed of six long, rectangular chambers in pairs, three on the east and three on the west. Originally it was probably a cairn, with chambers and passages added at a later date. A larger kerbed cairn was then built over them. Much of the site has been destroyed by generations of farmers for material to build fences but there are still some unusual T-shaped blocks around the edges which recall the design of the chambered mounds I had seen in the Boyne Valley. This is not surprising: as I have already mentioned, the Isle of Man has always been a staging post for mariners travelling between Ireland and the British mainland. Legend has it that a ghostly army of horsemen can sometimes be glimpsed riding by the ring.

The Isle of Man has been inhabited since Mesolithic times and there is a fine megalithic gallery grave at Cashtal yn Ard. The Manx language is closely related to Irish and Scottish Gaelic, and clearly shares the same cultural heritage. It was not until 1263 that the seafaring Manx lost the Western Isles of Scotland, till then part of their kingdom.

The island is said to be named after Manann Mac Lir. Manann was the sea god who ruled in the Land of Promise with his wife, the Pearl of Beauty. He usually appeared as a handsome warrior, but could also change shape and ride his chariot over the waves as if they were a plain. He was a god to be feared, causing storms as well as wrecking ships.

The Giantess's Apronful

We did not linger long at the Isle of Man for we were keen to head south to the Isle of Anglesey on the edge of North Wales. Ynys Môn, as it is called in Welsh, was the last stronghold of the Druids in Wales before they were defeated by the Romans. Not far from Holyhead, the main port to Dublin, there is a fine chambered cairn called Barclodiad-y-Gawres on a spectacular headland overlooking Trecastle Bay. Reflecting the ancient association of cairns with the Earth Goddess, and the belief that only people of extraordinary stature could have built the megaliths, the Welsh name means 'The Giantess's Apronful'. It would be difficult to imagine a more suggestive name to evoke its fertility symbolism. An old Welsh story has it that the stones themselves are giants, turned to stone by a spell, but on New Year's Eve the spell is lifted so that they can walk down to the nearest water and drink.

The original cairn of giant stones has long gone, and a concrete dome protects the large upright slabs which form the very rough cruciform shape of the chamber. The entrance is oriented to the north. Five of the slabs are carved with spirals, cupmarks, concentric circles, lozenges and zigzags, although some are now difficult to make out. It is the only remaining chamber in Wales displaying the same kind of megalithic art found in Ireland.

When it was excavated Barclodiad y Gawres revealed cremated bones, bone pins and a hearth containing the skeletal remains of reptiles, fish and small mammals. It was clearly used for the living as well as the dead, for ritual as well burial. It is still a place of pilgrimage and reverence, despite the concrete roof and iron grill which can only be opened with a key lent by a local farmer. When I visited it on the winter solstice someone had placed candles inside creating a magical effect as the light flickered across the great stones. I sat on its mound afterwards, watching the orange sun set on the shortest day into the wild Irish Sea and listening to the waves crash on the rocks below. Little has changed here in 5000 years.

The Mound of the Dark Grove

Further south on Anglesey, near Menai Bridge, is another chambered cairn called Bryn Celli Ddu, 'The Mound of the Dark Grove'. The large grass-covered mound is reached by a pleasant walk along a river and across a wooden bridge. It is undoubtedly the most impressive passage grave in Wales.

Originally, there was a henge with a ditch, bank and a circle of standing stones, although it was destroyed shortly afterwards when the cairn was built. Outside the cairn stands a replica of a pillar known as the Stone of Enigmas carved with zigzags and maze-like patterns on both faces and across the top. The original, now in the National Museum of Wales, probably formed part of the original circle but was taken down some time before 3500 BC and buried. Like the carvings at Barclodiad-y-Gawres, they shared the same metaphysical alphabet seen at Newgrange across the sea.

An unusual pit just beyond the chamber was found to contain a human ear bone. During excavations bones, flint tools, shells, a stone bead, a scraper and a flint arrowhead were uncovered. In the forecourt to the passage the remains of a hearth and a platform of white quartz pebbles were also discovered. They imply that it served as a ritual centre for shamanistic magic.

I entered the mound from the northeast. A narrow passageway 8 metres long leads to a small burial chamber no more than 3 metres across and about 2 metres high. Five large uprights hold up two large capstones. In the chamber I made an extraordinary discovery.

I went in at noon on a rare sunny day on the midwinter solstice. Rays of the winter sun shone through a 'roof box' to the south. It illuminated the middle part of a smooth central stone for an hour from 12.30 GMT; a golden glow gilded the greenish grain of the rock.

Elizabeth was with me. Putting her cheek against its surface, she quietly observed:

'It's a very, very sacred stone. No doubt about it!'

She stretched out her hand and the rays of the midwinter sun cast a shadow across the stone.

If it had not been for the supports for the new cement roof, the sun's rays would have touched the top of the stone. This would have occurred at a very special moment of cosmic time, when the sun was at its highest point during its most southerly position in the year. From then on, it would rise each day in the sky until it reached its zenith six months later, on the midsummer solstice.

This modest mound was orientated to the midwinter sun just like the great mounds at Maes Howe and Newgrange. These distant peoples of Scotland, Ireland and Wales clearly shared the same beliefs and the same concern with the power of Father Sun to fertilize Mother Earth.

From the centre of the original stone circle, which could date to as early as 4000 BC, the contours of the distant hills provide clear notches and gaps for possible alignments. It would seem that the position had been carefully chosen in order to plot to the east the extremes of the full moon's rising. Again, the Callanish site immediately comes to mind.

After my discovery of the light hitting the pillar, I came across the researches of Christopher Knight and Robert Lomas. They concluded that the passage of the mound was aligned on the equinoxes and the summer solstice to illuminate cup marks in the stonework. Above all, the pillar and roof box are positioned not only to measure the winter solstice but also the cycle of Venus, the third brightest heavenly body known as the morning and evening star. Every eight years towards the end of December Venus is at its maximum brilliance and follows the sun two and half hours after sunset. To a lesser extent, this occurs halfway through the eight-year cycle. At the maximum, with no moon in a clear sky, it would be possible to read a book by the light of Venus.[19] It would seem that Bryn Celli Ddu, like Newgrange in the Boyne Valley, served not only as a solar and lunar observatory plotting the main heavenly events of the year, but a place for observing Venus.

Druids' circles

It is common in Wales, as in the rest of the British Isles, to call a megalithic ring of stones a 'Druids' circle'. This is misleading for, as I've noted, they were built thousands of years before the Celts arrived in Britain around 500 BC. Far from being a mass migration of invaders, the Celts may well have influenced the local inhabitants through the interest their culture generated as much as through their force of arms.[20] It is also quite possible that the Celtic priests – the Druids – not only adopted some of the megalithic sites for their own rituals, but absorbed many of the beliefs of their builders which had been passed down the generations. The Druids may therefore offer a glimpse into the mind of the megalith builders.

The Celts made their last-ditch stand on Anglesey at Castell Ior against the Romans in AD 60. All we know of the Druids comes from ancient Roman accounts. These writers not only saw them from their own cultural perspective, but tended to demonize them in order to justify their conquest and the imposition of their own civilization. Nevertheless, Julius Caesar wrote respectfully of the Druids as priests, judges and astronomers whose doctrine he believed originated in Britain.

Because Druids were exempt from military service and taxes, Caesar claimed that many young people were attracted to Druidism, and that the Druids were held in great honour by the people. They were expected to memorize a great number of verses – so many that some of them spent twenty years at their studies. The Druids did not want to commit their teaching to writing, even though for other purposes they were already using the Greek alphabet. As I mentioned earlier, the initiates were also inculcated with the doctrine that 'the soul does not perish, but after death passes from one body to another', a belief which Caesar felt encouraged their bravery and disregard of death. The Druids claimed to be descended from the god of the underworld, whom they called Father Dis.

The most intriguing passage in Caesar's account, however, is where he describes their astronomical interests: 'They also hold long discussions about the heavenly bodies and their movements, the size of the universe and of the earth and the physical constitution of the world and the power and the properties of the gods'.[21] The Druids apparently measured the passage of time by night: when celebrating birthdays, the first of the month and New Year, the day began at sunset. They also adopted an accurate calendar based on lunar months.

The Roman historian Tacitus described one of the ceremonies of the Druids which evokes the joyous nature of their rites. It would almost certainly have occurred at the spring equinox; it could also possibly have taken place on Anglesey and been a reincarnation of the Great Goddess herself. Tacitus writes:

On an island of the ocean is a sacred grove and in it there is a consecrated chariot covered with a veil. Only the priest may approach it. He knows when the goddess appears in the sacred chariot. He becomes aware of the presence of the goddess in her holy place, and in deep reverence accompanies her chariot drawn by cows. Then there are days of joy and feasting in all places which the goddess honours with a visit. Then there are joyous days and wedding feasts. At those times no war is waged, no weapons are handled, the sword is sheathed. Only peace and quiet are at those times known or desired, until the goddess, tired of her sojourn among mortals, is led back into the shrine by the same priest.[22]

The cauldron of Cerridwen

The megalithic builders were active not only on Anglesey, but all along the Welsh coast. On Penmaenmawr – the 'Great Stone Headland' – near Conway, there is a fine stone circle, dating possibly from 3000 BC, at Cefn Goch. From the centre of the oval setting of stones, the two southern portals stand in line with the major southern moonset. Its long axis runs from ESE–WNW which is aligned to the setting sun on May Day (or Beltane in the Celtic calendar). Long associated with the Druids, local folklore has it that on one occasion, when a coven of witches was having an orgy inside the ring, the sudden booming from the stones frightened them so much that two went mad. The symbolism of the stone circle still reverberates down to the present day in Wales, with the Gorsedd ring of stones raised each year in different parts of the country to commemorate the bard of the year at the national Eisteddfod.

I was living in North Wales when I first began my voyage. One day my friend and neighbour Dei Hughes – Welsh-speaking sculptor, poet and shaman – placed into my hands two beautiful stone axes which he had been given in exchange for a sculpture. The first had an oval shape with a flattened top and a central perforated hole. It measured about 20 by 11 centimetres. As I turned it over in my hands, I appreciated its weighty solidity and carefully polished surface.

'It took me several years to realize its importance,' he told me. 'Only spiritual artists could do it. Although it is classified by archaeologists as an axe hammer, its use was probably more ritual than practical. Don't worry about logic, just feel it!'

The other axe he showed me was lozenge-shaped. It was 20.5 centimetres long and 7.5 centimetres wide. It too had a beautiful feel. Petrologists had classified it as a double-ended axe made from an agglomerate of arkose grit.

'It may not have been an axe at all,' said Dei, weighing it in his sculptor's hand. 'It was probably carried by a cord through its hole; it could even have been used as a sight for astronomical alignments. I place it on my altar at home!'

With Dei, I visited two impressive dolmens on a bed of white boulders at Dyffryn Ardudwy, not far from our homes, which stood on a hillside as if forever looking out to sea. As in Scotland and Ireland, dolmens are very common in Wales (except, as I've mentioned, that they are called cromlechs). These mounds have lost their stone and earth coverings to reveal the stark skeleton of their inner chambers, and truly look like the stone tables of giants. Some of them are massive. The Lligwy cromlech on Anglesey, for instance, has a gigantic capstone weighing 28 tonnes.

On the second leg of my voyage, I sailed from my old home port of Porthmadog with another neighbour, the architect David Lea, down the west coast of Wales. We sailed past the Neolithic burial chamber known as the Garreg Samson cromlech, which overlooks the wild

Strumble Head near Fishguard. This once great monument is now reduced to a capstone supported by three of seven upright stones. The best known monument in Wales, however, is the Pentre Ifan cromlech, southwest of Cardigan. It is sometimes called the Cauldron of Ceridwen, (Ceridwen being the Welsh goddess of the underworld), and locals say that fairies resembling little children dressed in red caps dance around its delicately balanced capstone. These gaunt stones have become the popular image of Stone Age Wales.

Although the Irish Sea is relatively calm in summer, it can still be capricious. As we left the wide-open harbour of Fishguard, it was calm and still. The only blot on the horizon was the possible threat of thunderstorms – and that wouldn't deter us. I was intent on visiting a very special site, further down the Welsh coast.

During the morning dark clouds rolled in and the wind inexorably picked up. After lunch, the threatened thunderstorm struck. It was an electric storm with great flashes of forked lightning streaking across the black sky. The breaking sea became a sinister dark steely blue. Then the heavens opened and heavy rain dropped in perpendicular streaks, hitting the surface of the water so hard they bounced off, in a spray of diamonds. One squall came in after the other, with winds gusting up to gale force. By the time we had rounded the islands off Pembrokeshire in southwest Wales and reached the protection of Milford Haven, both keels of my boat had sprung leaks which would be difficult to repair. The ancient mariners with their light skin boats may have fared better, for they could have easily hauled them out of the water onto the smallest of sheltering strands.

It was from Milford Haven that one of the greatest feats of engineering and seamanship took place in the megalithic age. Inland from the wide natural harbour on an expanse of open moorland called Gors Fawr – the 'Great Marsh' – at the foot of the Preseli Mountains, there is a large stone circle. Sixteen stones are carefully graded, with the tallest in the south. A short distance to the northeast are two taller standing stones set on a NE–SW axis, aligned towards the midsummer sunrise. One stone of the ring is made from a type of dolerite called bluestone.

It is now accepted that the first stone ring at Stonehenge in southern England was made from bluestone, taken from these very mountains. While the unique origin of the bluestone monoliths in South Wales is not disputed, the method by which they were moved is. The effort and ingenuity involved have led some to argue that they moved naturally during the Ice Age – sledged by glaciers – to Salisbury Plain.[23] There is no evidence, however, of Ice Age glaciers reaching as far south as Stonehenge, and no other post-glacial debris or deposited rocks have been found in the surrounding chalk uplands.

On the other hand, there is a growing consensus that the bluestones were brought by boat down from the Preseli Mountains along the River Cleddau to Milford Haven and then shipped across the sea. Divers have recently claimed to have seen a bluestone in the bottom of Milford Haven, and a small piece of spotted dolerite has turned up on Steep Holm, a small island in the Bristol Channel.

In the 1950s it was demonstrated that a bluestone, about 2 to 5 metres in length, could be lashed to canoes and carried up quite small waterways. A more recent attempt to carry one on two corracles failed because it proved top heavy in choppy water. If the experiment demonstrated anything, it was the incompetence of modern amateurs compared to the abilities of experienced Stone Age seafarers. A better way of transporting them might be to lash a bluestone to a boat underwater so that it could be partly buoyed up and act as ballast and a keel to stabilize the boat.

There are two possible routes for the transport of the twenty-three original bluestones from Milford Haven to Stonehenge. One is up the Bristol Channel, then along the River Kennet to Salisbury Plain; the other is around Land's End, along the Channel to Poole harbour and then up the River Avon, a journey of some 400 nautical miles.[24] Since the former would have involved a long passage across difficult terrain, the latter seems far more likely, especially as there is a long processional avenue leading from the bank of the River Avon. This was my next port of call.

CHAPTER SIX

The Proudest Singularity

Pile of Stonehenge! So proud to hint yet keep
Thy secrets . . .

WILLIAM WORDSWORTH

C hart on knee, I contemplated the route the Stonehenge bluestones would have followed from Milford Haven in South Wales. They would probably have been taken along the coast up the Bristol Channel, over to Steep Holm and then down the coasts of Devon and Cornwall. Travelling up the Channel after Land's End, my finger settled on the prehistoric port of Hengistbury Head near Christchurch, at the mouth of the Avon. From here the bluestones could have been transported upriver as far as Amesbury, just east of Stonehenge.

The long man-made avenue that runs up from the bank of the Avon follows the easiest contours, curving north and then running west to the main site at Stonehenge. It was probably built to commemorate the route along which the bluestones were taken on the last leg of their 650-kilometre journey around 2500 BC. And the reason for this extraordinary feat of engineering, seamanship and collective labour? Magic. The bluestones, composed mainly of spotted dolerite and ranging in colour from blotchy grey to reddish brown, were probably thought to have magical qualities by a people who worshipped the Great Goddess and wanted to build a temple to her on these wide open plains.

It is just possible that a circle of bluestones may have been removed complete from the Preseli Mountains and taken to Stonehenge in order to form the centrepiece of the earliest stone circle. A dim folk memory of this event may lie behind the suggestion in Geoffrey of

Monmouth's *History of the Kings of Britain* that the stones of
Stonehenge were brought by Merlin's magic from a Giant's Ring on
Mount Killarus in Ireland. Geoffrey was right in saying the stones
came from the west – he just got the country wrong.

The first inhabitants

The people who first raised the ring of bluestones at Stonehenge
around 2500 BC had inhabited the area for thousands of years, and
had already transformed the land and built many earthworks and
monuments. So the site, which stands on a slight spur above a dry
chalk valley on a southward-dipping plateau, was part of an already
highly developed ritual landscape. The range, variety and complexity
of monuments in the Stonehenge area are unique.

It seems that the first nomadic hunter-gatherers arrived here at the
end of the Ice Age around 9000 BC, when the land bridges to Europe
and Ireland were still intact. They would have hunted and gathered in
the thick forest and only slowly began to widen any clearings through
slashing and burning the surrounding trees. Their main tools were
knives, scrapers and arrows.

The recent discovery of four post holes near Stonehenge, dating
from around 8000 BC, shows that the site had been a sacred place for
a long time and that its early inhabitants had developed a strong social
and religious sense. These Mesolithic holes could well have held some
kind of totem pole used to commemorate ancestors, like those raised
by hunter-gatherers in North America who lived in a similar Boreal
landscape.

The first farmers did not arrive in Britain much before 4500 BC.
They brought with them domesticated animals – cattle, sheep, goats
and pigs. Since the land bridge to the continent had disappeared with
the sudden rise in sea level around 6500 BC, they would have had to
transport them by boat as elsewhere in the British Isles. It is not
entirely clear whether sections of the native population gradually
switched to agriculture or whether new people came in with the
skills; it was probably a combination of both. For a while, the new
farmers not only coexisted with the hunter-gatherers, but hunted
and gathered themselves.

Settled agriculture had enormous repercussions here. It not only
supported a rapidly increasing number of people but provided them
with the leisure to study the heavens and undertake great works of
monumental architecture. In their sophisticated medicine, they even

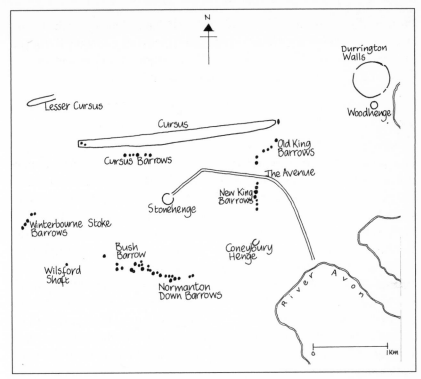

The principal megalithic monuments in the Stonehenge area

developed the art of trepanning, or cutting holes in the skull, to operate on the brain. Their barrows show they had a profound respect for the dead as well as the living.

The earliest major Neolithic work in the area is the enclosure with a causeway entrance at Robin Hood's Ball about 4 kilometres to the northwest of Stonehenge. It forms an open hilltop platform surrounded by two rings of ditches cut by a land bridge. Built in the first half of the fourth millennium and aligned to the sunrise, it was probably a ritual centre for a large tribal group living in the area. Human skeletons with the bones scattered about have been found in the ditches, together with the debris of feasts – pottery and animal bones – all suggesting that the site may have been used as a platform to commune with the dead as they were laid out to be picked clean by birds before being buried.

On a hill southeast of Stonehenge stands Coneybury Henge, the prototype of all henges. Although now flattened by ploughing, it was once entered, like Stonehenge, from the northeast, the direction of the rising sun at midsummer. Its shape is not circular but oval, like the stones of Stenness in Orkney. A recent find on a nearby hill hints at the lifestyle of the builders. Offering a remarkable cross-section of Neolithic culture in the early fourth millennium, the site yielded pottery, arrowheads, flint axes, the bones of domesticated cattle, emmer wheat grains, and other artefacts, probably of a ritual nature.

Among the most enigmatic features of the landscape surrounding Stonehenge is the linear earthwork to the north known as the Cursus – not a racecourse as its Latin name implies, but almost certainly used as a processional way. Stretching for nearly 3 kilometres, it was laid out around 3000 BC. Since it runs almost due east and west, it is roughly aligned to the sunrise on the equinoxes. A long barrow was built at its end.

By 3000 BC, the people of Salisbury Plain had cleared much of the wildwood of pine and hazel to create open grassland for their domesticated cattle. In their scattered arable plots, they grew emmer wheat and other cereal crops. By the middle of the third millennium, their domestic economy included textiles as well as carefully decorated jewellery and pottery.

They also developed wide trading links with the rest of the British Isles and Europe. Several examples (dating from around 2800 BC) of Grooved Ware pottery, possibly originating in Orkney and found throughout eastern Britain, have been discovered at Stonehenge. A perforated axe hammer made from the same Welsh stone as the bluestones has been found in a Wiltshire grave. An axe discovered in Hampshire was made from a precious stone, jadeite, only found in the Swiss Alps. Some of these would have been transported across land, but most undoubtedly would have come by boat.

Other Neolithic monuments in the area include the vast henge bank and ditch at Durrington Walls, built around 2800 to 2200 BC, northeast of Stonehenge. Half a kilometre in diameter, its outer ring almost brushes the bank of the River Avon. Nearby is the circular earthwork of Woodhenge, constructed a little before 2000 BC. It consists of six concentric rings of post holes within a bank and inner ditch and which has a northeastern entrance, facing the midsummer sunrise. Substantial caches of later Grooved Ware pottery have been discovered beneath the bank. The most intriguing find among a number of human burials discovered on the site is that of a three- or four-year-old child with its skull cleft in two. My most immediate thought was that it was part of some gruesome ritual, but since there is no evidence of human sacrifice in Neolithic times, this may well have been the result of a post-mortem.

South of Durrington Walls and Woodhenge is the beginning of the great Avenue along which the bluestones were transported from the River Avon. I can imagine them being escorted with great pomp and circumstance to their final resting place after their long and hazardous journey by sea and river from South Wales. I was intrigued to discover that the curving approach of the Avenue separates the older funerary monuments to the north from the ritual monuments to the south, thereby marking the boundary between the regions of the dead and the living. As with the building of Stonehenge itself, the actual process of constructing the avenue was probably as important as the goal: it was not just a means to an end, but a religious end in itself.

The building of Stonehenge

What we see at the main site of Stonehenge today represents the remains of the third stage of a complex development which took place over more than 2000 years. It is clear from the different phases of the development that the stones, despite their weight, were not fixed but part of a living, evolving ritual landscape.

In its first phase, Stonehenge consisted of an earthwork monument. A circular ditch enclosed by two earth banks intercut by two entrances was begun around 3000 BC, enclosing a space of around 85 metres in diameter. Animal bones were placed in the bottom of

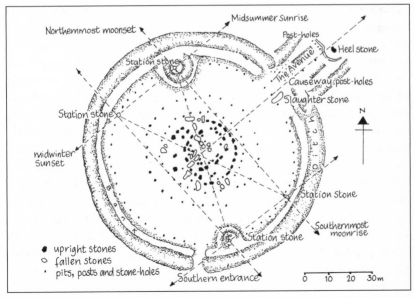

Ground plan of Stonehenge, showing some of its astronomical alignments

the ditch: two jawbones of cattle lying on either side of the southern entrance imply that they were highly revered objects. The principal entrance facing northeast was aligned to the midsummer sunrise. It seems that the lefthand side of the entrance-causeway also stood in line with the most northerly rising of the midwinter full moon.[1]

In the second phase of its development, from around 2900 BC, Stonehenge became a wooden monument. A complex setting of timber posts was put into place in the middle of the circle and in the southern and northeastern entrances. While their exact use is still unclear, the posts of the northeastern entrance, with its four outriders, may have formed a solar corridor through which the rising sun could be viewed at midsummer dawn. At this stage, the circle was also being used as a cremation cemetery.

The third phase of the building was the longest, involving the erection, dismantling and resetting of a variety of stones over at least six separate periods. This activity lasted from around 2550 BC to 1600 BC. Around 2400 BC, fifty-six holes – known as Aubrey Holes after the antiquarian who first spotted them in 1666 – were dug inside the inner bank to hold timber posts. They are now covered prosaically with concrete disks.

The famous bluestones were the first stones raised within the henge. Weighing about 4 tonnes each, they were the smallest in the present setting, although still taller than a man. They may have formed at first an arc on the northern and eastern sides or even a square with rounded edges within the circle.[2] A couple have tongue-and-groove sections cut into their sides, while others have mortise-and-tenon fixings. Both are still common joints in carpentry, and show the sophistication of the Neolithic stonemasons.

Almost certainly a larger stone was placed in the western portion of the circle of bluestones facing the northeastern entrance. This huge piece of Cosheston Beds sandstone, also thought to have been transported from South Wales by boat, now lies on its side and is erroneously called the Altar Stone.

All this was to be dismantled – perhaps within a hundred years – by the raising of enormous blocks of sarsen stone, an extremely hard form of sandstone found on the Marlborough Downs some 30 kilometres to the north of the site. Their name derives from the local habit of calling them 'Saracen' stones, no doubt due to their association with non-Christian beliefs. Shaped and dressed to about 4 metres of their height, thirty sarsens were erected to form a circle and crowned by a continuous lintel of stone blocks. Like the bluestones, they too were fitted together with mortise-and-tenon and tongue-and-groove joints.

They are not only beautifully upright, but great care was also taken in levelling off the stones, despite the gently sloping ground in which they stand. The lintels were carefully curved to form the lines of a circle, an extraordinary feat of engineering and design, especially as there was little room for error. And as in classical Greek temples, the stones in the circle have a slightly convex taper to counteract the foreshortening effect when looking up at them from the ground. The result of this subtle optical illusion is that the pillars look tall and straight.

A larger group of 'trilithons' were also raised within the circle: five separate pairs of standing stones, joined on top by lintels. They were set in a horseshoe shape facing the northeast entrance. The effect was to align the earlier monument a few degrees further east, lining up its central axis with the Avenue which bends down to the River Avon. It has been calculated that the axis was orientated towards the rising of the sun when half of its orb was above the horizon, about the time when sarsens were erected.[3]

The raising of the stones

Some of the largest stones are over 7 metres high and weigh 45 tonnes – in bulk alone raising the question of Stone Age technology. It was long thought they were moved on rollers, but this has been shown to be a cumbersome method. A more efficient way, requiring less manpower, would have been to surround the stones with a protective casing which acted like a cradle. Models of these have recently been found in the Egyptian pyramids. The most likely way, however, was to pull them on a sledge along a specially constructed wooden trackway, probably greased with animal fat. Experiments with this method in 1995 showed that a hundred people would be enough to pull such a sledge. Strong ropes were probably made from the bark of the small-leaved lime tree, the strongest plant fibre native to Britain. In this way, the builders of Stonehenge could have brought the sarsens down from the Marlborough Downs via the Vale of Pewsey, or more easily along the banks of the River Avon. Either way, it was another example of Stone Age engineering and ingenuity, not just brute force.

As in Orkney, the stones were probably raised by first digging a pit with a sloping edge. The base of the stone could then be eased in with the use of rollers and its top pulled into position by ropes with the possible help of an A frame on the other side to support it. Packing material was finally placed around the base to secure it in position;

some include the 'mauls', flattened spheres of stone, used to pound and dress the sarsens. That left the tricky job of placing the lintels, with their mortise-and-tenon joints, on top of the standing stones. This could have been done by lifting alternative ends of the lintel stone with levers and blocks while gradually building up a wooden platform under them until it was level with the tops of the upright stones. Whatever the exact method, the process would have involved the labour of hundreds over a considerable period of time; it has been estimated that it took 30 million man-hours of work to build Stonehenge.[4]

It has been observed that within the trilithon horseshoe, the left hand of each pair of stones is smoother than the one on the right. Could it be that they represent the eternal essence of Man and Woman? Linked together by the grooved lintel, they make a powerful symbol of the unity between lovers, connected and yet apart.

Four mysterious stones outside the main stone circle but within the earth bank were added some time during the third phase of Stonehenge's development. They are known as the Station Stones, two of which are still in place. Barrow mounds were built around the northern and southern ones. Forming a rectangle, their centre points to the centre of the circle.

Two other mysterious outlying stones were added, the so-called Slaughter Stone and the Heel Stone. The former, pitted with holes and marks, lies on its side by the entrance to the Avenue, and only became associated with sacrifice at the end of the eighteenth century. It may have been moved there to make way for a trackway for carts which once passed through the stone circle; it was certainly not flattened in order to slaughter young virgins or children to the gods. Indeed, there is no evidence that the Druids, let alone the megalith builders before them, ever sacrificed humans in stone circles, despite persistent myths.

The Heel Stone, a large undressed menhir, stands at the beginning of the Avenue and almost certainly had a twin in order to frame the sun rising on midsummer's day. It was erroneously thought to be named after the Greek word for the Sun, *helios*. A more likely derivation comes at a later date from the epithet 'Friar's Heel', given to an indentation on the stone which was made, so legend has it, after a friar lost a bout with the devil at its side.

The resulting form at Stonehenge was close to the one we know today. But subtle rearrangements continued to be made. Carefully shaped and dressed bluestones were probably set in an oval within the sarsen horseshoe, and a circle of rougher bluestones placed within the outer sarsen circle. Some new ones may have been taken from South

Wales at this stage to make up their number. Then, around 2000 BC, the inner bluestones were reset yet again, forming a horseshoe with a single standing stone – the Altar Stone – as a focal point for the whole monument. Two external circles of holes – now known as the Y and Z Holes – were dug, possibly to take another setting of stones; but they were never filled.

Not long after, the energy of the builders and worshippers finally ran out. Following more than a millennium and a half of building and use, the site of Stonehenge was abandoned around 1500 BC.

The Bronze Age

During the later phases in the building of Stonehenge some important social and cultural changes were taking place. Some archaeologists, looking at their own society, assume that only a stratified and territorial society could be capable of such monumental work. They argue that it would have been hard to marshal the necessary workforce without the strong leadership of a political elite.[5] But as we have seen in Orkney, there is no firm evidence to prove that Stone Age society was anything more than a loose confederation of affinity groups. Even if they did support a separate group of builders, astronomers, priests and healers, it does not follow that these had coercive power over the rest of the community. Indeed, it is probable that the megaliths were raised during a great collective surge of religious enthusiasm. The voluntary labour could be drawn on in the slack period in the agricultural year, after sowing and after harvest. As with the building of the Gothic cathedrals, it was no doubt considered an honour to participate in such a high spiritual endeavour.

As I've indicated, this society began to change dramatically around 2200 BC, with the growing influence of the Beaker people. Conflict, if not outright war, became part of everyday life. Hierarchy and domination began to emerge. Society became more individualistic: individual burials in round barrows replaced the older collective ones in long barrows. Powerful chieftains arose, and were buried with luxurious grave goods, especially battle axes.

A harbinger of the new order may well have been a man, buried at Amesbury near Stonehenge around 2300 BC, who came from what is now Switzerland. His recently excavated grave goods include two gold hair ornaments – the oldest gold to be found in Britain – and three copper knives from Spain or France. He was buried with five beakers. He was obviously a man of considerable power and wealth, and his lavish burial demonstrates the links between different parts of Europe at the time.[6]

Early in the nineteenth century, Sir Richard Colt Hoare unearthed at Bush Barrow near Stonehenge a marvellous collection of early Bronze Age artefacts buried with the remains of a tall man. Clearly a person of some distinction, he was laid out on his back with his head pointing north and with Stonehenge at his feet. The find, now in Devizes Museum, included a brass dagger, a gold breastplate decorated with lozenges and zigzags, and, most curious of all, a perforated stone composed of 'a mass of sea worms, or little serpents'.[7] The curious cult object was a mace head made from the fossil Tubularia, highly prized for its rarity.

The decoration on the wooden handle of the dagger was exquisite, consisting of thousands of gold rivets 'smaller than the smallest pin', as Colt Hoare put it. Does this mean that the craftsman of this work of art was using a crystal lens, since it would seem to be impossible to do it with the naked eye?

The enigmatic markings on the gold lozenge placed on the skeleton's chest have given rise to much speculation. Some, like Alexander Thom, have seen them as forming a solar and lunar calendar for Stonehenge, while others have interpreted them as rhomboid shapes defining segments of a circle which were used as a measuring instrument. It may not even be too fanciful to interpret the object as an idealized map of the ritual landscape at Stonehenge, or possibly, because of the curvature of its surface, as a chart of the night sky.

The notion that the Beaker people overran the native culture of the British Isles and conquered the local people by superior force is not absolutely certain. It is also possible, as it is for the Celts, that they lived alongside the indigenous population. The locals may then have gradually adopted the new technology of bronze working and the practice of individual burials. Either way, the Beaker people certainly introduced more than simply a 'fashion in fine pottery'.[8] At the same time, the newcomers probably took up many of the existing local beliefs and traditions: stone circles continued to be built in the Bronze Age throughout Britain, although on a less grandiose scale than before.

What is certain is that British culture became more warlike. The new warriors made their mark on the sarsen stones at Stonehenge. Their surfaces were dressed and smoothed, and twelve were also decorated with incised patterns. One of the central trilithons has at least fourteen carvings of an axe and a dagger, while another, from the eastern side of the stone circle, is decorated with many incised axeheads and some faded cup marks. The axeheads resemble the bronze-flanged axes of the Early Bronze Age dating from around 1500 BC, and were no doubt carved around this time. At the same time, one upright trilithon in the horseshoe appears to have the shape of a human female. Despite the new belligerent patriarchy, perhaps the presence of the Great Goddess was still felt at Stonehenge. Once carved on the stones, she would be difficult to erase.

Exactly why the builders and worshippers of Stonehenge abandoned the site sometime after 1500 BC remains a mystery. A combination of social and environmental factors was the most likely cause. There may have been a crisis of population, with the food supply unable to keep up with growing numbers – the total population of the British Isles at the time has been put at half a million. Furthermore, the massive eruption of the Hekla volcano in Iceland in 1159 BC could have caused acid rain and even temporarily blocked out the sun with a vast fallout of ash, resulting in a devastating change in the climate. The weather certainly began to deteriorate around this time, with heavier rainfall and cooler temperatures. The uplands became uninhabitable; the megaliths were abandoned; and the peat moved in.

The purpose of Stonehenge

Archaeologists more or less agree on the phases of the building of Stonehenge, but its exact function and purpose are far from settled. We know that Stonehenge was part of a ritual landscape; the causewayed enclosures, wood and stone henges all offered a protected circular space for dance, rituals, meetings and worship. As circles, they reflected the circle of the sun and the ring of the horizon. They embodied the rhythm of the year and and the cycle of human existence: the eternal wheel of life, death and rebirth. They were a microcosm on earth of the macrocosm of the universe.

Their sacred geometry includes the line as well as the circle. The early long barrows, avenues, stone rows and cursuses follow lines. Seafarers and wayfarers generally travel in straight lines, along the most direct route, or at least the line of least resistance. They observe how the crow – or seagull – flies. To walk in a straight line is to walk with a purpose. A line links one place with another. Virtually every ritual throughout the world involves walking in a line, whether it be a procession or a priest approaching an altar. The nomads walked in lines across the land, stopping at certain beneficial and special places. These no doubt became the sites of the first megaliths. When the nomads settled down, it would have been natural for them to embody their journeys in linear monuments and stone alignments.

It is widely believed that there are ancient trackways which crisscross the land and which act as conduits for the earth's energies. Alfred Watkins first called them 'ley lines' in his *The Old Straight Track*, published in 1925, and believed that they connected ancient sacred sites throughout Britain. He noticed that beacon hills, mark stones, camps, mounds, earthworks and moats seemed to fall into straight lines. Two such 'archaic whispers from the landscape' are said to cross Stonehenge: one running southwards through Old Sarum, Salisbury Cathedral, Clearbury Ring and Frankenbury Camp; the other connecting it with Castle Ditches and Grovely Castle to the southwest via the Avenue to Sidbury Camp and a string of barrows.

Some alleged ley lines may simply result from applying a grid to the map of the territory; some may be the result of pure coincidence. But when we consider that later monuments such as castles, churches and cathedrals were often built on megalithic sites, the idea of ancient links between sacred centres of energy does not appear so outlandish.

We still do not know exactly what rites took place at Stonehenge over the millennia. The number of barrows in the vicinity and the internment of disarticulated bones in the causewayed enclosures suggest that the site had long been a sacred space where the living celebrated the dead. Those who undertook the ceremonies were probably like shamans, combining the functions of priest, visionary and healer.

A man with a similar role may have been buried in a barrow at Upton Lovell, just 14 kilometres west of Stonehenge. Among his grave goods were not only delicate bone points in a necklace and on a fringe edging of his cloak, but also cult objects (now in Devizes Museum) which include a curious hammerstone, a stone axe and cups made from flint. Ritual objects such as jewellery, pottery, and animal and plant remains have also been found in a shaft at Wilsford sunk 30 metres deep into the earth and dating from 1380 BC. They were no doubt used in shamanistic rituals, which involved alcohol and drug use to induce prophetic visions. Many beakers containing traces of mead and probably decorated with cord made from cannabis hemp have been found in the area.

The Druids may have appeared about 1000 years after the abandonment of Stonehenge, but they no doubt continued the earlier shamanistic traditions and absorbed many of the beliefs. Although their Roman chroniclers say that they undertook their rites in woodland groves and clearings by streams and springs, local folklore all over Britain maintained that they conducted ceremonies among the stones.

As we have seen, many stone rings are still called 'Druids' circles'. The Druids certainly continued the ritual burial of objects with magical power such as swords and daggers, a practice stretching back to the first phase of Stonehenge with its buried deer antlers and cattle jawbones.

An astronomical observatory

There is a growing body of evidence to suggest that the Stonehenge site was used as an astronomical observatory as well as a sacred and social space.

At the beginning of the nineteenth century, Wordsworth recalled in *The Prelude* roaming among the ruins of Stonehenge and wondering whether it was indeed a work,

> By which the Druids covertly express'd
> Their knowledge of the heavens, and imaged forth
> The constellations . . .

A century later, indeed, the astronomer Sir Norman Lockyer argued persuasively that the ancient monuments were built 'to observe and mark the rising and setting places of the heavenly bodies'.[9] While books on archaeology have until recently ignored astronomy, books on astronomy usually open with Stonehenge. Its builders are rightly celebrated as among the earliest astronomers.

An important clue to the use of Stonehenge as an astronomical observatory is to be found in the rectangle of the four original Station Stones inside the circular earth bank circle. They not only pinpoint the centre of the monument but the short lines of the rectangle run parallel to the axis of the monument and are aligned to the midsummer sunrise and midwinter sunset. In addition, the long lines of the rectangle indicate exactly the most northerly and most southerly standstills of the full moon in its 18.6-year cycle. Again, this would seem to be far too precise a design to be a coincidence, especially as other megalithic sites like Callanish and Stenness were oriented to record the movements of the moon.

Only at Stonehenge's latitude do these alignments meet at right angles and form a rectangle. The possibility that all these alignments were the product of chance is remote indeed. As the Thoms have observed: 'Stonehenge may have been the centre of a huge accurate lunar observatory . . . perhaps a universal *backsight* from which distant marks on the horizon could be observed.'[10]

Even more extraordinary, it has been suggested that Stonehenge may represent the earth, with the long sides of the rectangle formed by the Station Stones reflecting the position of the Tropics of Cancer and Capricorn. Furthermore, for those interested in sacred geometry, a diagonal line drawn across the rectangle creates two triangles, the sides of which stand in a ratio of 5:12:13. Now, since there are twelve solar months and thirteen lunar months in a year, the numbers 12 and 13 can be considered 'solar' and 'lunar' numbers. As such, Stonehenge would appear to encode in its geometry the sacred marriage of Sol and Luna.[11]

There is some evidence to suggest that in its early phases Stonehenge was more focused on the movements of the moon than on those of the sun. Aubrey Burl, a recognized authority on stone circles, has shown that the vast majority of the long barrows were oriented within the range of the moon's cycle.[12] In addition, the cremations and human remains at Stonehenge were grouped mainly in the southeast of the circle, the position of the southernmost moonrise at its major standstill. Finally, the setting of the post holes in the second phase of Stonehenge at the northeastern entrance was aligned to the risings of the moon. The bluestones, with their assumed magical properties, may well have been associated with the Great Goddess and her heavenly symbol, the moon.

This aspect was lost in the third phase of the evolution of the monument, which took place after the arrival of the Beaker people, when the central axis was realigned towards the midsummer sunrise. Could it be that in the process a peaceful matrifocal society worshipping the Great Goddess was replaced by a warlike patriarchal society honouring the sun? Did Apollonian rationality replace Dionysian intuition? As we have seen, the archaeological record certainly shows that before the beginning of the Bronze Age, no weapons of war were found near the undefended megalithic sites at Stonehenge and elsewhere in Britain.

The most obvious feature of Stonehenge today is that its principal entrance points north east – the direction of the rising sun on the summer solstice. At this moment of the year in megalithic times, the rays of the sun would have been framed by the Heel Stone and its fallen partner and would shine down a stone corridor into the heart of the monument. At midwinter the sun sets in the opposite direction to the southwest, and its dying rays would have shone between the two vast stones of the great trilithon of the inner horseshoe. Clearly the people who designed Stonehenge and its neighbouring monuments were working to an overall pattern. It cannot be a simple coincidence that the majority of barrows, henges and cursuses within the vicinity of Stonehenge face east or northeast towards the rising sun.

The astronomers at Stonehenge would be interested in the stars as well. Their seafaring cousins would have navigated by them along the Atlantic seaboard. The stones and lintels of Stonehenge would have framed the stars as they moved across the night sky, and could have indicated the constellations which heralded the coming of summer and winter, the solstices and the equinoxes. It is possible, for instance, that the constellation of Cygnus within the triangle of the bright stars Deneb, Vega and Altar could have guided celebrants along the Avenue towards Stonehenge on early summer nights.

A Stone Age computer?

The application to Stonehenge of astro-archaeology, sometimes called archaeoastronomy, was given a boost by the American astrophysicist Gerald Hawkins, who attempted to decode Stonehenge using a computer in the 1960s. His calculations led him to conclude that it was designed as a lunar and solar observatory – a gigantic Neolithic computer, no less. He thought that the astronomical alignments were not only more accurate in the first phase of Stonehenge but that the fifty-six Aubrey Holes were used to predict lunar eclipses. This could be done, he argued, by first fixing three positions in the north of the circle, and then by moving six equidistant markers along one Aubrey Hole a year and a moon marker by one stone of the sarsen circle each day.[13]

The idea was at first dismissed by most archaeologists as 'moonshine'. Even if it were accurate, it could have only be used for a short period of time because the Aubrey Holes were filled in and used as cremation pits. Nevertheless, the fascinating hypothesis attracted the interest of the Cambridge-based astronomer Sir Fred Hoyle. Although his method differed from that of Hawkins, he too found a way of predicting lunar eclipses by counting and using the Aubrey Holes. The astronomer-priests of Stonehenge, he argued, moved large stones from hole to hole, at rates ranging from twice a day to three times a year.[14]

Like Hawkins's, Hoyle's interpretation has come under severe criticism – particularly his use of a 56-year cycle. But even if some of the details of their arguments are questionable, the broad thesis that Stonehenge could have worked as an astronomical observatory and calendar seems irrefutable.

Each generation tends to interpret Stonehenge in a different way. The site undoubtedly still hides many secrets. As the archaeologist Lieutenant Colonel William Hawley, who named the undeciphered Y and Z holes, observed: 'The more we dig, the more the mystery appears to deepen.'[15] I would add: the more we look up at the stars, the more the achievement of Stonehenge becomes awe-inspiring. Clearly its builders and users were not untutored savages but thoughtful, imaginative, religious and resourceful people who were capable of great works of engineering, architecture, astronomy, art and science.

The proudest singularity

When the Celts finally arrived at Stonehenge, the finer details of the original builders' sacred science would have been lost. But the Druids may have used the stones for their rituals and it seems that even during the Roman occupation of Europe, the megaliths were believed to have magical powers.

With the coming of Christianity, the new faith tried to devalue the old religion as much as possible. Imposing their rule, many Christian churches were built on megalithic sites. Chartres, for instance, was erected over a dolmen. In the Middle Ages, the megaliths were dismissed by the Church as rude stones left over from a barbarous age. Many sites were destroyed by agricultural improvers. What remained became the haunt of sheep, crows and the wayward traveller, but many folk stories continued to be told about the temples of the old gods.

It was only during the Renaissance in England that the abandoned stones on Salisbury Plain were noticed by the educated elite. In particular, they attracted the attention of Inigo Jones, architect and masque designer at the court of Charles I. He depicted Stonehenge as a Roman monument built in the shape of a precise circle. While inconsistent with the site, the design inspired the Georgian Circus now in Bath. Interest grew in the seventeenth century, when John Aubrey carefully surveyed the site of Stonehenge in 1666. Gripped by the new craze for topography, the antiquarian William Stukeley was the first to appreciate fully the megaliths in Britain. In his book *Stonehenge: A Temple Restor'd to the Druids* (1740), he declared the circle to be the 'proudest singularity' among the megalithic sites scattered throughout the British Isles. 'When you enter the building', he wrote in 1743,

Whether on foot or on horseback, and cast your eyes around the yawning ruins, you are struck into an ecstatic reverie, which none can describe, and they only can be sensible of it that feel it . . . When we advance farther, the dark part of the ponderous imposts over our heads, the chasm of the sky between the jambs of the cell, the odd construction of the whole, and the greatness of every part surprises.[16]

This same kind of sensibility led to the formation of the Ancient Order of Druids in 1781, and they eventually became self-proclaimed guardian of the stones.

During the Romantic era, Wordsworth declared: 'Pile of Stonehenge! So proud to hint yet keep/Thy secrets . . .' Blake saw them as the ruins of a great temple of the ancient Britons. Their Romantic appeal continued into the later nineteenth century. Constable and Turner painted them to good atmospheric effect, emphasizing their fallen grandeur on the forlorn plain under the wild sky. Tess of the d'Urbervilles, in Thomas Hardy's novel, spent her last night of freedom asleep on the Altar Stone before being arrested at daybreak by her persecutors.

Others have not always treated Stonehenge so well. A cart track was cut right through the ring by farmers, and during the First World War the Air Ministry wanted the stones demolished as a danger to low-flying aircraft. If they had had their way, it would have been an act of military vandalism on a par with the blowing up of explosives in the Parthenon in Greece or the use of the Sphinx in Egypt as a target for artillery practice.

Midsummer madness

Stonehenge has now been saved as a World Heritage Site and today it has become the most famous prehistoric monument in the world. It is an immediately recognizable symbol of the Stone Age; even my mother, who knows virtually nothing about the megaliths, knows about Stonehenge.

Until recently, the site was closed down to the general public on the summer solstice, leading to battles with police in neighbouring bean fields. However, all that has now changed and on the first summer solstice of the new millennium, I was able to travel down with Elizabeth to Stonehenge to witness the rising of the sun. About 6000 other people had the same idea, but the site was so large that there was enough space for us all.

Approaching from the south in the glow of midsummer night, we could hear the drumming in the distance. The dark stones on the hill gradually loomed out of the drizzle, with tiny human figures dancing in the light of torch flames. As we grew closer, we could see that each lichen-covered stone had an individual shape with a special texture and a subtle colouring. They felt warm and friendly in the cold, wet night.

Rain swept in from the west across the barren plain, but all night the drums ebbed and flowed in the inner circle, encouraged by the whoops, yells and leaps of the dancers. Like their distant forebears, many were drinking and taking drugs. The sweet smell of cannabis hung in the damp air. For all the growing excitement, the atmosphere remained peaceful and convivial. Just before dawn I saw a tame falcon stand on a stone in the rain, its feathers wet and its eyebrows unruly, completely at ease among the noise and bustle of the swarming humanity.

> Standing on
> The lichen-graced stone,
> Still as a heron,
> Alert as a tiger,
> The falcon blinks.
>
> A grey glow grows
> In the rain-drenched east,
> An orange fire drives
> the drum and dance.
> The falcon blinks.
>
> It is midsummer's morn
> Of the new millennium.

New Age worshippers, old-style travellers, exhausted children and hungry dogs; black and white witches; modern Druids dressed in long white robes, their staffs adorned with horns of deer and sprigs of oak; young women with garlands of flowers in their hair; nomads from Japan, Africa, America and India – we all took up our position inside the circle to witness the first rays of the sun light up the Heel Stone on the outer edge. But it was not to be. There was no break in the low clouds and drizzle, only a growing dull grey light in the universal gloom. Not to be dismayed, the drummers and dancers increased their energy. Their wild antics rose to a crescendo and continued long after the sun had risen over the cloud-soaked horizon.

Despite the dismal weather of a British summer, Stonehenge had come back to life. The spirits of the dead ancestors were being kept alive by the memories of the living. The sacred space within the circle vibrated with the music and dance of its celebrants. The careful alignments of the stones had fallen back into place for their original purpose: the creative power of the heavens was being channelled down to earth. By the celebration and prayer, the fertility of the world would once again be ensured for another year as the sun began its long journey south.

Whether in the frenzy of a midsummer dawn or in the stillness of an autumn evening, for those who are attuned to its special powers, Stonehenge will focus the sublime energies of the universe for a long time to come.

CHAPTER SEVEN

Merry Meet

The most august work at this day upon the globe of the earth.

WILLIAM STUKELEY

When I first visited Avebury it was on the eve of the winter solstice. The stones of the main site were eerily lit up by a full moon, standing out like ghostly mishappen giants. During the night, strong winds blew in from the southwest, bringing dark clouds and heavy rain. I visited the Red Lion Inn, reputedly haunted by a restless lady in a blue dress, where groups of megalith enthusiasts and pagans were gathering from all over Britain. The inn had been built, along with a small hamlet, right within the huge stone circle and its earthworks.

The Avebury site is located in the undulating countryside of the Marlborough Downs, due north of Stonehenge on the other side of Salisbury Plain. It was part of a unique network of megalithic monuments which spread across the old Anglo-Saxon kingdom of Wessex – an area roughly embracing present-day Wiltshire, Dorset and Somerset. The Stone Age civilization in the area produced a highly sophisticated and wealthy culture: Avebury, along with its neighbour Stonehenge, is a spectacular echo from this. Neither one diminishes the glory of the other.

The great henge at Avebury consists of a vast circular ditch and bank, within which is a ring of huge megaliths. Covering an area of 11.5 hectares, it is divided by four entrances roughly aligned to the four cardinal points of the compass. It took me a good half an hour to walk round its bank. The earthwork was begun around 3500 BC and in the following 1000 years, more than 180 standing stones were raised within it.

As at Stonehenge, the huge sarsen stones were taken locally from the downland surrounding Avebury. Many of the stones in the outer ring are either tall and pillar-shaped or squat and lozenge-shaped and as such are often identified as representing the male and female principles. Only twenty-seven of the original ninety-eight megaliths remain upright. Some reach 6 metres in height and weigh more than 40 tonnes. In the northwest sector, the great Swindon Stone weighs in at about 65 tonnes. The ingenuity and effort involved are truly mind-boggling: it has been estimated that it would have required 1.5 million man-hours to complete the enclosure.

If this is not enough, the great stone henge and bank of Avebury encircle two smaller circles. The more complete one in the southern half, known as the Sun Circle, originally formed a perfect ring of twenty-nine stones. Until recently, it had a central obelisk standing 7 metres high, around which villagers would dance on May Day.

The ring in the northeastern sector has only four stones of an original twenty-seven still standing. It is called the Moon Circle. It has within it two stones standing of an original three known as the Cove. They may have been aligned to the sunrise on the summer solstice as well as to the most northerly rising point of the moon.[1]

Ceremonies were no doubt performed in the central area of the henge, within the Sun Circle and the Moon Circle, depending on the time of year and the position of the planets. The henge could not only contain thousands of people, but spectators would have had a superb view from the top of the outer bank.

The serpent

The vast bank and stones enclosing the hamlet, the most visible aspect of Avebury today, are a strand in a complex web. Celebrants would have approached the central henge by two processional avenues: the West Kennet Avenue from the southwest, and the Beckhampton Avenue from the southeast. They were demarcated by two rows of huge standing stones and side ditches. When William Stukeley drew a map of Avebury and its avenues in 1743, he dramatically presented it as a vast snake, with its tail at the end of the Beckhampton Avenue, the main henge in the middle of its body and the West Kennet Avenue leading to its head crowned on Overton Hill by a small stone circle known as the Sanctuary.

All that remains standing of the Beckhampton Avenue are the Long Stones, also known as Adam and Eve. They stand in a field about a kilometre west of the main henge. Crop marks discovered there in 1997 led a team to discover an oval ditched enclosure (with one side straightened) measuring about 100 by 140 metres. The site not only contained early Neolithic pottery but also six huge standing stones buried as late as the eighteenth century. They had been arranged in pairs and spaced the same distance apart as those lining the West Kennet Avenue.

From the southern causeway entrance of the great henge, the West Kennet Avenue winds its way over 2 kilometres to the Sanctuary on Overton Hill. Although part of it crosses a road, it is still very impressive, consisting of 100 pairs of large stones approximately 15 metres apart. As in the main circle itself, the paired stones tend to be pillar and lozenge shapes, so representing male and female genitalia. It was probably built after the main henge around 2500 BC. Burial deposits have been found against some of stones, including human bones, a complete Grooved Ware pot and broken beakers.

The Sanctuary on the flat top of Overton Hill, which Stukeley mapped, no longer exists. In fact, Stukeley witnessed its destruction by farmers clearing the land for what he called 'a dirty little profit'. Recent excavations have revealed a mass of wooden posts and pits which show that about 5000 years ago a timber shrine was built on the hill. It was rebuilt and enlarged several times until it was finally replaced around 2000 BC by a double stone circle and linked by the West Kennet Avenue to the temple at Avebury.

The Sanctuary was constructed alongside the ancient trackway known as the Ridgeway. Such trackways, which crisscross England, were first marked out by nomadic hunter-gatherers in their migrations, and may form the underlying network of ley lines which traverse the country. They mainly followed the ridges of the hills but some timber trackways were laid across wetlands as early as 3800 BC. The Ridgeway track next to the Sanctuary runs north from Avebury and ends in the great White Horse of Uffington, a beautiful stylized figure cut into the chalk downs.

People of Avebury

Although the building of the main henge and ditch began around 3000 BC, the story of Avebury goes back to Mesolithic times. It seems that the earlier people who had walked across the land bridge from the rest of Europe before 8000 BC were tall and possibly dark. These nomadic hunter-gatherers and flint-workers were joined by a wave of Neolithic settlers who came around 5000 BC in boats with their animals and corn after the land bridge had submerged under the sea. From their skeletons, we can tell that the new farmers were about 1.6 metres tall, with a slender and athletic build. Their long hands and skulls suggest that they had delicate features. Since there was plenty of room for all, there does not seem to have been any resistance or conflict between the two groups. As elsewhere in Neolithic Britain, none of the early megalithic sites at Avebury were defended, and the enclosures and henges had open causeways.

What kind of society did they live in? The Avebury area supported a fairly dense population, probably consisting of several clans of extended families. Perhaps a population of 10,000 people occupied the Marlborough Downs, and five times that number lived in Wessex. From the available evidence, it would seem that in the Neolithic period, they lived in a peaceful, cooperative and egalitarian society. Long barrows were used as communal graves reflecting the communal nature of their way of life. There is no evidence of chiefs and the grave goods which have been unearthed are neither profuse nor rich.

It is often assumed by archaeologists that the great monuments of the later Stone Age required a more structured society with tribal chiefs but, as we have seen, this remains an unsubstantiated assumption. The building of the great henge at Avebury and its satellite monuments would not have been possible without a continuous supply of voluntary labour, extensive cooperation and a common religious purpose. Nor are there any grounds for arguing that there was growing social discord and conflict. While the last burial in the West Kennet barrow had an arrow embedded in the neck of his skeleton, this is insufficient evidence to maintain that warfare had become part of everyday life.[2]

Windmill Hill

The first monument built in the Avebury area was on Windmill Hill. Now a bare hilltop of rough pasture, where a few sheep graze and the odd crow soars, it lies about a kilometre and a half to the northwest of the main henge. In early Neolithic times the area would have been covered with a mixed woodland of hazel, blackthorn, oak and ash, which offered shelter to wild cattle, pigs and deer. Obviously appreciating its commanding views, the new settlers gradually widened the clearings to grow wheat and barley and to raise domesticated animals.

Around 3500 BC, the local farmers began work on a triple-ditch enclosure built just off-centre of the hill. Archaeologists now recognize it as a classic example of a 'causewayed enclosure' – that is, an enclosure with a wide gap in its bank which allows people to cross over an entrance causeway. Windmill Hill was not only the first enclosure to be excavated, but is the largest known, with a diameter averaging 400 metres and an area of 8.5 hectares.

Why should the local farmers have undertaken such a vast project? It seems that it was used as a centre for the clans in the neighbourhood to meet, feast, celebrate and above all to undertake collective rituals in their cult of the Great Goddess. Bones found at the site suggest they were used for magico-religious purposes. The activities may have been seasonal, for animals were slaughtered in the spring, as a part of rites surrounding sowing, and in the autumn, to mark the harvest and to kill off any animals which could not be supported in the coming winter. The enclosure continued as a space for ritual activity well into the Bronze Age for there are many small barrows, dating from around 1500 BC, still visible on the grassy hill.

West Kennet

From the windy summit of Windmill Hill, the stark winter landscape of the rolling Marlborough Downs stretched before me, the trees bare and the pasture a dull brownish green. I not only had an excellent view of the great henge at Avebury but could also make out the West Kennet chambered long barrow further south. Work started on it at the same time as the enclosure on Windmill Hill: where the latter celebrated the world of the living, the former remembered the dead.

More than 100 metres long, the West Kennet Barrow is the largest in the country. When first built around 3500 BC, it was deliberately set on an east-west axis in line with the spring and autumn equinoxes. The five inner burial chambers were entered from a semi-circular forecourt within an impressive façade of upright stones. A row of massive upright sarsen stones was used to seal the chamber 1000 years later. Successive excavations have revealed forty-six burials over the centuries, ranging from those of babies to the elderly. Some of the skulls and leg bones were removed for ceremonies elsewhere and possibly used for healing. In 1685, a Doctor Toope from Marlborough dug up some of the bones to make 'a noble medicine'.

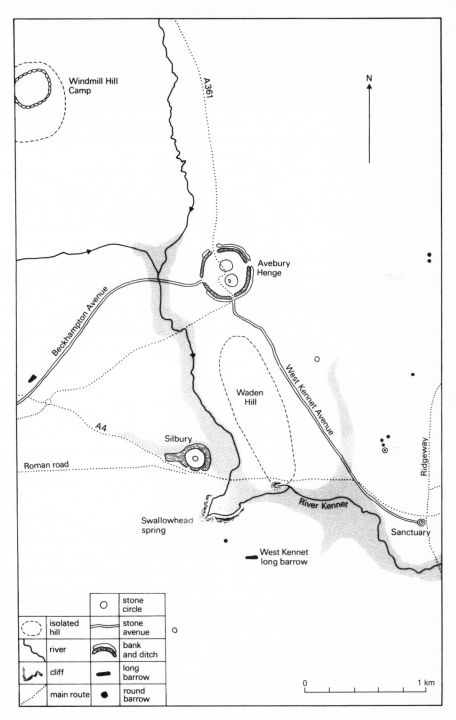

The principal megalithic monuments in the Avebury area

On a grey morning at the winter solstice, I climbed up the hill through a slippery and boot-clogging ploughed field to reach the site on the spur of the hill. Within the innermost chamber of the barrow, a string of worshippers stood in contemplation in front of an improvised altar made from a candle and a sprig of mistletoe placed on a stone. Incense filled the damp, cold chamber. There was a steady drip of water from the high corbelled ceiling but a shaft of light entered through a gap in the ancient stones illuminating the inner shrine.

'This is a very magical, very relaxed and very healing place', observed a young man in reverential tones, introducing himself as a member of the Cambridge Mystical Society. 'The energy is very female here. It feels like entering Mother Earth.' I could see what he meant.

The top of West Kennet long barrow afforded a magnificent view of the rolling hills all around. To the east, I could make out in the bare, sodden landscape the small private copse in which the East Kennet long barrow was hidden. It is said to be aligned to the sunrise on the winter solstice. To the west, I could also see a tall, flat-topped hill rising out of the the undulating landscape on a low spur by a swift-flowing river. After the henge itself, it was the crowning glory of the Avebury complex: Silbury Hill.

'That marvaillous hill'

William Stukeley was right when he declared: 'Silbury is that marvaillous hill . . . every way between the downs we are of a sudden saluted by its vast circumference'.[3]

While the enclosure on Windmill Hill was built on a natural feature, Silbury Hill, which lies just over a kilometre south of Avebury henge, is entirely artificial. Rising up 40 metres, it is the largest man-made mound in ancient Europe, and the centre of Neolithic England. Its construction took place over several centuries, from around 2800 to 2500 BC, and it was probably used until after 2000 BC. Built on a natural spur, the main portion of the hill was made from chalk carried up from the ditch at its base over a clay core with flints. Its base covers an area of more than 2 hectares. Again, it was a vast labour of love: it has been calculated that it took some 18 million man-hours to construct.

The artificial hill was built in three stages. In the first, turf was piled up on the low mound of clay and covered with layers of soil, gravel and chalk. We do not know the exact year (radiocarbon dating gives around 2660 BC), but we do know the season: a flying ant has been found in the first layer, indicating it must have been late July or August! In the second stage, the mound doubled in size with additions of chalk dug from the surrounding ditch. This immense engineering project was undertaken with the help of simple tools such as antlers for picks and cattle shoulderblades for shovels. In the third stage, a huge ditch was quarried up to 9 metres deep and a series of terraces was built, each one retained by inward-leaning chalk walls faced by an outer covering of chalk. Not only did the builders have a good understanding of soil mechanics, but the monument was also unique for its advanced design.[4]

Forming a polygon rather than a pyramid, with radial lines linked by straight lines, from above it would have looked rather like a spider's web.[5] Newly constructed, the brilliant white of the chalk-faced mound would have sparkled in the sun against the green landscape all around.

Despite at least six exploratory investigations, the exact purpose of the hill remains a mystery. The first possibility that comes to mind is that it could have been used as a gigantic sundial to determine the seasons and the length of the year. The shadow of a large pole placed on its flat summit could have indicated the movements of the sun like the gnomon on a sundial. The summit would also make an ideal platform for observing the night skies which, with better weather, would have been clearer than today.

At the beginning of the twentieth century, the English statistician Moses B. Cotsworth was convinced that it had been used as an astronomical observatory:

The 30° slope of Sylbury not only enabled the Druid astronomers to sight the visible daily elevation between the equinoxes and the winter solstice, but also as the midday sun rose from the spring equinoctal footing to its midsummer solstice height, it would be graded up the slopes to its turning point on the top of the north edge and down again to the autumnal equinox as autumn approached. In that way the four seasons of the year could be clearly indicated and comparative records kept by notching the daily and monthly points upon logs laid up the north meridian slope, as was done by the old clog almanacks which were used all over Northern Europe ages before printed almanacks were invented.[6]

The second possibility is that Silbury Hill was intended as a burial mound. John Aubrey, the English antiquary, recorded in 1663 the local tradition that 'King Sil, or Zel, as the country folke pronounce, was buried here on horseback, and that the hill was raysed while a posset [bowl] of milke was seething'.[7] When Stukeley saw it in the following century, he had 'no scruple to affirm Silbury is the most magnificent mausoleum in the world . . . the most astonishing collection of earth, artificially raised, worthy of the king who was the royal founder of Abury, as we may very plausibly affirm.'[8]

Although the hill has long been thought to contain human remains and gold treasure, repeated attempts to penetrate its interior over the last three centuries have failed to reveal anything more exciting than the remains of the winged ant. In the silt at the bottom of the ditch only the horns of red deer have been found, the abandoned picks of the original builders.

In fact, Silbury Hill predates the hierarchical society of the Bronze Age and there is no evidence to suggest it was intended as a burial mound or cenotaph for a great chief. The suggestion that it was intended to mark the territory of a tribe would also seem to project modern concepts of exclusive property into Stone Age mentality. Archaic thinking did not have a territorial drive.

It seem much more likely that Silbury Hill was used as a ritual centre and an open-air temple. A recent seismic survey has indicated that there may have been a processional pathway spiralling around the mound to the summit. Spirals have always symbolized the spiritual path to enlightenment. Indeed, the rounded shape of this great earth sculpture would appear to represent the Great Goddess herself, the supreme object of reverence of the dwellers in the land at the time it was built. No doubt rituals were held on top of the hill, visible from a long way off, at key moments in the calendar.

The fertility symbolism of the Great Goddess may well be encoded in the name of the river Kennet which runs close by. The waters which seep from the bottom of Silbury Hill emerge in the Swallowhead spring where the Kennet is born from the Winterbourne river. Stukeley recorded that country people called Swallowhead 'by the old name of Cunnit and it is not a little famous among them'.[9] The modern name of the river Kennet may have a common origin with the old Saxon word 'cunt', thereby underlining the female symbolism.[10]

Ever since Neolithic times, the Swallowhead spring has usually dried up from Samhain, at the end of October, to Imbolc, at the beginning of February, in the Celtic calendar. The waters of the holy spring have long thought to have healing powers: Stukeley observed that vessels of Swallowhead water were taken to Silbury at the time of the Eastertide assembly. And now, down the centuries, people still come to take its sacred waters and bedeck the fallen but living willow by the spring with colourful strips of rag to bring good luck and health.

The Avebury cycle

The discovery of the winged ant in the foundations of Silbury Hill indicates that the construction of the first mound began at the time of Lammas in the Celtic calendar in late July and early August, at the end of the harvest period. It was no doubt used thereafter to celebrate the bringing in of the harvest. Continuing the ancient tradition, the Chief Druid at Avebury continues to take a symbolic loaf of bread to the summit of the hill as an offering at Lammas after the grain has been harvested.

The megalith builders at Avebury, like all ancient farming peoples, would have followed a yearly cycle defined by the movement of the sun across the heavens and celebrated the key turning points in the year. These have come down to us through the Celts and been incorporated in the Christian calendar, but they are certainly much earlier. It would seem that each of the key solar events of the year is aligned to a monument in the Avebury complex.

At Yule, the winter solstice on 22 December, the East Kennet Long Barrow points southeast, to the sunrise. At the spring equinox on 20 March, the West Kennet Long Barrow points east to the sunrise. At Beltane on May Day, the obelisk in the southern inner circle of Avebury was used as a maypole. At midsummer, the summer solstice on 21 June, the three stones of the Cove in the northern inner circle were arranged towards the sunrise. At Lammas (also known as Lugnasadh), harvest time on 1 August, Silbury Hill was used for offerings. At the autumn equinox, 23 September, West Kennet Long Barrow points to sunrise again. At Samhain, 31 October (All Saints' Day, Winter's Eve and Hallowe'en), the old camp on Windmill Hill was used for a festival marking the end of summer. And on the winter solstice, 22 December, the cycle begins again.[11] Along with Samhain, the other 'quarter days' between the solstices and equinoxes were all traditionally celebrated with fires.

The cycle clearly reflects the relationship between Father Sun and Mother Earth, Sol and Luna, the God and the Goddess. The God as the Sun waxes and wanes in strength throughout the year, while the Goddess as Mother Earth changes her face but not her essence, becoming Maid, Mother and Old Woman in spring, summer and autumn.

Big hearts

It is, of course, impossible to say what the megalith builders of Avebury were like. But a persistent Cornish tale of the 'small people' may well be based on folk memories of them. It is said that they were star-worshippers and that they had no understanding of marriage. If a child was born, any one of the menfolk could have been the father and great celebrations were held at the arrival of new life into the community.[12] They may have been small people, but they had large minds and big hearts.

What were their beliefs? With the passage of time, it is difficult to be certain. But they probably shared many of the views held by other rural communities throughout the world who still live close to the land. From all the available evidence, we can assume that they were animistic, believing all that exists is alive – every rock, stream, cloud or wind. They would have been pantheistic in believing that nature is divine and that everything that lives is holy. They honoured the earth as a living, organic being, revering the Great Goddess as the source of all life and abundance.

A twelfth-century English herbal treatise, written in Latin, may well capture something of their belief. It includes a prayer to the Earth Goddess. As in the old Celtic religion, it pictures the earth as giving birth to the sun every day when it rises above the eastern horizon:

Earth, divine goddess, Mother Nature, who dost generate all things and bringest forth ever anew the sun which thou hast given to the nations; Guardian of sky and sea and of all Gods and powers; through thy influence all nature is hushed and sinks to sleep . . . Again, when it pleases thee, thou sendest forth the glad daylight and nurturest life with thine eternal surety; and when the spirit of man passes, to thee it returns.[13]

It would seem from what can be discerned of their architecture and art that the megalith builders of Wessex did not try to conquer nature, but sought rather to nurture and celebrate her in all her myriad forms. They accepted the kinship of all creatures and acknowledged unity with the natural world. They had a sense of belonging to the earth and a sense of wonderment when looking up at the stars. Within their sacred enclosures and their monuments, they gave thanks for the fertility and abundance of the land and worshipped the divine presence at the centre and circumference of the universe.

The dawn of civilization

Why the farmers of the Neolithic age at Avebury should engage in such immense works remains a mystery. Their nomadic forebears left no monuments: the megaliths went up when humans first settled down. Could it be that the great monuments of the Stone Age stand as works of expiation for having abandoned the old nomadic ways of life and for having violated Mother Earth by breaking up the land?

For the first humans, the earth gave all things spontaneously and they were content with its uncultivated produce. Guided and protected by the gods, they followed the migratory paths of their ancestors. They knew the cycles of the seasons and the movements of the heavenly bodies. They understood the lives of animals and plants. They respected life and took only what they needed. They lived lightly and wasted nothing.

For these wanderers on land and sea, guided by the stars, the sun and the moon, the universe was in a constant state of flux. Time was circular and all turned in the eternal wheel of life, death and rebirth. Then, after some 3 million years of this nomadic way of life, the farmers came with their ploughs and domesticated animals. They burnt and cut down the forests. They built permanent dwellings. They cut the bosom of Mother Earth with their sharp instruments. Time entered their lives in a linear way, for they had to plan and calculate, to sow and harvest.

Could it be that the first farmers, still surrounded by hunter-gatherers and still hunting and gathering themselves, felt like the nineteenth-century American Indian prophet Smohalla? He declared:

Men who work [the land] cannot dream; and wisdom comes to us in dreams.

You ask me to plough the ground? Shall I take a knife and tear my mother's breast? Then when I die she will not take me to her bosom to rest.

You ask me to dig for stone. Shall I dig under her skin for her bones? Then when I die I cannot enter her body to be born again.

You ask me to cut grass and make hay. . . But how dare I cut off my mother's hair?[14]

I suspect that the first farmers began digging their huge earthworks and erecting the great stones to the sky on the sacred sites of their nomadic ancestors to appease Mother Earth for what they had done and to draw down the healing energies from the heavens. And they deliberately built them at the sacred sites along the ancient trackways which their ancestors had followed in their cyclical migrations.

Dragon-slaying

What remains of Avebury today is not precisely as it was when built. Over the centuries the Christian Church and its agents have tried to destroy the energy and symbolism of the stones. They were partly saved in the 1930s, when the Dundee marmalade heir Alexander Keiller acquired the main site. But only partly. He not only had three-quarters of the village buildings pulled down, but also re-erected many of the fallen megaliths in cement – and not always in their correct position.

When Aubrey discovered the site in 1649, while out hunting, he declared that 'it does as much exceed in greatness the so renowned Stonehenge, as a cathedral doeth a parish Church'.[15] A century later Stukeley was no less impressed, calling it 'the most august work at this day upon the globe of the earth'. Yet he found local farmers trying to clear the megaliths from their fields by rapidly heating and cooling them so that they would break into more manageable pieces. 'The barbarous massacre of a stone here,' Stukeley wrote, 'with leavers and hammers, sledges and fire, is as terrible a sight as a Spanish Atto de fe.'[16] Much damage had already been done by the combined anti-pagan forces of church and manor.

The stones that exist today survived mainly because they were buried during the fourteenth century. The skeleton of a medieval barber-surgeon has been discovered in the southwestern sector under a toppled stone, having been accidentally crushed as it fell into a purpose-dug pit at its base. In a small pouch at his waist were found a pair of scissors, an iron probe and some coins dated to around 1315. The exact cause of another death remains a mystery: near the fallen slab known as the Devil's Chair by the southeastern entrance, the skeleton of a female dwarf was discovered in a shallow grave in the ditch.

Superstitions about the stones persist. Some people have reported seeing small figures moving among the megaliths on bright moonlit nights – the result, perhaps, of the combined effect of a fertile imagination and good ale from the Red Lion Inn. Others have seen 'earth lights' flickering among the stones, phenomena the Celts called 'fairy lights' or 'corpse candles', gateways to the underworld. A local legend has it that on midsummer's day the disturbed barrow at West Kennet is also visited by a ghostly priest and a large white hound.

Christianity has of course tried to stamp out such superstitions along with the stones. In the first millennium, a church was built at the western entrance to the main circle, partly from the deliberately shattered sarsens. If you go into the well-kept church, you will see a font carving of Christ with a book in one hand and a lance in the other. He is trampling two dragons, a traditional Christian symbol of the triumph of spirit over matter and of Christianity over paganism. Some see the story of St George slaying the dragon as a parable of Christian patriarchy killing off the old religion of the Great Goddess. At, a deeper and more esoteric level, however, dragon-slaying may have nothing to do with killing the powers of pagan darkness, but of drawing on the fiery dragon-energy of the earth. The serpent-dragon, moreover, is one of the oldest symbols of transformation: it regularly sloughs off its skin and disappears into the earth only to reappear as if reborn.

Hail and welcome

Rituals still take place at Avebury to mark the shedding of the old year and the birth of the new. On the winter solstice of 22 December, I joined one such ceremony with Elizabeth. In the early morning before dawn, a bedraggled band of revellers formed a circle around the stones. In the centre where the obelisk had once stood, a candle was burning, surrounded by sprigs of holly, mistletoe and ivy. When a couple of dogs began chasing each other among the stones, an imposing man stepped forward and suggested that they be kept under control; saying, 'This is the sacred Temple of the Ancient Britons. It is a very solemn time, the rebirth of the New Year!'

This was, in fact, the Chief Druid, a large man with a long grey beard and rounded belly. He wore a white tunic made from a sheet and a feather stuck in his flat tweed cap. Leaning on his staff, he meditated just before dawn with his face upturned towards the southeast. As the first glimmer of light appeared over the distant, rain-sodden hills, he strode into the centre of the circle. Striking the earth with his staff, he declared: 'Arwen, Arwen, Arwen! So may it be!'

He then began to 'open' the four quarters of the circle, welcoming in each of the four elements in turn. Facing east, he declaimed: 'Air, come join our circle. Bring us your knowledge and wisdom so we may learn. Hail and welcome!'

Turning to the south and west, he did the same for fire and water. Welcoming in the earth from the north, he intoned: 'Earth, from whence we come and whence we go. May we appreciate thee, work with thee and protect thee. Hail and welcome!' The motley group of celebrants, some spaced out and all the worse for rain and lack of sleep, repeated the refrain: 'Hail and welcome.'

Because of the low dark cloud and rain, the actual moment of sunrise was left to our imagination. But there could be no doubt that the sun was up at last and would begin its slow journey northwards.

'Now is the time for merriment and misrule!' declared the jolly Druid in the flat cap, white sheet and Wellington boots.

It was the signal for an improvised mummers' play, in which the forces of darkness, represented by a couple dressed in black, were chased inside the circle by the forces of light, symbolized by a couple dressed in white. After the dark forces were defeated and brought to the ground, an alchemical doctor with an elixir revitalized the Lord of Darkness and his Queen, Jenny Wren. The Queen of Light then helped the Queen of Darkness up from the ground, thereby symbolically affirming both dark and light are necessary for life on earth. Light and Darkness would later meet on equal terms in the coming spring equinox when day was the same length as the night.

This was completed by a serpentine dance of all the celebrants and dogs around the stones. The good-humoured and ancient ceremony was finished with the traditional words: 'Merry meet, merry met, and merry meet again!'

An official warden of the site told me later that the Druids were the best guardians of the stones at Avebury, keeping the old traditions alive and ensuring that the monuments would be protected as sacred places for future generations.

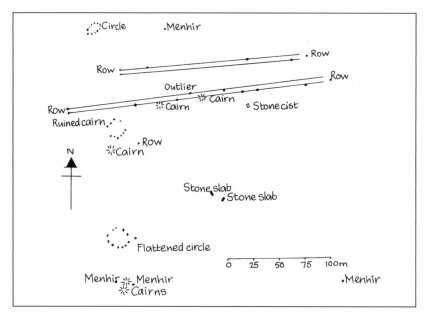

Ground plan of the stones at Merrivale, Dartmoor, Devon

CHAPTER EIGHT

The Civilized West

The people of that promontory called Belerion are friendly to strangers,
and from their contact with foreign merchants, are civilized in their
way of life.

DIODORUS SICULUS

The Preseli Mountains, Stonehenge, Avebury: it had been a long
and exhilarating journey. Now it was time to sail again. I returned
to Milford Haven to continue my voyage down to the West Country
– Devon and Cornwall. I chose to embark at night, under a full
moon and sailed over the oily sea of the Bristol Channel to Padstow,
the only safe harbour along the wild, wave-pounded coast of north
Cornwall. I avoided staying overnight at Lundy Island, an early
Christian community, pirate stronghold and penal colony, where I
had once almost been hurled on to the rocks below the lighthouse
when the wind suddenly shifted. I also kept clear of the notorious
Doom Bar in the wide estuary off Padstow.

The moors and high ground of Cornwall and Devon are dotted
with Neolithic monuments. The fact that they are found in bleak and
barren terrain attests to the deterioration of the weather around
1000 BC, which led to the sites being abandoned.

Merry vales

I now live near an intriguing collection of stones at Merrivale (see
opposite) on the west side of Dartmoor. It is one of the most important
sites in the south of England.[1] Despite its name – the Pleasant Valley
– locals called it the Plague Market or Potato Market, as in 1625

farmers left food there for the inhabitants of Tavistock, who were suffering from bubonic plague.

The stones stand on a plateau of scattered rocks and rough pasture with spectacular views of the surrounding hills. There are rows, circles, cairns, cists, stone slabs, hut circles and menhirs, the tallest of which rises to a splendid 3 metres. The stones of the southern circle are alternately pillars and slabs, like the Kennet Avenue at Avebury, and may equally represent male and female principles.

The most impressive feature at Merrivale are the stone rows: an avenue, a double row and one single row (there are more than sixty stone rows known on Dartmoor). The first from the road is a double row aligned almost east to west, 179 metres long by a breached leat, or small canal. Further south is the narrow avenue, 264 metres long and almost parallel to its northern neighbour, and like it ending with a 'blocking stone' in the east. It has an egg-shaped ring in its middle which may be the remains of a round barrow added at a later date. It is unlikely that either of them would have been a processional way since the parallel rows are too close to each other. Finally, there is a less spectacular row 42 metres long which runs from the SSW towards a cairn next to the longest avenue.

The remains (especially the stone cist and ruined cairn) date roughly from the late Neolithic to the early Bronze Age, showing that after the arrival of the Beaker people, the careful building and siting of stones continued to excite the imagination.

The exact function of the cluster of stones at Merrivale has not yet been satisfactorily deciphered, but their arrangement suggests that their geometrical and astronomical aspects were closely interlinked. There may well be an alignment to the star Arcturus and the Pleiades constellation. Alexander Thom thought the outlying stone of the southern circle could have been a meridian marker. At midsummer sunset, I also noticed an alignment from the circle to a notch in the horizon on Middle Staple Tor to the north. The east-west axis of the stone rows meant they were in line with the equinoxes.

An equally impressive collection of stones is to be found at Drizzlecombe on southwest Dartmoor, near the upper reaches of the river Plym. The path along the meandering river runs across stone-strewn land and through treacherous bogs. It emerges into a vast bowl under the arching sky, dominated on its northeastern side by lines of standing stones and barrows. The huge complex undoubtedly makes up one of the 'most elegant arrangements of tiny stone circles, long rows, standing stones, cists, cairns and pounds in Western Europe'.[2]

When I arrived in the late afternoon and went up to the northeastern lip of the bowl and looked down across the sides towards the setting sun, I could imagine thousands of people gathering here from all directions to celebrate the key events in the year.

There are some very clear alignments from the largest menhir, said to be the largest in Dartmoor and probably the finest in the West Country. Consisting of 7 tonnes of pointed granite, it now stands over 4 metres high. A southeastern ring 10 metres across is made up of thirteen low stones, from which a line of small stones runs southwest for 90 metres until it reaches the great menhir. To its south is a round cairn with a row of stones stretching 149 metres southwest to another menhir. For about two-thirds of its length, it has a double row of low stones. Close by is a huge, eroded cairn known as the Giant's Basin, badly battered for treasure over the centuries. Yet another row of stones, next to the first alignment ending with the great menhir, runs southwest for 159 metres, culminating in another blocking stone.

This would seem be aligned to the setting sun on the vernal equinox. The builders of the stones not only knew the four directions exactly, but carefully aligned the stones to celestial events. The alignment of the row from the great menhir to the northeast is close to the moon's most northerly rising.

A line from the great menhir runs precisely in a westerly direction through two outlying stones set far apart, until it hits a notch in a tor on the distant horizon. It has been further noticed that this magnificent complex at Drizzlecombe forms an enormous trapezoid in which sides are proportional to each other. The base is twice the length of the northeastern head, while the sides are six times as long: impressive surveying indeed. When I reluctantly trudged down the rock-strewn river valley, it felt as if I was turning my back on a magical place, which had somehow escaped the ravages of time.

The individual rows, cairns and circles at Merrivale and Drizzlecombe have to be seen as part of an integrated ritual landscape with a definite geometrical and astronomical pattern. Even today, they still form a splendid symmetry in the rugged and barren Dartmoor uplands.

Another atmospheric site on Dartmoor is the suitably named Grimspound north of Widecombe-in-the-Moor. Inhabited some 3000 years ago when the climate was much warmer and the uplands were covered in forest, it has a 3-metre-thick stone wall enclosing twenty-four circular huts. Several have raised places for beds. It is thought to have inspired the descriptions of the Stone Age settlement in which Sherlock Holmes camped in *The Hound of the Baskervilles*.

Cornovia

There are many other stones circles and rows worth a visit on
Dartmoor. Like the stones in Cornwall – known earlier as Cornovia
– they are on a smaller scale than in Wessex. But they equally show
resourceful and thoughtful minds at work, as well as a profound
appreciation of the correspondence between heaven and earth. Their
wild settings along the coasts or in the hills and moors make them
even more memorable.

On Bodmin Moor, just over the Cornish border, there are three
large stone circles standing in a NNE-SSW line set among rough
pasture and gorse. They are known as the Hurlers after a rough game
often played in the nineteenth century on Sunday afternoon, (after
church and the pub) which involved up to sixty young men from
opposing villages. The central ring is a little oval, with seventeen of the
twenty-eight stones still standing, the tallest of which is the height of a
man. In the smaller northern ring, I noticed on the inner face of a stone
next to a fallen slab what appeared to be a triple concentric ring. When
I visited the site, many cows were lying down among the stones:
perhaps they were sensitive to the benefic earth energies within the
ring, or perhaps they were just chewing the cud and awaiting rain . . .

At Carn Brea near Carnkie, there is a striking hill with three summits.
A castle in the Middle Ages and a mansion in the nineteenth century
were built here to take advantage of the dominating position and the
view. But there were predecessors: not long ago a prehistoric enclosure
was discovered on the tor. Dating from 3900 BC, it proved to be one of
the oldest settlements and most important archaeological sites in Britain.
In Neolithic times at least 200 people sheltered in a village by a
substantial wall, farming the southern slopes of the hill. For generations,
they lived and farmed peacefully until the village was suddenly attacked
and burnt to the ground. More than 700 arrowheads have been found
in the vicinity, suggesting a fierce battle. Since none of the Neolithic
sites were defended and no weapons of war have been found around
them, the devastation may have been the result of an attack of an
advance party of the invading Beaker people from the continent.

Land's End

After Padstow, we sailed along the rugged, savage coast of north
Cornwall, our boat rising in the Atlantic swell which has made
Newquay the surf capital of Europe. There is a small Elizabethan

harbour at Port Isaac, and a creek by Merlin's cave at Tintagel, but the only reasonable shelter is to be had at St Ives – although even that dries at low tide. We passed by the most spectacularly situated Neolithic site in England, perched high on a sea cliff near Cape Cornwall.

Ballowall Barrow, as it is known, is a huge, complex, multi-layered monument. The first monument under its green mound is thought to be a typical Neolithic chamber tomb. A T-shaped ritual pit was added in the Middle Bronze Age. Local legend says that the 'small people' dance around the barrow on moonlit nights – perhaps a folk memory of the rituals of the original Neolithic builders.

Ballowall Barrow is usually described as a 'Scillonian' chamber tomb, taking its name from the Isles of Scilly. During a previous voyage I had visited the barrows on the rocky islands off Land's End rising out of crystal-clear water. I was particularly struck by Innisidgen – the Giant's Grave – on a south-facing shore on St Mary's island. The Scillonian tombs are also known as 'entrance graves' because the passage-like stone chamber roofed by a number of flat slabs is usually open at one end. They are not only found in Cornwall and the Scilly Isles but also in Galicia in northwest Spain – compelling evidence of maritime links between these communities facing the Atlantic Ocean in megalithic times.

After sailing around Land's End in rough weather, where we were delighted to be joined by sharks, this time we made for the fishing port of Newlyn near Penzance, a good place to explore the many megalithic sites in west Cornwall. The area is rightly famous for its menhirs. They are still very much part of the living landscape and associated with music and dance. Unfortunately, they have not escaped the censure of puritanical Christianity. The beautiful, quartz-studded Blind Fiddler at Trenuggo stands over 3 metres tall, and is said to have been turned into stone for breaking the Sabbath with his life-affirming jigs. At Lamorna, two taller standing stones suffered a similar fate: they are said to be pipers turned to stone for providing music for the Merry Maidens of the nearby Rosemodress circle, who dared to dance on a Sunday. The maidens sometimes change sex: they are also known as the Dawns Men, no doubt deriving their name from the Cornish *don meyn*, meaning 'dance of stones'. They form a large circle of nineteen stones with a diameter of 24 metres. They are carefully graded, with the tallest erected in the southwest. They were probably raised around 2000 BC at the end of the Stone Age and the beginning of the Bronze Age.

The area is a megalith seeker's dream. Within a radius of a kilometre there are six menhirs, a number of barrows, and three holed stones. The cluster also includes the splendid Tregiffian entrance grave, dating from 1900 BC, which is decorated with cup marks.

The hostility of Christians to the stones as symbols of paganism and as places of worship for modern Druids continues unabated. At the time of the last solar eclipse, Christian fundamentalists were reported to be visiting sites at night in four-wheel drive vehicles and trying to pull out the stones with chains, until the local council blocked off access by placing large boulders along the paths.

Healing the earth

When I visited the Merry Maidens of the Rosemodress circle, I met a young blond woman moving around the stones with bent metal rods held out steadily in front of her. I asked her what she was doing.

'I'm dowsing. It's to feel the energy', she said. 'This is definitely a female site but it's lost its energy.'

It must have happened fairly recently. During a visit in the 1970s the dowser T.C. Lethbridge had experienced a tingling sensation, like a mild electric shock, from a stone he was touching. He even felt the stone rock and sway.[3]

From my own experience at the site, I tended to agree with the dowser I had met. She had an older companion with her who carried a pendulum made from a crystal dangling at the end of a silver chain. She held it near a stone, explaining that it could answer any question one wanted to ask: if the pendulum moved clockwise in a circle, the answer would be yes; if it moved from side to side, it was no. I asked her whether I should continue my journey. The crystal swung gently round in a circle. The answer – fortuitously – was yes.

My dowser said she was visiting the megalithic sites up and down the ley lines of Britain in an attempt to heal the wounds of the earth inflicted by our violent and grasping civilization. She did this by trying to integrate the male and female energies of the earth. She was working in a very ancient tradition: the Aborigines in Australia still follow their trackways – the 'songlines' – in order to restore the healthy flow of vital energy across the earth.

'By healing the earth,' she said, 'we also heal ourselves and integrate our own masculine and female sides. We can heal places and places can heal us.'

But it was a long and arduous task, and she admitted that there was a danger of becoming 'stoned out'. She gave her name as V. Mystical. Her personal card offered spiritual guidance on 'inner journeys to self-discovery'.

Dowsing

Dowsing has, of course, long been used with success by countrymen and women looking for underground watercourses and seams of minerals and metals. The traditional dowsing tool is a hazel rod in the shape of a two-pronged fork with a handle. I once had an old barn in North Wales surveyed by the chairman of the Dowsing Association of Great Britain, who was engaged in research at the university in Bangor. He used a circular disc with different colours on it, which indicated the kind of energy lines to be expected. As he doused with a rod with one hand, he moved the disc around his fingers in the other. He concluded that the overall site was beneficial, but a 'black line' of negative energy cut off one corner of the building. It was not a place to sleep, but its pernicious effect could be counteracted by well-placed metal bars in the earth nearby.

There does seem to be some kind of electrical or magnetic influence at work among megalithic stone circles. I have noticed at times that a compass will swing wildly due to a magnetic anomaly created by their presence. I have also dowsed with L-shaped metal rods held loosely in closed fists among the stones, and found that they swing inwards and outwards at different stones in a circle. They also sometimes twitch uncontrollably – a traditional sign that there is water underground. But I am not sensitive or imaginative enough to feel, like dowser Tom Graves, six 'energy bands' at different heights on standing stones. Nor have I found, like him, that the 'energy spiral' fluctuates in accordance with the phases of the moon.[4] And while I would like to see more research in this area, I simply cannot believe, as some claim, that they can dowse over the map of the terrain without ever visiting the site. How can there be 'earth energies' in an image on printed paper? Yet there are doubtless deep rhythms within the earth as there are in the heavens, and they must affect our lives intimately, even though it is difficult to quantify or demonstrate their influence.

Ley lines, songlines and shamanic pathways

In his book of 1925, *The Old Straight Track*, Alfred Watkins first popularised the notion of ley lines in Britain, which he thought followed ancient trackways linking sacred sites. He took a very practical view of them, and believed that they always followed the shortest route between one visible feature on the landscape and the next. But could it be that ley lines are sometimes created by inner experiences as much as by tramping across the countryside in a straight line?

As I've mentioned, the idea of ley lines has for me echoes of the songlines of the Australian Aborigines. The songlines are an expression of a dreaming consciousness as well as a metaphor for the living landscape. The Aborigines believe that in the mythical past of the First Time, semi-divine and semi-human beings descended from the sky or emerged from the earth and wandered across the land, thereby creating the lines. They left traces of their travels: white quartz, for instance, might be the remains of a torch; characters known as the Two Boys built Uluru (Ayers Rock) out of mud. By following their ancient tracks on foot, in ritual and song, the Aborigines hope to recreate the legendary journey of their Dreamtime ancestors. By singing the paths into existence, they recreate the landscape itself. And while walking along the songlines, the essential energy of life (called *kurunba*) could be evoked through ritual and song at the sacred sites, known as 'increase centres'. It would not surprise me if the megaliths in Europe were placed along the old trackways of the nomadic ancestors at such sacred centres of energy.

The author and researcher Paul Devereux, steeped in shamanistic ways, has further suggested that leys and alignments between stones may find their original source in the out-of-body experiences of shamans, the oldest priests and healers. By the controlled use of hallucinogens, they can enter trance states in which they experience the flight of their spirit. They usually travel in a straight line – 'as the crow flies' (the crow is a common 'power animal' who helps shamans in their trances), thereby creating lines of energy.[5] Leys could therefore have originally been shamanic pathways – outer expressions of inner experiences – and only at a later stage actual tracks defined by markers in the landscape.

None of this, of course, can be proven; but it supports the widely held view that there is a web of energy coursing through the veins of the earth's crust which the ancients knew how to channel and draw upon. In the 1978 *Needles of Stone*, the dowser Tom Graves makes the intriguing suggestion that the placing of standing stones into the earth may have been a kind of 'earth acupuncture, with the sacred sites as acupuncture points in energy channels both straight and sinuous'.[6] Dancing and other rituals at the sites would therefore be a way of massaging the earth! If this were the case, to pull down or to move standing stones would mean depleting or rerouting the energies of the earth. Similarly, to desecrate barrows and graves by digging them up would upset the field of force in the area. In their worship of the Great Goddess as Mother Earth, the megalith builders knew how to locate stones and mounds in order to maintain the balance and health of her body.[7]

Although such 'earth energies' can only be sensed rather than demonstrated, many dowsers like Graves talk in physical terms of 'electro-magnetic fields'. I suspect this is simply using modern 'scientific' language to describe an ancient experience of living nature. The Hindus called the vital energy which flows in all things *prana*; the Chinese call it *chi*. Indeed, the Chinese art of feng shui recognizes that there are subtle channels of energy in the land and that buildings should be built in harmony with them if their occupants are to have healthy and fulfilling lives. In the careful ways that they placed their monuments in the landscape, the megalith builders clearly followed many of the classic Chinese principles of feng shui, so much so that it might make sense to talk of an ancient British science of geomancy.[8]

Serpent lines

While I was in Cornwall I met the dowser Hamish Miller at a friend's house in Penzance. He had a gold serpent necklace around his neck and wore a colourful waistcoat. Having been a successful furniture maker, he had a near-death experience that changed his life and led him to settle in west Cornwall. He had written a book with Paul Broadhurst called *The Sun and the Serpent*, inspired by a walk along the so-called St Michael's Line, the ley line allegedly running from St Michael's Mount off the Cornish coast to Lowestoft on the Norfolk coast. On its way, it takes in Brent Tor, Glastonbury, Avebury and Bury St Edmunds.[9] On May Day or Beltane, the sun rises along this serpent line, lighting up hilltop and pond, sacred site and sanctuary. Since not all the sites are precisely aligned, it might best be described as a 'geomantic corridor' rather than a ley line in Watkin's definition as the width of a track.[10] When I met him Miller was about to set off on another journey along a ley line which he called the 'Apollo–St Michael Axis', from the island of Skellig Michael off southern Ireland to Armageddon in the Holy Land.

In Miller's view, the study of earth energies was once at the heart of an advanced science responsible for choosing the position and character of ancient sites. He was on the side of the 'earth energy' camp in the growing divide between those who take a mystical interest in megaliths and rely mainly on intuition and feeling, and those who take a more scientific interest and rely on deduction and experiment. At some sites such as Seahenge in the Holme-next-the-

Sea nature reserve in Norfolk, where an upturned oak tree root
encircled by the remains of timber posts was revealed after a storm,
the hostility between New Age enthusiasts and archaeologists has led
to abuse and physical fights.[11] The split is both unfortunate and
unnecessary. While I believe in sound reasoning based on firm
evidence, I am also open to thoughtful and imaginative hypotheses
and interpretations. One generation's absurdity can often become the
next generation's orthodoxy, as the development of astro-archaeology
so vividly demonstrates.

The holed stone

Throughout western Cornwall there are some extraordinary
megaliths, often in remote and wild places, which are the bare bones
of larger monuments. One of the most intriguing is to be found at
Mên-an-Tol near Chûn on the moors of West Penwith. It is found
along a narrow path which winds through impenetrable brambles
and gorse near a bog full of marsh cotton and sedges. Its name in
Cornish means 'holed stone'. Set on edge in line between two short
pillars (possibly moved from their original position), it resembles a
large wheel 1.3 metres across. With the two erect stones on either
side of the smooth orifice, the sexual symbolism is obvious. For some,
the holed stone represents the entrance and exit of the body of the
Great Goddess. By wriggling through the stone from the northeastern
side, one can emerge 'reborn' on the other. And according to the
artist Ian Cooke, who lives nearby, by touching the earth with one's
hands and knees as one crawls, disease is drawn deep into the ground,
deep into the lower world of death.[12] The archaeologist Marija
Gimbutas also claims that the holed stone in the European-wide
language of the Goddess is a symbol of initiation, renewal and health.
Crawling through the stone strengthens one with the energy of the
Goddess stored in the stone.[13]

Local folklore is full of tales about its healing powers. Children
used to be passed through it nine times as a cure for rickets, scrofula
and tuberculosis at certain seasons of the moon. Adults climbing
through it widdershins – against the sun – have found it beneficial for
back pain. I climbed through it myself and felt better. It is also
thought to have other magical powers: two pins placed crosswise on
the stone will allegedly answer any question by moving.

It was long thought that the stones at Mên-an-Tol were the remains
of a megalithic tomb with a porthole entrance, but it has recently been

discovered that they were part of a stone circle some 18 metres across. Even so, this does not change the symbolism of the holed stone.

Quoits

The chamber tombs of Cornwall have undergone a similar fate. Once covered in earth and stones, they are now denuded and stand as several massive upright slabs with a single capstone. They look like the stone tables of giants. These quaint structures, immediately recognizable symbols of the megalithic age, are variants of the portal dolmens I had seen in Scotland, Ireland and Wales during my journey. As I have mentioned, they are known locally as quoits – a word most likely of French origin, referring to a discus. By the beginning of the eighteenth century, the word was used to describe the flat covering stone of a cromlech, and then, by extension, the cromlech as a whole. Be that as it may, its sound evokes its angular shape perfectly.

There is a fine quoit to be seen at Lanyon, which has a capstone more than 5 metres across. A well-known local landmark by the side of an ancient road, it balances precariously on three uprights. It was restored in 1825.

Chûn Quoit has a much more atmospheric setting on an exposed hill looking westwards to the sea a short distance from the Iron Age ruins of Chûn Castle. It remains undamaged: its four slabs create a closed chamber surmounted by a thick convex capstone roughly 4 metres square. Looking like a mushroom, it is the best-preserved Neolithic chamber in Cornwall. Local legend has it that the builder of Chûn Castle was a character called Jack the Hammer or Jack the Tinner, a wandering tin prospector and giant-killer who settled in Penwith. This could well be a veiled reference to the incoming Beaker people who took over the Neolithic sites and knew the art of metal smelting.

On a wild, wet day, I trudged up a steep hill across rough fields, then moorland in a swirling mist. Without the help of my compass, I would have missed it. Chûn Quoit was not large – about a metre high – but beautifully shaped with slabs on all sides. I crawled inside the chamber to discover the remains of a fire. It felt very cosy sitting under the 30-tonne stone, which had not moved for 5000 years. While I was taking my ease listening to a distant lark, two young women came along and sat outside. Their shadows flitted on the walls through the cracks in the stones. At first, I thought they would move on but they stayed to eat their lunch and to discuss the most intimate details of their lives. I was in quite a quandary; I did not want to frighten them, nor did I want to eavesdrop. In the end, I coughed and said: 'Don't worry, I'm not a ghost. I'm just a walker taking a rest from the rain!'

They jumped up, laughing, and one of them said: 'Are you sure you're not a gnome?'

I recalled that the Irish believe that the dolmens are gateways to the underworld and gnomes are considered to be spirits of earth. They are one of four 'elementals', the others being sylphs (spirits of air), salamanders (spirits of fire) and undines (spirits of water). They are part of a pantheon of nature spirits, sometimes called *devas* or fairies, who inhabit the natural world: dryads in the trees, naiads in the waterfalls, nereids in the sea and oreads in the mountains. These elemental forces still kept alive by folklore undoubtedly hark back to the polytheism of ancient Britain.

The Dwelling of the Elder Tree

For all its wealth of megalithic ruins, the most evocative site for me in the West Country is the small sheltered stone circle at Boscawen-ûn which means in Cornish 'The Dwelling of the Elder Tree'. It can only be reached from the road to Land's End by crossing rough and neglected fields, in summer full of bracken, gorse, thorn bushes, campion, foxgloves and wild orchids. It is surrounded by a circular stone wall overgrown with thorn bushes, which was built in 1862 when the circle was restored. The result today is a hidden and intimate space. I counted nineteen upright stones in an ellipse 25 metres across at its widest point. A stone, leaning sharply to the northeast, is situated just off-centre.

The circle has a wide entrance to the west. It is clearly part of a wider network of stones, for there are still some outlying menhirs to the northeast and there were others across the valley to the west which have been recently pulled down. An aerial view has shown six standing stones in the vicinity.

On my first visit, it immediately reminded me of the stone circles raised at the National Eisteddfod festivals held each year in Wales. In fact, I found out later that it was reputed to be one of the three Gorsedds (thrones for the bards) of Britain, taken up by the Welshman Iolo Morgannwg (Edward Williams) in the Romantic Celtic Revival of the early nineteenth century. It may have even been the moot assembly place of 'West Wales' since AD 926.[14] The modern Cornish

Gorsedd was inaugurated here in 1928. A fiftieth anniversary was held in 1978 within the circle.

During my visit, I was particularly struck by a whitish quartz stone with pinkish veins on the perimeter of the circle. The megalith builders valued quartz for its magical qualities and the pillar had clearly been carefully chosen. It could have served as a backsight for observing the May Day sunrise. As I examined it, I noticed that someone else had felt its power and had left a candle to burn on the top of the stone. Under the leaning central stone in the middle, I also found burnt paper, sea shells, coloured snail shells, pieces of quartz, garlands, flowers and ribbons – all left by passing wayfarers to mark their presence and to expedite their prayers. It was indeed a magical and inspiring place. Swallows dived in the air, a thrush sang in a thicket, bees buzzed all around me. After sitting in the circle and meditating for a while, I returned from a deep place and felt as light as air and relaxed as the breeze.

I went back to Boscawen-ûn on the summer solstice. I wanted to see whether the rising midsummer sun leaves in shadow two elongated triangular 'axeheads' at the bottom of the north face of one of the stones in the circle. It is said that they cannot be seen at other times of the year.[15]

In the middle of the night, as Elizabeth and I trampled across the moonlit fields, we could hear drumming in the distance. On our arrival, we found three other couples in the intimate circle, leaning against the stones, facing east, waiting for the rising of the sun. Just before dawn one ageing hippy said to his companion, 'Let's have earth sex!' but she took another swig from a bottle and ignored him. Another woman, looking the worse for having stayed up all night, said to me: 'What are you interested in – the zodiac?' A third said: 'They're very strong energies here . . .' and gave a beatific smile. We settled down by the white quartzstone and kept our peace.

One, then two, then countless birds opened their throats for the dawn chorus on midsummer's day. A weak yellow streak of light gradually began to glow on the eastern horizon. The rays of the sun passed up the hills, across the fields and gently touched the top of the stones. Glory to the Sun!

> Thank you sun for your light and heat.
> Go well on your journey to the south.
> May the harvest be good.
> May the people be warm and content
> In the coming winter.

Although on that occasion, I was unable to confirm whether the two 'axes' could be made out, I left the Dwelling of the Elder Tree with much greater understanding of the meaning of stone circles.

Moon shadow rising

The highlight of my journey through Cornwall was the solar eclipse on 19 August 1999. A solar eclipse was the event most feared in the ancient world, for it could augur the end of the earth if the sun did not reappear and light return. Since a total eclipse occurs every 350 to 390 years or so in any one place, and the average lifespan in Stone Age Britain was about forty years, its memory would have been passed down from generation to generation. The event would no doubt grow all the more terrible in the telling. As a result, one of the central tasks of the early astronomers was to predict the eclipses in order to prepare the people.

We were fortunate that the band of 'totality' – complete darkness – passed directly through Cornwall that year. I travelled with Elizabeth, my daughter Emily and her boyfriend Tom to a camp on a hill above Land's End with a view of the sea on three sides: the Celtic Sea, the Atlantic Ocean and the English Channel. The gathering was called 'Moon Shadow Rising' in honour of the fact that it was a solar eclipse in which female Luna covers male Sol. After a night of torrential summer rain, we gathered on a spur on the hilltop to watch the awesome event. The moon rose in the west and like an arrow in slow motion, arched towards the sun, a light-yellow orb in the swirling cloud.

In the penumbra preceding totality, I noticed my daughter's breath turn to steam. A daisy at my feet began to close its white petals. As the world grew dark, the birds fell silent. The faraway street lights of Penzance automatically came on, white pinpricks in a distant black velvet cushion. The full moon shadow fell on the earth – it was the moment of the umbra, of totality. My watch said it was 11.10 am British Summer Time.

A hush spread across the land lost in darkness. I could hear my heart beat. It felt terribly cold: the cold travelled up my spine; the cold of death; the cold of dread; the cold of a world without the sun. Would totality turn into finality? Was it the end of the world?

Hidden by light cloud, we could not see the sun's ghostly outer atmosphere, the corona. Then, after a few minutes, light began to spread across the earth. The gloaming became a second dawn of silvery, shimmering light. The clouds cleared for a moment to reveal the sun half-covered by the moon. Life and warmth came back hand in hand to the barren land. The stunned people around me began to talk excitedly.

'Wow', said my daughter, shivering and laughing with relief. 'That was really eerie!'

A young woman nearby, holding a baby to her breast, said: 'If my baby lives to 2099, he should see it again in England. But none of us will!'

In the distance, down by the tipis set around the campfire, the drums began to beat and the didgeridoos boom. The shamanic dancing, encircling the sacred land, continued long afterwards as the reinvigorated sun climbed boldly into the sky.

I could see why solar eclipses were considered such omens of doom – and how important it was for early astronomers to predict their coming for their people. The ancient Chinese, who recorded the first eclipse in writing in 2136 BC, would beat drums and send fireworks into the sky to scare away the heavenly dragon as he devoured the sun. In that way, they hoped to restore the universal balance between Yin and Yang which had been so severely disturbed. No doubt our own distant ancestors had performed similar ceremonies among the megaliths.

Rock Valley

The last place I visited before leaving Cornwall was an ivy-strewn cliff face by a ruined mill in Rock Valley, near Tintagel on the north coast. It stands among trees on the bank of a rushing steam which plunges across jagged rocks into the sea. Carved on the fissured rock face are two amazing hand-sized carvings of labyrinths. A plaque suggests that they 'proably' date from the early Bronze Age (1800–1400 BC), but they could have been carved much earlier. They reminded me of the concentric circles cut to the centre by a straight line I had seen on the rocks of Kilmartin. Over the years, pilgrims had squeezed coins into seams in the rock and tied ribbons to the surrounding twigs of the trees and branches of ivy – offerings and symbols of ritual cleansing and healing. Someone had unsuccessfully tried to deface the carvings; but they had already withstood the ravages of more than 4000 years. The sheltered site is a truly magical place: the stillness and permanence of the rock carvings contrast wonderfully with the ever-changing water music of the tumbling stream.

Some years ago I once showed the labyrinths to a friend of mine, a rationalist and humanist philosopher. He admitted that he was moved to tears. This may have been because after a long cliff-top walk by the pounding sea he had been touched by the power of an archetype deep within his psyche. Perhaps, like Theseus facing the Minotaur, he was hoping that the thread of Ariadne would lead him out of the difficulties in his life.

I traced with my finger the path along the rings made by two continuous lines to the centre. Its shape reminded me again of the great labyrinth carved on the flagstones in Chartres Cathedral. It had also inspired a friend of mine, Lucy Rees, to make a journey after a personal catastrophe to the Hopi Indians in Arizona, who possess a carved labyrinth on a stone identical to the one in Rock Valley. It was a perilous journey, both physically and emotionally, which she described brilliantly in her book *The Maze* (1992).

For me, the carvings in Rock Valley symbolize the labyrinth of the world through which we all have to pass to reach the paradise of the heart. There is an indirect and a direct line to the centre. As in alchemy and Zen, there is a gradual, moist path and a fast, hot path to enlightenment. Most of the us take the slow one, and some get lost on the way, but a few can aim straight at the centre and attain sudden liberation.

Labyrinth at Rock Valley, near Tintagel, Cornwall

Axes, tin and saffron

At the time I visited the labyrinth in Rock Valley, a young Japanese man had been swept into the sea by waves as he stood on a rock a few hundred metres downstream. One of the coastguards told me that after crossing the Atlantic, an American yacht had also crashed into a rocky cliff nearby, and then sunk on a calm day. The incidents reminded me not only how easy it is for the sea to take life but how the Cornish coast has seen visitors from distant shores for millennia.

In prehistoric times, the mineral wealth of Cornwall and its strategic position jutting out into the Atlantic made it an important trading centre. Cornish axes, made from granite and greenstone and often highly polished, were sent to many parts of Britain. But it was during the Bronze Age that Cornwall became celebrated for its rare deposits of tin and copper which, mixed together, make bronze. It was not long before the trade, already well developed with Brittany, extended right down the west coast of Europe and into the Mediterranean.

Around 1900 BC a small group of tin merchants from Brittany settled in Cornwall and began the prosperous trade in bronze. Indeed, it seems that the technique of bronze making in Britain developed near St Just, not far from Land's End, where deposits of copper and tin occur together naturally. The word spread and by the middle of the second millennium BC, countries from areas as far afield as Mycenean Greece and the Baltic were trading for Cornish tin.

After the Celts, a tall warrior people from Central Europe, arrived on British shores around 500 BC, the trade in tin continued. Barter was the custom, for in Britain no currency was used until well into the Roman period. Even the Phoenicians, who from their base in Carthage (present-day Tunis) threatened the Romans in the two Punic Wars, became interested in Cornish tin. Their great seafarer Hanno is said to have travelled to Cornwall and Ireland around 500 BC.

Another visitor was the Greek astronomer and geographer Pytheas of Massilia (modern-day Marseilles) who visited Cornwall around 325 BC in an expedition to 'Thule', thought to be the most northerly place in the world. He is said to be the first Greek to use the stars to determine latitude and to have made the connection between the tides with the moon, but the northern megalithic seafarers would have discovered that long before him. Although his works have been lost, his observations were used by the first-century BC historian Diodorus Siculus in a remarkable passage from one of the first written records mentioning Britain. It gives a fascinating portrait of life in

Cornwall, enriched by thousands of years of maritime trade from megalithic times:

The people of that promontory called Belerion are friendly to strangers and, from their contact with foreign merchants, are civilized in their way of life. They carefully work the ground from which they extract the tin. It is rocky but contains earthy veins, the produce of which they grind down, smelt and purify. The metal is then beaten into ingots shaped like astragli and carried to a certain island lying off the coast of Britain which is called Iktis. During the ebb of the tide, the intervening space is left dry and they carry the tin, in abundance, over to this island in their wagons. Here, then, the merchants buy the tin from the natives and carry it over to Gaul. . . .[16]

The island of Iktis is almost certainly St Michael's Mount in Penzance Bay. Diodorus also mentions later Narbonne and Marseilles as places receiving Cornish tin on the Mediterranean coast. It was probably transported down to present-day Bordeaux, up the river Garonne and across the Carcassone Gap to Narbonne.

The foreign merchants visiting Cornwall included the Veneti, a tribe of Breton Celts, who had large, heavily built oaken boats with leather sails. Their high poop and foredecks were ideally suited to Atlantic conditions. Their powerful fleet was only defeated by Julius Caesar in 56 BC at the battle of Quiberon Bay in Brittany, when the oar-propelled Roman galleys could take advantage of the becalmed Veneti ships.

My local baker in Tavistock, West Devon, sells what he calls saffron bread, bright yellow and filled with raisins. He tells me that foreign sailors would come to a particular cliff in Cornwall and barter saffron for tin with the locals. But they were suspicious of each other. The locals would lower empty baskets from the cliff top, which were then filled on the sea shore with a quantity of saffron and other spices. The basket would be hauled up and then returned with what they thought to be a quantity of tin of equivalent value.

'And who were the foreigners?' I asked him. 'Venetians', he replied emphatically.

He could well have been referring to the Veneti from Brittany who traded up and down the Atlantic coast. But then further west in Cornwall, the same spicy, yellow bread is sometimes called Phoenician bread – named after the greatest maritime people and traders of the ancient world, who came from the eastern Mediterranean and sailed all the way up the Atlantic seaboard to the British Isles.

CHAPTER NINE

A Place of Sadness

*The sea is so large
And my boat is so small.*

BRETON PRAYER

I t took a long time to leave Cornwall for Brittany, in northwest France. Although it was midsummer, the weather continued unsettled and low after low blew in from the southwest. But the weather alone wasn't to blame for the delay. Before sailing down the west coast of the continent, I had decided to investigate megalithic culture in the north of Europe which reached as far as Sweden. Apart from those in Brittany, the first Stone Age farming communities had emerged in northern Europe along the river basin of the Danube. One settlement at Geelen in Holland dates from just after 5000 BC and many long dolmens for collective burials known locally as *hunebedden* were built soon after. This 'Danubian culture' seems to have spread from Bohemia across central Germany to the North Sea: many isolated menhirs stand in the region as an eloquent testimony of this diffusion. In the following millennium, Wéris in Belgium became a major megalithic site with long alignments of stones as well as dolmens. But it was Denmark, with all its islands, which became most active in megalithic building. It has more dolmens than any other country in Europe: 3500 compared to 2000 in the British Isles. I was intrigued to learn that at Breddyssen on Zealand, there are carvings of two ships, encircled by cup marks, on a capstone. Clearly the Vikings who sailed down into the Mediterranean were simply carrying on the seafaring skills of their megalithic ancestors.

While fascinating and confirming my thesis that the megalithic sites were linked by the sea and waterways, my foray north had been a diversion, however. Now it was time for me to head south. So when at last the wind eased and turned westerly, we decided to set off in the late afternoon for an overnight sail across the Channel to the port of Aber-Vrac'h on the Brittany coast. The late afternoon sun was warm on our faces and with the steady breeze we relaxed to think that we were at last heading for France where we could expect to see some of the best megaliths in the world.

It was not to be. As it was beginning to get dark, the wind shifted north and started to blow hard. The spectacular coastline of Brittany is notorious for its rocky, unforgiving nature and the entrance to Aber-Vrac'h involved careful navigation through a long, narrow leg between rocks and islets. I did not fancy being caught in such a place after a hard night's sail in strong onshore winds. About thirty nautical miles out at sea, a third of the way across, I therefore reluctantly decided to turn round and head for the shelter of Falmouth on the other side of the Lizard. And here we stayed: the bad weather continued for a week.

The enforced wait reminded me how important it is for navigators to be patient; for millennia, we have had to wait for the right winds and sea conditions before setting sail. 'Be present in the moment,' I wrote in my journal. 'Life continues whatever happens. Clouds come and go. Tides come and go. Ships come and go. I've come into this world and will soon be going. Why speed up the process?'

Eventually there was a window in the endless lows and gales sweeping up the Channel: 20 July, Elizabeth's birthday. It was a great relief to be able to shake out the sails again. I was now leaving the British Isles once and for all for continental Europe. It marked another turning point in my sea quest to uncover the mysteries of the megaliths.

Since megalithic times, there has been a long tradition of the Cornish going to live in Brittany and Bretons taking refuge in Cornwall. In fact, the Celtic language of the Bretons, Cornish and Welsh are closer to each other than to Irish and Scots Gaelic. Even as late as the early 1980s, I can remember Breton onion sellers coming over to Cornwall and Wales to peddle their bikes and wares – the last in a long line of traders stretching over 7000 years.

I had planned to sail to Roscoff and to visit one of the earliest megalithic monuments in France – the Barnenez megalithic complex, sited on a headland on the opposite side of the Baie de Morlaix near Plouézoc'h in Finistère. A huge pile, it resembles an elongated, stepped pyramid, but has a complex structure consisting of two cairns next to each other, the western part built around 4700 BC and the eastern up to 400 years later. The magnificent construction of its wall is a fine testimony to the skill of its builders right at the beginning of the megalithic era. André Malraux rightly called it a 'Megalithic Parthenon'.

The imposing long-stepped cairn has long passages leading to its eleven stone chambers. The one at the extreme northeast contained a carved 'figure' with wavy lines on the underside of the first capstone, probably representing the Great Goddess who watched over the dead. I was all the more intrigued because the whole looks like a funerary boat with its prow pointing southeast, toward the direction of the midwinter sunrise.[1] The exact purpose of the eleven adjoining chambers remains as elusive as ever; local legend has it that it was once the home of fairies, and the north and south cairns were linked to the sea by an underground passage.

Because of the direction of the winds, I decided to miss Barnenez for the time being and head due south from Falmouth to try for Aber-Vrac'h yet again. The 100-mile Channel crossing proved comparatively easy in rolling seas under a dark starlit night. There was one memorable incident. The Channel is now one of the busiest stretches of water in the world, and it was particularly busy that night. I was semi-dozing, with one eye open around 2 am during the so-called 'dead man's watch', when I espied two white lights on my starboard side. But I could not make out a red port light or a green starboard light which would tell me the direction of the vessel.

The white lights got closer and closer, but there were still no red port light or starboard green light to be seen. Suddenly I was wide awake: the huge dark bows of a great ship seemed to be almost on top of me and I felt I was about to be crushed. I pushed the tiller hard to starboard. At that moment, almost instantaneously, the great ship also altered course. Miraculously, we missed each other. Its vast wake tossed our little boat about like a cork. The fearful sound of its thudding engines rapidly faded as the ship disappeared into the dark night. It was a phenomenally lucky escape.

It was not long before dawn began to break, cold and grey. I could just make out a darker line of the coast on the horizon as the strong tide began to turn against us. Only when I was quite close to the coast could I make out, among the rocks, the Vierge lighthouse, reputed to be the largest in the world. Aber-Vrac'h was indeed a tricky entrance and it was difficult to make out the buoys in the driving drizzle which had descended with gusty winds soon after dawn. The appearance of a belfry heralded the entrance into the small harbour, and we sailed in – just as a thick sea mist descended. We had only just made it.

Our next port of call was Brest, in a deep inlet around the great rounded stretch of land which points out to the Île d'Ouessant or Ushant, the most westerly point of France. The sail demanded careful calculations of the tides: on a spring tide, a current of 6 knots can sweep you down the narrow Chenal du Four, with a rocky coastline on one side and rocks and islets on the other. Eddies and overflows swirl around submerged rocks. The ancient mariners who travelled up and down the western seaboard of Europe would have been equally careful in getting the tides right. With their knowledge of the cycles of sun and moon, encoded in their monuments, they would have known the twice-daily movement of the tides and the coming and going of the spring and neap tides with the waxing and waning of the moon.

It has been argued that the parallel of latitude 45 to 50 degrees north in France roughly formed the southern boundary of the region where skin boats were used in ancient times. This includes the area of Ushant where, according to the early fragment of a pilot called the Massiliote Periplus, goods being transported north in the fifth century BC were transferred from planked to skin boats.[2]

Certainly by the time of the Roman invasion of Brittany, the Celtic Veneti were using large wooden sailing boats. Julius Caesar was impressed by their flat bottoms and leather sails. They had no doubt evolved from dugouts, which were first used for the rivers and estuaries and then strengthened with crosspieces and higher stems in order to venture out into the open seas of the Atlantic. They were possibly influenced by the Phoenicians, who by the end of the 2nd millennium BC were sailing their flat-bottomed 'hippos' with leather sails as far north as the British Isles. The wooden boats of the Veneti, however, may have been a late development from skin boats: a carving on a megalith at Mané Lud in Brittany and a painting in the Las Figuras rock shelter in Andalusia have both been taken to represent skin-boats.[3]

There was an early morning mist when we left Aber-Vrac'h for Brest, but it soon lifted and we had a pleasant voyage in a northwesterly breeze. The sun blazed as we sailed past the menhirs near Porspoder. The most impressive ones, however, are the giant menhirs at Kerloas, or the Place of Sadness, at a site a little inland near Plouarzel in Finistère, 16 kilometres west of Brest. It has the tallest surviving menhir not only in Brittany but in the whole of Western Europe. Once a staggering 12 metres high, it had a couple of metres knocked off during a thunderstorm about two centuries ago. For years, the broken part was used as a cattle-trough in a neighbouring farm.[4] The menhir has on either side of its base two enormous balls – or possibly breasts – in relief, indicating its fertility symbolism. In the past, newlyweds would go to the stone, strip off, and rub themselves against these bosses in the hope of having sons. Another local legend maintained that if a young naked couple rubbed against the menhir at the full moon, the man would have beautiful children and the wife would wear the trousers![5]

That afternoon, off the aptly named and dangerous Pierres Noires, we saw a pod of about a dozen dolphins playing in the water. Their apparent joy at being alive mirrored our own after all our delays, and the long slog down the west coast of Wales and round Cornwall. We were now blessed by what the French sailors called *le vent solaire*, the wind of the sun. With its perfect shelter and deep-water harbour, I could see why Brest was the principal naval base of France in the northwest.

With every nautical mile south, I felt we were leaving the persistent wind, rain, drizzle and cloud of the last few months behind us. In my diary I wrote ecstatically: '*Enfin, le soleil!*'

All along the coast of Brittany, stone structures can be found from the beginning to the end of the period of megalithic building. There are dolmens, stepped cairns, earth-covered passage graves and alignments of standing stones. Giant single menhirs are also widely scattered. One of the tallest stones, 9 metres high, is to be found at Dol, on the borders of Brittany and Normandy not far from le Mont-St-Michel. Broad in one direction, it is flattened and narrow in the other, no doubt for astronomical sightings.

The Crozon Peninsula

We next sailed from Brest to Morgat, a small fishing village just around the corner in Baie de Douarnenez on the Crozon Peninsula. Off Camaret-sur-Mer, we were overtaken by a flotilla of sailing boats which appeared over the horizon like an armada of Viking long ships, with their brightly coloured spinnakers billowing in the gentle wind.

To visit the famed local megalithic sites, we travelled overland northwest, back to Camaret-sur-Mer which we had sailed past. We walked up the hill overlooking the fishing harbour with its colourful boats, and there, among the coarse grass on the headland, we found the fine collection of stones known as the Lagatjar alignments, shaped like a huge open rectangle. It would have made an ideal prehistoric football pitch. The two sides, which ran for about 82 metres, were oriented towards the northeast, the direction of the rising sun on the summer solstice. The baseline stones ran for about 112 metres, according to my strides at least. The tallest stones were more than 2 metres high, two of them made from quartzite. On a clear day, the inhabitants would have had a commanding view of the entrance to the Rade de Brest and far along the coast in both directions. It felt very peaceful and ordered, but I could well imagine the wild chaos of the headland in darkest winter.

On the Crozon Peninsula there is a fine dolmen at Saint-Nic Pentrez and a cracked one at Sainte-Barbe which dates from around 450 BC. Standing stones from that time are extremely rare, but the fact that it is there demonstrates the continuity of the megalithic tradition in the area. This is also reflected in a procession which takes place every six years at Locronan near Douarnenez. Known as La Grande Troménie, it brings together megalithic, Celtic and Christian beliefs. The procession moves in a circular direction over 12 kilometres through plains and mountains, stopping at 12 stations which represent the 12 months of the year. Each month is consecrated to a god of the Celtic pantheon, and by walking the stations the pilgrims would ensure the fecundity of the land throughout the year.

The Druidic calendar consisted of two seasons: the cold, wet, feminine season which began on 1 November with Samhain, and the warm, dry, masculine season which began on May Day with the festival of Beltane. The months of the year were defined by the waxing and waning of the moon. Christians retained one aspect of the Celtic lunar calendar by continuing to calculate the date of Easter (which changes each solar year). At Locronan, Christians continued the practice of walking the twelve stations in the Middle Ages but prayed to the Irish bishop Ronan who calculated the date of Easter rather than to the Celtic gods of nature. The Celtic 'temple' became a Benedictine priory: the word *troménie* comes from the Breton for 'the tour of the refuge'. I was not surprised to find out that the stations not only included sacred Christian sites such as a church, an abbey, and several chapels but also holy fountains and megaliths. The Christianized Celtic practices around the Baie de Douarnenez undoubtedly have Neolithic foundations.

We next investigated the sites near the town of Crozon itself. We took a bus ride and then walked along a dusty road to a hamlet called Landaoudec in rolling countryside which was reputed to have some interesting alignments of stones. When we arrived in the late afternoon, the place appeared deserted. Many of the fine stone houses were shuttered, and the stone-walled fields looked neglected or abandoned. Just as I was about to give up, I saw a fit-looking man with a shock of white hair working in a garden. I went up to him and explained our interest; his pale-blue eyes immediately lit up. I noticed a fine rosy-coloured stone about waist high in the middle of his lawn. It was one of the most beautiful stones I had ever seen in my travels.

'Yes, it's a menhir,' he said in answer to my first question, and pointed out the rosettes which looked like stars on the white rock.

'We call it *"quartz étoilé,"* ' he observed. 'At night, it shines beautifully under the sky.'

His name was Jean-Claude le Bretton and his parents had until recently lived in the old stone house and worked the few surrounding fields. They were among a dying breed of Breton peasants who could no longer earn a reasonable living from the small, stony fields, which had been continually subdivided down the generations. Jean-Claude was living in Paris and only came to his old Breton home for holidays.

He took us on a tour of the local megaliths – the ones, that is, that remained. There were a few near a fort on a hill and there was a ruined dolmen which Jean-Claude said had been split by lightning. Early illustrations, which he sent on to me later, show that in 1835 it had consisted of five supporting stones and a capstone in the form of a triangle about 2 metres long and 3 metres wide. Jean-Claude also sent me a copy of an engraving made in 1843 which showed two huge stones about 9 metres tall, also allegedly split by lightning.

Other engravings of the period showed a great number of stones in alignments in open countryside, but now the area has returned to rough moorland and most of the menhirs have been brought down.[6]

'The general pattern of the alignments is now lost,' Jean-Claude said. 'One hundred and fifty years ago, there were many sanctuaries in this area. Our ancestors pulled most of them down to clear the land and then added a few here and there. I can still remember, only thirty years ago, when farmers dynamited the menhirs in their fields. There are many more lost in *la lande*.'

He pointed to the rough, stony moorland scattered with stunted trees.

It turned out that Jean-Claude was a sailor too and when he heard of my voyage, he said: 'You know, before the Celts, the Bretons invaded Cornwall and settled there. Many generations later they then came back and invaded Brittany!'

The ancient memories of the relationships between the two lands on either side of the Channel die slowly.

After leaving Morgat and the Crozon Peninsula, we sailed between the Île-de-Sein and the Pointe du Raz and across the Baie d' Audierne. Rounding the Penmarc'h Peninsula, we were unable to see the broken menhir at Kerscaven on the southwestern corner of Brittany, which once stood 6 metres high and would have been a distinctive landmark for the ancient mariners. Our destination was Concarneau, which had a fine fort overlooking the harbour. On the way, I was fascinated to find marked on the chart about one mile off the Cap de la Chèvre a rock called the Roche du Dolmen; it certainly looked like one. It was beautifully hot and the water was as smooth as a mill pond. I felt we were like a white feather drifting on a glassy sea. But we did not linger for we were drawn by the promise of Carnac in the Baie de Quiberon, on what the French call the Côte de Mégalithes.

If Brittany is outstanding in France for its megaliths, the region around Carnac is doubly exceptional for the number, size and variety of its share of them. Over twenty-five centuries, from 4500 to 2000 BC, successive generations built the first stone architecture and created the greatest concentration of megaliths in the world.

CHAPTER TEN

The Pillar and the Axe

*Covered with bizarre designs, curves, lines, straight, broken, sketched,
and combined in a hundred different ways.*

PROSPER MÉRIMÉE

I n circles of megalith lovers, the very mention of Carnac inspires
awe and enthusiasm in equal measure. It is one of the oldest
continuously inhabited places on earth. On the seashore at Saint-
Colombin, choppers and worked flints (now in the Carnac Museum
of Prehistory) have been found dating from around half a million BC.
These were left by *Homo erectus. Homo sapiens,* who were the first to
bury their dead, did not appear until around 500,000 BC. Remnants
of mammoths, rhinos, lions, wolves and reindeer from this period
have been found in the region. Thereafter little physical evolution
occurred since our direct ancestors, the Cro-Magnons, merged with
or replaced the Neanderthals around 40,000 BC.

Fascinating remnants of the Mesolithic culture that flourished along
the coasts of Brittany have been found on the nearby islands of
Tréviec and Hoedic, which were at the time attached to the mainland.
They show that the nomadic population not only lived from hunting,
fishing and gathering shellfish, but made jewellery from perforated
shells and stags' teeth, and decorated bones with geometric lines.
They also made double graves (with a woman and child or a man and
child) and, as a decorated human rib suggests, undertook ritualized
secondary burials.[1] Their skeletons, dating from around 6000 BC,
show that they were short and slender, with small feet, sturdy hands
and narrow skulls which broadened at the face.[2] Although mainly
hunter-gatherers, they kept dogs and perhaps sheep.

While the domestication of plants and animals appeared around

8000 BC in the Middle East, it seems that it reached Brittany a couple of thousand years later along two main routes. One was from the Mediterranean region along the coasts, reaching the Atlantic seaboard through the Strait of Gibraltar. This was the route I was following in reverse. The other was via the so-called 'Danubian' culture I have mentioned, which came up the Danube from the shores of the Black Sea. In the west of France, the mingling of the two currents led to a new way of producing food which involved the clearing of the forests and the growing of wheat and barley.

Agriculture was not simply a new stage in evolution during which humans began to direct and control nature. It also stimulated techno-logical innovation, especially in the polishing of stone, pottery, weaving and wicker work, and the manufacture of agricultural implements such as reaping hooks and mills. In the Carnac region, the inhabitants ground their cereal into flour, from which they made a kind of pancake and gruel. They supplemented their meat diet from sheep, cattle, pigs, wild boars, rabbit and to a lesser extent deer and small horses, with seabirds, fish and molluscs gathered along the shores.

The first stone architecture

Not long after settling down, the local farmers produced sufficient food by the new methods to have the leisure and surplus energy to build stone monuments on a massive scale. Yet despite the grandeur of their works, there were probably no more than 30,000 people living in Brittany and half a million in France as a whole.

The working population must have supported architects and engineers who understood measurements and materials, as well as astronomers and priests who observed the movements of the celestial bodies and focused the creative and spiritual energies of the people. There is, however, no direct evidence that these specialists crystallized into an elite or that the communities were led by chiefs. As in the British Isles, until the coming of the Bronze Age the megalithic builders of Carnac lived in peaceful, egalitarian and cooperative settlements. Yet they were clearly able to organize themselves for large-scale endeavours. The raising of the stones, some of which weigh up to 300 tonnes, must have involved hundreds of men at a time.[3]

The French megalithic monuments fall into two main categories. Those in the first concern the world of the dead: mounds, cairns, barrow, dolmens and passage graves. The second concern the world of the living: standing stones and alignments which stretch for several kilometres. Both were clearly used for ceremonial and religious purposes. In terms of chronology, it would seem that giant standing stones were first raised in the fifth millennium BC, followed by tombs with rectangular chambers around 4000 BC. A third phase in building was marked by tombs with long chambers, from around 3000 BC.

There are four distinct types of stones erected around Carnac. The oldest is the tumulus, usually containing a closed grave under a mound. The other three have been given Breton names which have now entered common archaeological parlance. Collective burial sites are called dolmens, from the Breton *dol*, meaning 'stone', and *men*, meaning 'table'. These skeletons of monuments, which resemble stone tables, have an entry to a passage leading to a higher and larger space originally surrounded by stones under a cairn. The third type are menhirs, from the Breton words *men*, meaning 'stone', and *hir*, meaning 'long', which stand on their own or near a grave. For some reason, one side is invariably rounded and the other side flatter. They are set into circles, quadrangles or in alignments. Another local word for menhir, now falling into disuse, is *pelvan*. Much rarer are the cromlechs, from the Breton words *crom* for 'circle', and *lech* for 'stone'. The term is often used to describe semicircles of stones. As we have seen, in Wales the word is mainly applied to dolmens. Clearly, Breton has many words for 'stone', no doubt because many different shapes and sizes are scattered across the land.

The world of the dead

The earliest known date for a megalithic monument in the world is the Kercado passage grave, which has been carbon-dated to 4700 BC. Set on a slight hill in a glade of pine trees near a manor house, this impressive and well-preserved mound has a standing stone on its summit. I could not help thinking that it looked like a phallus placed above the womb of the dolmen. It is also encircled by a ring of stones – a very rare configuration in Brittany.

Its entrance is oriented south of east, pointing almost exactly towards the midwinter sunrise when the light would have penetrated deep into the inner chamber, as in Newgrange in Ireland and Maes Howe in Scotland. Excavations have revealed polished axes, arrowheads, jadeite beads, a rare green variscite bead necklace and the remains of human bones (teeth and a fragment of a skull), now all held in the Carnac Museum. Because of the acidity of Brittany's soil, very few human remains of any size have survived.

Soon after the Kercado mound was built, the local people raised an immense hill now known as the Tumulus Saint-Michel, just outside the town of Carnac. It is so called because early Christians, wishing to make the holy site their own, placed a chapel on its summit. It has a commanding view of the flat plain all around. Shaped rather like a stone axe, its narrowest end points southwest, towards the setting of the sun on the winter solstice. It was built around 4500 BC and contains the earliest form of burial site: a pit containing square cists made from stone slabs deep within the massive long barrow. A beautifully polished dark-green jadeite axe, now in the Carnac Museum, was found in the mound. Although not as awe-inspiring as Silbury Hill at Avebury, its height of 12 metres is still impressive.

The exact purpose of the mound is mysterious, but it was almost certainly more than a tomb. Neolithic people specifically sited major monuments in special configurations of hills and lowlands. For a newly settled people, the shape of the landscape, the passage of the seasons, the movement of the heavenly bodies and the forces of nature were central to their religion. Their ceremonies in sacred spaces were undoubtedly intended to bring together the energies of the earth and heaven in order to ensure the fecundity of the soil and the continuation of life.

Locmariaquer

We next visited the famed broken menhir of Locmariaquer, now on the shore of a peninsula, but once part of the ritual landscape which has drowned in the waters of the Golfe du Morbihan. The peninsula forms the western arm of the entrance to the gulf. In megalithic times, when the present sea level was about 9 metres lower, the gulf would have appeared as a series of hills cut by two river valleys. The peninsula alone, just 13 kilometres long, had seventy monuments recorded at the beginning of the twentieth century, of which forty now remain; there are no doubt countless many more under the water, waiting to be discovered.

Near Locmariaquer there is a tumulus at Mané Lud, 80 metres long and 50 metres wide, which dates from the middle of the fifth millennium BC. I was excited to discover some remarkable carvings on the stone slabs of the inner tomb, not only of axes and bull's horns but of boats. In fact, they are the oldest known images of boats. With an elevated prow and poop, they recall the long seagoing skin boats such as the curraghs of Western Ireland.[4] Beautifully polished beads of a variscite necklace were found at the site, and are now housed at the Carnac Museum. No less beautiful are the great polished axe and bracelet made from greenish jadeite, now in the Museum of Vannes.[5]

The site at Locmariaquer is rightly world famous for three megalithic monuments dating from 4300 to 3800 BC, built more than a thousand years before Stonehenge. The most famous of all is Le Grand Menhir Brisé, now fallen and broken into four pieces, but once a staggering 20 metres high. I could see that it had been tall and slender, with flattened sides and a polished rounded tip. Weighing about 280 tonnes, it is not only the first great standing stone but also the largest dressed stone in the world. It was originally part of a row of nineteen menhirs running for 55 metres, decreasing in size and oriented towards the north. It would have been an important landmark for ancient mariners travelling up and down the west coast of France.

To have raised the stone was an achievement in itself, but I was astounded to learn that the type of quartzite granite from which it is made (known as orthogneiss) isn't found locally.[6] Unless it was mined from a submerged seam, the nearest known source is 10 kilometres from the site; some authorities, however, say that it was transported 80 kilometres from a quarry in Finistère.[7] If so, given its length and weight, we are left with a transport and engineering problem from the fifth millennium BC far greater than the movement of the 5-tonne bluestones from South Wales to Stonehenge. The likely solution is that the Locmariaquer menhir was brought by sea, slung underneath an enormous raft of wood guided by skin-covered boats. It could then have been moved forward by rocking from side to side, or pulled over wooden rollers by teams of oxen and men.

What was its purpose? Nothing is certain, but with its feet in the soil and its tip pointing to the sky, it could well have represented the axis of the world around which all turns. It may also have been a phallic fertility symbol. Professor Thom and his son, following up the work of the nineteenth-century archaeologist Félix Gaillard, have further claimed that it was the centre of a lunar observatory based on a series of alignments with other monuments scattered in the region used to trace the maximum and minimum risings and settings of the moon.[8]

Although the backsights indicated by the Thoms are dissimilar, ranging from passage graves to single menhirs, they could well have provided viewing stations. By sinking stakes in the ground to plot the settings of the moon on successive nights, the resulting curve could be continued when the moon disappeared over the horizon. Such observations, recorded over a hundred years or more, could be used to forecast eclipses, celestial events which proved so frightening and

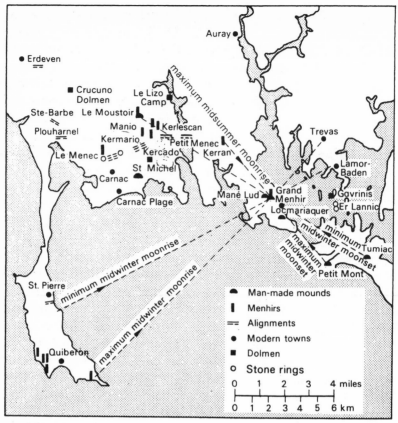

The principal megalithic monuments in the Carnac region, Brittany,
with possible lunar alignments

ominous to ancient peoples. If so, it demonstrates once again the
sophisticated scientific understanding and knowledge of the builders.

Although tradition has it that Le Grand Menhir Brisé was broken
by lightning, it now seems more likely that it was deliberately knocked
down along with other menhirs in the alignment, only a few centuries
after their erection. Their destruction possibly indicates a change in
the religious practice of the local inhabitants or the arrival of a new
people with different beliefs.[9]

Around 4000 BC, one of the stones of the alignment was reused to
build a huge dolmen nearby, La Table des Marchand. Now restored,
this round barrow, about 30 metres in diameter, contains a passage
leading into a four-sided chamber. A remarkable slab forms the
backstone of this chamber: shaped like a shield and looking like an
idol, it is decorated with four levels of axes. The whole structure was
built around it.

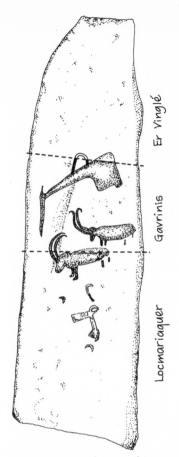

The engraved menhir at Locmariaquer which was re-used in neighbouring monuments when broken into three parts

In 1984 the archaeologist Charles-Tanguy Le Roux made the stunning discovery that the capstone, decorated with a magnificent axe, crook and an animal's head with swept-back horns, was taken from a broken menhir which originally stood near Le Grand Menhir Brisé. Even more intriguing was the discovery that the middle part of the same broken menhir was reused for the roof of a tumulus on the nearby island of Gavrinis, and the top part became part of the vault of the tumulus of Er Grah (also known as Er Vinglé) at the Locmariaquer site.

My young and enthusiastic female guide to the site argued that the dolmen of La Table des Marchand signified the 'cult of the Mother Goddess who gives and takes life,' and that the reason why the entrance to the cairn was so low was to make the person entering bend down low and thereby show respect. The axes and crook were symbols of authority. She also interpreted a dolmen as a tomb for a family and a tumulus as a chief's grave and argued that the society which built them was hierarchical, with chiefs, priests, architects and artisans. And she claimed that the monuments were intended to mark the territory of the people who built them. While this was a widely held view amongst earlier generation of archaeologists, as we have seen, there is in fact no direct evidence to support the hypothesis. Indeed, since none of the sites are defended nor show any signs of weapons of war, it seems unlikely that the megalithic builders were driven by a 'territorial imperative'. A more plausible explanation is that the monuments were intended as religious buildings creating sacred spaces for worship and ritual as well as for burying the dead – not unlike a medieval cathedral.

To the west of La Table and Le Grand Menhir, the Tumulus d'Er Grah stretches some 140 metres. Probably built at the end of the fifth millennium BC, it is now in a sorry state, with two ends partially razed to the ground. The oldest part once contained the bones of two bulls. A green variscite pendant and beads (now in the Carnac Museum) were also discovered.

A couple of kilometres away, on the southern tip of the Locmariaquer peninsula, is an elongated burial chamber on the edge of the sea among the sand dunes. It is known as the Dolmen des Pierres Plates – the flat stones – because the cairn stones have been removed to reveal the great slabs underneath. Constructed around 3000 BC, it is one of the few existing examples of an angled gallery grave; as such, it has an L-shaped structure.

The walls of the monument are beautifully decorated with stylized depictions of the human form, becoming increasingly elaborate as they approach the inner chamber. One of the most intriguing looks like a stylized face with eyes, while another looks like a human ribcage.[10] I was struck by the great fluidity of the lines. None of the carved panels are identical; they offer a rare example of Stone Age sculptors making individual designs. Not far away at Chrac'h near the village of Luffang, there is a similar carved stone with an elongated face and staring eyes (now in the Carnac Museum). They may well represent that supreme Neolithic divinity, the Great Goddess.

Islands in the gulf

After Locmariaquer, we sailed our boat from Trinité-sur-Mer in the Baie de Quiberon to enter the Golfe du Morbihan, Breton for 'Little Sea'. It can be tricky sailing into the gulf: strong currents swirl through the narrow stretch of water at its entrance. We had to make sure that we arrived when the water was slack so that the rising tide could take us through. The gulf itself is virtually an inland lake 10 kilometres square and is scattered with pine-covered islands. Rocks emerge from the swirling waters at low tide, although it was not always like this. About 10,000 years ago, global warming provoked the great melting of the glaciers and ice sheets which resulted in a rise in sea level around 6500 BC. Then, around 3000 BC, it rose again by some 6 metres. The event may have partly inspired the old Breton legend of the drowned island of Ynys. After a few minor changes, the sea level stabilized to its present height about 2000 years ago, during Roman times. There are undoubtedly still many submerged megalithic treasures waiting to be discovered.

So around 4000 BC, when the megaliths were being built, the

Golfe du Morbihan was not under water. An undulating fertile plain with wide, slow-moving rivers, it would have supported a dense population of farmers. When the sea level rose it seems to have broken through the narrow entrance to the gulf and flooded their fields, settlements and monuments.

After negotiating the rocks and islets at its entrance, we sailed across the gulf in glorious sunshine and with a stiff breeze to Île-aux-Moines, the Island of Monks. We anchored off the northeastern tip of this largeish island and went ashore to find the site at Kergonan. It proved difficult since it was overgrown with rough vegetation and hidden by houses and pine trees. Yet this vast U-shaped cromlech, known locally as Er Anké (the 'Goddess of Death'), has been called 'the finest cromlech in Brittany'.[11] At 70 metres deep and 95 metres wide, it is open to the southeast, the direction of the midwinter sunrise. The tallest stones also stand in line with the midsummer sunset to the northwest. Although I searched, I was unable to find an axe and an anthropomorphic rectangle reported to be carved on two of the stones. Nor did I see, thankfully, Er Anké, who is said to appear as a skeleton in a white shroud driving a cart with groaning wheels.

The most intriguing site in the Golfe du Morbihan is on the privately owned islet of Er Lannic near its entrance. It is protected by fierce currents which can run up to 9 knots around it.[12] Late one afternoon, as the tide was going out, we rowed in a dinghy from our anchorage off the nearby Île de la Jument to investigate the megaliths which rise out of the sea and march up the shore like so many petrified mermen. Three-quarters of this megalithic complex is now underwater. Dating from around 3500 BC, the stones originally would have formed two intersecting 'horseshoes' of standing stones on a fairly steep slope. Now the stones of one horseshoe step down into the sea, while those of the other are completely submerged except at spring tides.

The visible horseshoe, measuring about 72 by 54 metres, is in the shape of a flattened circle.[13] It is oriented towards the southeast – the rising sun on the winter solstice. It could also be positioned to track the cycle of the moon, for the long SE-NW axis puts it in line with the major northern moonset. At the centre of the horseshoe an observer would have been able to see the major northern moonrise, roughly at right angles to the main axis over an eastern outlying stone. A preoccupation with the moon would be natural for a seafaring people dependent on the tides, especially as they associated it with the Great Goddess.

I could only see the weed-strewn stones marching up the beach but divers have discovered a submerged horseshoe 61 metres long and open to the east. I was even unable to see seven or eight of the stones which are visible at spring tides. Two huge outliers, now fallen, apparently mark out its east-west axis which would have been in line with the sunrises and sunsets on the equinoxes. One fallen stone has cup marks which are said to form a rough pattern of the stars in the constellation of Ursa Major (the Great Bear). If so, they could have been used to indicate north until about 3000 BC.

Due south of the horseshoe was a huge pillar which the local fishermen called Men-ar-Gou or the Blacksmith's Stone. The largest menhir – now broken and visible at low tide – stood 8.2 metres tall. Some of the stones, like those at Locmariaquer, are made from orthogneiss of unknown origin, again suggesting that the megalithic builders did not hesitate to bring stones by boat over long distances.

Zacharie Le Rouzic thoroughly investigated the site in the 1920s and discovered traces of huts and stone cists. The latter contained human bones and decorated cylindrical vases with bowls, which may have been used as perfume burners, as well as some pottery with two beautifully decorated vase-supports.[14] The finds all imply ritual activities took place on the island. Hearths containing charcoal dated to around 2500 BC have been found near the visible horseshoe. I was intrigued to discover that some fragments of clay now in the Carnac Museum retain the fingerprints of the potter, a uniquely personal sign from our distant ancestors. Thousands of flint fragments and some polished axes suggest that it may have been the site of an axe workshop with long-distance trading links. A few standing stones have carvings of axes.

The island of the abyss

We saved the greatest delight in the Golfe du Morbihan for the end. A little to the north of Er Lannic lies the island of Gavrinis, justly famed as one of the most outstanding examples of the earliest architecture in the West, and one of the oldest and most beautiful monuments in the world. When the passage grave covered by a rocky cairn was built on Gavrinis around 3100 BC, it would have been a hill in a coastal plain dominating a narrow river estuary. Today, it is sometimes called the Île de la Chèvre or Goat Island, but its name probably comes from a Celtic root found in the modern French word *gouffre*, meaning 'island of the torrent' or 'island of the abyss'. It was no doubt so named because of the swift and treacherous currents which swirl around it.[15]

Passage graves of this type were fairly common in Brittany between 4500 and 3000 BC, and further along the Atlantic seaboard in Ireland, England, Spain and Portugal. The restored masterpiece of Gavrinis, however, is the longest passage grave in Brittany, running for nearly 16 metres. It has a roughly square inner chamber measuring approximately 2.5 metres on each side. Now covered over with a cairn, it is outstanding for its size: more than 50 metres in diameter and almost 8 metres high. The mass of stones of the cairn are held together by facing stones on each side of the inner dolmen, creating a monument with regular tiers. It may originally have appeared like a pyramid with rounded edges, with sides about 30 metres long.

The entrance is oriented towards the southeast, roughly in the direction of the rising sun on the winter solstice. It was blocked off with stones around 3000 BC, according to some carbon-dated ash from a burnt timber structure, which implies that its was used for only a few centuries. A layer of sand was added on top, thereby turning the cairn into a formless mound and hiding the dolmen with its exquisite carvings within. They were intended for the eyes of the deities and the deceased.

In the interior, I made out on the 17-tonne capstone sections of a plough and horned bull which matched with the stone in La Table des Marchand and in the Er Grah vault. It had originally been taken from the broken menhir at Locmariaquer, 4 kilometres to the west as the seagull flies – a considerable feat even for the megalith builders. A few other stones were clearly recycled from earlier buildings since their carvings are now placed below floor level. All the stones are made from local granite, except for two on the top of the passage which are quartz, a type of stone highly revered at the time. As no quartz seams are known in the region, they must have been transported from afar by boat.

Megalithic art

The gently rising passage at Gavrinis is a masterpiece of megalithic art. Indeed, it is the most sumptuously decorated passage grave in existence, comparable only to the one at Newgrange in Ireland. The great stone slabs of its walls, carefully chosen to fit together, are covered with marvellous carvings. Of the twenty-nine stones, twenty-three are decorated with spirals, intersecting circles, chevrons, triangles, snakes and other whorled designs. It is abstract megalithic art at its most supreme, executed with extraordinary facility and expression, sometimes very controlled, sometimes very fluid, but always inter-woven and interrelated. Perhaps created in a trance, they superficially recall the psychedelic art of the 1960s, although much more profound and accomplished.

Dating from the fifth to the fourth millennium, the main motifs (probably created by picking at the slabs with tiny quartz pebbles) represent agricultural tools and hunting weapons such as ploughs, axes, crooks and bows and arrows. There are also abstract patterns such as zigzags, herringbones, crosses, chevrons, and inverted U-shapes.[16] The carved forms are pure and stylized, celebrating life, energy and beauty. Clearly, they were important symbols for farming people who had only recently cut down the forests and begun to plough up the earth's surface.

As I mentioned in a previous chapter, megalithic art is quite different from that found in Palaeolithic caves such as Lascaux in France. Most of the earlier cave art is figurative, whereas megalithic art is, on the whole, abstract. Since the granite used is very hard rock and difficult to carve, the artists may have reduced the carvings to their bare essentials, and then painted them. It is more likely, however, that they simply preferred to work in a symbolic way. The fine carving on the capstone at Gavrinis of an animal with swept-back horns shows that the artists were quite capable of depicting more natural representations if they so desired.

Although most archaeologists say that the geometrical motifs of megalithic art cannot be interpreted, most feel free to speculate about its function. Ralph Bradley, drawing on a Darwinist notion of territoriality, has argued that it was a method of 'signing the land' and ensuring cooperation between different groups who were 'exploiting' the same resources and who would not meet very often.[17]

Taking a more sociological approach, the archaeologist Elizabeth Shee Twohig sees the symbols as creating a bond between the members of a group by reinforcing the status of the 'leaders' and by providing a focal point for the group. But as we have seen, there is simply no evidence that leaders existed at the time, yet alone used art to legitimatize their rule. Equally, it is pure speculation to claim that the symbolism of megalithic tomb art acted as a bond between the 'initiated' and was intended to isolate the 'uninitiated'.[18]

Despairing of ever being able to understand, the expert in prehistoric art Paul Bahn dismisses 'the fruitless search of meaning', and compares the symbols of prehistoric art to musical symbols, which are just dots on paper until played by someone who can read them.[19]

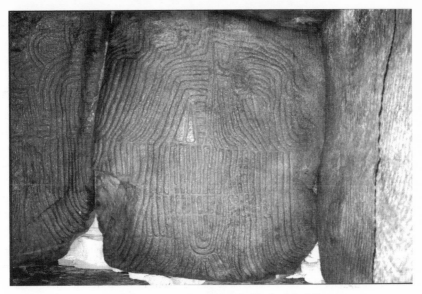

Megalithic art at Gavrinis, Golfe du Morbihan

Even if many archeologists are content to record and not interpret megalithic art, it doesn't mean that the attempt to decipher it is not worth undertaking. Clearly their art was deeply significant for the artists and their audience. In my view, the megalithic art at Gavrinis formed part of a magical and religious symbolism used to protect and help the deceased in the afterlife, like the hieroglyphs carved and painted in Egyptian tombs. As such, it is part of a universal symbolic language.

Since the code of megalithic art has not yet been fully deciphered, varied interpretations have inevitably been put forward. Yet they are not necessarily mutually exclusive. The great value of symbolic and abstract art is that by its very nature it is ambiguous and multilayered.

Many of the symbols were obviously inspired by natural pheno-mena, such as crescents by the moon, or zigzags by lightning, or concentric circles by the ripples of a pool after a stone has been thrown into it. But as universal symbols of the collective unconscious, they probably appeared in the trance visions of the artist-shamans who no doubt made use of hallucogens. The engravings may well depict inner optical effects (called entoptics) created within the visual cortex of the brain during such drug-induced trances.[20]

The axe is undoubtedly the most universal symbol of the Stone Age, since it was essential for the new farmers to cut down the forests and break up the land. At the same time it is not necessarily an emblem of authority. Polished axes, too small or too big for everyday use, were clearly symbolic. They were not only used as grave offerings but as a means of exchange and as gifts between the scattered communities. Unlike the Bronze Age dagger, the stone axe is a symbol of peace, not war.

Other symbols at Gavrinis are more ambiguous. A bull, a boat or the moon may be represented by the U shape. Again, a bull is not necessarily just a male symbol, for it can represent the life force in general. A boat, as in Egyptian symbolism, can be a vehicle for the deceased in the afterlife, as well as a means of transport. And since the crescent shape of the moon is closely associated with the Great Goddess, it is a symbol of life, death and regeneration.[21]

Today, the crook, originally used to control animals, has become a symbol of religious and political power, but its presence on the carved walls of Gavrinis can hardly be considered evidence for a stratified society with an elite of priests and chiefs. For the megalithic artists it could represent a sickle or even a boomerang. Indeed, it would seem primarily to be an energy symbol related to the horn and spiral.

In Christianity, the cross has become a symbol of suffering whereas in the ancient world it was a widespread symbol of continuous life. In Egyptian hieroglyphs, for instance, it stands for 'living' and forms part of such words as 'health' and 'happiness'.[22]

The snake that appears on the walls of Gavrinis was one of the dominant motifs of ancient European art. While snakes are sometimes used to represent water or even long hair, they are also associated with the phallus and, by extension, with male fertility. At the same time, they are widespread symbols of life after death since snakes seem to have the power of rejuvenation by sloughing off their old skin and reappearing with a new one. As such, the snake is a universal symbol of transformation.

Many of the symbols at Gavrinis would appear to be associated with the cult of the Great Goddess. At the entrance, there is a fine slab which suggests a female form. Some other slabs have carvings apparently depicting women with their hair standing on end like ferns. These are accompanied by snakes and cattle horns, usually taken as symbols of male fertility. According to Gimbutas, however, women are depicted much more often than men in Neolithic art, and when present they tend to dominate the symbols of male power: bows, axes, crooks, bulls and snakes.[23]

The astronomical alignments of the Gavrinis monument would seem to support this interpretation. As you look out of the inner chamber, a stone on the right-hand side of the chamber entrance lines up with the first stone on the left-hand side of the main entrance and indicates the midwinter sunrise on the horizon. The principal axis of the passage however is oriented towards the southernmost moonrise on its major standstill. What is even more extraordinary is that these solar and lunar lines cross in the middle of the passage opposite one of the few uncarved stones. Being made of rock crystal, it may have glowed at the significant moments in cycles of the sun and the moon; a truly magical effect!

My young female guide to Gavrinis observed: 'Since the passage grave was finally covered up, some claim that to enter it is a violation of the *Déesse Mère*. By visiting it too often, we only create negative energy inside.' I could see her point, but I could not help feeling that the anonymous carvers of this megalithic art would also have appreciated their work being celebrated throughout the world thousands of years later. And the builders no doubt would have been impressed by our rediscovery of their careful astronomical orientations.

The central mysteries of Gravinis remain. Why was it built only to be sealed up a few centuries later? What purpose did the carvings serve? Why was it made partly from recycled stones taken from earlier monuments in the area?

Gavrinis was clearly part of a wider family of passage graves along the Western Atlantic seaboard which have been traditionally considered to be collective burial sites. It is the only Breton one with carvings of spirals. Since these are a common motif among the Irish passage graves in the Boyne Valley, their presence at Gavrinis suggests that the two communities may well have been in contact with each other. Indeed, both Newgrange and Gavrinis face the midwinter sunrise and there are similar carvings of chevrons at the entrances of the chambers.[24]

Like Newgrange, Gavrinis was undoubtedly more than a burial site. No human bones have been found inside. Its huge cairn on a hill above the original estuary would have been seen from afar. Although there is no firm evidence to support the view that it served as a territorial marker, it may well have been a symbol of religious identity for the people who built it and lived in the area.

Its primary purpose was almost certainly to provide a site for sacred rituals. The fact that the carvings are more sumptuous closer to the inner chamber implies that it was used for initiation rites for the living as well as for the dead, and perhaps to ease communication between the two states. From the inner fastness of the crypt, the gentle slope of the passage moreover enables one to see both sea and sky, bringing together heaven and earth in an eternal embrace. Whatever its exact purpose, there can be no doubt that Gavrinis represents the apotheosis of the earliest megalithic art in Europe.

CHAPTER ELEVEN

The Large Stones

If I were to be asked, after so many opinions, what is mine, I would give one, irrefutable, undeniable, irresistible . . . It is as follows: the stones of Carnac are large stones!

GUSTAVE FLAUBERT

Having visited the principal chambers in the Carnac region, I next turned my attention – and my bicycle – to the justly famous alignments. They are the most intriguing monumental series in the world and attract more than a million visitors a year. There is nothing quite like their scale and number. Raised between 4000 and 3800 BC, there are some 3000 stones forming part of three great menhir systems – Kerlescan, Kermario and Le Ménec. But while these are the most spectacular, there are four other interrelated smaller alignments which, taken as a whole, show the grandeur of the vision and the brilliance of the execution of the original architects and builders.

What is the meaning of the alignments? The question has puzzled people for millennia, and has still not been fully answered. As bizarre anomalies of nature, they have, unsurprisingly, been associated with the invisible, the sacred and the uncanny. Confronted with their silent and imperturbable mystery, many legends have grown up about them among the local people. One of the most persistent concerns St Cornelius, who became Pope in the third century. Pursued by Roman soldiers to the seashore, and finding no boat to escape in, St Cornelius is said to have turned round and turned his pursuers to stone. Given the military precision of the alignments, the association with soldiers is understandable.

The church at Carnac is dedicated to St Cornelius, and several other churches in the region have images of the saint accompanied by oxen. An engaging variation of the legend is that he hid from the Roman soldiers in an ox's ear and after turning them to stone established a cult of the ox in gratitude. Could there be an echo here of an ancient bull cult from megalithic times? The bull was certainly a masculine symbol of fertility and played an essential role alongside the Mother Goddess in the Neolithic religions of Europe and the Mediterranean region.[1]

As with legends in Scotland, Ireland, Wales and Cornwall, the stones are thought by local people at Carnac to be petrified humans. Some, it is said, actually come alive on Christmas Eve and go down to the sea to drink. Goblins (*kerions* or *korrigans* in Breton) are also said to haunt the megaliths and dolmens; they are so strong they can move the stones, especially on the Sabbath when their magical powers are at their height. The legends continue to proliferate.

It was not until the eighteenth century that the stones were taken seriously by scholars in France, but extravagant claims continued to abound. A widespread view was that they were the remains of Caesar's camp when he came to conquer the Veneti during the Gallic Wars. The Comte Anne-Claude-Philippe de Tubieras de Caylus, one of the founders of French archaeology, argued that their different shapes formed the signs of a lost code waiting to be deciphered like the Egyptian hieroglyphs.[2] A musical interpretation held that the form of each stone corresponded to a note, allowing the alignments to act as a vehicle for processions of worshippers singing hymns.

During the Romantic Celtic Revival of the nineteenth century, they were hailed as Celtic temples presided over by Druids. The methods of carbon-dating organic material and of testing the thermoluminescence of potsherds in the late twentieth century, however, demonstrated that they were built thousands of years before the arrival of the Celts in France around 500 BC.

In recent times, local school children have come up with their own imaginative ideas about the meaning of the countless stones all around them. One suggests that the stones represent giants' teeth which fell out when they became old. Another surmises that when a man was lost at sea and his body could not be recovered, a standing stone was raised in his memory. Clearly the mystery of the stones continues to beguile the human imagination, generation after generation. One modern myth claims the alignments were intended to act as runways for flying saucers or extraterrestrials in search of uranium!

The raising of the stones

The stones used at Carnac once formed part of a huge geological fold known as the Cornish anticlinal zone, which affected Brittany and Southwest England. The bedrock naturally forms slabs. While natural menhirs created by erosion were used, most of the stone was extracted from the bedrock with the help of quartz hammerstones, wooden wedges and levers. After making a hole in the stone and knocking in a wedge, water would be added so that when the wood expanded it split the rock. Some of the stones, weighing up to 125 tonnes, were then dragged over 4 kilometres from their original positions.

It would have been a major undertaking. An experiment in 1979 demonstrated that a 32-tonne block could be dragged 100 metres a day by 200 people using wooden rollers and ropes. Remains of rope have been found, made from hemp and the bark of lime trees, linen and ivy.

The fine-grained granite stones were then wedged in shallow dug-out hollows and filled with small packing stones, with about a tenth of their height underground. Clearly a foundation ceremony took place, for charcoal, potsherds, flint flakes and tools, polished stone axes, querns, grinders, polishers and spindle-whorls have all been found as ritual deposits at the base of the stones.

Since Neolithic times, the megaliths have been eroded continuously by wind and rain, forming intricate networks of hollows and grooves on their surfaces. In this rain-drenched land, they are also covered by beautiful arrays of lichens and mosses in subtle hues of grey, yellow, green and brown. They now form weird and wonderful figures, often with a small foot and big head or a large belly and arched back. No wonder they have been associated with giants over the centuries.

Le Petit Ménec and Kerlescan

There are so many alignments around Carnac that it can, at first sight, all seem very bewildering, especially as many of the stones are hidden in recently grown woods. The alignments gradually settle, however, into a discernible pattern in the undulating landscape and reveal definite relationships to each other.

I began my exploration by cycling to Le Petit Ménec, the smallest of the Carnac alignments, situated to the northeast of the Tumulus St-Michel and not far from the port of Trinité-sur-Mer where I had left my boat. Although it was difficult to make out all the stones, as many

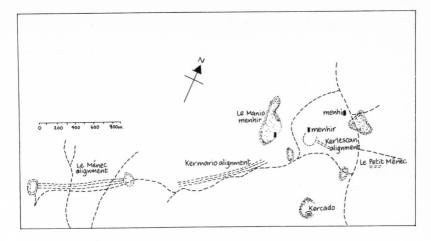

The principal stone alignments at Carnac

are hidden in an oak and chestnut wood, I could see that their general orientation was from southwest to northeast.

To the west in more open ground is the Kerlescan alignment, the best preserved of the Carnac rows, with 579 menhirs still standing. Their configuration is comparatively easy to read: thirteen rows of stones are arranged in a fan shape over a length of 350 metres, converging in the east. As a whole, the alignment is set on an east-west axis.

The avenues open out, on the west, to a large barrel-shaped enclosure, 80 by 90 metres, demarcated on three sides by granite pillars stones standing 2 to 2.5 metres high. It appears like an open court or a sacred place for gatherings. The remains of a wooden table have been found here, which could have acted as an altar.

In a wood immediately to the north of the Kerlescan rows are the ruins of an enormous megalithic horseshoe, known as Kerlescan North. Open to the ESE, it is now almost entirely lost among the trees and thick undergrowth.

When asked what the Kerlescan stones mean, my guide replied that they were principally territorial markers, as if to say: 'We are the owners! Look how powerful we are!' But once again, such an interpretation would seem to be imposing our own attitudes about property and political power on to our remote ancestors. Such narrow motives could hardly have inspired the kind of spiritual energy and vision embodied in the Carnac megaliths.

Kermario, Le Manio and Le Ménec

Southwest of Kerlescan lies the Kermario system of alignments bordered by a road on one side and pine trees on the other. The longest and most impressive of all the Carnac rows, it extends for more than 1100 metres and contains 982 standing menhirs. Generally oriented northeast to southwest, it consists of ten roughly parallel rows of stones set about 100 metres apart which run down into a hollow from the east. A house stands incongruously in the middle. The ground then rises to a high point in the west where the stones are the tallest and where there was once an enclosure.

For the walker striding west towards the setting sun, this distorts the usual perspective and gives the impression that the stones in the distance are the same size as the ones nearby. They rise like spreading fans. The enclosure at the end also appears closer than it really is. The effect was clearly intentional. I once again marvelled at the ingenuity and care taken by the megalith builders, similar to that of the Greek architects who played with the effects of perspective in designing their temples and columns.

I felt a strong presence among the tall stones at the western end of the alignment, some almost three times my height. I was not surprised to learn later that dowsers have felt a high charge from the earth energies among them. As I sat on the rough grass, leaning against one of the stones, it was very pleasant to feel their solidity after so many weeks bobbing around at sea. Perhaps that was why I was drawn to the megaliths: they seem so immobile and permanent in a world of constant change.

In a tranquil clearing in the pine and chestnut woods in the northeastern section of the Kermario alignment there is Le Manio enclosure (100 by 30 metres) with a small semicircle of stones in its middle. It is easily identified by Le Géant du Manio, a menhir 3.5 metres tall which dominates the landscape. When I visited the site, entertained by the erratic flight of butterflies in the dappled shade, I noticed that someone had managed to place pebbles and pine cones on the top of the giant.

Thom suggested that it was originally the backsight and foresight of a vast astronomical observatory in the area, marking the settings of the sun and the moon. The base of the giant stone is carved with the images of five snakes, three with their heads inverted and one upright. They no doubt represent the serpentine energies of Mother Earth into which the megaliths were plunged and were perhaps intended to channel. Five polished axes were also found as offerings at its base.

Further west lies the Le Ménec alignments. Although not the longest at over 950 metres, it has, with 1169 menhirs, the greatest number of stones still standing. Towards the western end, the aligned stones are taller, some more than 3.6 metres high. Like Kermario, the eleven rows of standing stones are oriented in a southwestern to northeastern direction, with possible sightlines to the midwinter sunset and midsummer sunrise.

At both ends of the alignment, egg-shaped enclosures have been found, the eastern one with its narrow end pointing northwest and the western one with its narrow end pointing southeast. The western enclosure, shaped like an inverted egg, is made of up of joined slabs of stone and measures 90 by 70 metres, easily accommodating a thousand people in its heyday. The overall shape is still just visible despite the thoughtless encroachment of houses from the neighbouring hamlet, which has standing stones scattered about its alleys and gardens. Seen from the high point at the west end, the unrolling rows of stones are spectacular. I noticed two special lines of stones marking out a distinctive alley which could have provided a processional way to the sacred space of the western enclosure. The same occurs at Kerlescan.[3]

The Sacred Way

Although the alignments I have just described are the stars in the Carnac firmament, there are seven series of stone rows in the region. Not too fine an interpretation can be put on their exact positions as 60 per cent of the stones have been resurrected since the 1920s. Nevertheless, they all have certain features in common. The rows of stones are generally parallel. An enclosure on higher ground is sometimes found at their eastern end, but more usually in the west. The menhirs increase in size, as they are set closer to the enclosure, thereby playing with perspective and creating an optical illusion. They are aligned towards the sun on key moments of the year: Kerlescan to the equinoxes, the others to the solstices. It would seem that the alignments are oriented so that the rays of the rising sun follow the avenues to the western enclosures and during the evening bathe them with their dying rays. The west, where the sun sets, has always been associated with the end of life.

In my view, the alignments round Carnac provide a ceremonial and sacred way leading to an open-air temple used for rituals and ceremonies. This confirms the idea that the principal purpose of the alignments was religious. It would be natural for the first farmers to pray to the divine forces in nature and to the sun and the moon to ensure the fertility of the soil and a good harvest. A sacred space to contact the divine, usually on high ground and clearly separated from the surrounding wilderness, and a sacred way providing privileged access for initiates to reach the sacred space, are the two fundamental elements of all religious architecture. The enclosures no doubt provided a form of security and were a symbol of permanence and stability. There was no need to defend them, for no weapons suitable for making war have been found in the region during the Stone Age.

But there are differences with modern Christianity. Churches and cathedrals are directed towards the rising sun in the east, stressing the resurrection of Christ. The stones of the Carnac alignments, on the other hand, point to sacred enclosures situated towards the setting of the sun in the west, suggesting that their worshippers were more concerned with the process of death as a transition to the afterlife. They would therefore be ideal places to conduct ceremonies and rituals to launch the souls of the deceased into the Great Unknown.

Mathematicians and astronomers

The alignments at Carnac are not only embedded into the earth; they also offer ways of reading the sky. The British astronomer Sir Norman Lockyer made a study of the alignments between 1906 and 1909, and concluded that they were oriented mainly towards the sun and to a lesser extent the moon. His and Félix Gaillard's research was then taken up and developed by Alexander Thom and his son, in the 1970s. They argued convincingly that the stones were laid out like the monuments in Orkney and Wessex, according to the standard unit of measurement which they called the 'megalithic yard' (see page 15) and which corresponded roughly to a human pace. They further identified another unit more specific to Carnac which they called the *toise*, the French word for 6 feet or 2.07 metres.[4] It is the same as the English fathom, used until recently for measuring depths on British charts.

In each of the lines at Le Ménec and Kermario, the gap between each stone in every row is equal to the megalithic *toise*. Thom also believed that a simple multiple of it was also used to define the diameter of the circles of standing stones. My own measurements, made by striding between the stones, confirmed his hypothesis. Clearly the megalith builders were masters of geometry and mathematics. Their achievement is all the more impressive when one considers the

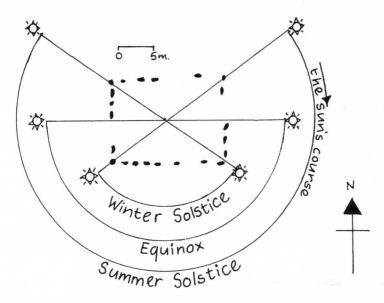

The megalithic rectangle at Crucuno, near Carnac, showing the alignments with the annual movement of the sun

variations between measurements in Europe until the recent adoption of the metric system. It also confirms my thesis of a pan-European Neolithic civilization.

The builders of Carnac, like their counterparts in Scotland and southern England, were astronomers as well as mathematicians. As we have seen, the Kerlescan alignments based on an east-west axis could have been used to indicate the equinoxes, while the southwest-northeast alignments of Le Ménec, Kermario and Le Petit Ménec point to the sun rising on the winter solstice and setting on the summer solstice. Taken together, the alignments could have marked a seasonal calendar of agricultural activities. And if Thom is right about Le Grand Menhir Brisé at Locmariaquer being the centre of lunar observatory, they would have been able to predict eclipses as well.

The most remarkable example of the astronomical function of the megaliths is found at Crucuno near Plouharnel, northwest of Le Ménec. The corners and sides of the quadrilateral enclosure are oriented so perfectly to the solstices and equinoxes in the solar year that it cannot be a mere coincidence. Measuring 33.3 by 24.9 metres, its sides form an exact ratio of 3:4. Although it was long suspected that a restoration in 1882 had tightened its amazing precision, the discovery of a survey made fifteen years earlier demonstrated that it was closely following the original plan.[5] It has an obvious affinity with the four stations of Stonehenge and undoubtedly served a similar astronomical function.And it would not surprise me if the astronomers at Carnac were in touch with those in Stonehenge, Avebury, Newgrange, Callanish and Orkney.

The Celtic twilight

The Neolithic period came to an end in Brittany, as elsewhere, around 2000 BC with the arrival of the Beaker people who brought with them the use of the first metals, copper and gold. While lead, silver and gold is found in Brittany, copper and tin had to be imported to be made into bronze. During the Bronze Age, tin was brought over from Cornwall, and a large number of worked objects were exported to Wessex.

The strong trading links forged in the Neolithic era right down the western Atlantic seaboard and deep into the Mediterranean continued. A delightful ring bead from the Bronze Age, found at the Parc Guren dolmen and held in the Carnac Museum, is an imitation of ones found in Tell el-Amarna in Egypt during the reign of Pharaoh Amenhotep IV, also known as Akhenaten. It shows that there were connections between Egypt and Brittany at the time, and confirms my general thesis that the ancient mariners travelled much wider afield than was previously supposed.

It was during the latter half of the Iron Age, round 500 BC, that the nomadic Celts swept down on their horses from the Middle Danube region and settled in Brittany. Although they traded with the Romans, the Celtic Gauls fought for their independence from Roman colonization under the leadership of the Veneti, the tribe from the Morbihan area, then known as Venetia. Once their heavy wooden ships were defeated in a naval battle in 56 BC recorded by Julius Caesar, the long prehistory in the Brittany region came to an end.

Garden of sculptures

Today the vast array of stones, too numerous to be counted, set among the moorland and woods of Carnac create a huge garden of sculptures marking the daily voyage of the sun and the key moments in the solar year and the lunar cycle. The mounds, graves and align-ments were clearly arranged to be seen as an interrelated whole in a ritual landscape oriented towards the heavens. When I saw them for the last time, I had no doubt in my mind that the ceremonies conducted among them were intended to bring about harmony between heaven and earth and to ease the transition between life and death.

One of my young guides exclaimed in despair: 'At Carnac, we have lost the keys!' Exactly why the stones were built still remains a mystery, but we are beginning to decipher their meaning. As I wandered through the great avenues of stone stretching to the horizon, it occurred to me that just as the purpose of a garden is the act of creating the garden, so the meaning for the people who raised the stones was not just the final arrangement but the creative process itself. As in most spiritual practices, the means was as important as the ends; indeed, the means were ends-in-the-making.

I left the Golfe du Morbihan and the Baie de Quiberon deeply impressed by the first known stone architecture on earth. To have the imagination to design the alignments on such a vast scale and to have the skills to realize the vision was truly amazing. The fact they were built long before Stonehenge and Callanish suggests that the skills may have been first developed in Brittany and then taken over by boat to the British Isles and along the Atlantic seaboard.

CHAPTER TWELVE

The Bay of Biscay

A free man will always seek out the sea.

CHARLES BAUDELAIRE

Before I left the Carnac region for good I sailed back to Trinité-sur-Mer, where I met one of the great sailors of the world. He stands in a long tradition which stretched back to megalithic times when Stone Age argonauts sailed the seas.

His name was Thierry Dubois. He was a short, fit, handsome man in his mid-thirties, with a shock of black hair and steady blue eyes. I first noticed him when I saw his enormous 18-metre long blue and white yacht with its 26-metre high mast and tiny cockpit on the other side of the harbour wall. He had sailed around the world in the famous solo Vendée Globe 2002 race which saw Ellen MacArthur come second and earn the title of the fastest woman to circumnavigate the globe.

As a young man, he had worked on the fishing boats in Trinité. He soon realized that his real passion was for sailing, and by winning races he was gradually able to get bigger yachts without sponsorship. I was attracted to him not only because he was, like the ancient mariners, a nomad of the sea but because of his maritime philosophy.

'The sea teaches you,' he told me, 'one simple rule: to help your fellow man. That's what I call "*la solidarité maritime*". I would like to transpose that simple rule to the land. Perhaps I'm a dreamer but one must dream.'

I asked him what he thought of the importance of the sea: 'The sea makes up seventy per cent of the world's surface. From space, the world looks blue. It's not *planète terre* but *planète mer*.'

And did he think the sea was cruel? 'The sea isn't cruel but it's a special element; it must be respected. Man is not made for the sea. In order to survive, we must understand it and adapt to it. You can't cheat with the sea.'

The sea was also a symbol of freedom for him: 'On the sea, there is freedom of circulation. The sea is without frontiers. It cannot be controlled.'

I felt sure the ancient mariners would have felt the same: the sea was free and for all and linked the different peoples of the world along its shores. As I listened to Thierry Dubois, I felt I could hear the authentic voice of his seafaring ancestors.

He quoted a *bon mot* which I had already heard attributed to Plato: 'There are three types of men: the living, the dead and those who go to sea.' It was indeed a special calling.

On the bow of his yacht, *Solidaire*, he had painted the first article of the French Declaration of the Rights of Man: 'We are all born free and equal'. Wherever he went around the world he tried to promote the liberty and equality of all peoples. 'It is the one idea in my heart,' he said. It was a view which would have been shared by the first megalith builders whose society shows no signs of hierarchy or domination. And the ancient mariners would have agreed with his view: 'May the wind blow in a good direction for all!'

In a way, Thierry Dubois is a foil to the cynicism of those archaeologists who project their own hierarchical views into the past and argue that the megaliths were raised to show the power and authority of the chiefs and the control of their territory. I had as yet seen no convincing evidence to suggest that the late Stone Age from around the sixth to the third millennium along the Atlantic seaboard was anything other than a peaceful civilization based on an equal and cooperative society.

Temple-dolmens

From Trinité-sur-Mer, I carefully planned to sail to Belle Île, a large island off the Baie de Quiberon. I thought it would make a perfect stopping-off point before attempting to cross the Bay of Biscay to La Coruña in northwest Spain. Moreover, it was wise not to go too far south before crossing the Bay, since it is dangerous to be caught in a strong onshore wind on a lee shore. In the elbow between France and Spain, there is little shelter and vast stretches of surf-pounded beaches. It would also have involved, as the ancient mariners knew, a long detour along the north coast of Spain if one wanted to continue down towards the Mediterranean.

Although I was leaving the megaliths on mainland France, they did not, of course, stop at Carnac. It's just that there was nothing like Carnac's concentration and richness of megaliths elsewhere. Nevertheless, there are some massive dolmens around Saumur on the river Loire, which might best be called 'temple-dolmens' since they were apparently never covered with earth.[1] The largest capstoned dolmen ever built is to be found in the garden of the Café du Dolmen in a back street of Bagneux, a suburb of Saumur. The chamber is almost rectangular, more than 18 metres long, 6 wide and 3 high; its largest capstone, one of four, is said to weigh 86 tonnes. These dolmens were probably erected around 3000 BC. The dates of the dolmens, as I would have expected, tend to be earlier along the coast of France (4000 to 2700 BC) and later inland (2700 to 2200 BC).[2]

Some sailors, fearful of crossing the Bay of Biscay and sailing down the exposed coasts of Portugal, take a shortcut to the Mediterranean via the Gironde and the Garonne river, which today connects to a canal which comes out at Sète in southwest France. Early traders from the Mediterranean region also went cross-country here and picked up boats in Bordeaux to continue their journey further north. The Greek astronomer and geographer Pytheas of Massilia (modern-day Marseilles) came this way around 325 BC before sailing to Cornwall and beyond. And when the Phoenicians blocked the entrance to the Mediterranean at the Pillars of Hercules, the overland route was the only safe one.

Along these ancient overland routes in the neck of France, between the Bay of Biscay and the Mediterranean, many chambered mounds and long barrows containing stone chambers of local Jurassic limestone were built in megalithic times. The dolmens, surrounded by circles of stone slabs, often stand out sharply on carefully chosen hills. Although these megaliths in France were the farthest from the sea and among the highest above sea level, their similarity with those of southern Britain and Brittany shows that they still shared a common culture.

Crossing the Bay

We left for Belle Île just after dawn on a day in early August. It was plain sailing close-hauled on a stiff northwesterly wind and it did not take as long to reach Le Palais, the principal harbour on the island. It was strategically important, and strongly defended by a great citadel.

In Neolithic times, however, the inhabitants lived in peace. All that remains of their civilization are two menhirs known as Jean and Jeanne near Anvorte in the middle of the island, and three ragged lines of small stones. Nineteen of the stones were used to build the island's lighthouse, but the two menhirs remain the stars of a local legend. A nineteenth-century story claims that Jean, a pillar of red schist 4 metres high, and Jeanne, a granite block and squatter in stature, were a couple petrified by a witch. Yet they were still able to make love on a full moon, when they came alive, and their offspring became the stones of Carnac. Another tale has it that they were petrified because Jean was a bard and disapproved of by the Druids for loving a woman, but they were released by a fairy.[3]

Once again the weather left us stranded. We holed up in the inner harbour of Le Palais on Belle Île for more than a week waiting for it to improve. In the Bay of Biscay, the prevailing winds in August are from the northeast, ideal for sailing down to northwest Spain. A high usually settles over the Azores, with a heat low over central Spain. The normal weather is warm, settled and sunny, just as it was in Neolithic times. So despite its evil reputation, the Bay in summer should not be too much of a challenge for an experienced crew and well-equipped boat.

Unfortunately, the weather during the summer we sailed down the west coast of France was extremely unsettled. Low after low brought southwesterlies in across 3000 miles of the Atlantic. As I went down to the harbour master every morning to check the weather, I began to wonder whether I would ever be able to cross the Bay. The intended voyage from Belle Île to La Coruña at the northwest tip of Spain was about 400 nautical miles. I sailed at 3 or 4 knots, the same average as the ancient mariners in their curraghs, and I would need at least four days of reasonable weather to make the crossing.

To stem my rising frustration, I wrote in my notebook: 'Take it easy. Be bold but careful. Be thorough but prudent. Be true and sincere. It doesn't matter if you don't make it to the Med. Don't push the world too hard. Take it easy.'

While waiting on the weather in Le Plaisant, I met another extraordinary navigator. He lived on board a metal boat that looked like a pointed beer barrel – Olivier Pitroset, the first Frenchman to sail across the Arctic Ocean. He was a quiet man with bare feet and thick spectacles. He had sailed from Vancouver to Brest via the

Northwest Passage, a voyage of some 1200 nautical miles, and had
written up his experience in a book called *La Voie de Glaces* (*The Way
of Ice*). He loved the frozen Arctic, had married an Inuit and was
heading north the day I left to go south. Such chance encounters,
spanning the globe, would have been made by the megalithic seafarers,
and would have provided ideal opportunities to discuss the finer
points of navigation and to learn about other communities.

His last words to me were, '*Bons vents! Bonne continuation!*' I wished
him the same. We all need fair winds and plain sailing.

At last a window opened in the weather. The forecast predicted that
the wind in Biscay would be North West, Force 4 to 5, decreasing to
3 or 4 later. Visibility would be mainly fair. This is what I had been
waiting for and I decided to leave at first light. But we had a rude
awakening. As we left the shelter of harbour, the sea was still lumpy
from a week's bad weather and when we cleared the southwestern
headland of the island, the breaking rollers and deep swell really hit us.
We glimpsed another yacht making heavy weather of it, disappearing
from sight in the deep troughs of the wild waves.

There was more west than north in the wind, so we had to sail
close-hauled on our southwesterly course to La Coruña. And it was
not long before I felt sick, then really sick – over the side, and many
times. There is nothing more debilitating that prolonged seasickness
and that is what I had, retching hour after hour, retching until there
was not even any bile left to retch. But we continued on our course
and made reasonable progress. Since there were only the two of us,
we shared the four-hour watches. This meant we did not get much
more than a few hours' fitful sleep in one go. I took the 'dead man's
watch' from 1200 to 0400 and I certainly felt like a dead man. For the
first and last time, I wondered why on earth I had embarked on this
crazy voyage. I steadied myself by imagining leaning against a Carnac
megalith, solid and static in the deep earth, as we rolled and pitched
on the heaving waters of the Atlantic.

The next morning, the wind abated a little and the sight of two
dolphins diving through the waves lifted our spirits. But we felt even
more lonely in the vast expanse of the ocean after they left. I recalled
the prayer of the Breton fishermen, which must have been expressed
countless times since humans first raised a sail some 10,000 years ago:

> O Lord please protect me.
> The sea is so large
> And my boat is so small.

As *Celtic Gold* rolled and pitched wildly, I wrote in my notebook:
'The sea is vast, beyond human comprehension. We have tamed and
domesticated most of the land, but the sea is untamable. It will always
escape us. The vastness of the sea makes me feel giddy. It is easy to be
overwhelmed. I am like a butterfly on a blade of straw in a huge
expanse of water. If something goes wrong, there is just the universe
and me – and Elizabeth.'

At least by now, our second day at sea, I was able to hold
down some water and dry biscuits. Things could only get better.
Then, at 1600 hours, I received a forecast which announced that
there would be strong north or northeast winds in southwest Biscay
in the next twenty-four hours. I did not relish the idea of hitting
the rocky Galician coast in onshore gale force winds, megaliths or
not. I decided to continue for the time being. When I went down at
nightfall for a sleep in my bunk in the groaning cabin, the wind
seemed to be picking up, and the breaking waves rolling in from the
pitch-black night looked more sinister than ever.

I was dreaming of lying down inside the chamber of a cairn when
I suddenly heard the engine fire and then stop. I went up into the
cockpit to see a huge container ship, its lights ablaze, bearing down
on us in the dark night. We had been sailing with closely reefed sails
and Elizabeth had tried to start the engine to change course swiftly.
She tried again but again the engine fired and died after a few strokes.
I quickly let go the sails and managed to swing the yacht out of
harm's way. But that left us bobbing up and down in a strong swell
with the threat of gale force winds, and without an engine.

The ancient mariners would not have been able to predict the
weather apart from what they read in the sky and the sea. Perhaps a
degree of ignorance is sometimes not a bad thing after all. Anticipating
a gale can sometimes be worse than experiencing the gale itself.

I found that the yacht was not responding to the tiller properly.
When I shone a torch in our wake, I realized that we had picked up
a huge green fishing net. It was wrapped around our propeller and
steering gear. At first light on that cold, grey morning, I climbed over
the back of the boat in the great Atlantic swell and tried to cut away
as much of the net as I could. It had been floating in the ocean for so
long that it was covered in seaweed and a whole community of
minute marine life lived amongst it. The net was slimy and cold, but
I managed after many stabs to cut away the bulk of it.

What to do next? To the southwest there was a treacherous coastline
which in the summer experiences fog for 20 per cent of the time.
There was a forecast of near-gale-strength winds. We had no engine

to get us out of trouble. By this time we were almost a third of our way across the Bay, but there seemed only one sensible thing to do in the circumstances: to sail back to the French coast. It was a huge disappointment, and it could mean that I might not be able to get down to the Mediterranean that year after all.

Funnily enough, I had asked myself several times the day before what I would do if the engine failed. When it happened, it was almost as if I had expected it to happen. I felt no panic nor fear. I consoled myself with the thought that the ancient mariners would be more at the mercy of the sea than I was. They would have enjoyed clearer skies and calmer seas but they would have had no engines, no weather forecasts, no radio, no charts, only the natural signs to read in the sea and sky and the behaviour of the fish and the birds, and their faith in their gods to see them through.

We turned due east and steered for France. Without an engine, we were, like the early seafarers, more vulnerable to the strength and direction of the winds. I checked the entrances and tides to the ports of La Rochelle and Royan at the entrance to the Gironde. Further south was the shelterless coastline of Les Landes. In the event we managed, after a couple of days' sail, to reach Les Sables d'Olonne, the starting point and end of the the round-the-world solo Vendée Globe race which Thierry Dubois and Ellen MacArthur had entered. During the day we saw many shearwaters and storm petrels skimming across the waves and at dusk an orange-red moon appeared over the bows. Shooting stars lit up the night sky and moonbeams played on the white-capped waves.

Seven miles southwest of the entrance to Les Sables d'Olonne, the wind dropped entirely. We decided to have lunch in the flat calm. The boat slowly turned around on itself. I thought of the song of Uvavnuk, an Inuit shamaness:

> The great sea
> Has sent me adrift
> It moves me
> As the weed in a great river
> Earth and the great weather
> Move me
> Have carried me away
> And moved my inward parts with joy.

After lunch, I decided to go overboard to try and cut the rest of the net away. As I dived into the crystal-clear water sparkling in the

Skara Brae settlement, Orkney, inhabited from 3100 to 2500 BC. It is the best preserved Stone Age village in Northern Europe

Dwelling at Skara Brae, with central hearth, stone dresser and bed box, reflecting a high standard of living

Inner circle at Callanish, Isle of Lewis, dating from 3000 BC. It may well have served as a lunar observatory

Entrance to the mound at Newgrange, Ireland, built around 3250 BC.
The rising sun on the winter solstice shines through the roof box into
the inner chamber

Author by the Géant du Manio, Carnac, one of the many impressive menhirs in the region with possible astronomical alignments. Five snakes are carved on the base of the stone

The Kermario alignment, one of several at Carnac. Raised between 4000 and 3800 BC, the rows run for more than 1100 metres and lead to a sacred enclosure in the west

Chûn Quoit, the best preserved Neolithic dolmen in Cornwall, roughly 4 metres square. It would have been originally covered by a mound

Dolmen de Axeitos, (circa 4000 BC), Oleiros, Galicia. A granite carving, probably of the Great Goddess, was found on the site

Dolmen de Fontanaccia or the Stazzona di u Diavalu ('Devil's Forge'), Cauria, Corsica. It faces the rising sun

Collapsed dolmen, part of the Bugibba temple complex, Malta. The wide distribution of dolmens shows how Europe shared a common megalithic culture

Taula in the Torralba d'en Salord sanctuary in Menorca. Such unique monuments were built all over the island from 1400 to 800 BC

La Naveta des Tudons ('Boat of the Wood Pigeons'), Menorca. Built around 1400 BC, it was used for rituals and secondary burials

Statue-menhirs surrounding the central monument, Filitosa, Corsica. Carved from around 1800 BC, they are the first stone sculptures with human features

Tomba di Giganti ('Giants' Tomb'), Coddu Vecchiu, Arzachena, Sardinia. Built around 1500 BC, it was used for collective burials and ceremonies

Neolithic anchors dating from the third millennium BC. Archaeology Museum, Palermo, Sicily

Split stone egg, symbol of rebirth, at Monte d'Accoddi sanctuary, near Porto Tórres, Sardinia

Limestone altar, with carved 'Tree of Life', found in the Hagar Qim temples, Malta. Archaeology Museum, Valletta, Malta

Known as the 'Sleeping Lady', this beautiful terracotta of the Great Goddess was found in the Hypogeum at Hal Saflieni. Archaeology Museum, Malta

Author at the main entrance to the Hagar Qim temples, Malta. The colossal dressed stones are made from local limestone

The three Mnajdra temples, Malta, dating from 3000 BC. They are aligned with the rising sun on the equinoxes and solstices

sun, I could not believe my eyes: the net which I had seen still trailing before lunch was gone! It must have unravelled itself as the becalmed boat gently turned on itself. Soon after, the wind picked up and we sailed to the harbour entrance of Les Sables d'Olonne. We had sailed 250 nautical miles in four days and three nights, only to end up about 80 miles further south along the coast. But we were content.

Another extraordinary coincidence took place: the first person we saw on the pontoon in the harbour was Jean-Claude from Crozon, who had a rosy megalith in his garden. He kept his yacht at Les Sables d'Olonne. Breton sailors still travel far. J.C., as we called him, was, like Jesus Christ, close to the sea and a friend of fishermen. It seemed miraculous that he should be there at that very moment after our long and unexpected loop around the Bay. Sailors have always been suspicious and ready to read signs in the sea and the sky.

He was a philosophical man, now living alone. As we shared a meal on board with his good bottle of wine, he observed: '*La mort est le retour au Néant avant d'être né.*' ('Death is a return to the Nothingness before being born.') He also reminded me of Baudelaire's famous line: '*Homme libre, toujours tu chercheras la mer.*' ('A free man will always seek out the sea').

The next day the weather turned bad once again. We spent our time sitting on the dock of the bay, watching the tide roll in and hoping that the wind would turn north. I had the boat lifted out of the water and the keel bolts retightened, as they were leaking again after all the movement since leaving Belle Île. With such capricious forecasts and strong winds, I thought it best to err, if at all, on the side of caution.

The second attempt

The chances of crossing the Bay, let alone of reaching the Mediterranean, seemed to be slipping away day by day. We were approaching the end of August, the period of depressions. After eight days, we at last had another window in the weather and left at noon on an easterly wind. There was a lot of swell but the wind was gentle and the weather warm and sunny. There is a lovely French phrase for it: '*la mer belle*'. On watch at night, I was regaled by the movement of the stars across the great orb of the sky, with the Milky Way clearly visible. Shooting stars fell all around us on the endless horizon. As the boat cut through the long swell, with 150 metres between crests, the phosphorescence of the disturbed plankton sparkled in streaks and spirals in the water.

On the second day we were joined by a group of killer whales, one jumping clear of the water and showing its white underbelly as it turned to dive back into the boisterous waves. A porpoise and its offspring came later and made a perfect synchronised leap. The appearance of flying fish showed us that we were now heading down towards warmer climes and the tropics. A rare voice from an unseen yacht on the crackling radio declared that he was heading for Chile in South America. I had once travelled across the Atlantic with my brother; it had taken us just over three weeks, the same time it took Columbus. It would not surprise me that Neolithic seafarers had crossed the Atlantic to the Caribbean. Once they had travelled south to the coast of Africa, it would have been comparatively easy, with the ocean currents and trade winds behind them.

On the third day, a beautiful little land bird with a white chest and black and white wings flew into the cabin. It stayed for half an hour and then flew southwest towards our own destination. Land could not be far away. Vikings and no doubt their Stone Age ancestors used the flight of birds at sea to guide them to shelter.

On the morning of the fourth day, my fifty-fifth birthday, I reckoned that we were getting close to the Galician coast with its deeply indented *rías*, or flooded river valleys. By midmorning it was a beautiful, hot day with a dark, steely-blue horizon. As we set course for La Coruña, I could feel the perfect northeasterly breeze on the back of my neck as *Celtic Gold* glided steadily over the long, gentle swell. The worry over surviving the trip was over; now we felt pure delight. At night, we could see the silver flash of fish in the deep, black curve of the steady waves.

I wondered what the ancient mariners must have felt after dead reckoning their position at this stage in their voyage across the Bay. Without charts and compasses, they would have had to rely on their oral knowledge, skill and luck. Where the modern navigator with his electrical equipment is cut off from the sea and sky, the ancient mariners would have been much more closely attuned to the colour and direction of the sea, the weather signs in the sky, the daily movement of the sun, moon and stars, and the meaning of passing birds, fish, seaweed and flotsam. Like all good navigators, they no doubt had a sixth intuitive sense which kept them out of danger. An old and wise saying of navigators is that it is more important to know *where you are not* rather than where you are – in other words, not near rocks or shoals, but with ample sea room.

Not long after dawn, banks of fog rolled in and it became impossible to make out the coast. Then, suddenly, the most extraordinary thing happened: an overwhelming smell of sweet pine and warm earth reached me. The mist lifted for a moment and I noticed close by – too close for comfort – rocky pinnacles fronting high cliffs. I calculated it to be the Punta Estaca de Bares, the most northwesterly tip of Spain.

The warmth of the southern sun caressed the back of my neck and shoulders. I noticed a small apple in the water – another sign of our closeness to land. A rare sea eagle swooped across our bows and a dozen porpoises joined us.

Several hours later, at dusk, we entered the wide-open harbour of La Coruña. Visibility was poor, and as soon as we arrived, thick fog descended. After two attempts, six nights and eight days at sea, we had only just made it in time. According to our log, in our first attempt to cross the Bay of Biscay we had sailed 254 nautical miles; in our second, 402. Since the log under-read by about 10 per cent, I reckoned that we must have sailed about 700 miles – over eight days. In large, firm letters, Elizabeth wrote in the logbook after the last entry: 'Arrived – which says it all!'

Like countless sailors before me, from Scotland, Ireland, Wales, Cornwall and Brittany, I made a pilgrimage inland to Santiago de Compostela to give thanks for our safe arrival. I bought a scallop shell there like the one St James had used as a cup after landing on the shore and trekking up to the hill where he founded his church and died. The end of a voyage is as important as the beginning. In the Reliquias chapel, there was a poignant fifteenth-century carving in alabaster of the corpse of St James lying in a small boat with two angels holding the sails and a third looking down at him. I wondered whether any guardian angels had helped us across.

I would now be following in the wake of the ancient mariners and St James down the rocky coastline of Spain and Portugal and into the Mediterranean. The cold waters and grey skies of the north of Scotland seemed a long way away, but, as I was soon to find out, the megaliths of Iberia were inspired by the same beliefs and built in a similar manner.

CHAPTER THIRTEEN

The Coast of Death

To die at sea among the waves is terrible.

HESIOD

The links between Galicia and Brittany, Cornwall, Wales, Ireland and Scotland are strong. They not only face the pounding waves of the Atlantic, but share a Celtic tongue that survived the Roman conquest. The scattered remains of their megalithic monuments also show that long before the arrival of the Celts and Romans, they had a common civilization and long-distant trading links stretching right down the western Atlantic seaboard and into the Mediterranean.

La Coruña is now a major city with a bustling waterfront. In the old quarter the houses have glassed-in balconies to withstand the winter rain brought by the Atlantic depressions. The city's recorded history goes back to Phoenician times, when tin was mined nearby. Its first charter was granted by the Romans. The Phoenicians and the Romans, like the megalithic seafarers before them, realized only too well its strategic importance for traffic crossing the Bay of Biscay from the north or the south.

Outside the harbour on a prominent cliff stands the Torre de Hércules, the oldest working lighthouse in the world. It was built at the time of Julius Caesar, when the city was called Brigantium Flavium, in order to keep watch on the route to the British Isles. The remains of many North African amphoras, a kind of vase, from the first to the sixth centuries, have been found. The fact that this continued to be an important route is attested by the fact that it was the Spanish Armada's departure point.

A museum of archaeology and history is conveniently situated next to the harbour in the Renaissance fort of Castillo de San Antón.

It contains an intriguing exhibition of megalithic art from around 5000 BC which includes human figures and a horse with a rider. I was particularly interested in a replica of an ocean-going boat in the museum.

In Mesolithic times along the Galician coast, humans had begun fishing using light, finely cut flints for fish spears. They used simple but perfectly seaworthy canoes – one dates from around 8000 BC – made from tree trunks hollowed out with the controlled use of fire. I had seen one made in a similar way at the site of Locmariaquer near Carnac.

The boat in the museum in La Coruña, however, was made like an Irish curragh from animal skins stretched over a wicker frame. It had oars as well as a leather sail but unlike the Irish curraghs, it had a curved bow reminiscent of ancient Mediterranean and Egyptian boats. It had been built in the mid-1970s by the professors and students of the Faculty of Geography and History at the University of Santiago de Compostela. It was called the *Borna* after the site at Borna-Meira by the Ría de Vigo. Here, stone carvings of megalithic boats had been found and it was these that had inspired the boat's design.

I was delighted to learn that classical authors had testified that such boats were still used in the maritime relations between Galicia, Brittany, Cornwall, Wales, Ireland and Scotland in the Bronze Age. It was not only good to see such a boat capable of long-distance navigation in Galicia but to have my own argument supported for early maritime links along the Atlantic seaboard.

The boat had been painted with *oculi*, or eyes, on its bows, just like the ones on the boat depicted on the Bronze Age bowl founded in Caergwrle in Wales. Similar *oculi* can be seen on old Breton, Galician and Portuguese fishing boats.

In the hills around La Coruña, there is ample evidence of megaliths, but they are not always easily accessible. At a private golf club inland above the port the megalithic tumulus of A Zapateira still stands among the links. Dating from around 2500 BC, it commands tremendous views of the sea as well as the surrounding hills. Some of the ritual objects found at the site can be seen in the La Coruña museum.

I tried to find a rumoured megalithic site – according to my taxi driver – in the vicinity of the nearby fort of Castro de Elviña. It was the scene of an important battle between the British and the French during the Peninsula Wars of the early nineteenth century, during which General Sir John Moore was killed; his body now lies buried in the Jardines de San Carlos in La Coruña. Unfortunately, the area is now so overgrown and off the beaten track that I was unable to find either the megalith or the ruined fort.

Throughout Galicia there are mounds of earth called *mámoas* and said to be frequented by fairies. But the most visible type of megalithic monument in the region is the uncovered dolmen, revealing its heavy bones to the sky. The impressive Dolmen de Dombate in the Cabana district inspired a poem by the nineteenth-century Romantic poet Eduardo Pondal, composer of Galicia's anthem. It consists of an earth tumulus covered by a well-constructed shell 21.5 metres across and 1.8 metres high. Inside there is a corridor almost 7 metres long opening into a chamber 3 metres high. Its entrance faces the setting sun over the sea. Several votive axes and anthropomorphic 'idols' engraved on slabs of stone have been found at the site.[1]

Costa da Morte

Galicia is a wet place, with weather that for most of the year resembles the damp, mild weather of Southwest England, where I live. In the summer, however, it can become very hot, and this can result in a sudden descent of thick coastal fog. It can occur any time and last for at least a week. The region moreover is entirely exposed to the full fetch of the Atlantic, and its high cliffs and offshore pinnacle rocks can be extremely dangerous for mariners. This wild, magnificent and forbidding coast is known locally as the Costa da Morte, or Coast of Death, and with good reason.

There are spectacular *rías* between the bold headlands along the Galician coast. These wide and deeply indented bays resemble Scottish sea lochs, and were once river estuaries, flooded at the end of the Ice Age.

We left La Coruña to explore this spectacular coastline in a light sea mist through which the silvery sun threatened to break at any minute. As we sailed south, I noted the high, curved bows of the painted fishing boats, designed to ride Atlantic swells. Even in the summer in light winds, we were experiencing a swell of 2 metres.

As we were about to enter the Ría de Camariñas, our next port of call, a thick band of fog descended. Visibility was reduced to about 200 metres, and we had to inch our way slowly forward. Four porpoises, undisturbed by the fog, came and played around our boat. It was ominous to hear the sound of a fishing vessel in the eerie gloom, and even more so when we were hit by its bow wave rolling across the still waters of the loch. We must have been very close.

Suddenly, the fog lifted to reveal a couple of old men fishing in rowing boats; they stood up and pointed the way to the harbour entrance just before the fog descended again, as thick as before. We just managed to nudge our way in. When the fog lifted that evening, I saw that we were surrounded by a wild and rugged hillside scattered with large boulders, rough bush and pine trees. The hill was purple in the setting sun. Soon after dusk a great thunderstorm broke out – lightning flashed across the black sky, thunder echoed around the hills, and torrential rain thudded and bounced on the deck of our boat.

The next day we rounded Cabo Finisterre, the westernmost point of the Spanish mainland, another exposed point with strong currents out in the Atlantic. It is feared by mariners, ancient and modern, with good reason. I expected something rugged and wild, but it resembled the rounded back of a stranded whale.

The cape marked another stage in our long voyage south. Like a good omen, a dozen porpoises joined us, leaping out of the water with a few flicks of their tails. I could even lean over the bows and touch them as they swam alongside.

It was a great relief to have the Bay of Biscay behind us. We would now have plenty of shelter – the natural harbours, *rías* and estuaries of Western Iberia are only about a day's sail apart. We turned into the Ría de Muros y Noya and reached the picturesque harbour on the north side. After the swell of the Atlantic, it was delightfully calm and bathed in the sweet-smelling fragrance of pines and eucalyptus trees.

The Grave of Wheels

Muros is an old fishing town with narrow streets, colonnaded pavements, a Romanesque church, and famous petroglyphs and rock art in the surrounding hills. We set out to find them, taking a short bus ride along the coast to Louro, then walking by well-tended homesteads set in small stone-walled fields and up through dappled woodlands of pine, eucalyptus and stunted oaks. We eventually came to a rough, rocky plateau with magnificent views down to the azure sea and inland to grey mountains. Above the incessant dry tick of cicadas, I could hear the muffled boom of the Atlantic surf crashing on a small rocky peninsula below. Scratching my arms and legs, I forced a way through the tangled bush of tufted grass, gorse, briars, broom and bracken until I reached the outcrop I was looking for. A Laxe das Rodas, the Grave of Wheels, had only been discovered in 1956 but it is typical of Galician rock art which is invariably found on an advantage point with extended views. Some archaeologists have argued that the carvings were intended to lay claim to territory and control access to strategic areas of landscape, but to me they seem more likely to mark special places for celebrations and rituals and the gathering of the clans.[2]

Facing southwest, the group consisted of nine figures, two spirals, and seven circular motifs with concentric circles. One circle had dots carved into the rock all around it, perhaps to mark the annual movement of the sun. The two spirals have been interpreted as one of the earliest solar and lunar calendars used to mark the agricultural year.[3] They may also represent the male and female principles, the labyrinth of the world, the movement of the starry night, and the mystical path to enlightenment. Perhaps, they are all of these – and more.

Similar motifs were carved throughout Europe in megalithic times. The situation and design of A Laxe das Rodas, however, immediately reminded me of the circles and cup-and-ring marks I had seen at Kilmartin, set in a similar landscape 2000 nautical miles to the north. The mazes were also similar to the ones I had seen near Tintagel in Cornwall. Sitting on the rock, and looking out towards the sun setting over the sea, I wondered what had made those ancient artists climb to such beautiful places overlooking the sea in order to carve their cherished symbols in the hardest granite – so hard that their energy has remained undiminished after several thousand years of wind, rain and sun.

These were not the only stone carvings in the vicinity. At the site of Cova da Bruxa, about 9 kilometres from Muros, I came across an extraordinary profusion of stags and does, carved among the circles and mazes. Although made by settled agriculturalists, the carvings showed clearly that the hunt was still an important part of everyday life. The many images of male and female deer suggest that they may also have been carved as magical symbols of fertility: many of the stags are shown with erect penises. Moreover, the scattered discs carved among them were undoubtedly intended to represent the sun, the source of all life on earth. There were even some beautiful and evocative carvings of stags carrying solar discs in their antlers. These were probably drawn by the warlike Indo-Europeans who spread across Europe in the Bronze Age, replacing the cult of the Great Goddess with their male sun gods.

In the museum in La Coruña, I had seen other drawings taken from the rock art in the area. These included two 'idols' shaped like phalluses: one had an upturned crescent like a smile at its top; the other, three such lines topped by two dots resembling eyes. I was astonished to discover that there was also a swastika carved on a rock. Its leading edges pointed in a clockwise direction like those in India, which symbolize good luck – the opposite direction and meaning of the Nazi version.[4] Then there were rectangles divided into four with a dot in the middle of each part, groups of three wavy lines and even a foot with five toes. The rock artists of Galicia clearly not only had great skill and perseverance in working the granite outcrops, but had extremely fertile imaginations and could draw readily on archetypes deep within their collective unconscious.

The rutting stag

After Muros, we sailed past the deeply indented and beautifully named Ría de Arosa and Ría de Pontevedra. It was difficult to resist their seductive embrace. We were sorely tempted to land at the Islas Cíes which appeared like a magical apparition of Shangri La, their wooded slopes rising high out of a sparkling sea. But we resisted the temptation: no megaliths had yet been discovered on their shores. Passing Bayona, I saw an exact replica of Columbus's boat *La Pinta*, which made its first landfall here in 1493 after returning from the New World. It would not surprise me that megalithic mariners had beaten him to it by several millennia.

Our destination was Vigo, an ancient and well-heeled town on the southern shore of the *ría* of the same name. After disembarking, we travelled from there north overland to visit the *rías* we had just sailed by. We visited the justly famous Dolmen de Axeitos, hidden in the dappled light in a pine, oak and eucalyptus wood near Oleiros on the northern shore of Ría de Arosa. A huge capstone, 4.5 metres by 3.5 metres, was supported by eight vertical stones. It was about 2 metres high and, according to an old man who suddenly emerged out of the foliage like a leprechaun, was built around 4000 BC. He pointed out the faint carving of a fish which was used by early Christians as a symbol of their new faith. A granite 'idol' had also been found at the site, no doubt of the Great Goddess herself.[5]

Although there was a gentle sea breeze smelling faintly of seaweed and fennel, as I sat inside the mushroom-shaped dolmen I was reminded immediately of Chûn Quoit on its wild and rainswept hill in Cornwall. They were almost identical to the ones I had seen during my voyage in Ireland, Wales and Brittany. There could not have been a more eloquent

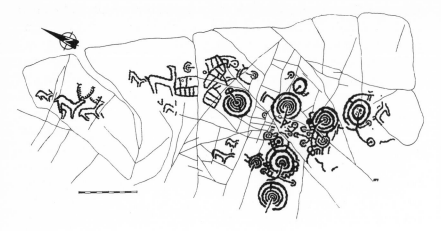

Rock art at Os Cogoludos, Paredes, Campo Lameiro, Galicia

testimony of the common culture and beliefs which linked the regions of the Atlantic seaboard in megalithic times.

We then visited the Castro de Baroña on the southern shore of the Ría de Muros, an impressive Iron Age fortified town with circular walls and houses strategically built on a small rocky peninsula. It faced southwest, its back sheltered from the northerly winds. Begun in the sixth century BC during an economic boom driven by tin, gold, copper and iron mining, it was later occupied by the Celts. It was a stark reminder of the centuries of war following the end of the Stone Age. I could not resist joining the local sun worshippers at a nearby nudist beach for a dive in the crashing Atlantic surf.

Another foray inland from Pontevedra to study the remarkable collection of petroglyphs at Campo Lameiro proved even more memorable. Set high up in the mountains, it has not only been called 'the capital of Galician rock art' but the capital of European rock art as a whole.[6] The carvings engraved on the granite rocks are both naturalistic and geometrical. The abstract shapes are the most common, and include concentric circles, spirals, labyrinths and squares with rounded corners, which are often grouped together to form complex patterns. Although thought to belong to the Bronze Age, more recently it has been argued that they were carved at the end of the third millennium BC.[7]

The naturalistic carvings consists mainly of deer (some standing, others running), anthropomorphic forms, human figures on horseback, and what Spanish archaeologists call *idolos-cilíndricos* – cylindrical idols. There are also carvings of daggers, swords and shields, almost certainly

Bronze Age additions. Some short swords at the complex of Conxo even appear to be borrowed from British models from the same period found in Wessex.

The rock art of Galicia would appear to be expressed in two languages, one geometrical and esoteric, the other naturalistic and open.[8] The former, which seems to be the earlier, can be found all down the Atlantic seaboard and doubtless has a religious significance. Circles, spirals and mazes, associated with the cult of the Great Goddess, are all symbols of the spiritual path towards enlightenment.

The naturalistic figures, on the other hand, with deer, humans on horseback and weapons, reflect hunting scenes. They were probably intended as a kind of sympathetic magic for the hunter as well as marking control of territory. The antlers of the rutting stag had the same significance as the drawing of weapons: they are undoubtedly signs of male aggression.[9] This development in Galician art would seem to mirror the shift around 2000 BC to a more hierarchical and complex society with leaders and chiefs. A greater stress on the individual is also reflected about the same time in the move from communal burials to single ones with metal grave goods. The emerging elite no doubt wished to affirm its power through the depiction of prestigious activities such as hunting and riding, and to declare its status through fearsome objects like metal arms and shields.

We started our explorations of the Campo Lameiro rock art from the village of Paredes, set on a steep hill above a valley covered in pines, oaks and self-seeded mimosas. The dahlias were in bloom, the cicadas noisy, and the grapes ripening in the family vineyards. In summer, this was a forgotten world of rural tranquillity, although in winter life was harsh and the valley was often cut off by snow. After climbing a narrow stone path through the woods, we came across Lax Dos Cabalos, two beautiful horses carved on a large flat granite rock; they had been loafing there for 4000 years. In the vicinity of the village, we also found deer, circles and labyrinths at the great complex of Os Cogoludos, more men on horseback at Outeiro dos Cogolos and large stags at Os Carballos.

We were fortunate enough to meet in the local bar a warden of the national park who led us along the narrow, twisting roads through dark forests until we reached the wide open space of the high plateau. It provided wonderful panoramic views of the surrounding mountains cut by deep valleys with homesteads nestling on their wooded sides. Continuing our search alone, we discovered an extraordinary array of carvings on the flat granite boulders scattered amongst the wild heather. The artists here must have been consumed by a frenzy of energy: the carvings are spread over some 400 rock outcrops covering a huge area.

But this is not all. The largest concentration of rock art is to be found in As Fragas where the Pedra da Boullosa has an enormous complex of circles, labyrinths, deer (with and without antlers) and a large snake. One stag is mounted by a man – an apt symbol of the growing domination of humans over nature in the Bronze Age and of their new male-oriented religion.

CHAPTER FOURTEEN

The Portuguese Trades

At sea by such rough storms and griefs forespent!
So many a moment when Death stands alert!

LUÍS DE CAMÕES

V igo was our last port of call in northwest Spain. As we passed
the wide estuary of the River Miño, which marked the border
with Portugal, I switched the Spanish flag flying from the mast to a
Portuguese one. It was a formality which the ancient mariners, part
of a common culture well before Europe was divided into nation
states, would not have had to do. The coastline is extremely jagged
in Galicia and flat in northern Portugal, but they share the same
climate, wet and mild, and have mountainous hinterlands.

We were now beginning to pick up the Portuguese trade winds
which blow down the coast from the north, making a southerly
voyage a pleasure, but a northerly one hard work involving much
tacking and overnight sails. The winds are caused by the diurnal
change in temperature in the Sahara: they tend to blow hardest in the
afternoon when the desert has heated up, and die out at dusk as it
cools.

After a lovely sail on an emerald sea in the hot sunshine, we sailed
up the river Lima to the old town of Viana do Castelo, our first stop
in Portugal. The old fishing port has a long tree-lined esplanade along
the river front, with white stucco houses ranged along narrow streets,
leading up to little cobbled squares overlooked by ornate balconies.

The town still has an active fishing fleet. The fishermen stand in a
long tradition – their ancestors have journeyed far since megalithic
times. In the sixteenth century, the town grew rich from trade with
Brazil and from cod fishing on the Newfoundland Banks. It was there

that the local fishermen swapped their fortified wine – the local wine did not keep well, so they added some brandy – for nets brought out by Englishmen from Brixham in Southwest England. In those interminable winters fishing in the icy sea, it no doubt tasted liked bottled sunlight. The Portuguese wine – eventually abbreviated to port – became so popular that English merchants came out to Viana to develop the trade. It was only when the harbour silted up that the centre moved to Porto on the Douro river further south.

In Viana do Castelo, we met David Lumby, the brother of a friend of mine. A strong, good-natured man, he was an experienced sailor who had written the section on Portuguese waters for the main British nautical almanac. He had also a deep interest in Portuguese history, archaeology and architecture, and was to prove a mine of information, an attentive host and an excellent guide to the archaeological sites during our stay in northern Portugal.

In megalithic times, of course, the people living along the western coasts of Iberia shared the same culture and language. It is not therefore surprising that the remains discovered in northern Portugal should be similar to the ones found in northwestern Spain. Although they have been separate states from the twelfth century, they still have strikingly similar cultural traits. Euan MacKie believes that the megalithic tradition began in Iberia and spread out from there, but as we have seen it began more or less at the same time along the Atlantic seaboard when hunter-gatherers first settled in the British Isles and Brittany.[1]

The megaliths in northern Portugal consist mainly of *antas* (dolmens) and *mámoas* (mounds), and date from 4500 BC onwards. In addition to complex passage graves, there are a range of chamber types – polygonal, single, rectangular and long. The coastal mounds on the whole were wealthier than their counterparts inland, reflecting the greater fertility of the land and ease of communications along the coast.[2] The presence of flaked tools made from flint, such as arrowheads and large blades, suggests that the coastal communities must have built up exchange networks to obtain such a scarce raw material.

Unfortunately, most of these monuments have been ransacked and plundered, and the most common artefacts left in them are flaked or ground stones. These might include stone idols, beads, querns, blades, arrowheads, maces, or veritable Neolithic toolkits – hoe-blades, double adzes and chisels.

The oldest mounds usually contain single polygonal chambers. New developments began to take place from around 2700 BC, when the passage graves become longer and larger. The stone artefacts began to grow in number and variety, especially in the case of ground objects such as axes, and to a lesser extent adzes and maces, which probably served as prestigious objects. At the very end of the third millennium, pottery striking for its fine shape and intricate decoration emerges, made by coiling strips of clay and moulding them together.

During the Chalcolithic period, which lasted from about 2500 to 1700 BC, the introduction of copper smelting meant stone grave goods began to give way to metal ones. Bell beakers, named after their shape, spread throughout the region. There was also a shift towards single burials, as elsewhere in Western Europe. Nevertheless, the kind of dolmens which had appeared in the third millennium continued to be erected. Constructed on plains or hills, they were clearly intended to be conspicuous from afar.

The Early Bronze Age in the Iberian Peninsula began around 1700 BC and lasted to about 1200 BC. As elsewhere, the changes in technology and burial customs and the development of a more hierarchical society may have been the result not of large-scale immigrations or conquests, but the diffusion of techniques and ideas, especially along the coasts and up the rivers, which affected different local communities at varying periods.[3]

During the Early Iron Age, roughly from 700 to 200 BC, the impact of traders from the Mediterranean increased, supplementing existing, long-established trading links with the communities along the Atlantic seaboard to the north. The Phoenicians reached Portugal at this time. A Semitic people occupying much of the coastal plain of Lebanon, they established settlements on both shores of the Mediterranean, particularly at Carthage on the site of present-day Tunis. They brought with them writing and the use of the wheel for making pottery. Rather then conquering local populations, they probably set up trading centres along the coasts and bartered for their mineral wealth. Through them, the distant cultural influence of Egypt and Mesopotamia began to be felt.

The most visible prehistoric remains in northern Portugal, as in northwestern Spain, are the *castros* like the one I had seen at Baroña. These oval fortified Iron Age villages dated from the end of the second millennium BC. Some were inhabited continuously from 1500 BC to AD 1500. At first, circular buildings were built within circular walls but rectangular shapes were added later as can be seen at Briteiros near Braga on the Costa Verde. It seems they were first built by Mediterranean peoples but were taken over by Celtic tribes who arrived in the fifth century BC all down the Atlantic coast, and later by the Romans.

The Lusitanians from this region of northern Portugal, who were probably Celts, put up a famous and spirited fight against the Romans in the second century BC. There is a fine stone carving of a Lusitanian warrior holding a circular shield in front of him in the National Museum of Archaeology in Lisbon. A story goes that the Lusitanians made a final defence at the river Lima and claimed that whoever tried to cross it would lose their memories. The Roman general Decimus Junius Brutus Gallaecus crossed the river at the head of his troops and defied the superstition once and for all.

Although these movements of peoples out of the Mediterranean into the Atlantic occurred after my main period of interest, they were undoubtedly following in the wake of the earlier megalithic seafarers.

The Lumby Stone

My guide, David Lumby, kicked off our archaeological tour of northern Portugal by taking us to some little-known abandoned sites along the coast. The first, called Anta da Barrosa, was hidden in rough bush at the side of a road not far from the sea near Âncora. The dolmen was a passage grave about 8 metres wide with outer stones nearly 3 metres high, very similar to the one I had seen at Los Axeitos de Ribiera north of the border. An axe, arrowhead and ceramic fragments had been found on the site. The last time David visited, he had lost his dog there for two days; it was even more neglected now.

We then visited a mound not far away, in Afife, grandly called the Mámoa da Eireira. It too was overgrown with gorse, heather and bracken among abandoned olive trees and pines a few hundred metres from the sea. An old plaque on the site dated it to between the third and second millennium BC. Excavated in 1985 and now consisting of ten large slabs lining an open trench, it would have originally been a huge mound with a diameter of 36 metres, covering a collective burial site. We managed to find carvings of three vertical wavy lines or snakes, a cross, two six-pointed stars with dots between each line, and what I called 'flying stars' made from four lines forming an off-centred cross. I felt that they were clearly intended to help the deceased in his or her voyage in the next life.

The next trip David proposed was to the Parque Nacional da Peneda-Gerês, which is part of a granite mountain range in the hinterlands of northern Portugal traversed by the river Lima. A few days earlier, he had made a remarkable discovery. Walking along a stone-strewn track outside a remote village in the park called Ermida, he had stumbled, fallen and found himself holding on to a large oval stone. It had a strange 'waist' about a third from its pointed top. It was certainly unlike any other of the grey stones in the vicinity. A geologist who was with him at the time immediately asked: 'Could it be an axe?'

David still had the extraordinary stone and showed it to me. It was made from grey granite with some shining mica in it, but was much bigger than any axe I had seen before in my travels. A narrow ellipse in shape, it was about 35 centimetres high and 30 centimetres at its widest point, and weighed some 2 kilos. It was certainly axe-like in appearance and we both felt that the circular 'waist' could not have been accidental. David took me to the very spot where he had found it. Without his fateful stumble, it would still be there today.

The village of Ermida was situated over 1000 metres above the Lima on a plateau not far from the Spanish border. Half the population were working abroad, and only old men, women and children remained. Only recently had a road financed by the European Union reached them. The villagers saw the men leave along it, and electricity, beds and the first tractor arrive – along with the destruction of a self-sufficient, sustainable, democratic and cooperative way of life stretching back to megalithic times. Even money had been a recent novelty: for thousands of years the people of Ermida had exchanged goods by barter or placed them in a common store for people to draw on according to their needs. They had farmed communally, and met on a flat rock outside the village to discuss their affairs and solve their disputes without the law.

'I love this place,' David said. 'It's so wild and the people are so wise.'

They were still deeply superstitious: on the first of May, they put brooms outside every door to keep the devil away. People from down in the valley would come up to a spring to get water they thought was good for their ailments, especially sexual problems.

As in Africa, the women worked in the fields. David joked: 'The men meet during the day in the village to decide what they might do tomorrow!' I saw old women dressed in black carrying great piles of hay and wood on their heads along the rough stony tracks. A woman's lot was not a happy one. 'If you've got a wife, you don't need a donkey' was a local saying.

In a stark bar run by an old blind man, who seemed miraculously able to work out the exact change, I met a few of the young men who had returned from working in France – Paris now being the second largest 'Portuguese' city in Europe. They had been drinking all day. I felt they were lost souls, no longer part of the village they came from, nor part of the city where they spent most of their lives working and dreaming of home.

Pine, oak and cork trees grew among the small stone-walled fields, but because of the high altitude they were festooned in lichens and mosses. Bracken and heather grew in the alpine fields. In the summer, small, well-built stone canals brought water to irrigate them but for the rest of the year the weather was cold and wet. It would, of course, have been much milder in megalithic times when the region was widely populated and barley and wheat were grown. The shepherds brought in their sheep and goats at night because wolves still roamed the mountains. It was a way of life that had hardly changed for thousand of years until recently.

An old man had set up a little 'museum' in a disused barn in the village. When I asked him about a stele which had once served as a lintel, he replied: 'Ask David – he knows more than us.' There was a statue-menhir discovered in a nearby field, said to be 4000 years old. Another stone about 1.8 metres high depicted two 'lovers' holding hands; it had been found holding up the wall of a villager's house. It probably dated from around 300 BC.

A local warden working for the national park who had spent thirty years working in Paris took us for a walk above a steep ravine to show us some carvings on slabs of rock facing the setting sun. Here, once again, were the circles and spirals I had seen in Scotland, Ireland, Brittany and Galicia.

The park had several clusters of megalithic graves – *antas* and *mámoas* – especially in the high plateau regions in the northeast and southeast. There was also an impressive *mámoa* for all to see by the side of the road at Mezio among pines and chestnut trees just as you enter the park. Dated to between the fourth and the third millennium BC, its polygonal chamber was still intact, with an access corridor which pointed east to the rising sun. It was also still covered by a tumulus made from rocky stones. Offerings of decorated vases had been found among the remains of corpses. There were more than a dozen such mounds in the area, all reachable on foot.

Before we left, we travelled to the huge dam at the Vale do Salas in the northeast of the park. An accessible dolmen stood on each side of the dam wall. There were no doubt many more, submerged under the water of the artificial lake, and they might reappear in thousands of years' time, when the civilization which flooded the valley will be a distant memory.

During our visit to the mountains, we presented the 'Lumby Stone' David had found near the village of Ermida to the archeology section of the national park office at Arcos de Valdevez. They were delighted and honoured, and impressed by David's honesty, observing that few people ever brought in any artefacts. I later heard that it was confirmed to be a Neolithic axehead dating from around 3000 BC. My own researches confirmed that a similarly shaped axehead had been found at A Cova da Moura in Noia.[4] Given its great size, it had almost certainly been a ceremonial axe. It was good to have held a work of such immense antiquity in my hands, and to have been involved in saving it for the Portuguese nation.

Up the Douro to the Palaeolithic

After leaving Viana we decided to make the best of the Portuguese trade winds, which regularly blew in the afternoon to a Force 6, and a near 1-knot current in our favour. On our way along the hilly Costa Verde, lush enough to live up to its name, we called in at Póvoa de Varzim, a large fishing harbour and seaside resort with sandy beaches set between rocky ledges.

Checking the rigging at the top of the mast in Póvoa, I broke a front tooth while holding a rope between my teeth. It fell on to Elizabeth below on deck; at least it wasn't me who was falling . . .

Our next stop was Leixões, the main port for Porto, Portugal's second city, which lies at the estuary of the river Douro.

Moored outside the bodegas of Porto, which unsurprisingly specialize in port, bobbed a few remaining examples of the traditional sailing boats which used to bring the wine down the river. Their flat bottoms, prominent bows and large square sails were designed to navigate the turbulent river, notorious for its deep pools, treacherous rapids and raging currents. The paddle-like rudder, which in the larger boats needed a dozen men to control it, was very similar to those of the Phoenician sailing boats which had once sailed up the Portuguese coast to Brittany and Cornwall.

David had arranged a special steam-train journey up the Douro valley. We joined it at Vila Real station. The old locomotive, built in Germany in 1925, dripped oil, poured out water and belched great clouds of black smoke as it slowly puffed along the tortuous narrow-gauge line which wound its way above the Douro. Black flakes from the funnel and drizzle from the overflowing water tank came through the open windows and spattered our shirts, which soon dried in the hot sun. We gazed down at the river's deep green pools and rapids, flashing in the sun like a succession of mirrors. Small stone-walled

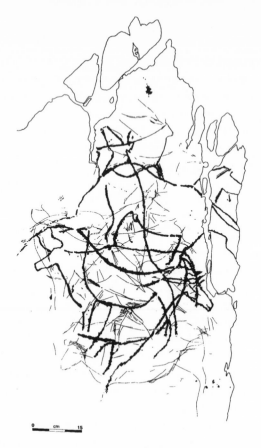

Palaeolithic rock art in the Parque Arqueológico Vale do Côa, Portugal, with aurochs, ibexes and a horse superimposed on each other

olive groves and vineyards on terraces had been etched out of the lower slopes of the steep valley sides. Chestnuts, cork and pine trees grew higher up; chestnuts had been the staple diet of the hardy inhabitants before the recent arrival of potatoes and maize. Higher still were the barren, sun-baked sides of the mountain summits.

This rugged region had been inhabited since Palaeolithic times. In the barren mountains just south of the Douro river, which marks the border with Spain, there is the Parque Arqueológico Vale do Côa, which has recently been designated a World Heritage Site. It is a huge Palaeolithic open-air art gallery running for 17 kilometres along the banks of the river Côa. It is unique for having the largest collection of Palaeolithic images in the world and for being the only known place where rock art can be seen from many different prehistoric and historic periods. Although some of the paintings and carvings have disappeared under water in the partially flooded valley, it was the discovery of the rock carvings on slabs of granite that saved the site from being drowned altogether by a dam.

The images include beautiful outlines of aurochs (extinct long-horned cattle), ibexes (wild goats with twisted horns), horses, red deer and other animals. They were made by nomadic groups of hunter-gathers between 10,000 and 30,000 BC, no doubt as a form of sympathetic hunting magic. These ancient artists relied mainly on pecking, rubbing, scraping and fine-line incision to achieve their superb effects. Some of the figurative works are so detailed you can see the head, mane, nape, legs, tail, and sex of the animals. At Penascos, there is even an image of a mare being mounted by a stallion. The male has three heads, one above the other, to show a downward movement, anticipating a now-familiar technique in modern animated comics.[5]

As with the cave paintings of the Pyrenees, there are often many images superimposed one over the other, rather like a palimpsest. At the Canada do Inferno site, for example, so many different figures have been superimposed at different times that at first sight it looks like a mass of doodles; when unravelled, it reveals a lively tableau of aurochs, ibexes and a horse.

There are at Faia some very stylized paintings in red ochre of human beings and deer exhibiting their sexual organs. They date from the Neolithic and Copper Age, and show that the art in the valley was clearly appreciated and developed over thousands of years. At Vermelhosa, an Iron Age knight holding a spear in his upstretched hand is superimposed on a Palaeolithic deer; he would have been a Lusitanian warrior whose people lived in fortified *castros* before the Roman conquest. Christian crosses were added in the seventeenth century, and a petroglyph from 1944 depicts a steam train of the Douro line crossing a railway bridge, just like the one I had travelled in!

In general, caves decorated with rock art have been interpreted as sanctuaries for performing the rites of a cult and as a means of expressing the religious beliefs of the artists.[6] In the Côa valley, however, the open-air art gallery may have had a social as well as a spiritual dimension, as in the art of the Australian Aborigines which records the exceptional deeds of the ancestors.[7]

Ancient sea-craft

We left David Lumby and his mountain treasures with some reluctance, but once again the weather was all important and we had to continue our journey south before it turned. After Leixões the coast was generally sandy and low, and I missed the wild ruggedness of Galicia. We were still dogged by banks of fog and sea mist, but the winds remained steady and we made good progress. After a day's sail we called into Figueira da Foz, a pleasant seaside town on the north bank of the Mondego river, the longest waterway to rise in Portugal.

On a hill to the northeast of the town was a well-preserved collective grave in a Neolithic necropolis. Known as the Dolmen das Carniçosas, it has an unusual feature: when it was acquired by the local archaeological society in 1898, a protective wall was built right over the mound which covers the chamber and corridor! To the east of the town are the ruins of a seventh-century BC Phoenician settlement, the Castro de Santa Olaia, on a small hill overlooking the Mondego estuary. The local museum houses ceramic and metallic objects found at the site, including great amphora vases once used for storage and for transporting provisions.

Along the section of the coast north of Figueira, a local boat known as a *saveiro* was in use until very recently. It may well have had features dating back to the earliest times of navigation. Boats used along sandy stretches of beach are often very conservative in design; if they work, they tend to change very little. This particular craft had high ends at bow and stern, with a flattish bottom and horizontal strakes. It was launched off the beach into the breaking Atlantic rollers by oxen pushing a wooden fork against the stern post. A fine example of the *saveiro* has been preserved in the Exeter Maritime Museum in England.

The boat would appear to be a remarkable survival and a crucial link, combining elements of Atlantic and Mediterranean design which no doubt reflect the meeting ground of the ancient mariners along the Portuguese coast. Its origins no doubt lie in dugouts used in the estuaries, which were strengthened by cross-pieces and had high bows and sterns, allowing them to ride the rollers breaking on the shore and to venture out into the swell of the Atlantic. Like the Irish curraghs, the *saveiro* had a tholepin for each oar and no provision for steering. Like the traditional Breton fishing boats, it often had *oculi* painted on it bows. Its Mediterranean elements are probably its horizontal strakes and forward-facing oar positions.[8]

It has been suggested that the *saveiros* were descendants of twelfth-century BC boats from the lost Phoenician city of Tartessus near Huelva in Seville, and in turn inspired wooden ships of the Veneti in Brittany which took on the Roman Navy and so impressed Julius Caesar.[9] There is no reason, however, that they should not have

evolved locally and fine-tuned their design and method of construction from passing mariners in ancient times. There is a painting in
the Dolmen dos Antelas at Viseu, which looks like a comb but
probably represents a boat. It suggests that the same sort of high
double-end craft as the *saveiro* was in use off the West Iberian coast
as early as 3000 BC.[10]

Explorations

Another day's sail down the Portuguese coast brought us to Nazaré, a
busy fishing port with a long beach and high headland. The locals
proudly claim to have Phoenician origins. Some of the fishermen still
wear plaid trousers – a possible echo of long-ago trading with Scottish
fishermen. The reason the women traditionally wore seven petticoats
remains a mystery, but it may have been something to do with the
passing sailors . . .

Up on the headland was a fort with a plaque dedicated to the
navigator Vasco da Gama who came to pray before the Virgin of
Nazaré before setting off on his first voyage to India – another local
seafarer standing in a great and ancient tradition of sailing. Not far
inland was the fifteenth-century abbey of Batalha, a masterpiece of
Portuguese Baroque architecture which contains the tomb of Prince
Henry the Navigator, the younger son of King João I and his English
wife Philippa of Lancaster, who sparked off the age of exploration.
Long before these relatively modern explorers, the ancients had of
course opened up the sea routes.

At Nazaré, a couple whom we had last seen in Belle Île took our
ropes as we berthed alongside another yacht. The world shrinks for
those at sea. It also turned out that the harbour master was Michael
Hadley, a retired English captain with a bushy beard, who had been
sailing down with his wife from the Isle of Man to the Mediterranean
but had decided to stay for a while.

As with most seafarers, his talk often centred on the weather: 'In
the last five years, the weather's been more erratic,' he told me. 'You
can't rely on the trades anymore. Usually the sun shines from May, but
it didn't arrive until July this year.'

'Can it get very rough along the coast?' I asked him.

'What happens in the Atlantic ends up on the Portuguese coast,' he
replied emphatically. 'From east to west there's three thousand miles
of open ocean; from north to south, infinity. As a result, we often get
cross-seas and a swell up to four or five metres.'

'And what was it like in southern Portugal?'

'You can still have big seas there. When the easterly *levanter* wind blows the skies suddenly go dark. All you can do is reef in, go down below, make a cup of coffee and wish you had gone by plane!'

'And the Mediterranean?'

'In the Med,' he declared with a smile, 'West is worst, centre is good, East is best!'

I looked forward to seeing if he was right.

His yacht, which he built himself in the Isle of Man, was based on the same design as the *Spray*, the boat Joshua Slocum sailed in the first single-handed voyage round the world. Small boats can go far.

We did not tarry, for there were no noteworthy megalithic sites in the vicinity. It was becoming notably hotter and shoals of sardines flashed in the clear green sea. We sailed between the beckoning island of Berlenga with its gulls, puffins and cormorants and the rocky Cabo Carvoeiro. The coastline then rose steadily to form a plateau inland of Cabo da Roca, the most westerly point of Europe and another key landmark in our voyage.

After this point the land dropped steeply to a low headland at the wide estuary of the Tagus, one of the great rivers of the world. After passing the Boca do Infierno or 'Mouth of Hell', which can boom and send spray high into the screaming wind but on that day was as quiet as a mouse, we anchored off Cascais, an expensive suburb of Lisbon.

Lisbon has, of course, many ancient maritime connections, from its megalithic, Phoenician and then Roman roots. The florid white limestone fortress of the Torre de Belém on the northern shore of the Tagus was the last landmark for the early Portuguese explorers who were the first Europeans to see South America and South Africa, and to find the passage to India.

Lisbon contains an interesting but small archaeological museum which mentions Portugal's megalithic past, and a maritime museum which covers traditional sailing craft. Both are housed in the west wing of the Mosteiro dos Jerónimos, the city's most famous monument. The monastery was built on the site of the chapel founded by Prince Henry the Navigator in memory of Vasco da Gama and his successful journey to India. This vast limestone building is another superb example of Portuguese Baroque architecture.

Ancient remains abound round Lisbon. There are many rock-cut tombs made from around 4000 to 2000 BC, and interesting rock art is to be found near the Tagus at Vila Velha de Rodâo. Along the banks of the river there are also many Copper Age tombs, such as the one at Vila Nova de São Pedro, which contain dark brown pots known locally as *copos*. They are ornamented with channelled decorations which are very similar to those on pots found in Anatolia and the Aegean in the Early Bronze Age. They are usually hemispherical but some have a flat base. This implies links with the Mediterranean, but what is more intriguing is that some of the pots' shape and decoration are strongly reminiscent of Grooved Ware found in Britain – another hint of strong links between Portugal and Britain at the beginning of the third millennium.[11]

Southeast of Lisbon there are several important megalithic sites near Évora which reveal a flourishing Stone Age civilization in Portugal. On the Guadiana river east of Évora is a well-known group of seven early round-chambered mounds. Their sides are made from large slabs up to 1.5 metres high, while their roofs, now collapsed, were probably corbelled with small stones rather than the more usual single capstone. Two of the *antas* near the river have dolmens built next to them of a later type – long, corbelled tombs – which may date from 3500 BC.

North and west of Évora there are two more famous large dolmens: Anta Grande and the Anta do Silval. The latter is a passage grave facing southeast, and topped with a capstone. Not far away, at Herdade dos Almendres, is one of the most impressive megalithic sites in the Iberian peninsula. Inhabited from the fifth to the third millennium BC, it has several rare stone circles which were at first single, then double. Some of the stones are decorated with chipped-out circles. Further southeast of Évora, there is an interesting cave at Escoural with paintings and carvings dating from the Palaeolithic era. It was also an important Neolithic necropolis, partially sealed off by a large stalagmite. And it was fortified during the Copper Age, when a megalithic burial chamber with a false cupola roof was built nearby.

The megaliths around Évora are among the earliest and most impressive in Europe.[12] Near the village of Reguengos de Monsaraz, grave goods (including pottery bowls, stone axes and flint blades) have been discovered in the Anta do Poço da Gateira. They have been dated to 4150 BC using thermoluminescence tests, which determine the age of old materials by the amount of phosphorence generated when gently heated. The goods were so arranged to suggest that there were twelve burials, but since the earth is acid and corrosive no human bones were found. The nearby Anta dos Gorginos has been dated to around 4440 BC; only the Kercado monument in Carnac has given an earlier date.[13] So while the megalithic phenomenon did not necessarily begin in Portugal, it saw one of the earliest flowerings of its extraordinary architecture and art.

CHAPTER FIFTEEN

Eastward Bound

The Kinetic cape, where the starry light dims, rises loftily as Europe's last post, only to lose itself in the salty waters of the monster-filled oceans.

RUFUS FESTUS AVIENUS

The colourful fishing boats heading out to sea from the Tagus reminded me of a voyage I had undertaken from Lisbon nine years earlier. I had first sailed on board the *Boa Esperança*, a replica of the caravels used by early Portuguese explorers. I then transferred to a Moroccan trawler followed by a series of working boats until I returned seven months later, having circumnavigated Africa.[1] Then I was a passenger; now it was good to be the skipper of my own boat, however small and vulnerable. And it was good to experience the sea as the ancient mariners had – to feel the wind on the nape of my neck and to balance my body against the rolling deck in the long Atlantic swell.

We left Cascais for Sines further south, in the Baía de Setúbal. It was a clear morning, but thick fog soon descended in the Tagus estuary. As we slowly edged our way forwards, we could hear the great ships blasting their foghorns all around us. It was eerie and very disconcerting. Having no radar we could not see them; I simply hoped they could see us before running us down.

The fog eventually lifted after lunch and we sailed down the Costa Azul, the Blue Coast of Portugal, in bright sunshine with a fair wind. By nightfall we had reached the entrance of Sines after passing a long stretch of sandy shore. It was difficult again to escape signs of that cruel and intrepid mariner Vasco da Gama. Sines was, in fact, his birthplace, and the crescent beach below the small castle was named after the first European to find a way around South Africa to reach India. It was a good departure point for sailing down to the infamous Cabo de São Vicente or Cape St Vincent, respected by all mariners ancient and modern for its strong winds and treacherous currents.

We made good progress from Sines in a steadily strengthening wind. By late afternoon, we could make out the sheer brown cliffs of the notorious Cape, the most southwesterly point of Europe, which dropped 100 metres into the roaring Atlantic surf. Its tall lighthouse had helped guide countless ships into the funnel between Europe and Africa which led to the Strait of Gibraltar and the Mediterranean beyond. It was not long before we began to pitch and roll in the breaking waves of a 3-metre swell; one or two unceremoniously broke over our cockpit and soaked us. I wondered how the Stone Age mariners would have managed. Very well, no doubt, if the experience and example of the Irish Aran islanders, facing the Atlantic rollers in their buoyant curraghs, is anything to go by.

As we swept around the cape, the wind whipped round the headland and I had to reef the sails down hard. We were soon running in front of the wind with virtually bare poles. Spray swept across the tops of the foaming waves and the winds gusted to more than 50 knots, the strength of a severe gale. I decided to seek shelter round the next headland. As I put the tiller hard over to starboard, nothing happened. I immediately thought that I had lost my steering, but I then realized that it was the strength of the wind on the hull pushing us to leeward. I resigned myself to the possibility of being blown down towards Africa. But slowly, inch by inch, *Celtic Gold* began to turn, and then suddenly we were sailing into the shelter of the bay. I anchored just under a sheer cliff in shallow water, safe and sound after a hard day's sail.

The sacred promontory

The Roman writers of antiquity, such as Pliny the Elder, called Cape St Vincent the Promontorium Sacrum, the sacred promontory. Drawing on information from the Greek geographer Artemidorus of Ephesus, who visited the place around 100 BC, Strabo refers to the Cape St Vincent in his *Geography* (circa 28 BC) as a place of holy rites. Strabo recorded that worshippers would 'turn over' – perhaps walk round – stones that were placed in groups of three and four.[2] For this ceremony, they brought their own water and did not stay overnight on the site as this was the time when the gods assembled there. Considering the many megaliths found in the area, it is quite possible that some cult involving the stones had continued down the ages from Neolithic times.

The fourth-century AD Latin poet Rufus Festus Avienus speaks of the cape as rising 'loftily as Europe's last post, only to lose itself in the salty waters of the monster-filled oceans'.[3] He mentions that the cape was dedicated to *sacra Saturni*, possibly referring to the Phoenician god Baal Hammon. The Phoenician link is confirmed by the first-century AD Hispanic author Pomponius Mela, who mentions in his *De Chorographia* (circa 41) a village called Portus Hannibalis on the Promontorium Sacrum, named after the famous third-century BC Phoenician general from Carthage who took on the might of the Roman Empire and managed to get his elephants and men over the Alps. As late as the sixteenth century the cape was known as Terçanabal, possibly a corruption of the Arabic *tarf anabal*, meaning 'the cape of Hannibal'. The Phoenicians, of course, reached as far north as Brittany, Cornwall and Ireland as early as the fifth century BC in their pursuit of tin and gold, following routes already opened up by the megalithic sailors.

There's no doubt that for thousands of years crews had climbed the promontory and prayed to their gods before venturing forth into the unknown and endless seas of the Atlantic. Both the Moors and the Christians considered it a sacred place and made pilgrimages to it. Even today it has a very special atmosphere, placed as it is on the windswept edge of Europe, close to Africa but facing 3000 miles of open sea to the Americas.

The first navigation school

We had in fact anchored immediately under the fortress at Sagres, right at the tip of the cape, which was reputed to be the site of Henry the Navigator's navigation school. The following morning, we sailed around the next rocky headland in near-gale force winds and anchored in the harbour of Baleeira, the port for Sagres. The strong winds continued to blow for days on end, so much so that in the end I put in ear plugs to reduce the incessant howling. The only other sailing boat anchored in the bay was owned by a Canadian who had sailed from Vancouver. In the previous week he had recorded winds gusting up to 67 knots.

Sagres was the last 'sheltered' port, where shipping from the Mediterranean would put in before setting out into the open Atlantic.

It was also the first for the mariners, like myself from the north, looking for refuge after sailing down the exposed coast of Portugal and round the formidable cape. It was a place where seafarers of all ages would take shelter and wait for favourable winds. And for thousands of years, fisherman would perch on perilous cliff ledges like seagulls, plucking fish from the crashing surf off the Atlantic rollers below.

It was the second time that I had visited the fortress at Sagres. It is is set on a wild escarpment covered with jagged outcrops and coarse vegetation, constantly buffeted by the wind. I could see the sheer cliffs of Cape St Vincent from its ramparts and shuddered at the thought of being swept upon their rocks. I gave thanks for our safe arrival in a small, salty chapel, the very opposite of the ornate opulence of the Cathedral of Santiago de Compostela at the other end of the Iberian Peninsula. I was fascinated to learn that a former Devon neighbour of mine, Sir Francis Drake, had personally led the attack and occupied the fortress in 1587 as part of his campaign to harry the supply lines of the Armada. Further havoc was wrought on the site in 1755 by an earthquake and tidal wave which destroyed much of Lisbon.

I admired once again in the central courtyard of the fortress the huge mysterious circle with radial lines running from its centre. It was about 40 metres in diameter and made from unhewn stones placed on the ground. Although coins from the sixteenth century have been discovered on the site, it probably dates from much earlier. It would appear to be intended as a sundial used in conjunction with a vertical gnomon.[3] For me, it had strong echoes of megalithic circles like Stonehenge, which were used in a similar way.

The so-called 'navigation school' at Sagres, allegedly the first in Europe, was probably more of an informal meeting place than an academy for seafarers to share their knowledge and experience and to discuss the finer points of navigation. And thereby it carried on a tradition which had been established in megalithic times.

The first inhabitants

There are traces of very ancient settlements in the southwestern Algarve. Going by the findings from some shallow graves, they go back to the Palaeolithic era, when Europe was connected to Africa by an isthmus. Since it is now well established that humans first evolved in Africa and spread out to populate the world, they would inevitably have come by this route as well as through the Middle East. In the Santo valley at Sagres, excavations have also revealed rich pottery remains dating from the Mesolithic. But the Neolithic produced the greatest remains still standing.

We walked the 7 kilometres from Sagres across rough rolling countryside to a sleepy town on a hill close to the Atlantic Ocean – Vila do Bispo. On the way, we passed a few silent homesteads, surrounded by clumps of bamboo and fig trees. Cows with bells around their necks tried to graze on the parched and barren land. Yet it was a fine place for menhir-hunting, cooled by a sea breeze and freshened by the clean smell of wild fennel under the wide open sky.

There is an extraordinary concentration of menhirs around Vila do Bispo in the Monte dos Amantes area. Their conical shapes were hewn and carved out of the local white limestone. Dating from 4000 to 3000 BC, they tended to be raised on conspicuous sites in the shallow bottoms of valleys or on the low hills. There is, for example, a fine hilltop menhir called Pedra Escorregadia. Carved at the base of this well-known landmark is a series of ellipses running from a central axis. There are not only two other decorated menhirs nearby, but also a collective burial chamber excavated in 1994. It consists of eight stone slabs with a metre-long central corridor facing southeast. It held ten bodies but few artefacts have been found. It was used over 500 years from the late Neolithic to the Bronze Age.

Not far away stand the remains of more than forty menhirs. Some formed part of two circles, rare for Portugal and Spain. The smaller, oval in shape, was 35 metres long and 26 wide. One stone is decorated with wavy lines, like the serpents I had seen on the stones in Carnac. Along the horizon there were outlying menhirs which may have been used as markers for astronomical alignments. The most striking, however, is an immense broken menhir near the top of a hill which looks like a giant's petrified penis, with a crown of half circles surrounding the glans. Many other menhirs around Vila do Bispo are decorated with a similar pattern, which suggests that they may have been erected in the Bronze Age by a patriarchal people who replaced the earlier cult of the Great Goddess with their male sun gods.

The catalogue of Portugal's National Museum of Archaeology and Ethnology in Lisbon makes no bones about the symbolism of the menhirs: they are 'undoubtedly phallic, plain or decorated with symbolic motifs that evoke life-giving energies and the myth of regeneration.'[4]

The word *amantes* means 'lovers', and the valley is so named because in the winter the mandrake flowers there. Since ancient times, this plant has been thought to have aphrodisiacal powers because of its roots, which resemble the human body. In the spring, the phallic menhirs are surrounded by a carpet of flowers, including the *Paeonia lusitanica* brought back from West Africa by the early explorers. It is indeed a seductive and beautiful place, conducive to the taking of love potions.

Most of the menhirs come in groups of twos and threes, but near the village of Raposeira further east, one has as many as twenty-one menhirs, some of which are decorated. A few, as at Ladeiras, reach 2.5 metres high. But there are not only menhirs in the region. Further east again, Bronze Age burial sites consisting of chambers made from sandstone slabs have been found at Almedeninha e Figueira near the village of Budens. They show that the area was continuously inhabited for thousands of years.

While a few of the sites are well indicated, we spent hours being scratched by rough gorse, heather, blackberry briars and sea holly looking for the outlying menhirs around Vila do Bispo. But it was a very memorable day, and well worth the effort. Thorns weren't the only impediment, however. Many of the stones have fallen or been deliberately pushed over. Ever since the Council of Nantes in 658 AD, which ordered menhirs to be destroyed or buried underground in an effort to root out pagan rituals, fanatical Christians have been at work in the Algarve, as they have elsewhere in Europe.

The Algarve

Both weather and sea changed perceptively after we left Sagres and Cape St Vincent. The Atlantic swell gradually diminished, the tidal streams weakened, the winds abated and, above all, it grew hotter. There was a lovely rush, gush and slap of water as we cut through the small, playful waves glittering in the sun. For the first time for weeks, we were able to put all our sails out.

We were definitely approaching North Africa and the Mediterranean. But it was a safe coast to cruise, for the harbours along the Algarve and southwestern Andalucia are sheltered from all but the infrequent southerly winds.

The Algarve, the most southerly stretch of Portugal's coastline, is Arabic for 'the West'. It was so named by the Moors who lived there for 500 years from the eighth century. It is a beautiful coastline, its sandy beaches a magnet for northern sun worshippers. And because it is still washed by the plankton-rich waters of the Atlantic, the ancient tradition of inshore fishing continues. On our way, we saw several groups of dolphins rounding up shoals of fish to feed on.

Portimão was our first port of call. It has long been a stopping-off point on the maritime routes from the Mediterranean to North Europe. Like the lost village on Cape St Vincent, it too has been identified with the Portus Hannibalis mentioned by Pomponius Mela.

Portimão stands on the wide estuary of the Arade river up which Phoenicians, Greeks, Romans, Normans and Moors have sailed in the wake of the megalithic seafarers to trade with or conquer the ancient city of Silves. Not far inland at Alcalar there is an important and well-managed site dating from the Stone Age and the Copper Age. There is a necropolis with some eighteen graves of several types, ranging from megalithic chambers to tombs with false cupolas and side alcoves. There is another burial ground nearby at Monte Canelas.

Travelling inland from the coast, we found the rolling countryside to be much more fertile than around Sagres. In the groves among the well-tended fields, olives, oranges and almonds ripened in the hot sun. An old Algarve legend says that a king once married a princess from northern Europe and when she complained of missing the snow of her native country, he planted almond trees all over the Algarve so that she could enjoy their thick white blossom in winter.

The less said about Vilamoura the better, except that it had echoes of that Old Testament city, Gomorrah. We passed the gap in the low-lying dunes at Cabo de Santa María which leads to the lagoons and channels round Faro, one of the main ports for the early Portuguese explorers. We also ventured up the channel to the unspoilt fishing town of Tavira near the Spanish border. Set among salt pans, it is thronged with a profusion of egrets, herons, storks and other birds. It is a very old town: one of its bridges is said to have been built by the Romans, while the only Greek inscription found in Portugal was discovered at nearby Santa Luzia.

As we were swinging at anchor one night in the river under a full moon, the sound of drumming came across the salt pans, merging with the gurgling and slapping of the ebb tide. I could have been in Africa, up the Congo, listening to pagan rites or back in megalithic times when the worship of the Great Goddess would have reached its zenith as her silver symbol in the night sky shone at its brightest.

Atlantis and the Phoenicians

Further along the Andalusian coast from Tavira lies the port of Huelva on the Río Tinto, now a city of oil refineries and heavy industry but once the departure point for Columbus's voyage in 1492 'across the ocean blue'. It may well have been the site of the ancient city of Tartessus, established in the eighth century BC, whose wealth and sophistication were so admired by ancient Greek writers. Around 600 BC, the inhabitants are thought to have blocked the Strait of Gibraltar to protect the local silver deposits and to monopolize the rich mineral resources which lay to the north. They exported the metals to their markets in the Middle East, particularly Syria. The trade was not only one way: Greek and Etruscan ceramics have been found in southern Spain dating from about the same time.

It is thought that Phoenicians from Carthage took over and destroyed Tartessus around 500 BC. At the same time, the Phoenician explorer Himilco sailed from here up the Iberian coast and across the Bay of Biscay to reach Armorica – now Brittany – where he described the skin-covered curraghs still in use in the region. Another great Phoenician navigator, Hanno, sailed from here in 425 BC down the coast of West Africa as far as Cameroon where he described its active volcano.

Clearly, Huelva was an important trading centre from antiquity. A cemetery of nineteen tombs from Phoenician times on the hill of La Joya above Huelva has yielded a rich assemblage of grave goods in gold, bronze and alabaster, all with strong eastern Mediterranean influences. An even older and more fascinating find was brought up from the mud of the harbour, probably originating from a sunken ship. Dating from the late Bronze Age, the hoard contained spears cast in the British Isles, brooches from Sicily and many swords and ornaments from the Atlantic seaboard. It all confirms the existence of ancient long-distance trading links between northwestern Europe and the Mediterranean.

The German archaeologist Adolf Schulten believed that Plato's description of Atlantis drew on an imaginative picture of the rich and fortunate city of Tartessus, which he placed further east near the mouth of the Guadalquivir river.[5] Certainly in the first mention of the myth in Plato's *Timaeus*, the Egyptian priest who narrates the story to the Greek legislator Solon says that the Atlanteans, from their base in the 'outer ocean', entered the Mediterranean and 'attempted to enslave, at a single stroke, your country [Greece] and ours [Egypt] and all the territory within the strait . . . which you call (so you say) the pillars of Heracles'.[6]

The destruction of Tartessus by the Carthaginians was, according to Schulten, the equivalent of the sinking of Atlantis in 'a sea of mud'. I do not, however, find the case convincing. Solon brought the story back from Egypt in 560 BC, before the alleged disappearance of Tartessus in 500 BC. Moreover, many classical authors mention

Tartessus as being in existence after 500 BC, including Rufus Festus Avienus in his book *Ora Maritima*, which was based on a lost Greek pilot book known as a *periplus*.

In their long-distance voyages, the Phoenicians used the wooden *hippoi*, an ancient craft common in the Mediterranean. It had two raised ends and a carved horse's head in the bows (*hippos* in Greek means 'horse'). The geographer Euxodus, during his second return voyage to India about 112 BC, found on the shores of what is now Somalia, near Cape Guardafui, the wooden prow of a ship with a horse's head. It originally came from the ancient city of Gades in southern Spain. The implication is that it had sailed around the Cape of Good Hope in the opposite direction from the Phoenicians, who had left the Red Sea and come back via the Pillars of Hercules around 500 BC. A silver brooch from the seventh century BC found at Aliseda in Spain depicts a horse-headed, double-ended craft just like the *hippoi*.

There may well be a direct link between the *hippoi* and the ships of the Veneti, who later took on the might of the Roman Navy off Brittany. A gold coin from Gaul, dated to about 100 BC and now in France's Bibliothèque Nationale in Paris, depicts a chariot driver holding up a model ship. It not only has a mast with a yard amidships, but the upright stem and stern have horned animal heads, giving it a strong resemblance to the *hippoi*.[7] And the seafarers of the *hippoi* were simply carrying on a much older tradition of sailing which went back to megalithic times.

After sailing across the wide Golfo de Cádiz, I went up the mouth of the Guadalete river to El Puerto de Santa María, the point of export for the best Andalusian sherry and, in ancient times, for minerals, olive oil and wool. It is opposite the great port of Cádiz, which is usually taken to be the ancient harbour of Gades, sometimes also called Gadir. After being driven from Sicily by the Romans, a force of Carthaginians under the general Hamilcar Barca – Hannibal's father – established itself in Gadir in 237 BC. From there they captured and held the south of Spain until 206 BC, when the Romans finally took over the city.

The shelter at Cádiz, before and after sailing through the Pillars of Hercules, would have been much appreciated by the megalithic seafarers going to and from the Mediterranean. It was from here that Columbus made his second voyage to America. For centuries, it handled nearly all of Spain's trade with the New World: its resplendent Baroque buildings, which include the Santa Cruz church with its gold-covered dome, are the result. Its beautiful botanical gardens by the sea have plants and trees brought by ships from all over the world. Walking around the heavily fortified near island, I thought again of Sir Francis Drake, who took advantage of the harbour's accessibility and 'singed the King of Spain's beard' with a daring raid which delayed the departure of the Armada for British waters.

The Pillars of Hercules

The prevailing winds along the southern coast of Iberia blow from the west and are known locally as the *poniente*. Since they were holding steady, I decided to sail directly from Cádiz to Gibraltar and into the Mediterranean without more ado.

The very mention of the word Trafalgar conjures up that key episode in British history, when Nelson defeated the French navy during the Napoleonic Wars. Although it figures so large in the imagination, in reality Cape Trafalgar is just a long sandy spit. I kept clear of the dangerous banks and rocky shoals round the lighthouse; in heavy weather, the sea breaks and a race can form eight miles offshore here. Although northwestern Scotland makes a similar claim, this section of the coast is reputed to be the windiest place in Europe. Certainly the windmills in the hills beyond the flat cape were making the best of it as we sailed by.

As soon as we had turned Cape Trafalgar, the winds began to change. I had carefully calculated the tides to get their maximum help to pass through the Strait of Gibraltar; to go against them would have been impossible in any small boat. The ancient mariners would have had to do the same, and stay wary of the wind too. East of Cádiz the wind effect of the Strait of Gibraltar, with its narrow channel and steep-sided mountains, becomes more pronounced. Most of the winds are either the westerly *poniente* or the east-northeast *levanter*. We had started with the *poniente*, but now it seemed that a *levanter* was about to begin. This was the last thing I wanted. It can blow up to 60 knots and last several days, with visibility dropping in the warm drizzle to a mile or less.

There is a permanent east-going current through the Strait which effectively makes up the water loss in the Mediterranean through evaporation, but the tidal streams on the surface can run up to 4 knots in each direction. With wind against tide, the waves can quickly build up. Since I was well underway and reluctant to turn back for Cádiz, I decided to press on.

After a while, I began to see yachts sailing from the Mediterranean taking advantage of the wind, which had turned in their favour. The waves increased as we headed into the narrow stretch of water which cuts Europe off from Africa, about the same width as the Straits of Dover separating Britain from the continent.

I thought again of the Greek navigator and geographer Pytheas of Massalia, who had sailed through the Strait some time before 320 BC and reached Brittany, Cornwall and possibly Scotland. As I have mentioned, he was the first to introduce astronomical observation and mathematical calculations into geography. His major work *Periton Okeanou* or *On the Ocean* has been lost, but many ancient authors quoted from it. He is said to have travelled to the regions where the longest days last seventeen or eighteen hours, and commented: 'the barbarians showed me the sleeping place of the sun'.[8] I suspect that his land of the Hyperboreans was none other than the island of Lewis in the Outer Hebrides, where I had begun my voyage.

At Tarifa, which claims to be the board-sailing capital of Europe, the only other yacht going with me in an easterly direction gave up the struggle and took shelter behind the small island just off the town. Strong winds funnelled down the mountains and through the strait. It was already dusk but since we were still making some headway, I decided to continue. The currents around the Isla de Tarifa swirled and turned the boat, but we just managed to get through. We headed for the steep cliffs of southern Europe, where the wind was not so strong and the water not so rough. Since the tidal stream turns earlier closer to the coast, I was able to get the benefit of an east-going tide. Eventually, after many more hours of hard sailing, we reached an open bay. Beyond it the Rock of Gibraltar loomed like a great ship in the night.

It was another major turning point in my long voyage. Sailing from the cold grey waters of northern Scotland, after more than 2300 nautical miles I had finally reached the threshold of the Mediterranean. To my own satisfaction at least, I had proved that there was no reason why the ancient mariners should not have done likewise.

CHAPTER SIXTEEN

Mediterranean Spain

An immense and unbeatable museum of prehistory and protohistory.

LUIS SIRET

The Pillars of Hercules, as the ancient Greeks called the two rocks on either side of the Strait of Gibraltar, were the limit of the known world to the seafarers of the eastern Mediterranean. But the envoys of the megalithic civilization that stretched down the Atlantic seaboard penetrated the western Mediterranean along the south Spanish coast and visited the North African shore.

The museum in Gibraltar shows that 'the Rock' has been inhabited since prehistoric times. In St Michael's Cave there is a large natural grotto which was once home to Neolithic inhabitants. In fact, southwestern Spain was one of the last strongholds of the Neanderthals. Recent research indicates that they disappeared from the rest of Europe between 40,000 and 35,000 years ago as a result of the immigration of people known as Cro-magnons with a fully modern anatomy from the Middle East.

A white-painted mosque and its tall minaret are prominently visible from the sea near the lighthouse of Europa Point, a reminder that the Rock of Gibraltar was occupied by the Moors in 711 AD; they remained for more than seven centuries. Indeed, its name derives from the name of the Arabic conqueror, Tariq. *Jebel Tariq* means 'Tariq's mountain'. The famous Barbary apes on the Rock are named after the Barbary coast of Algeria: here, not only does the Atlantic embrace the Mediterranean, but Europe faces Africa. And in megalithic times the two were united by the sea, not separated as now.

On leaving Gibraltar, I decided to hop from one Pillar of Hercules to the other. The passage from Gibraltar to Ceuta in Morocco is only about twenty nautical miles long, the same as the narrowest point of the English Channel. The crossing was perfect: the sky a light blue, the sea a deep azure, with a warm gentle breeze blowing from the west. Dolphins leaping with their young provided the entertainment; the great ships passing in either direction, the navigational challenge. When we reached Ceuta we found a rich mixture of Arab and Spanish – as perhaps mainland Spain would have been before the Christian reconquest. It was surrounded by mountains and hills, beyond which stretched the lone sands of the desert.

It is well known that there are many megalithic sites along the coast of North Africa and down West Africa as far as Senegal. The civilization of the megaliths, connected by sea, did not stop at the southern coast of Europe. I had lived in Senegal many years before, and knew of the necropolis at Sine-Ngayene in the southern part of the country, which is marked by circles and standing stones. Within each of the circles, a filled-in ditch contained the remains of successive Iron Age burials, but the practice was probably established much earlier in other parts along the coast.[1]

In Morocco, two extraordinary necropolises are to be found at the edge of the Sahara Desert close to the frontier with Algeria. The one at Foum al Rhjam, a mountain pass near a bend in the Drâa River, has many hundreds of tumuli. Most are simple cairns but on the highest places on the crests and tops of the mountains there are some intriguing ones with 'skylights'. They are too small for humans to pass through and some have been closed with a large flat stone. They have a clear view of the eastern horizon and most are oriented towards the southeast and the midwinter sunrise.[2]

In neighbouring Algeria, there is also an important group of dolmens at Beni-Messous, a dozen kilometres west of Algiers and a couple of kilometres from the sea. These simple dolmens with rectangular chambers, mostly facing the eastern horizon like the skylight tumuli in Morocco, probably date from around 1000 BC.

Religion and culture now form an almost inseparable barrier between southern Europe and North Africa, but in ancient times they were part of a common seaborne civilization along the coasts of the Mediterranean basin. Moreover, the ancient maritime connections between North Africa and northwestern Europe persisted until recent times. As late as 1631, pirates from Algiers sailed up to Baltimore in southern Ireland and took the entire population of 163 souls back with them to the Barbary coast. Around the same time, three Algerian ships sailed as far north as Iceland and left with 300 captives.[3] From a navigational point of view it would have been easy: after rounding Cape St Vincent, all you need do is follow the Pole Star until you hit Ireland.

We sailed back from Africa to the Costa del Sol of southern Spain, where the 'barbarian hordes' from the North come to worship the sun during the day and engage in wild rituals with loud music, hallucinatory drugs and intoxicating drinks during the night, no doubt just like their distant ancestors. We briefly visited the old fishing ports, now transformed into graceless and futuristic marinas, of Puerto de Fuengirola and Puerto de Benalmádena. The quiet fishing harbour of Puerto Caleta de Vélez, a little east of Málaga, was a welcome respite, with its unspoilt beaches where fishermen still push out their brightly painted wooden boats from the shore.

During our sail we came across yet more pods of dolphin, this time engaged in frenzied feeding, herding shoals of fish into ever-tightening circles. Like humans, they hunted the shoals of fish until they were all gone – only there are many more of us and we hunt the seas until they are exhausted. Earlier hunter-gatherers were fewer in number, lighter on the ground, and knew when to stop.

Antequera

We left the boat at Puerto Caleta de Vélez and travelled to Málaga. An ancient city originally called Malaca, it was founded by the Phoenicians as a trading station in the eighth century BC. Our destination, however, was inland up a river valley which leads to the dry plateau of the interior. We were heading for Antequera, some 35 kilometres north of Málaga on the rim of a fertile plain at the foot of the Sierra de los Torcales. The wheat had already been harvested and farmers were gathering in the onion fields among the groves of olives. Out of the golden plain rose a number of extraordinary eroded outcrops of calcareous rock which reminded me of the tors of Dartmoor in Devon. And on the outskirts of Antequera there are three huge megalithic monuments which really did seem to have been built by giants.

Two of these are to be found together among pine trees in an enclosed park on the eastern edge of this hilly town. The oldest, dating from the end of the Neolithic and the beginning of the Copper Age (around 2500 BC), is the Cueva de Menga, a magnificent mound containing a dolmen misleadingly called a *cueva* or cave. It was discovered in the seventeenth century and long thought to be a Druid temple.

A large oval chamber 25 metres long, the Cueva de Menga has a covered gallery which is slightly narrower at the entrance. The chamber is made up of massive square monoliths covered by gigantic slabs, so large that three extra pillars support them where they meet. The largest topstone weighs about 170 tonnes. Even the builders of the trilithons of Stonehenge would have been overawed by them. On one of the slabs, perhaps engraved after it was built, are carvings of a five-pointed star, a human-shaped figure and crosses.

The stones were originally separated from the bedrock by a technique I have already mentioned – knocking wooden wedges in cracks and then wetting them so that the slabs split off when the wood has expanded. Considerable engineering skill and a great deal of labour would have been involved in rolling them on thick tree trunks from the quarry to the chosen site. Trenches were then dug and the blocks raised by means of ropes. In order to set the covering slabs on, the internal space was probably filled with earth, forming a ramp up which they could be hauled into position; or else the slabs were progressively levered up on a wooden scaffold which was built higher as necessary.

The view from the top of the mound was spectacular in all directions. A surveyor friend of mine, Paul Green, who was with us at the site suddenly exclaimed: 'I'm feeling an overwhelming desire to build a trig point here!' The entrance to the dolmen is unusually oriented north of the midsummer sunrise, which implies that it is not astronomically aligned. Why then did the megalith builders take such care to position it where they did? All becomes clear if you follow the direction of the corridor: it is directly in line with an outcrop of rock on the horizon, which looks exactly like the head of a sleeping giant laid out on his back.

This spectacular outcrop is now called La Pena de los Amantes – the suffering of the lovers. A local story relates that a Christian girl fell in love with a handsome young Moor, and when her father forbade the match she threw herself off the rock to her death.

The second dolmen in the park outside Antequera is the Cueva de Viera, which takes its name from the two brothers who discovered it in 1905. It probably dates from around 2000 BC. There is a covered gallery made up of a 19-metre-long corridor which leads into a small square chamber with rounded edges, nearly 2 metres square. Set in the corridor close to the chamber entrance is a monolith with a small, square-framed opening. The slabs used are smaller than those of its neighbour. A section of the gallery's side walls, which are not exactly straight, points to the equinox sunrise.

But the most spectacular megalithic monument outside Antequera is the Cueva de Romeral. It is to be found 3 kilometres from the others, down a dusty track and around the back of a sprawling cement factory. The Restaurante del Dolmen on the nearby main road is much more frequented than this site. It is tragic that its original setting in a dramatic landscape was lost, especially since its builders had such a wonderful sense of place.

Despite its unfortunate position, it has rightly been called 'the grandest architectural achievement of Iberia in the late Neolithic period or early Copper Age'.[4] Although the date of the dolmen remains uncertain, it is thought to have been built around 1800 BC. Under a great tumulus 85 metres in diameter and once 10 metres high, there is a long access corridor which was formerly twice its present length of 14.5 metres. A framed door at the end leads into a large round chamber with a false cupola dome. From this, a short corridor leads into another, smaller circular chamber which was used for offerings. What makes Romeral unique amongst its sisters is that its internal walls were constructed entirely from small yellow stones. Large stones form the roof, with massive slabs placed on top of the chambers. The precision and beauty of the stone-walling reminded me of Maes Howe in Orkney, but Romeral faces due south to the midday sun, not to the midwinter sunrise.

The Cueva de Menga and the Cueva de Viera are usually called burial chambers, but the doors into the chambers suggest that they were used repeatedly for religious rites and not just for the burial of the dead. The Cueva de Romeral in particular feels like an underground chapel with its additional small chamber. It remains a mystery why the local megalith builders should have built such huge chambers so close to each other over a period of eight centuries and yet left nothing else in the area. A sign at the site in English reads: 'They are mad by using big stones.' If they were, it was an inspired folly.

When I asked two young women who were 'restoring' one of the monuments what they thought of the civilization which built them, one of them replied: 'We know nothing about it. We are just restorers.' They could not even recommend a book about them in the town's library. I hoped they knew what they were doing to some of the most spectacular monuments of Europe's lost civilization.

I did track down a local leaflet that recognized the strong sense of cooperation among all the individuals who built the dolmens, but provided no evidence for its claim that this society was 'based on chiefs or the overriding authority of certain individuals who coordinated and directed the work'. I had come across the same unfounded prejudice, reflecting our own stratified society, in the works of many archaeologists throughout Europe. Despite the obstruction of a cement factory and a nearby petrol station, at least the local town council of Antequera calls its three dolmens 'the most important megalithic complex in Europe'. This is an exaggeration, but they are undoubtedly the most impressive megalithic monuments to be found on Spanish soil.

Los Millares

Back on board *Celtic Gold*, we embarked to sail further down the Costa del Sol to Motril, a small fishing harbour which had developed into a large commercial port for Granada, and then on to Aguadulce, a little man-made harbour under a great cliff next to the old city of Almería. This fine city of wide palm-lined pavements, still resplendent from its wealthy colonial past, is situated close to the river Andarax. From the large commercial port, ferries regularly sail to the Spanish enclave of Melilla in Morocco, on the north coast of Africa.

From Almería, we travelled some 17 kilometres up the valley of the river Andarax towards Santa Fé de Mondújar, where a sensational megalithic site from the Copper Age can be seen nearby. Los Millares lies on the spur of a plateau protected by a ravine on one side and by a steep cliff which drops down to the riverbed of the Andarax, which would have been navigable in ancient times. For nearly 1000 years, from 2700 to 1800 BC, a large settlement of pastoralists flourished here thanks to the once-fertile land and abundant game. With the copper mines of the Sierra de Gádor nearby, they pioneered the introduction of copper smelting in the western Mediterranean. Prospectors had been searching for the ore in Europe as early as the fourth millennium.

The site was first explored in 1891 by the Belgian engineer Luis Siret after it had been disturbed by a railway company. In the 1950s it was more widely excavated. It is now a well-managed site with a little museum. Some of its most important finds have been taken to the library of the University of Almería.

At first glance the site looks chaotic, with mounds, ditches, holes, scattered rocks and half-collapsed walls littering the forbidding landscape. The only life seems to reside in the odd swallowtail butterfly flitting over the piles of dry and broken stones. Our feet raised dust wherever we walked. It is difficult to imagine that 4000 years earlier it had been a thriving township in a green and fertile land. But as we continued to walk, a pattern gradually emerged. It had clearly been a strongly defended site. Indeed, the site boasts the longest wall of the European Copper Age, stretching some 310 metres across the exposed western side of the spur.

In the middle of the wall, much of which is still standing, is a well-fortified gateway behind a ditch. It is flanked by bastions, and at a later date two barbicans were added with loopholes, that is, small slits set in the walls probably used for archers or guards. But this is not all: the settlement was protected by four lines of thick walls, some with circular turrets. It even boasts a dozen fortified outposts with two bastioned walls, strategically located on a series of hilltops and ridges to survey and guard the approaches. Clearly the inhabitants lived in turbulent times, and felt the need to protect their valuable copper industry from the seafarers and traders who travelled along the coast. Yet surprisingly enough, there are no signs of war here. Even the outlying fortresses, which were protected by a 6-metre ditch and two walls with six bastions each, doubled up as granaries and mills. Water was brought down to them by a canal from faraway springs.

The whole complex of more than 5 hectares shows a highly sophisticated megalithic society; indeed, it might not be too far-fetched to talk of Los Millares as having the status of a megalithic town.

Within the third wall, I came across a silo, the remains of a large rectangular building 12 metres long, and a metal workshop. Scattered around its hearth abundant copper workings and mineral residues have been found. The space within the fourth wall was the first to be settled and the last to be abandoned. It seems the settlement expanded out from here. The detritus from the site contains evidence that there were at least five phases of occupation.

The inhabitants lived in round stone huts 4 to 6 metres in diameter and probably covered in thatch or turf. They contained sherds of pottery, handmills and even a cheese maker. One famous piece of pottery has at its base *ojos soles* – eyes with solar rays fanning out from them – below a chevron design in the middle and dots around the rim.

I was astonished to find that this same eye motif is to be found on pottery from a vessel found in a Danish passage grave dating to about 2000 BC. Even the number and arrangement of the 'sun rays' or 'eyelashes' which go out from each eye are exactly the same.[5] They are no doubt depictions of the 'owl' eyes of the Great Goddess who was still worshipped throughout Europe at the time, despite the growing influence of the patriarchal Beaker culture and its sun gods.

The inhabitants of Los Millares were involved primarily in agriculture, growing barley, wheat and vegetables and herding sheep, pigs and goats. They also continued to hunt deer and wild boar. But it was smelting copper and shaping it into adornments, utensils, tools and weapons which made them prosperous.

The settlement also had an immense necropolis unparalleled for its age, consisting of more than 100 beehive tombs, usually with one central chamber but some with lateral ones. These were sited outside the walls on the plateau towards the east. It would seem that each contained the ancestors of a particular clan.

Most of the tombs are now decayed, but one that has been reconstructed shows the general design: a corridor leading to an inner chamber lined with more slabs. It has a corbelled vault made from smaller stones which makes it resemble the Mycenaean *tholos*, except that it was built much earlier. The whole was covered by a tumulus of stonework and earth, and outside there was a courtyard where funeral rites would have taken place.

I found the most interesting features, however, were the three slabs placed across the corridor with hollowed-out 'portholes'. Climbing through them on bended knees felt like going through a passage to another world. I also felt that I was somehow passing into a womb – the inner chamber. Sitting at its centre, I strongly sensed the presence of these remarkable people who took so much care of their dead.

All cultures have recognized that birth and death are difficult journeys. The ancients of Los Millares knew that it is important to be well prepared and equipped. Having lost their flesh, the bones of the deceased were carefully buried a second time in the foetal position, accompanied by jars, utensils and tools. Virtually all the tombs face towards the east and may possibly be aligned with distant mountain peaks. After studying their orientations, Hoskin found that only six out of sixty-six faced outside the range of sunrise.[6] And sunrise is universally associated with rebirth and new life.

The 'Millarian' culture reached much of southeastern Spain. As the first excavator of Los Millares, Luis Siret observed, all the region needs is 'a roof to make it into an immense and unbeatable museum of prehistory and protohistory'.[7]

The White Coast

After Los Millares, we headed up the east coast of Spain towards Cataluña. Here, around Gerona, a megalithic culture which left many dolmens had developed. But for now we enjoyed the gentle breeze and the warm, clear, deep-blue waters as we sailed up the rugged coastlines of the Costa Calida and the Costa Blanca with its light-grey rock and small coves. We rounded the magnificent Cabo de Gata and called in at the small picturesque fishing harbour of Garrucha before reaching the splendid port and naval base of Cartagena.

The city is protected by rugged mountains on all sides except for its narrow entrance. This 'New Carthage' was founded in 228 BC by Hasdrubal, Hannibal's brother, and became an important centre of Carthaginian influence in Europe. Hannibal used it as his base for his trek with elephants across the Alps to attack Rome. It is said that the disciple James also landed here in AD 36, bringing Christianity to Spain from Palestine. Although the Phoenicians regularly sailed the route, the legend that James completed the passage in four days is a little far-fetched. My old neighbour Drake turned up here yet again, stealing the city's cannon in 1585 and sailing away with them to Jamaica. If I had stayed, I was told that the hull of my boat would soon be covered in coral; I could hear the coral making a cracking sound in the water.

After Cabo de Palos, the still and sparkling inland waters of the Mar Menor enticed us, but we continued along what was now the Costa Blanca, with its broken cliffs and long sandy beaches. We anchored overnight in the wide harbour of Torrevieja, which has beaches on either side, and then passed next morning the old pirate base on the Isla de Tabarca. We sailed passed Alicante (another Phoenician city, occupied by the British as a mercantile colony in the eighteenth century) and Benidorm (a once small fishing harbour taken over by the British in the late twentieth century) to Calpe. Nestling under a spectacular rock just south of Cabo de la Nao, it too has Phoenician and no doubt megalithic foundations. On the way, I spotted a Westerly Centaur like my own boat – the only other I'd seen since leaving British waters – appropriately called *Perseverance*. I was not the only one to do long-distance navigation from northern Europe in a small yacht but, as the ancient mariners knew only too well, it certainly required stamina and determination.

From Cabo de la Nao, the coast turns northwest towards Barcelona. But our route lay elsewhere. From under the great sheltering rock of Calpe, I headed east across the open water to the Balearic Islands. Although I stayed over night at anchor in the wide sheltered creek of San Antonio in Ibiza, I did not linger there; like its smaller neighbour Formentera, it has no known megalithic sites. I hopped over to Andraitx on the rocky western tip of its larger neighbour Mallorca. It was only another day's sail to the capital Palma on the fertile south coast: a good place from which to explore the island's unique megalithic past.

CHAPTER SEVENTEEN

Islands in the Sun

The time for men to sail is fifty days
After the solstice, when the exhausting heat
Of summertime is over...
At this time winds are steady, and the sea
Untroublesome; so trust to the winds, and drag
Your swift ship to the sea with confidence.

HESIOD

A fter travelling along the Iberian coast, it was a delight to be island-hopping once again in the Balearics. The sandy beaches along the east coast of Mallorca contrasted strongly with the rocky coves and jagged cliffs of the northwest and southwest coasts. Inland, pine woods covered much of the hills and mountains, while vineyards, orange and olive groves were scattered among the terraced and care-fully cultivated fields. It was on a lovely human scale, easily traversed on foot or circumnavigated by boat. But then I was biased, for I have always had a love of islands, especially for those basking in the sun.

A unique megalithic culture developed in the Balearic Islands. Lightly established on Mallorca, it had its greatest flowering on the small easterly island of Menorca.

Settlers first arrived in the Balearics at the beginning of the fifth millennium BC: the earliest communities have been radio-carbon dated to 4900 BC. They lived in caves or in wooden huts. By the third millennium, they had begun to carve out caves to live in and bury their dead.[1] During this period the population was scattered lightly across Mallorca and Menorca, living in extended families within communities which had a strong egalitarian base.[2] Their principal diet was fish, although they also kept some sheep, pigs and cows. Their life expectancy was about thirty-five years. These seafaring people seem to have lived in peace; there are no signs of defensive fortifications around their settlements.[3]

They left little behind them except subterranean vaults and some unique stone structures built above ground and known locally as *navetas* (Catalan for 'boats'). On Mallorca, there is an extensive cluster of boat-shaped stone buildings about 18 metres long and 8 metres wide, to be found at Es Figueral de Son Real near the Badia d'Alcúdia. They date from 1700 to 1400 BC. Shorter ones can be seen at Closos de Can Gaià near Porto Colom on the southeast coast. It would seem that the navetas were used for burying the dead.

It seems that their builders had a sophisticated understanding of the movement of the stars and attached special meaning to the Southern Cross, which is close to the constellation of Centaurus. At Son Mas settlement near Valldemossa in the north of Mallorca, there is a huge boulder with a large groove on its side which looks man-made and points up a valley to the south. Around 2000 BC the hills on either side would have spectacularly framed the Southern Cross. Due to the phenomenon known as the precession of the equinoxes, caused by the slight wobble in the earth's axis, the lowest star of the cross would have disappeared from view around 1700 BC – exactly the time when radio-carbon dating of the site shows that it was abandoned.[4]

Only a few true dolmens from this period can be found in the Balearic Islands – four in Menorca and one in Mallorca at Son Bauló. The latter originally had a tumulus within a stone circle 6.5 metres wide, dating from 1750 BC. They may have been erected during the brief occupation of people from mainland Spain or southern France, who arrived some time before 2000 BC. The similar shape of the dolmens in these countries shows that they shared a common Neolithic civilization with the rest of Western Europe.

The Talayotic culture

The second phase in the prehistory of the Balearics is called the 'talayotic' period, named after its characteristic megalithic building, a round tower known locally as a *talaiot* (from the Arabic for 'watch tower'). They were built by a new wave of warrior people from around 1400 BC – a date coinciding with the Bronze Age.

Who were these people and where did they come from? It seems likely that they were among the so-called 'Sea Peoples' who attacked

Egypt in the twelfth century BC. They were known as the Shardana, probably came from Sardis in the eastern Mediterranean, and occupied Sardinia and southern Corsica not long before 1500 BC on their way to the Balearic Islands.[5] The traffic between these islands – only two days' sailing apart – undoubtedly went in both directions; within recorded history, there was a tribe called the Balari living in Sardinia. In any case the Shardana, in the words of Menorcan prehistorian Luis Casanovas Marqués, were a 'bellicose and organized people who dedicated themselves to piracy'.[6] They may well be represented by some remarkable bronze statues of nude warriors with lances which have been found on Mallorca among the bronze horns and heads of bulls.[7]

There can be no doubt that the arrival of these warlike people with their bronze weapons brought about a profound change to the Neolithic population of the Balearics. As they came from the east, they settled first on Menorca and then went over to the eastern part of Mallorca. They soon began constructing talayot towers within the defensive ramparts of their settlements.

What was immediately apparent was that these megaliths were different from any we'd seen along the Atlantic seaboard and southern Iberian coast. The stones are much rougher, fashioned from local limestone. Rather than large stone slabs placed one on top of the other, the central Mediterranean method of construction generally consists of irregular blocks forming walls and corbelled vaulting. They are known as examples of so-called Cyclopean architecture, which is characterized by large, undressed blocks of stone. The term comes from the mythical Cyclopes, a race of fearsome giants with a single eye in the middle of their foreheads whom Ulysses encountered during his *Odyssey*.

The talayots – circular towers made from such rough blocks of limestone – were the most significant buildings of Menorcan and Mallorcan prehistory, and continued to be occupied until the Roman conquest in 123 BC. This means that the Balearics were the last place in Europe to have an unbroken tradition of megalith building. The mounds, now generally eroded to between 8 and 10 metres high, were usually built on high ground with clear views of the surrounding countryside. They usually had a corridor and central chamber like a tumulus in northern Europe.

Their exact purpose, however, remains a mystery. Their commanding position implies that they were primarily built for defensive purposes, but they may also have had a symbolic role. Erected at a time of rapidly expanding population and growing conflict, they may have acted as territorial markers for a particular clan and provided a focus for their social and religious activities. Perhaps the settlements were caught up in rivalry with their neighbours, rather like the statue carvers of Easter Island, with each community trying to outdo the others with their towers. At the same time, they could have provided a platform for observing the movement of the heavenly bodies. The fact that entrances to the settlements are invariably from the north and the entrances to the talayots face south suggests that the people who built them had a strong sense of astronomical alignments.

Only a few talayot sites are to be found in Mallorca, mainly in the south and east. As I've noted, on its smaller neighbour Menorca many more survive – more than 200, in fact. From the summit of one, it is even possible to see eight others in the surrounding countryside. Moreover, Menorca developed a unique structure known as a *taula* – an immediately recognizable T-shaped megalith erected within a sanctuary. The island undoubtedly possesses the most striking and memorable megalithic monuments on Spanish soil.

The windy isle

Menorca is known as the 'windy isle'. It is regularly buffeted during the winter by strong northerly winds from the Golfe du Lion. In the summer, it is generally calm. In Palma, the capital of Mallorca, I was joined by my 20-year-old son Dylan and we sailed first to the wide, shallow Porto Colom and then across the sea to Mahón in Menorca. The weather was so settled that I could pull him behind me in the warm, limpid waters on a rope.

Menorca is a sailor's paradise. It has splendid sheltered creeks known as *calas*, carved out during the Ice Age. The capital Mahón also boasts the best natural harbour in the western Mediterranean. The British seized it in the eighteenth century to use it as a naval base – as the Romans, Greeks, Phoenicians, Bronze Age seafarers and megalith settlers had done before them.

The northern part of Menorca is rugged and infertile, while much of the southern areas, where most of the megalithic sites are to be found, consist of sedimentary rock from the Tertiary era, with Miocene limestone forming the largest part. It not only provides the best soil, but the bedrock is also easy to cut out to form caves, underground cisterns and houses.

I started my exploration of Menorca at the necropolis at Cales Coves in the southeastern part of the island, where two glacial ravines

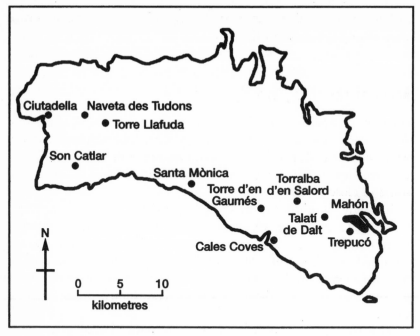

Map of Menorca, with the principal megalithic sites and modern towns

meet. They form a beautiful creek where sailing boats have anchored from megalithic times. Divers have recovered a pottery figure of the Phoenician fertility goddess Tanit from the seabed, which is now held in the Menorca Museum in Mahón.

The limestone cliffs around the creek have more than 100 caves which were dug out from the end of the third millennium BC, first for living in and then as communal tombs. The earlier ones have rectangular doors and occasionally rectangular windows. The typical chamber is one large circular room no more than 2 metres high and about 10 metres in diameter. Some of the larger ones have central support pillars and niches cut into the side walls. Reflecting the seafaring life of the people who sculpted them, many are made like the navetas, in the shape of upturned boats. Since no major settlement has been found in the vicinity, it suggests that the dead were brought here for burial from all over the island.

The caves continued to be used down to the Iron Age, when lime was added to the bodies during cremations. Engraved stones suggest that they continued to be used after Roman times as a place of pilgrimage. Even today, some of them have been taken over by modern nomads from all over Europe in search of a Stone Age lifestyle. I was invited into one, and it seemed very cosy, but I would not like to have slept among the spirits of the dead.

Boats of the living and the dead

Menorca undoubtedly has the most impressive navetas in the Balearics. A very early one survives at the Santa Mònica settlement close to the west coast. It is shaped like an elongated horse shoe, with a slightly concave façade, and is entered by small doorway which once had a stone to close it off.

In nearly all of the navetas there is a vestibule or corridor leading to the main oval chamber, above which there is sometimes another chamber. The earliest settlements, before the building of the talayots, consisted of a cluster of navetas, often connected to each other. The first megalithic settlers on the island no doubt built them in this shape to commemorate their older seafaring days, as they had done in their caves.

The navetas were also used for communal burial. The most striking on Menorca is the Naveta des Tudons (Catalan for 'boat of the wood pigeons') which is situated to the east of the old Moorish capital of Ciutadella. Erected on a slight spur in a rolling plain, the monument is in an excellent state of preservation; indeed, it has been called the oldest intact building in Europe.[8] With its simple lines and harmonious shape, it is, to my mind, one of the most beautiful and evocative megalithic monuments of the Mediterranean.

If you look at it carefully, you realize that large slabs were used at the base of the naveta, but halfway up smaller worked stones were incorporated among the Cyclopean masonry. They are placed with great precision to form a corbelled vault: its outside measurements are roughly 13.5 metres wide, 4.25 metres high with a width which varies from 6.4 metres at the base to 3.25 metres at the crown. Built at the end of the pre-talayotic period – just before 1400 BC – it eloquently demonstrates that the builders had reached the height of their skills not long after settling on the island. As with the Egyptian pyramids, later megalithic monuments on Menorca show a decline rather than an improvement in workmanship. It implies that the settlers came in the third millennium with their megalithic skills already fully developed elsewhere.

The Naveta des Tudons was a collective tomb used for secondary burial. As such, it was primarily an ossuary, a place to lay the bones of the ancestors once the flesh had rotted away from them. When excavated in 1959, it was found to contain the remains of 100 people, carefully placed on a bed of pebbles, together with bronze bracelets, bone buttons and ceramic pots.

The monument can be entered by a small porthole entrance in its slightly concave 'stern' which faces west–southwest. I found it strangely disorienting to move from the blinding glare of the midday sun into its cool and dark interior. Nothing but dust and bare stones remained. The existence of a small antechamber and an apsidal recess suggests that rites were carried out when the bones were placed in the monument. A second chamber above the main one may have been intended to store as many bones as possible. It could even have served as a place to let the flesh rot away from the bones of the deceased before they were rearranged in a secondary burial.

I could not help thinking that the naveta was shaped like a boat not only because it mirrored the seafaring nature of its builders but because it was intended as a symbolic vehicle for the voyage of the soul into the afterlife. The Egyptians believed that after passing through the underworld we would join the sun god Re and sail in his 'Boat of a Million Years' across the heavens. The Vikings too, I recalled, used to launch their dead in burning boats into the sea.

Tables of the sun and the stars

Not far from the Naveta des Tudons on Menorca is the large Torre Llafuda megalithic site, inhabited between 1400 and 1300 BC. It is reached across fields, and is tucked away in a copse of holm oak. A quiet, rarely visited place, it is bathed in the cool, dappled light of the evergreen trees. A decayed talayot stands there, looking like a tumbled-down ziggurat from which the surrounding fields and olive groves can be viewed. There are also dwellings, two artificial caves and the remains of a rampart to explore. Dylan and my 23-year-old daughter Emily who accompanied me during my visit, had fun disappearing down the holes in the ground.

The site also has a taula, the spectacular megalithic monument unique to Menorca. The taula takes its name from the Catalan for 'table', and you can easily see why: it is a T-shaped structure, with a horizontal slab balanced on top of a vertical rectangular pillar placed in a slot in the bedrock. It is never placed in the centre of its sanctuary but a little to the north, while the flat face of the vertical stone is directed towards the entrance. The precinct wall invariably curves in the shape of a horse shoe around the central taula, thereby creating a sacred space within. Except for one exception, all the taulas face south, with an unimpeded view of the horizon.

At present no heavenly bodies can be seen rising on the southern horizon in Menorca. Taking into account the precession of the equinoxes, the British archaeologist Michael Hoskin has, however, calculated that the lintels and side pillars of the precinct entrances to the taulas framed the Southern Cross and two other bright stars of Centaurus around 1000 BC.[9] The fact that the megalithic settlements in Mallorca were located in fertile valleys and plains without a clear southern horizon in the surrounding mountains may explain the fact that no taulas are to be found on that island.

Apparently, each settlement had its own taula set in its own sanctuary, which was the focus of their worship. It may have served as the altar of a sun cult or have been a symbol of an unknown divinity. The T shape could even have been a stylized symbol of the bull which was associated with sun rites throughout the Mediterranean at the time.

The highest taula can be seen at the settlement of Trepucó, situated on the outskirts of the capital Mahón, which dates from around 1400 BC. Its main column rises to 4 metres and its topstone makes it even higher. The site also boasts the largest talayot in the Balearics, 40 metres in diameter. After an excavation during the 1930s led by the Cambridge archaeologist Margaret Murray, the taula had to be reinforced with cement.

Another outstanding taula near Mahón can be found at Talatí de Dalt. This settlement developed around 1300 BC and was continuously inhabited well into Roman times. One side of this taula's massive topstone is supported by a leaning pillar. The standing stones forming the sanctuary around it are also massive. There are rooms attached to the western side of its defensive wall, and a much deteriorated talayot on a slight hill. In addition, the site has an underground hypostyle chamber supported by a central pillar, with horizontal stones fanning out like sun rays. A single menhir, pierced by a hole, greets you as you approach the site. All in all, it is one of the most evocative megalithic sites in southern Europe.

Bulls and horses

It is difficult to tire of taula-hunting on Menorca because of their mysterious presence and their beautiful setting in this rolling landscape.

The best preserved one, dating from around 1000 BC, is to be found at Torralba d'en Salord settlement near Alaior west of Mahón. In a large circular hearth in front of the taula, ceramic vessels and the chopped bones of pigs, goats and cattle have been found – undoubtedly the remains of ritual offerings. Large quantities of amphorae have also been unearthed. They were deliberately broken, just as many Greeks today still break all the crockery after a special celebration.

The Spanish archaeologist Manuel Férnandez-Miranda concluded after excavating the site that the taula enclosure was not roofed as sometimes has been argued.[10] There is no evidence of stone slabs to span the side walls, and a wooden roof would have been impossible given the size of the fires made in the large hearths during the rituals.

A fascinating find from the site is the bronze figurine of a bull, no doubt part of the cult of the bull which was prevalent throughout the ancient Mediterranean. After the decline of the Great Goddess cult, this symbol of male virility was often associated with sun worship in the region.

Even more intriguing was the discovery of a plinth with three holes, each containing a fragment of bronze in the shape of a hoof secured by molten lead. What could it represent? Although figurines of horses are fairly common, no evidence for a horse god in Mediterranean cultures has been found. Hoskin, however, has persuasively suggested that it could have represented not a horse but the wise and kind centaur Chiron, the Greek god of healing. As a sanctuary, the site would have been a place of healing as well as worship.

There is one anomaly about Torralba. Constructed around 1000 BC at the peak of talayotic building, it is the only known taula sanctuary to face east. As Hoskin has pointed out, it would have been aligned at the time exactly towards the east, where Rigel, the brightest star in the constellation of Orion, would have risen, followed shortly after by Sirius.[11] There may well be an Egyptian influence here: Sirius was identified with Isis and Orion with her husband Osiris, and Isis and Osiris were the two most important gods of the Egyptian pantheon.

Another fascinating find at Torralba next to the altar stone were two ceramic figurines of the Phoenician fertility goddess Tanit, now in the Menorca Museum. Knowing the sacred nature of the Torralba sanctuary, passing Phoenician seafarers may well have left their own idol or perhaps even taken it over during a brief occupation of the area.

Imhotep, Asclepius and Chiron

The most fascinating megalithic settlement on Menorca, and the second largest on the island, is to be found at Torre d'en Gaumés west of Mahón. Its position made it a centre for much of the south coast. The site was inhabited continuously from pre-talayotic times to the Roman conquest – the topstone of its taula was actually reused in a Roman tomb. The site was not completely abandoned until the Middle Ages.

In the public area of the settlement, three talayots still stand on a hill. The outer wall, now incomplete, had sections added to the circular walls of the original houses. The remains of the dwellings show that they were separated by radial walls, which converged on a central courtyard where a water tank was sunk. There is even a storage and filtration system for the water which flowed down the hill, consisting of a number of cavities of different sizes hollowed out of the rock. In the southern part of the settlement there is a hypostyle hall – the best preserved on the island – with pillars and the stone cross support of the roof still intact. It may have been used as a storehouse. The inhabitants of the settlement clearly lived comfortable and sophisticated lives, congregating in the central public spaces for social gatherings and religious ceremonies.

Outside the walls of the Torre d'en Gaumés settlement is a talayotic sepulchre, the most beautiful of its kind, made from six large upright slabs placed on the ground. The capstone is missing. A porthole entrance has been cut in a huge oval stone at one end. It reminded me of the circular entrances to the underground tombs at Los Millares in southern Spain, and I could see no reason why the two peoples could not have been in touch during the Bronze Age.

The most intriguing aspect of Torre d'en Gaumés was the discovery, during an excavation of the sanctuary in 1974, of a bronze statuette some 15 centimetres high showing a man sitting on a throne. An inscription in Egyptian hieroglyphs declares him to be Imhotep, the legendary Egyptian founder of astronomy, architecture and healing. No more appropriate figure could be placed next to a taula in a sanctuary oriented towards the constellation of Centaurus. The ancient Greeks identified Imhotep with their god Asclepius and it was the Chiron, a centaur associated with the constellation of Centaurus, who taught him medicine.

These extraordinary Egyptian and Greek associations with healing and astronomy in taula sanctuaries on Menorca show the extent of the trading and cultural links across the Mediterranean in the second and first millennium BC. To find echoes of the centaur Chiron and the Centaurus constellation in two megalithic sites on Menorca would seem more than a coincidence. I further enjoyed the synchronicity of having reached the island in my boat *Celtic Gold* which was officially called a Westerly Centaur.

There are many more megalithic settlements with talayots and taulas in Menorca, but I finished my explorations at Son Catlar in the southwest of the island. It is the largest megalithic site still surviving in Menorca and one of the oldest: a pre-talayotic rectangular hypogeum has been discovered outside the walls which dates from 1800 BC.[12] Now set in a landscape of stone walls, rough fields and olive groves, the settlement covers an area of about 6 hectares. It is surrounded by a massive rampart of Cyclopean masonry which runs for nearly a kilometre. It is constructed of two parallel walls of large stone slabs, with an infill of smaller stones between them, sometimes as much as 2 metres thick. The resulting rampart is not, however, uniform: some turrets and walls were added at a later date.

The only known entrance is to the north, through a small once-roofed corridor near a watch tower. It has five talayots like stepped pyramids, some inside and others built into the perimeter wall, which may have been a part of the defence system of the settlement. Tombs were cut into the ground rock within the settlement's walls. The central sanctuary once contained a massive taula; its capital stone, weighing 20 tonnes, is now broken and fallen to the earth. There was a cave 3 metres deep under the central pillar, which must have been used for ritual purposes.

War and peace

Broken Phoenician and Roman pottery has been found on the floor inside a hypostyle building at Son Catlar. Towards the end of the talayotic period, around 700 BC, Phoenician influences were increasingly felt on the island. The military prowess of the islanders was well known throughout the Mediterranean; Diodorus Siculus mentions in particular their famous sling-throwers, who were sought after as mercenaries from 400 BC onwards. From their base in Carthage in present-day Tunis, the Phoenicians would enlist them to form the vanguard of their armies against Rome during the Punic Wars. Two hundred accompanied Hannibal and his elephants in their long journey from Cádiz through Spain and France and across the Alps in the 3rd century BC. It was the Roman conquest of the island in

123 BC, however, which finally put an end to the longest-lasting megalithic culture in Europe.

As I wandered round the remains at Son Catlar, the sun was casting long shadows among the rough white walls and the dark-green olive trees. I sat alone in the inner sanctuary, listening to the crickets and watching the birds leap from branch to branch in the surrounding pines. There was a hint of the sea in the warm evening breeze. I thought of the megalith builders of Menorca who had built their navetas in an era of peace, but whose descendants had seen great scenes of bloodshed. I was pleased that their ancient ruins were now once again places of solitude and tranquillity.

Eastward bound

We left the harbour of Mahón in Menorca and sailed to the islands where the talayot civilization may well have come from: Sardinia and Corsica. Sardinia lay due east, but as the winds were favourable we decided to head northeast to Corsica, a voyage of some 230 nautical miles. We saw no ships but halfway across I saw a dragonfly vainly flapping its four filigree wings, doomed to a watery grave. After spotting a turtle resolutely swimming east, we heaved to and went for a swim at midday in the centre of the great, deep, blue expanse of the Mediterranean, over a hundred miles from any shore. I was naked and vulnerable in the water as the ancient mariners had been before me.

Compared to northwest Europe, with its strong tides and currents, it was easy sailing. As there is no magnetic variation in this part of the planet, no adjustment had to be made to our compass. The main drawback in the Mediterranean is that there is either not enough wind or too much. Without doubt the most difficult thing to bear for a northerner is the implacable heat of the midsummer sun: the temperature in our cabin regularly rose to more than 42 degrees Celsius.

The tideless inland sea of the Mediterranean, interrupted by numerous islands and peninsulas, has always enticed the seafarer. In the summer, the days are long, the sea is generally calm and the visibility good. The Greek poet Hesiod, writing in the eighth century BC, restricted the recommended period of navigation to fifty days after the summer solstice in late August, but the season usually lasted from March to October. Some more hardy travellers, however, would take to the sea in winter, always ready to make for harbour if storm clouds veiled the stars.

After we had sailed for two days and nights – the days hot and sticky, the nights cool and bright with stars – the first rays of the yellow sun rose at dawn behind the tall mountain peaks of Corsica. The land below remained obscured by haze until early morning, when the forbidding mountains and the beckoning coasts appeared in all their glory. We made for the bright waters of the Golfe de Valinco and landed at Propriano, a small, bustling seaside resort in the southwest of the island. It was an ideal spot from which to explore the justly famed megalithic sites of Corsica.

Not long after our arrival, the dreaded mistral descended, the strong wind that whistles down from the Alps and can blow for a week. We had arrived just in time.

CHAPTER EIGHTEEN

The Granite Isle

A profound obscurity covers the first ages of Corsica.

PROSPER MÉRIMÉE

C orsica is, to say the least, a place of drama. Its two mighty granite mountain ranges, separated by a central depression, surge ferociously out of the sea. In its densely wooded interior herds of wild pigs still live off chestnuts. In the summer, it can be baking hot along the coasts; in the winter, snow falls. It is a hostile land, a back-breaking land, only partially tamed by humans. Not surprisingly, the dwellers of this unforgiving place are austere and independent. With good reason, Dorothy Carrington called her rich portrait of Corsica, published in 1971, *Granite Island*.

The island is the fourth largest in the Mediterranean. Its importance has always been as an indispensable refuge for those sailing across the sea; from the earliest times, it developed trading links both to the east and the west. Yet because of its difficult terrain and forbidding hinterland, ancient beliefs have lived on here among the country folk far longer than elsewhere in the Mediterranean. Despite the impact of Christianity, many still believe in an implacable Destiny, in prophetic visions and in the interfering and dangerous spirits of the dead. Then there are the *mazzeri*, feared individuals who against their will are compelled to become night hunters of souls. They set off to hunt an animal in their dreams; if, after killing it, they turn it over and recognize someone they know, within a year he or she will die. Some of these beliefs may well harken back to megalithic times.[1]

When the French novelist Prosper Mérimée visited the island in 1839, as an inspector of historic monuments, he wrote: 'The Corsicans have never cultivated the arts. There are no great buildings there . . . One can only look in Corsica for imitations or importations of their happier neighbours.' The megalithic monuments were simply not recognized as relevant to the island's prehistory. Indeed, as Mérimée observed, a 'profound obscurity covers the first ages of Corsica'.[2] Only in recent times has the mist begun to lift and farmers been prevented from knocking down megaliths to clear the land and build their houses. Such a wealth of prehistoric remains have come to light that Corsica is now considered, second in importance – after Carnac – among the megalithic regions of France.[3]

Seashell potters and dreamers

The oldest known skeleton found on the island, known as the Dame de Bonifacio and housed in the Lévie museum, dates back to 6610 BC. Although the island was sparsely inhabited in Palaeolithic times, Neolithic seafarers and farmers settled there in the fifth millennium BC, bringing with them seeds and domesticated animals. They decorated their round pots with narrow necks by pressing Cardium seashells into the damp clay and making dotted lines with a sharp tool. A similar design has been found all along the coastal regions of the Atlantic seaboard in Portugal, Andalusia and Morocco, and along the littoral of the South of France, Tuscany and Sardinia.[4]

Beautiful pottery made by their descendants from the fourth and third millennium BC has been found at Basi in the south of the island. It is decorated with triangles, chevrons and friezes, among other motifs; some fragments have beautiful sun rays fanning outwards. The inventive people of this *culture Basien*, as it is known, used obsidian for their arrowheads, knives and tools. Obsidian is a kind of organic glass which can produce razor-sharp blades. Unavailable on the island, it must have been brought by boat from Monte Arci from Sardinia or from the Aeolian Islands to the north of Sicily. To a lesser extent, they also imported flint for their tools. They were pastoralists as well as farmers, driving their livestock up and down the mountain spines according to the season, just as Corsican shepherds continue to do today.

The remains of a man aged sixty-five or seventy, found buried in a neolithic tomb under the fireplace of a hut at Araguina-Sennola, suggests that the ancient Corsicans practised the worship of family ancestors. By sleeping over the bones of their ancestors – as at Skara Brae in Scotland – they could draw on their wisdom and strength in dreams. A beautiful female statuette in steatite or soapstone, with rounded forms and crossed arms (discovered at Campu-Fiurelli near Grossa in southern Corsica and now in the British Museum) shows that the Great Goddess, source of life and guarantor of the continuation of the human race, was also revered on this island.

It was the people living along the coasts, most exposed to outside influences, who were converted to megalith building, for nearly all the megaliths were erected in valleys and plateaux only a little way from the sea. Although divided by the strong currents of the Strait of Bonifacio, which runs between Corsica and Sardinia, it seems that from 4500 BC the southern part of the island was influenced by the Ozieri culture which developed in the northern part of Sardinia.[5] The Ozieri buried their dead singly in cists surrounded by low circles of standing stones.

The fascinating site at Terrina behind the plateau of Aléria has given its name to the *culture Terrinien* which developed at the beginning of the third millennium. Excavations show that the megalith builders in this area grew barley and wheat and had a rich diet of pork, fish, oysters, eggs, honey, nuts and olives.[6] Most megalithic settlements on Corsica, however, had mediocre soil, and sites were chosen as much for herding livestock as growing crops.

The devils' forges

The most well-known Corsican megaliths are to be found in the south and southwest of the island, especially in the Sartenais and Taravo regions. Those so far discovered include 18 closed stone chambers or cists (*bancali*), 25 alignments (*filarate*) and 46 dolmens (*stazzone*), a great number of menhirs standing alone or in groups (*stantari*) and 83 statue-menhirs (*paladani*). Another local variation is the *tafoni*, granite rocks carved by erosion, which were often further carved out and used as tombs (from 2900 to 2000 BC, according to the carbon-dating of ash taken from those at Calanchi).

None of the Corsican megaliths are huge like their counterparts in northwestern Europe: the menhirs rarely rise above 4 metres and the dolmens average about 2 metres in height. But they are exceptional, carefully shaped and dressed, and even on some occasions, polished. The stone is granite. As for the skeletons in the neolithic tombs, none remain: they were either plundered, or dissolved in the acid soil.

What are the Corsican dolmens like? Their chamber is nearly always rectangular, with side walls made from one or more slabs, a single backstone and a single capstone. The entrance is usually completely open, although some are made with vertical stones on either side. They are invariably oriented within the southeast quadrant, towards the midwinter sunrise.[7] It's probable that they grew out of the earlier local tradition of cist building, stimulated by ideas brought by seafarers from the Atlantic seaboard.

Corsican dolmens are of two types. The first, sometimes called 'paradolmens', are constructed partly underground and surrounded by a ring of substantial stones, the remains of the retaining kerb of a tumulus. A wonderful example is the Dolmen de Settiva, near the town of Petreto-Bicchisano about 20 kilometres in the direction of Ajaccio from Propriano, where I had left my boat. I spent six hours with David and Elizabeth on a boiling hot July day hunting it down. No one in the local village commune who had recently acquired it knew where it was. I knocked on the door of an old lady nearby who pointed me up an ancient track which had long been used to take cattle into the mountains for summer grazing. Having got lost in the sprawling chestnut wood on the lower slopes, I was about to give up when I spied an old man in a lower field. He turned out to be the owner of the land. With a few mumbled words and an imperious gesture, he directed me to the exact location of the elusive dolmen.

It was on a brow of a hill, hidden in a grove of oak trees illuminated by the setting sun. The site was very small and delicate, on a human scale, 'almost feminine' as Elizabeth observed. The small sunken dolmen was surrounded by a circle of standing stones about eight metres in diameter. Its entrance, which had a tall menhir in front of it, faced a dramatic mountain peak in the distance. David, an architect, said: 'It's a beautifully selected site. I can see now how classical architecture in Greece stood in a very ancient tradition.' It was a beautiful, tranquil spot and well worth the effort we'd taken under the midsummer sun to reach it. The words 'sylvan' and 'Arcadian' came to mind as I sat dreaming in the dappled light.

The second kind of dolmen in Corsica is constructed above ground level, as in northwest Europe. The most beautiful and the best preserved is the Dolmen de Fontanaccia, sometimes called the Stazzona di u Diavalu, or the Devil's Forge. It is situated near Cauria, south of Propriano, on a gentle rise a few kilometres from the sea. After a pleasant walk along a track and across fields through a wide undulating valley, you see it standing up on a slight rise – a striking monument with a thin capstone resting on six slabs. There is a fine panoramic view from the site. I had to crouch to enter the spacious interior, as it's only 1.8 metres high. The entrance faces the rising sun, a good direction for the soul of the deceased as it begins its journey in the afterlife.

Menhirs and alignments

The Dolmen de Fontanaccia is at right angles to two impressive alignments nearby. The first group, known as I Stantari, contain statue-menhirs facing east; two have beatific faces. But there is a mystery. The figures have swords carved downwards on their bodies, which clash with their calm expressions. Could these carvings have been added at a later date?

There are several more alignments at Rinaiu, further south across a few more fields. They nestle among a grove of holm oaks growing under a massive granite outcrop. Some of the rows run north-south, others east-west; many stones lean crazily or have tumbled ignomini-ously to the earth. The broken slabs of a dolmen show that the place was long used as a ritual site. Sitting on a fallen menhir under the towering rock as the shadows lengthened, I felt profoundly at peace in this open-air sanctuary.

A few kilometres to the northwest as the seagull flies, there is another intriguing series of alignments at Pelaggiu in a valley leading up from the creek at Tizzano. Set on a plateau surrounded by hills, it is reached by a long sandy track through the rough, herb-scented scrubland which Corsicans call *le maquis*. There are seven groups so far known to archaeologists in the area, totalling 258 menhirs in all, although a local landowner told me that there are many more menhirs lost in the scrub, known only to the hunters who occasionally stumble across them.

At the main Pelaggiu site, three alignments stand close to each other, surrounded by some fine holm oaks. Two, the longest of which has 142 menhirs, are oriented on a north-south axis. The third, consisting of thirty-one menhirs, runs east-west. Since they make up the four cardinal points of the compass, they could well have been used as a calendar tracking the movement of the sun.

Many of them have fallen or are leaning over perilously; they look like teeth drawn from the jawbone of some great prehistoric carnivore. As I walked among the menhirs, an artist drew them while his wife and children waited patiently in the shade. I could see why he would be so attracted by these abstract forms in a state of withheld collapse. Having once been so carefully ordered by man – all of the menhirs were dressed and placed perfectly in line – an element of chaos is now breaking them up and nature is slowly but triumphantly reclaiming them as her own.

The great majority of the menhirs at Pelaggiu are about human height. Although none of them have the outline of a head, they do have round tops and from a distance look like human silhouettes. The archaeologist Roger Grosjean, who uncovered them in the 1960s, aptly called them '*protoanthropomorphes*'.[8] They probably date back to the beginning of the second millennium. A stone box nearby, surrounded by a crown of large blocks of stone, was found to contain material which dated back to the end of the Stone Age.

As with the I Stantari alignment, the site poses a riddle. Daggers or swords are engraved on three of the 258 menhirs. These engraved, headless menhirs are unique on the island. Again, could it be that the weapons were added when this part of the island was occupied by warlike invaders wanting to impose their mark on the existing culture?

The alignments of standing stones are the most striking feature of Corsica's megaliths. Around 600 have been discovered so far, of which 100 were carefully dressed. Most of the alignments are found near dolmens, cists and the granite tafoni tombs or significant places such as crossroads, river fords and wells. On seeing them for the first time, I was immediately reminded of the alignments of Merrivale on Dartmoor near my home, but unlike the ones at Carnac, they tend to run north-south rather than east-west, or north-east to south-west. This does not mean, however, that they have no astronomical purpose.

All the menhirs on Corsica have been carefully chosen. Many are much larger than the average height of a man: some are 3 metres high and the largest is almost 4. The most intriguing and striking are the statue-menhirs I have mentioned, which are carved with the outline of human faces. Local people believed that statue-menhirs were persons turned into stone for having transgressed the moral code laid down by Christianity. While most are of men, some are clearly female with breasts. One, called La Pierre d'Apriciani, with carved hair, mouth, nose and far-seeing eyes, is particularly serene and beautiful. During the Christian era, it was said that the female statue-menhirs (as at Cambia in northern Corsica) were young girls turned into stone for daring to break the barrier between the sexes by committing an act of bravery – the sole prerogative of Corsican men! This is not surprising in a society which is still chauvinist in the remoter parts of the country: a wife traditionally calls her husband *mio padrone*, 'my master', and when he dies, she dresses in black and rarely leaves the house.

Filitosa

The most celebrated megalithic site on Corsica, and the best one for statue-menhirs, is at Filitosa in the southwest of the island, just north of Propriano. Situated on a spur which ends in a rocky escarpment, and above a fertile plain, it is protected on three sides by the sheltering arms of mountains. The river Taravo is close by, providing easy access to the sea. Its location not only reflects the traditional preference of the megalith builders for high places with panoramic views, but is in keeping with the ancient Chinese principles of feng shui.

As my architect friend David Lea, who accompanied me to the site, sagely observed: 'This is a wonderful site which has been very carefully chosen. The main monument seems to grow out of the spur and is carefully lodged in the landscape, raised up under the sky yet nestling in a bowl created by the surrounding hills. It has a powerful presence overlooking the plain just like many classical temples built on raised platforms. It's a very special place and feels good!'

The sacred space at Filitosa was inhabited for more than 8000 years. The first group, arriving in around 6000 BC, were hunter-gatherers who set up shelters under the eroded rocks and made pottery impressed with Cardium shells. They used tools of flint and imported obsidian. They began sowing crops around 4500 BC; many grindstones and small pestles have been found on the site. And they kept oxen, sheep and pigs, fished for trout in the river, and hunted wild boar in the densely wooded interior. Their dwellings were stone huts with roofs made of branches filled with clay. From around 2300 BC, they began to carve statue-menhirs, at first only hinting at human features, but then gradually making them more individualized and pronounced.

Around 1500 BC, a tower-building and metal-using people arrived and occupied the site. They were probably the Shardana originally from the eastern Mediterranean – the same people who occupied Sardinia, where they built the towers called *nuraghi*. They were almost certainly among the 'Sea Peoples' who attacked Egypt around 1190 BC during the reign of Ramesses II. Their defeat by the Egyptians was commemorated on a bas-relief in the temple of Medinet-Habu.[9]

The new occupiers of Filitosa rebuilt the site entirely. They knocked down the statue-menhirs and incorporated them into the foundations of a huge Cyclopean round tower (known locally as a *torra*) which they placed on the highest point, as if to demonstrate their conquest and rule. There are in fact some tower-like monuments in Corsica said to date from the end of the third millennium, but they were probably a localized development from the circles built around the cists. The full-blown torra built at Filitosa definitely marks a new departure from the earlier megalithic culture and shows all the signs of foreign influence at work. The *Toréens* or Tower People stayed until after 800 BC, and possibly as late as 500 BC, by which time the island had come under the sway of the Phoenicians.

The mystery of the statue-menhirs

The carving of statue-menhirs seems to have been an unparalleled megalithic development in Corsica. The skills of the carvers gradually became more refined: the best are like Picasso's drawings, in which simple lines create a bold and haunting image. Some are quite naturalistic, with nose, eyes, mouth, chin and shoulders delineated, anticipating the classical Greek style of sculpture and the aesthetic principles of all later European art.[10] While revealing a true appreciation of the ideal human form, each retains its own individuality. As such, they are the apogee of megalithic art.

But, to return to those enigmatic statue-menhirs at Filitosa: what are we to make of them? Many bear daggers and swords and seem to be draped with shoulder armour. Who are these people? Are they heroic ancestors or protective guardians? Are they gods in stylized human form, or dead warriors and chiefs? Could they be, as the archaeologist Roger Grosjean suggested, enemies killed in battle? Or could it be that the armed menhirs at Filitosa represent the invading Tower People, carved by the threatened islanders to act as magical effigies to counter the destructive power of their enemies? I find this latter view the most persuasive. None of the actual daggers or swords depicted on the menhirs, which resemble bronze weapons made in the Aegean around 1450 BC, have yet been found in Corsica.

The fact that the invaders knocked the menhir-statues down and used them in the foundations of their tower at Filitosa suggests that they saw them as powerful icons and wanted to demonstrate their own power by destroying them. In this, they were acting like modern soldiers, who pull down the flag of their conquered foes and raise their own.

The other possibility is that the weapons were added to the statue-menhirs long after they were erected as a symbol of conquest by the new invaders – in the same way that pharaohs in Egypt would add their names to existing temples in order to claim them as their own. The fact that there are only two statue-menhirs found in Sardinia, where the Tower People developed a major presence, and seventy-three known ones in Corsica, suggests that the art form was a local development.

Some of the menhirs on the site at Filitosa are distinctly phallic, suggesting that the Bronze Age invaders may have also imposed their own aggressive patriarchy on the earlier peaceful, matrifocal society of Stone Age Corsica.

The rock statue

The site at Filitosa was discovered in 1954; for twenty years the local farmer had been sitting on a fallen menhir without being aware of its importance. It is now a well-developed site with a small museum. You enter it by a narrow gateway in the eastern platform built by the Tower People. Since the spur on which the site is located drops away on three sides, this is the side which most needed to be defended after their arrival in the violent Bronze Age. There is on site a great arching rock here which once housed the shelters of the earliest inhabitants.

The central monument now consists of a decayed chambered round tower. It was built around 1300 BC on a circular platform about 2 metres high, and may have had a false vault. A number of standing stones and statue-menhirs, dating from 2000 to 1500 BC, have been placed around it. They may originally have formed a circle around a cist at the centre of a sanctuary, or been arranged in alignments. No one can be certain. During the excavations in the 1950s, the statue-menhirs found in the foundations of the central tower were re-erected at the whim of the archaeologists. Megalithic sites continue to suffer from injudicious rebuilding, restoration and the good intentions of some misguided archaeologists.

The west monument on the edge of the spur which drops down to a valley is the most intriguing and striking of the structures at Filitosa. Sculped by erosion, it is a beautifully shaped natural outcrop standing about 6 metres high, with curved gullies. It has a large, round carved niche on one side and three small underground chambers on the other. A complex of Cyclopean chambers forming a roundish platform was probably added later by the Tower People.

With its dramatic setting, drawing in the energies of the earth and sky and facing out to sea, this rock-statue must have been an object of great reverence for the original megalith builders of Corsica and the centre of their cult. Its antique and sacred presence reminded me of the so-called Devil's Stone at Avebury in England. The Aborigines of

Australia probably felt the same about their own sacred rocks which rise out of the earth under the arching sky.

From the rock escarpment, a semicircle of five statue-menhirs can be seen in front of a 1000-year-old olive grove which lies at the foot of a hill on the other side of a little valley and a mint-bordered stream. Casting shadows in the bright sun, they look as if they are guarding a sacred grove. But as before, they are not in their original positions, and were placed there entirely at the fancy of the excavators.

A fantastically shaped outcrop of rock tops the hill and is thought to have been used as a quarry. Some of the rocks are massive and round, forming perfect shelters, while others are so fractured they create natural, free-standing menhirs. It would not have required a great effort to remove and transport them to the main site. If I were a stonemason, I would have loved to get out my tools; instead, I stroked the smooth rock and admired the beauty of the close-grained granite.

I share the view of Roger Grosjean in believing that Corsica was influenced during the Bronze Age by the nuraghi culture of the warlike Tower People in neighbouring Sardinia.[11] I was intrigued to find out that there was a definite decline in the quality of pottery during this period. The archaeological museum at Sartène in the hills above Propriano shows that pots made in the fourth millennium had fine and polished sides, and those from the following millennium were finely decorated with chevrons on their sides and perforations around the borders. However, during the Bronze Age, when the Tower People made their presence felt on Corsica, there is a clear deterioration in artistic taste and skill: the rough pots have simple forms with few decorations, and stand on heavy and crude bases. Entirely utilitarian, they are intended for nothing more than storage and cooking.[12] Their makers had no time for the delicate artistry of the earlier potters and the carvers of the statue-menhirs.

An usual respect for justice

Corsica emerged from prehistory around 565 BC when, according to Herodotus, the Phoenicians established themselves on the island. Greeks from Phocaea in what is now Turkey also founded a colony around 560 BC at Alalia on the island's flat eastern plain, although the Etruscans from mainland Italy and the Carthaginians joined forces to crush their westward thrust. Romans eventually conquered the city, renamed it Aléria and made it their capital. But their culture had little immediate impact. Writing in the first century BC, Diodorus Siculus described the Corsicans as pastoralists and food gatherers with an unusual respect for justice.[13]

The turbulence of the late antique world undoubtedly left its mark on the island. Well into the Middle Ages bloody quarrels were common between groups of shepherds and farmers from neighbouring regions. Vendettas between families and clans became an entrenched part of Corsican life, immortalised in Prosper Mérimée's novel of 1841, *Colomba*. Dorothy Carrington has suggested that Napoleon, the island's most famous son, was 'the lineal descendant of the warriors of Filitosa'.[14] But he did little for his fellow Corsicans. When asked why they should not have roads, he replied that they should travel as they had always done – by sea.

For all the rivalry between families and the cult of the hero on Corsica, a sense of democratic cooperation harking back to megalithic times came through in the medieval rural communes. The constitution conceived by the nationalist Pasquale Paoli in the middle of the eighteenth century declared unequivocally that 'the General Diet of the people of Corsica' is 'legitimately master of itself'. Although annexed by France in 1769, many young people in Corsica continue to call for independence.

Despite the coming of Christianity to Corsica, the legacy of the megalithic civilization made itself felt in other ways. Gregory the Great complained in the sixth century that the Corsicans still worshipped stones. Until recently, funeral rites involved wailing, verse-improvisation and dancing, and the dead were buried collectively in the vaults of churches or family sepulchres rather than in individual graves. Village assemblies and tribunals in the past often used to meet around a slab of stone, known as the *petra l'arringo*, laid over a tomb or above a burial ground so that the spirits of the dead could influence the judgments of the living.

I left Corsica not with the image of the Shardana Bronze Age daggers in my mind, but with the vision of the smiling steatite statuette of the Goddess from Campu-Fiurelli. But I was to learn much more about the warrior people who left their violent mark on the island as I headed south along the southwest coast of Corsica to Sardinia.

CHAPTER NINETEEN

The Sky-Exposed Land

A savage, dark-bushed, sky-exposed land.

D. H. LAWRENCE

We slipped down towards Sardinia along Corsica's indented western coastline with its many gulfs and *calanques*, or deep narrow creeks, in which generations of mariners have taken shelter. In the Baie de Figari we landed just as the mistral began to blow again, sending white horses up the bay and bending the olive, oak and cork trees dotted on the rocky hills around.

It was only a short journey to the fortress of Bonifacio, built into cliffs 70 metres high, which commanded the entrance to the narrow strait of that name that divides Corsica from Sardinia. The unearthing of the remains of the Dame de Bonifacio, a young woman who lived near the town about 8500 years ago, shows that this area had been inhabited from the earliest times. It had not developed during the Neolithic and Bronze Ages, as the dolmens and alignments of menhirs along the coast show, but it had a sizeable population during classical antiquity. The passage in the *Odyssey* where the hero encounters the Laestrygonians, a race of giant cannibals, at the foot of 'sheer cliffs on either side' could well have been inspired by the entrance to the Goulet de Bonifacio, the Bonifacio Narrows. Its fierce currents and high winds funnel between the two points of the islands, and can hurl an unwary boat onto the scattered rocks and islets beyond. Although Corsica and Sardinia shared a common culture in megalithic times, their present occupiers – France and Italy – make sure the two islands remain apart and linked to their respective mainlands.

Although the mistral had blown over, the sea was still choppy and we gave the entrance to the Bonifacio Narrows a wide berth. We

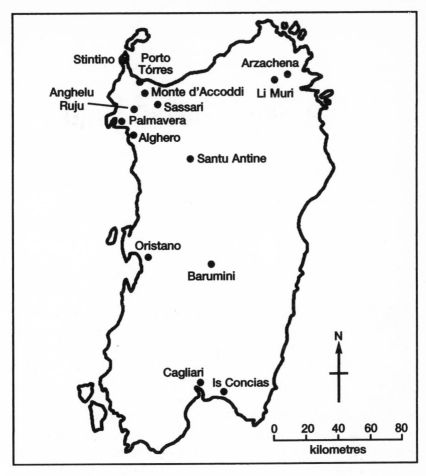

Map of Sardinia, with the principal megalithic sites and modern towns

made for the old port of Stintino, a small fishing village on the finger-shaped peninsula to the west of the Golfo dell'Asinara. Being well sheltered, it proved a good place from which to explore the northern and western parts of Sardinia, where megaliths abound. As in Corsica, rugged granite mountains run along much of the east and southwest coasts. Travelling through the country in the 1920s, D. H. Lawrence called it, in *Sea and Sardinia*, a 'savage, dark-bushed, sky-exposed land'.

Placed strategically in the middle of the Mediterranean, the windswept island has always been a landing place for seafarers. On a clear day, the shores of Africa can be seen from its southern tip. Although now part of Italy, its people jealously guard their distinctive culture, and in the interior, many still speak an ancient Latin-based dialect. They disparagingly call the mainland *il continente*.

The Ozieri culture

Sardinia, like Corsica, was inhabited later than the rest of Italy. The first settlers developed what has been called the Ozieri culture, named after a village in the north of the island where a cluster of their stone and pottery goods was first found in a cave.[1] While earlier believed to date from 2500 BC, it is now thought that the Ozieri culture flourished from 4000 BC to 3200 BC. Their earliest free-standing megalithic tombs date from the fourth millennium.[2]

Who were the Ozieri? They travelled wherever it was possible to develop their skills on Sardinia – agriculture, gathering, animal husbandry and the working of flint and obsidian for tools and utensils. They lived in open settlements or in natural caves (*tafoni*) eroded in granite outcrops. They decorated their beautiful pots with zigzag geometric patterns, arcs, segments of circles and spirals, and buried their dead in small artificial caves, stone cists enclosed within circles or *tafoni*. The latter were still being used as graves in the nineteenth century and as temporary shelters by shepherds within living memory.

The Ozieri had links with both the eastern and the western parts of the Mediterranean and shared the common worship of the Great Goddess. Many mysterious female figurines have been found on the island: some have flat fronts with only the nose and breasts in relief like statuettes from the Cyclades islands of Greece, while others are more curved and ample like the ones found in mainland France and in northwestern Europe. In the G. A. Sanna Museum of Archaeology and Ethnography in Sassari, there are two charming round statuettes with smiling faces and vaginas dating from the fifth millennium BC.

Fairy houses

Not far from the Catalan-speaking port of Alghero in the northwest of the island – a legacy of its time as a Catalan colony – I visited the most famous and striking of the Ozieri rock-cut tombs at a site called Anghelu Ruju.[3] Used from 3500 to 1800 BC, the tombs of the necropolis are carved into a low, flat-topped hill. Twenty-seven of the thirty-eight tombs were built during the Ozieri period. They are known locally as *domus de janas* or 'fairy houses', and I could see why. Some of the small entrances look like upright manholes while the grander ones are carved to look like dressed trilithons. Many have several chambers leading off a central rectangular room reached by a passageway, while a few have developed architectural features like false doors and cupolas. Tomb 20 of the necropolis is so large that it has wide steps leading down to its entrance and pillars within to hold up the ceiling. It feels more like an underground temple than a tomb. But for the most part you have to crawl into them if you want to join the lizards and spiders in the cool shade and avoid the baking heat of the midsummer sun. The people who used them 5000 years ago practised secondary inhumation, that is, they buried the skull and long bones of the deceased after the flesh had rotted away. All that remains now is dust.

Around the entrance and inside three of the tombs, there are carvings of the long-horned bulls' heads associated with the cult of the Great Goddess, the giver and taker of life. The bull was revered as the incarnation of male procreativity. Tomb 27 has two beautiful pairs of horns on either side of its entrance carved above a square containing three concentric rings. Several tombs are painted with red ochre, suggesting menstrual blood in the womb of the earth and symbolizing rebirth.

There is a relief in Tomb 30 which could be a set of very wide horns but is more likely a boat. Rich grave goods have been excavated in the necropolis which show the wide maritime trading links of the Ozieri people. Dating from 2200 BC, they include many typical Stone Age artefacts – flint tools, mace heads, arrowheads and beads. But there were surprises in the cache: silver rings and copper daggers, probably imported from Spain, an awl from southern France, a copper ring of an Eastern European type, and an axe from the British Isles.

The ziggurat of the Goddess

Further north near the coast between Sassari and Porto Tórres I came across the most intriguing megalithic site in Sardinia. Monte d'Accoddi rises up on a rolling plain close to a stream, surrounded by distant mountains and facing the sea. Like Silbury Hill in England and Tumulus St Michel in Carnac, it is a painstakingly man-made mound. Squareish in plan at 36 by 29 metres, and oriented towards the cardinal points of the compass, it has been likened to a truncated pyramid. Yet to my mind it looks more like a ziggurat with its two-stepped terraces made from skilfully laid dry stone walling. Built at the end of the fourth millennium BC, its top structure is now decayed, but it still stands about 9 metres high.

A wide, straight ramp about 41 metres long and held in by stone walls rises from the south-facing side of the mound to the first terrace. A flight of steps then leads up two stages to reach a platform on the summit, which has a spectacular view of the sea under a great arc of Mediterranean sky.

This unique monument was built by the Ozieri people on a site which had been occupied from the second half of the fifth millennium. On top of the platform, they first erected a sanctuary – known as the Red Temple – made from small limestone slabs bonded with mortar and decorated in red ochre. This was probably destroyed by fire and a second altar was built on its ruins around 2700 BC.[4] A granite pedestal depicting the Great Goddess was found on the north side of the structure near three small chapels used for votive offerings. A fragment of the pedestal has the spiral decorations on either side of a triangle similar to the ones I had seen engraved on megaliths during the whole of my journey from northern Europe.

Although this extraordinary monument is called by local archaeologists an altar, it could equally have been an observatory, especially since the orientation of its ground plan to the four cardinal points of the compass is the same as the Great Pyramid in Egypt. A small stone found at the site (now in the museum in Sassari) is incised with parallel marks which could well represent a tally recording the movement of celestial bodies during the yearly cycle.

A dolmen still stands near the southeastern corner of the ziggurat, with a large flat capstone balanced on small slabs. It has some holes cut into its sides which may have been used to lift and transport it; some say it was to tie up animals which were to be sacrificed but I find this unlikely. On the other side of the ramp of the mount, there is a slender dressed menhir, standing 4.7 metres high and weighing almost 6 tonnes, one of several in the area. These probably went up around the end of the fourth millennium before the main structure.

Strange carved stones have been found on the site. The most intriguing is a huge boulder carved in the shape of an egg and then cut through two-thirds along its body by a curving line of great geometrical subtlety.[5] Some have seen it as a solar symbol but it most likely represents the primordial egg, the universal symbol of birth, from which the gods and goddesses first emerged.

Monte d'Accoddi stands at the centre of a ritual landscape, with other necropolises dating from the Ozieri culture nearby. A hypogeum, disturbed by the laying of a railway line, has a pillar with bull's horns carved on it as at Anghelu Ruju. The site has also yielded up a beautiful statuette of the Great Goddess, with small breasts and shoulders and arms forming a square. It is so elegant that it has been reproduced in silver as a necklace for visitors. I bought one for Elizabeth's birthday.

Circles, cists and dolmens

More ruins of these worshippers of the Great Goddess can be found in the megalith-rich area around Arzachena in Gallura in the northeast of Sardinia. They lie in the mountainous granite region just inland of the beautiful Costa Smeralda or Emerald Coast, with its outlying islands. The area was inhabited in the early Neolithic period, from the sixth to the fifth millennium. So-called Impressed Ware pottery, decorated with impressions of Cardium shells, date from this time.[6] Small stone objects made from flint and obsidian were also used to impress geometric forms – half-moons, triangles and trapeziums – on the clay before firing. The obsidian, valued for its colour and hardness, no doubt came from important deposits in the centre of the island. This 'black gold' of antiquity was exported to Neolithic settlements on the Italian and French mainlands.

Just outside Arzachena, a dirt road leads past a farmhouse to Li Muri where there is a famous group of five small rectangular tombs built by the Ozieri people in the late Neolithic period. Four are closed stone chests or cists. They are surrounded by four intersecting circles – the largest with a diameter of 8.5 metres – made from slabs mixed with thin standing stones. They were no doubt originally intended to hold in the mound of earth and stones laid over the cists.[7] Unique to this site in Sardinia, there is a menhir standing in the external circle of each tomb. The fifth tomb, probably added later, is a gallery with a west-facing entrance.

Three of the tombs are oriented on a north–south axis, while one lies roughly east–west and another points towards the northeast. As such, they could mark the equinoxes and the rising of the sun on the summer solstice. The location is high, but like many other sites in Europe it is situated on a platform on the slope of a spur, surrounded by hills and open on one side.

Pebbles covered in red ochre stain were placed in the graves. The colour of blood and symbol of regeneration, red ochre may also have been used to paint the bodies of the deceased. Finds on altars in the cists reveal skilful workmanship: they include flint axes, beads, mace-heads, sherds of pottery, and a large number of soapstone beads. There is even a soapstone cup with two splayed handles. Spherical pommels made of green and blue soapstone may have come from abroad: similar ones have been found in Anatolia, Italy, France and Iberia. Human remains were found in only one cist.

To bury their dead, the Ozieri people built many paradolmens, incorporating conveniently shaped natural rocks. Only five truly free-standing dolmens (usually called *stazzone* in Sardinia as in Corsica) are known to have survived from the early period before the second millennium; each has a rectangular chamber and massive capstone.

A magnificent example and one of the most beautiful of all Mediterranean dolmens is at Sa Coveccada near Mores in the central part of north Sardinia. Measuring 5 metres long and 2.7 metres high, walls and its roof are all made from massive single slabs of stone. There is a small niche inside on the west wall for votive offerings. Its curved entrance stone is remarkably similar to the dolmen Coste-Rouge in eastern Languedoc in the South of France.[8]

The Tower People

After the demise of the Ozieri culture, an extraordinarily megalithic culture developed in Sardinia during the Bronze Age which, as we have seen, colonized southwestern Corsica and may have reached Menorca. It takes its name from the towers or *nuraghi* which scatter the island. The builders are sometimes called the Tower People. They may have actually been the Shardana, one of the Sea Peoples who attacked Egypt during the reign of Ramesses II. The Shardana certainly live on in the island's name.

More than 7000 of an estimated 20,000 nuraghi still exist. Dating from 1700 BC in the early Bronze Age, they were built even after the Phoenician and Roman incursions for a period of nearly 2000 years.[9] They first emerged with the increasing threat of war after the arrival of Bronze Age warriors. Islanders began to build their villages on rugged highlands, and to defend their weakest sides with huge megalithic walls. No doubt inspired by the earlier dolmen design, they then began to build flat-topped conical towers. Their masons completed the roofs by oversailing the layers of stones until they could be covered with a single capstone, thereby creating a false dome or cupola. Unlike the beehive-shaped *tholoi* graves of Mycenae, which were erected inside mounds, the nuraghi were built entirely above ground.

As they grew larger and more complex, internal corridors, different chambers, niches, wells and silos were added. Small embrasures let in some air and light and could be used as loopholes for archers. The largest of the nuraghi had three storeys, and it proved necessary to incorporate winding stairways in the structure to reach the summit of the central tower. It was not long before other towers were added, then joined together by curtain walls to form massive bastions. The result was to create an almost impregnable fortress.

The nuraghi were clearly the seats of powerful military groups centred on a tribal chief who controlled the land and resources of the surrounding territory. Around the fortified towers the common people huddled in circular stone huts with pointed roofs made from branches. They were protected by lower outer walls, but under attack they would have had to take refuge in the nuraghi. Theirs was not an open life of free exchange, as in ancient Greece. Although some larger huts may have been used for meetings, no common area or public square, no common well or gutter have been found in these haphazard villages. The inhabitants must have lived a harsh and uncertainty life in an authoritarian, hierarchical society.

An exceptionally fine nuraghe is sited at Palmavera, 11 kilometres west along the coast from Alghero and not far from Anghelu Ruju. Situated on the side of a hill running down to the sea, Palmavera was occupied from 1500 to 800 BC. It had one central tower to which was added a second tower; between the two a small courtyard stairway led to the upper floors. The whole structure was surrounded by a pentagonal defensive wall.

Outside this menacing castle huddles a village originally consisting of 150 circular huts (now reduced to the ruins of about fifty) inhabited in the late Bronze Age, from about 1000 to 900 BC. The most interesting feature of the site is a large round hut enclosing an internal space 9 metres in diameter, called by some archaeologists the Hall of Reunion. Stone benches circle round the interior, and a stone statue in the shape of a nuraghe stands in the middle. A box made from slabs of stones found in the hut reminded me of the ones I had seen at Skara Brae. Bronze buttons, clasps and bracelets have also been found on the site during recent excavations.[10]

The entrance faces southeast, to the rising sun on the winter solstice. It was probably used as a meeting place for elders who implemented the orders of the chief and who were encouraged to venerate his authority in its most visible form – the model of the tower itself.

As I roamed the site, I met a visiting professor of archaeology from Spain who maintained that the nuraghic civilization was a home-grown affair, although he admitted that it could have influenced tower-building in southwestern Corsica and Menorca.

I then travelled inland to visit the famed nuraghe tower of Santu Antine near Torralba in the centre of the northern part of the island. Surrounded by hills, it dominates the fertile plain for kilometres around. The tower is named after St Constantine but locals call it Dom de su Re – the 'House of the King'.[11] The first drawings of it in its dilapidated state were made by an English traveller called W.H. Smith, who passed by in 1827.

The nuraghe at Santa Antine has a large triangular base with sides 39 metres long, enclosing a courtyard and well in front of a huge tower in the shape of a truncated cone. It now rises to 17.5 metres; originally it must have reached a massive 25 metres before the site was raided for building material by neighbouring villagers. It is the tallest nuraghe in Sardinia and by far the most imposing. While the lower courses are made from large rough blocks of local basalt, the last third of the keep is made from dressed blocks, similar to the Cyclopean technique seen in Greece. The central tower has three chambers built at different levels, one on top of each other. Bastions with three outlying towers at the corners of the triangular base were added at a later date. Although there does not seem to have been an overall architect's design, the whole demonstrates a high degree of engineering ability for the time.

Only when you enter from a courtyard and wander around its labyrinthine corridors and dark chambers do you realize the size of the task. The circular corridor on the ground floor is tall enough for a horse and rider to pass through. An internal winding stairway leads you clockwise up to the chambers of the central tower with their high false vaults. They are dark and heavy inside, even with artificial light. The claustrophobic atmosphere created by the lack of light and air is no doubt reinforced by the peculiar magnetic field of the huge grey basaltic rocks: they can can cause an error of up to 20 degrees on the needle of a compass, making a proper survey very difficult.

The nuraghe fort was clearly intended as a utilitarian building for displaying the military power of the local chief; and in that, it succeeds. But while imposing, I did not find it either aesthetically pleasing or spiritually uplifting. Indeed, its massive and menacing bulk was intended to create fear in its subject people and enemies. And it still does.

The most sophisticated complex is Su Nuraxi at Barumini further south in the island's centre. It is now a World Heritage Site. Set on a terrace overlooking a fertile plain, the 20-metre-high central tower dates from 1500 BC – the Middle Bronze Age. It was first surrounded by a defensive wall with four towers, but in the thirteenth century BC the site was rebuilt with a new wall and seven towers. It was used down to Punic and Roman times. What now remains are its square lower section, central tower and four towers protruding at the corners of a bastion.

The nuraghe at Su Nuraxi was clearly at the centre of a well-

defended tribal territory: the hills around are dotted by minor groups
of satellite nuraghi which form a 'star system'.[12] With its monumental
size, the central nuraghe was a fearful symbol of power and prestige to
reinforce the chief's domination over the people and his control of
the lands and livestock. It was a long way from the egalitarian,
matrifocal communities of the early megalithic period.

Around the bastion of the nuraghe huddles a disordered array of
poor circular huts. They are closely grouped, as the archaeologist
Giovanni Lilliu aptly puts it, as if they were a 'termitary'.[13] A large
room with a ring seat for thirty people, built in the eighth century BC,
implies that at this late phase elders gathered to discuss the orders
issued from the castle and the affairs of the village. As in Palmavera, a
baetyl or sacred stone found in the hut, made from limestone in the
form of a miniature nuraghe, suggests that it was made an object of
awe and veneration. The high spirituality of the early megalith builders
had degenerated into a means of controlling the masses. With good
reason, the Sardinian people later called the nuraghe Sa Domu e
s'Orku, the 'Ogre's House'.

As we left the bleak and decayed monument, my young female
guide observed proudly: 'We're weak now but we were powerful
then!' Who were the 'we', I wondered. Certainly not the people
huddled in their huts below that vast and barren keep.

Excavations suggest the villagers had a simple and frugal life. Meat
was scarce, and the staple food consisted of wheat and barley made
into bread and enhanced by legumes, tubers, wild fruits and acorns. A
few mussels and crustaceans were brought up from the sea. Lentisk
(mastic) and wild olive oil was used for the lamps. As elsewhere, men
were mainly responsible for the supply of raw materials for pottery,
while the women fashioned the pots, dishes and terracotta braziers.

For me, the nuraghi have none of the calm and inspiring atmosphere
of a religious sanctuary. On the contrary, their massive grey walls and
towering keeps form a heavy, brooding presence in the landscape.
Inside they are dark, airless and cramped; there is no sense of comfort
or ease. Unlike any other megalithic building I had entered on my
voyage, I felt the weight of the huge, rough stones above me and
feared being entombed in their cavernous depths. They were
undoubtedly places of war and strife, of the petty cruelties of the
barracks, of the dull discipline of military life. I did not find that they
expanded the mind like most megalithic buildings, but rather drained
the body of its energy. It was a great pleasure to leave their dark,
malevolent atmosphere and to emerge into the light and warmth of
the Mediterranean sun.

The giants' tombs

The complex towers were not the only architectural legacy of the Shardana. They also built unique structures known locally as the *tombe di giganti* – 'giants' tombs'. Their design probably developed from the *corridoi dolmenici*, which in turn were doubtless inspired by the simple dolmens of the earliest megalithic period. They consist of extended rectangular tombs with open entrances facing the southeast, which are very similar to the French *allées couvertes*. Evidence of both primary and secondary burials have been found inside them. The number of bones and lack of grave goods suggest that at first they were for all members of the community, although as society became more hierarchical they probably became reserved for the families of the chiefs.

The giants' tombs were almost certainly more than communal burial sites. They have a forecourt (sometimes called an 'exedra') with a curved frontage made from high slabs or Cyclopean walls. The Tower People no doubt used them as open-air temples for religious ceremonies in front of the houses of their dead. Several classic authors mentioned the Sardinian custom of sleeping near the graves of the ancestors for magical or therapeutic reasons.[14]

Close to the cists and stone circles of Li Muri near Arzachena in Gallura, there is a magnificent example of a giants' tomb. It is set on a small hill in a plain surrounded by mountains. Known as Li Lolghi, the gallery, some 27 metres long, dates from the Early Bronze Age. It has lost its covering mound of stones and earth to reveal its stark rectangular slabs of granite. The imposing central stone on the façade was added later. Having been partly broken off, it now looks like a giant's head on a body with a small entrance like a porthole cut between its 'feet'. The low entrance, decorated with a frame in relief around it, suggests a threshold into another world, marking the passage from the living to the dead.

Nearby is another equally impressive giants' tomb – Coddu Vecchiu. Not far from two decayed nuraghi, it has a beautiful arched stele as the centrepiece of its forecourt. Composed of two granite slabs, one placed on top of the other, it rises to 4 metres. The lower one is rectangular with an arched entrance and the upper one a rounded slab. I had to crawl on all fours to pass through the threshold. It might be a giants' tomb, but the entrance was for elves.

In a study of the orientation of the giants' tombs in Sardinia, Michael Hoskin found that in the centre of the island, where they are concentrated, virtually all of them face east. An examination of

252 tombs distributed all over the island further showed that most face the south-east quadrant, especially in the north of the island. One in three in the south, however, fail to confirm to the general pattern: some are aligned well west of due south, while others face to the north of the midsummer sunrise. The giants' tomb of Is Concias near Cagliari on the south coast is a rare example of a Mediterranean communal tomb which faces close to north.[15] Unusually, its façade consists of rectangular blocks laid like bricks, and has a square entrance below a lintel.

The local differences may well be due to greater foreign contacts in the south. The farming was better here and it had one of the richest deposits of minerals in the Mediterranean. Obsidian mined at Monte Arci was shipped abroad and has been found during the Neolithic and Copper Ages in sites as far afield as Spain, France and mainland Italy.

Sanctuaries and holy wells

Towers and tombs are not all the nuraghi culture produced. Among their megalithic remains are five intriguing free-standing temples. One is elliptical in form while the others are called 'megaron' because their sides extend beyond the front or back wall in the manner of the Greek megaron temples. Two fine examples close to the ruins of a megalithic village can be seen at Serra Orrios near Dorgali on the east coast, an area which also boasts a giants' tomb and dolmens.[16] The megaron feature has led some to see Greek influence at work from the middle of the first millennium in Sardinia, but more recent research indicates a much earlier date and suggests that it was a local innovation. All five free-standing temples are oriented towards the south-east quadrant, like the dolmens, the *corridoi dolmenici* and most of the *tombe di giganti*.

This is not all. Many mysterious sanctuaries dating from the beginning of the first millennium have been found scattered over the island. They consist of stone domes built over sacred springs and wells. Such holy springs and wells with their life-giving and purifying waters were long associated with the Great Goddess, and in Sardinia may well represent a continuation of her cult despite the overall turbulence of the Bronze Age. Baetyls with mammalian bosses or cavities have been found near the giants' tombs, while double-axes have been discovered at the water sanctuaries, symbol of the Great Goddess in her twofold guise as provider and terrifier.

A large number of bronze statuettes discovered in their vicinity were no doubt intended as votive offerings; one represents a demon with four eyes and four arms, while others are quite realistic portrayals of animals. The waters from the sanctuaries are still considered by local people to have healing properties. A fine example I visited is in the village of Sant' Anastasia, not far from Bavumini. Situated next to a nuraghic settlement, it has a flight of twelve steps going down to the well and a dome to protect it. Part of the sanctuary was dismantled to build the church, which still stands – another example of the Christian religion imposing itself on a pagan site while being unintentionally affected by its sacred nature.

There can be no doubt that the tower-building people of Sardinia were great seafarers. Seagoing craft figure among the most interesting of their bronze statuettes. Of the thousands of scale models of boats produced up to the sixth century BC, 120 remain. They were probably used as oil lamps and have been found in areas populated by Etruscans on mainland Italy. Their existence imply that there was a nuraghic navy equipped with at least two kinds of large craft: one with a flat bottom for navigating inland waters, and one with a convex keel, mast and animal-headed bow for carrying cargo and warriors, similar to the Phoenician *hippoi*.[17] It was the latter which no doubt formed part of the navy of the Sea Peoples.

As early as 700 BC, the name Shardan was given to the island. The tower-building Shardana were feared as mercenaries throughout the Mediterranean: bronze statues depict them as fierce warriors with highly ornate helmets and daggers slung about their necks. Strabo comments on their attacks on the Etruscans. But they met a far more powerful foe: the Carthaginians who took on the might of the Roman empire during the Punic Wars. Diodorus Siculus records how they formed settlements on Sardinia after 800 BC and eventually an expedition from Carthage sacked the major nuraghi around 500 BC. The shock led to the demise of their culture in the following century: more than 3000 years of megalithic building on the island came to an abrupt end.

CHAPTER TWENTY

Africa and Back

Delenda est Carthago!

CATO THE ELDER

W e followed in the wake of the Shardana and Phoenicians down the exposed and windy west coast of Sardinia. From our northern base, Stintino, we sailed through the tricky passage between the peninsula and the small island of Asinara, uninhabited by humans but teeming with a splendid array of birds. Good winds took us past Alghero – as I've mentioned, a Catalan-speaking anomaly – and its nearby nuraghe fortress at Palmavera. We revelled in the sight of the bold headlands along the coast and called in at Bosa along the way, a city of elegant Baroque churches.

In complete contrast, we landed on the beautiful, uninhabited Isola di Mal di Ventre – Bad Stomach Island. It is not clear why it is so called. The island would have been a natural resting place for ancient mariners, but perhaps its water was contaminated. Opposite the island, on the southern tip of the Sinis Peninsula, there are still ruins to be seen of the ancient Phoenician port of Tharros, later occupied by the Romans. The site was abandoned in the seventh century AD when it was attacked by Moorish pirates and its inhabitants moved to Oristano further inland.

The wide Golfo di Oristano gives way to the magnificent green coastline of the Costa Verde, all rugged mountains running down to the sea. We visited the former mining port of Buggerru with its silted harbour set below a series of imposing peaks. After calling in at Portoscuso in the southwestern corner of the island, we passed over the shallows between two more islands, San Pietro and Sant' Antioco, and rounded the Capo Teulada, the most southerly point of Sardinia.

We then sailed passed the strategically placed ancient port of Nora, founded in the ninth century BC by the Phoenicians and later taken over by the Romans. The impressive ruins of this evocative site run right down into the sea.

Our next port of call was the befittingly small Porto Piccolo, with its lovely beach half-covered in sunbathers and its nearby salt lake full of pink flamingos. It is on the edge of the handsome city of Cagliari, the capital of Sardinia, with its Phoenician necropolis and vast Roman amphitheatre. It has a well-kept archaeological museum full of nuraghic bronzes. From our base here we made forays inland to visit the megalithic sites of southern Sardinia, which are much fewer than in the north.

I had intended to travel from Cagliari directly to the Isole Egadi just off the western tip of Sicily, but looking at the chart, I realized that it was just a day's sail to the ruins of Carthage in Tunisia, the former centre of the ancient world's greatest maritime empire. Nearby was the tiny volcanic island of Pantalleria, reputed to harbour mysterious megalithic remains. It was all too enticing to resist.

At first light we left our quiet anchorage off a white sandy beach in the Golfo di Cagliari. It was a calm, clear day and I took an early morning dip in the limpid water before setting sail for Africa. I sighted flying fish that day, and during the night saw shooting stars falling out of the pin-pricked sky. The light of the moon danced on the smooth waters. At dawn, the sudden smell of warm earth heralded the beguiling sight of the rocky African shore. The shallow seabed made this part of the Mediterranean dangerous in rough weather, but rich in fish and fishermen. As we entered the Gulf of Tunis, we were entertained by hundreds of seagulls in an aerial display – a rare and memorable sight for the Mediterranean. The inland sea is something like a semi-arid desert, and its famed clarity is due to the lack of plankton – the starting point of all fish and bird life.

The first Hiroshima

Tunis lies at the edge of a vast inland lake which is entered through La Goulette, the Narrows. I hesitated at its entrance and then decided to sail along the coast to the little harbour below the white walls and turquoise doors of Sidi Bou Said, towering high on a cliff. On the way, we passed the ruins of the ancient Punic Ports, the President's Palace, and high on a hill the remains of Carthage itself, now dominated by a deconsecrated cathedral.

Ever since I had left Britain, I had been aware of the pre-sence of the Phoenicians as I followed in their wake down the Atlantic seaboard and across the Mediterranean. Without doubt they were the greatest seafarers of the ancient world: some time before 480 BC, Hanno reached the Bight of Benin in West Africa where he saw Mount Cameroon, and Himilco came to Brittany and Cornwall, thereby controlling the gold and tin routes. According to Herodotus, the Egyptian pharaoh Nechos II had employed Phoenicians around 500 BC to sail from the Red Sea down the east coast of Africa. Three years later they came back through the Strait of Gibraltar, thereby making the first known circumnavigation of Africa.[1] And it was the Phoenicians who halted the megalith building in the Iberian Peninsula and the Mediterranean islands.

The Phoenicians founded Carthage in 814 BC as one of their colonies along the north African coast, spreading from their original city-state of Tyre in Phoenicia (present-day Lebanon). Legend has it that the founder was Princess Elissa, immortalized as Dido, Queen of Carthage, in Virgil's *Aeneid*, who threw herself into a fire rather than marry a Berber king. Her ancestors had been visiting the coast of North Africa since 2000 BC.[2] By the end of the fourth century BC, the city had become the greatest power in the western Mediterranean and inevitably came into conflict first with the Greeks and then with the Romans. The Phoenicians took on the growing might of the Roman empire in the three Punic Wars, the high point of which was when Hannibal, whom Napoleon called 'the greatest captain in the world', took an army from Gades (Cádiz) across the Alps with several hundred elephants. But Hannibal hesitated outside Rome, and was doomed. The Romans eventually took Carthage in 146 BC and burnt it to the ground, and in a symbolic gesture cursed, and spread salt over, its fertile soil. This world war of antiquity ended with its own version of Hiroshima and the first holocaust in history. The deadly phrase '*Delenda est Carthago!*' ('Carthage must be destroyed') has reverberated down the ages ever since.

Of the original Carthage on Myrsa Hill, only a few sparse remnants exist – ruins of ruins. At the height of its power, Carthage would have boasted six-storied houses set alongside wide avenues which ran down to the sea. Behind it vast ramparts and their towers – 34 kilometres long – were stables for more than 4000 horses and 300 elephants. They would have been no match for the remaining megalith builders along the coasts and islands of the Mediterranean.

The Punic Ports from which their mighty navy sailed at the bottom of the hill have been reduced to two small lagoons. The artificial harbour originally consisted of an outer rectangular basin for the merchant fleet which communicated via a canal to a round port with an island in the middle where the admiralty once stood.[3] I wondered what the peaceful fishermen in the Gulf of Tunis, bobbing up and down in their brightly coloured boats, would have thought of their feared ancestors.

Near the Punic Ports are the ruins of the sacred enclosure known as the Tophet where the Phoenicians sacrificed children to Baal and Tanit, the guardian gods of the city. The practice was based on the principle of *Anima pro anima, sanguine pro sanguine, vita pro vita* ('Spirit for spirit, blood for blood, life for life'). Different layers of the site reveal that the ashes of the children were collected in urns and placed in small dolmens made with a kind of stucco accompanied by a stele commemorating the sacrifice.[4] In the Bardo Museum in a former king's palace in a suburb of Tunis, there is a stele taken from the Tophet which shows a priest holding a child about to be sacrificed. Despite a common misapprehension associated with the Druids, there is no evidence that megalithic peoples ever practised such human sacrifice.

While the Phoenicians were developing Carthage, the people of the interior – the Berbers – continued to build real dolmens for their dead. As the *Atlas Préhistorique de la Tunisie* makes clear, there are numerous dolmens in Tunisia. They are not, however, thought to be earlier than the first millennium BC, thereby making them proto-historic rather than prehistoric. The British archaeologist Michael Hoskin however has recently found at Kesra, on a stony plateau 16 kilometres southeast of Makthar in northern Tunisia, the remains of two monuments which resemble the French *allées couvertes*. They have a corridor leading to a rectangular chamber, and a backstone with a carefully smoothed centre. They are oriented towards the east. Hoskin dated them to the early or middle second millennium BC.

Another extraordinary site 12 kilometres west of Makthar at Henchir Midad has some 200 dolmens in rows on a hill above a watercourse. Typically, they have a rectangular chamber formed of five massive and carefully shaped stones, the one in front with a rectangular hole at ground level for access. They tend to face south, that is, downhill.[5] Unfortunately, little is known of the megaliths of Tunisia and even less of the people who built them. But as elsewhere in the Mediterranean, their culture was brought to an end by the Phoenicians and then by the Romans who occupied their land.

The volcanic island

I had been fascinated by my foray into Tunisia, but not to the point where I forgot my plan to stop off on the nearby island of Pantelleria. From Cap Bon, it lies 70 nautical miles away and about 50 from the African coast – closer to Tunisia than Sicily. A grey volcanic place that bursts into flower in spring, Pantelleria is scattered with intriguing late megalithic tombs. The local inhabitants think nothing of them, apart from their being rough stones in the way, or useful for making the walls that demarcate their fields.

After an overnight sail during which our navigation aids, radio, engine and even clock packed up within about ten minutes, we searched for the tiny island on the empty horizon shimmering in the African heat. Apart from the help of a compass we were as alone and vulnerable as the megalithic seafarer. At midday it appeared as a speck ahead which came and went like an illusion. It eventually turned out to be a great black rock rising out of the azure sea. Without a decent chart we edged our way along its steep, dark cliffs until we found the entrance to the wide harbour. As soon as we moored in an empty space in the 'free' inner port, we were asked to move by an aggressive local boat owner who claimed it was his. 'You're now in southern Italy!' joked an onlooker on the deserted and neglected quay. In town, where there were no taxis, we were fortunate enough to meet a Sicilian who offered to show us the archaeological sites of the island.

On the northwestern tip of Pantelleria, near Mursia, a major settlement from the early Bronze Age (1800 to 1600 BC) has been discovered on a low cliff. A good part of its defensive wall on the land side is still standing; it was about 8 metres high and 200 metres long. Originally, it boasted a population of some 2000 inhabitants. Intriguingly, the site lies atop the lava flow of an extinct volcano, beyond which stretches fertile agricultural land. On an island which now experiences serious shortages of water in the hot summer months, the settlement could enjoy cool water from springs in the area.

The necropolis, now mostly hidden in thorny vegetation and cacti, lies on a slope of lava outside the walls of the settlement. It has over fifty communal tombs known locally as *sesi*, roughly constructed from blocks of black lava. The largest, known as the Sese Grande, is 20 metres across and has twelve passages, each leading to its own chamber deep inside the mound. One entrance from the north is divided into two passages with small chambers. There is no obvious astronomical orientation.[6]

The Sese Grande is stepped like a small ziggurat. My kindly guide Francesco Ferrera thought the people who built them came from the Middle East. It is tempting but fanciful to compare the sesi with the nuraghi of Sardinia or the navetas of Menorca. Local guidebooks suggest that the Neolithic people who first settled on Pantelleria around 3000 BC probably came from Tunisia or Spain. It is equally possible that they came from Sicily, where you can also find tombs cut into cliffs. I learned later that Pantelleria alone shares a common lizard with Malta, which indicates a maritime connection. Given the strategic position of the island in the middle of the Strait of Sicily between Africa and Europe, it is not surprising that the Phoenicians occupied it in the ninth century BC, followed by the Carthaginians who minted their own money and built an acropolis, the ruins of which can still be seen near the airport.

As we sailed away we saw the local *carabinieri* towing a dozen Arabs in a small dinghy. They had been drifting at sea in the hope of being washed onto European shores. If they could attempt it in such a haphazard fashion, the crossing would have been no major feat for experienced ancient mariners in seaworthy boats who knew how to sail and navigate by the stars.

Sicily

The distance from Pantelleria to Sicily is 65 nautical miles. Usually it is a heavenly stretch of azure water, but dark clouds gathered on the horizon soon after we set sail, shooting great zigzags of lightning across the brooding sky. We managed to escape the thunderstorm and sailed fast – for us at least – across the strait to the fishing port of Sciacca in southwestern Sicily, a journey of fourteen hours. It confirmed yet again how easy it would have been for the ancient mariners to hop from one island to the other.

The largest island in the Mediterranean and strategically placed in the middle, Sicily has always been a target for successive waves of settlers and invaders. It has been inhabited from the Upper Palaeolithic times at the end of the Würm glaciation: incised or painted figures of humans and animals from this period can be seen in a cave at Addaura near the capital Palermo. I admired the grace and energy of the prehistoric dancers of Addaura in finely executed drawings held in the archaeology museum at Palermo, housed in a beautiful villa. There I also lingered in front of a handsome prehistoric jug found in the grotto of Moarda near Palermo dating from the early Bronze Age.

The museum contains the famous Palermo Stone, a fragment of black diorite engraved in the middle of the third millennium with hieroglyphs containing the annals of the first five dynasties of the Old Kingdom of Egypt. But although prosaic, the most evocative artefacts for me were some Neolithic anchors, scattered around the gardens of the inner courtyard. Dating from the third millennium, they were made from great stones with carved holes for attaching leather cords. At the same time it was amusing to come across a mosaic of Orpheus taming wild animals with music taken from a Roman villa in Palermo which was an exact replica of one I had seen in the Bardo Museum in Tunis.

It was long thought that the first peoples to settle in Sicily, around Syracuse, arrived in the fourth millennium and established the so-called Stentinello culture. Recent excavations near Palma di Montechiaro and Licata along the south coast however have shown that the earliest Neolithic pottery dates back to the seventh millennium. Just inland from where I had landed at Sciacca on the southwestern coast, ceramics dating back to around 6000 BC have also been found at Monte Kronio which is honeycombed with caves. Much of the pottery is decorated with zigzag bands.

The people of the Stentinello culture decorated their pottery with impressions of cockle shells and friezes fashioned with specially made bone tools.[7] The lozenge stamps, symbolizing the vulva, and zigzags, representing streams of water, are among their most characteristic designs, suggesting that they too worshipped the Great Goddess. Where these people came from remains a mystery. T. Eric Peet believed that the 'lake-dwelling terramara people' from the Danube valley in Central Europe invaded Sicily, while Margaret Guido felt they came from the Eastern Mediterranean.[8]

The first users of copper, who buried their dead in rock-cut tombs, arrived in Sicily during the third millennium BC. They had trade connections with Western Europe and imported beakers from Spain and France. The widespread maritime links continued into the middle Bronze Age. On Salina in the Lipari or Aeolian Islands off the north coast of Sicily, a necklace has been discovered which includes some segmented faience beads of an Egyptian type. These were popular throughout the Mycenaean world, and have been found as far afield as the Wessex culture in England.[9]

There is a settlement at Castelluccio, inland from Syracuse, which sits on a spur above a steep valley like Los Millares in Spain. More than 200 tombs are cut into the cliffs, and although no dwellings have survived large amounts of pottery have been found scattered on the site. Since some of the pottery dates from the Helladic period of

Greece, it has been customary to date the site to between 1800 and 1400 BC, but it was probably built much earlier. There are even some carvings of spirals and other motifs similar to ones which I was to see in the Tarxien temples in Malta, which date from the fourth millennium.

Although it lies south of Italy and between the dolmen-rich lands of Sardinia and Tunisia, Sicily has so far yielded no true dolmens. Indeed, few tombs from the megalithic era have been found. Those discovered are either true hypogea cut in the bedrock, 'dolmenic hypogea' that are partly underground, or 'paradolmens' which incorporate natural features of the surrounding rock.

On the western tip of the island at Roccazzo a necropolis of some 200 graves has been discovered on a plateau dating from the fourth and third millennium BC. The builders simply cut a circular shaft in the limestone bedrock to around a metre and then struck sideways, in no consistent direction, to carve out an oval chamber large enough for a single body. They then sealed off the entrance with a vertical slab. Tombs of a necropolis at Ciachea at Capaci near Palermo dating from the second half of the third millennium are similarly sunk in the bedrock, although here multiple chambers lead off from each shaft.

Opposing the main trend in Western Europe, early Bronze Age builders in Sicily moved from constructing single graves to communal ones at the end of the third millennium. They were still fundamentally hypogeic in construction, but incorporated megaliths in their structure. One in Paolina in the southeast of the island is a fine example. A little later the roofs of the sunken communal tombs were capped with a megalithic slab.

There a few paradolmens still surviving on the island, two of which are to be found at Cava dei Servi near Modica in the southeast. Nevertheless, it is still accurate to say that no true dolmens have been found so far on Sicily.[10]

The Phoenicians occupied Sicily in the eighth century BC, founding a settlement called Ziz (the Phoenician word for 'flower') on the site of present-day Palermo. At the same time, these great seafarers established a colony on the island of Mozia in a lagoon just above Marsala on the island's western tip. It remained their main maritime base in the central Mediterranean until it was burnt down by the Greek tyrant Dionysius of Syracuse in 397 BC. Many ruins still remain and there is a museum on the island named after Joseph Whittaker, an English wine merchant who excavated the site at the end of the nineteenth century. In the lagoon, which is still used to make salt and has many windmills on its shores, a headless Egyptian figure was discovered holding a caduceus, a rod with two entwined snakes. It is usually thought to represent Hermes, the Greek god of travel and trade and the counterpart of the Egyptian god Thoth, reflecting yet again the close cultural exchanges and maritime connections across the ancient Mediterranean.

Mainland Italy

I was fascinated to find out that, apart from a small group of minor chamber tombs in the region around Rome and Naples, the only megaliths on mainland Italy are concentrated in its southeastern heel. Since this cannot be explained by prevailing winds and currents, the only reasonable explanation can be that the existing culture in central and northern Italy was strong enough and sufficiently entrenched to resist the religion of any megalithic-building visitors. In the heel of Italy, however, megalithic seafarers must have landed and persuaded the local inhabitants of their beliefs, or local seafarers must have travelled to neighbouring Corsica and Sardinia, possibly even to France and Spain.

There is a celebrated group of dolmens scattered amongst the olive groves west of Bari in Puglia. These gallery graves, believed to date from before 2000 BC, have long structures and a single capstone; an impressive one is to be found close to a service station called Dolmen on the Bari–Naples road. I took this route once during a journey around Africa: it is the most direct one from one major port to another in southern Italy.

The most outstanding of the ruins is the Giovinazzo gallery grave, not far from the seaside town of the same name in Puglia. Stretching some 27 metres, it has a cairn of carefully dressed drystone masonry which was covered with earth until it was crushed in the middle by a bulldozer. Many skeletons were unearthed. Although curving slightly, it is aligned on a north–south axis. Mycenaean pottery, in use around 1800 BC, has been discovered amongst the grave goods, but the main structure was probably built much earlier.

Finally, on the very tip of Italy around the port of Otranto lies a group of dolmens thought to date from around 2000 BC, together with standing stones which once reached 3 metres high. Clearly, the heel of Italy was little more than a foothold for the megalith builders. Malta was an entirely different story. There, the first free-standing architecture in the world was built in the fourth millennium BC, and I could not wait to explore it.

CHAPTER TWENTY-ONE

Temples of the Goddess

This is none other but the house of God and this is the gate of heaven. And Jacob rose up early in the morning, and took the stone that he had put for his pillows, and set it up for a pillar, and poured oil upon the top of it.

GENESIS

W e sailed overnight from Licata on the south coast of Sicily. It was an easy jaunt of 76 nautical miles, helped along by the southeast-flowing current which picks up to more than a knot in the Malta Channel. On a clear day, it is possible to see the low-lying Maltese islands from mountainous Sicily, but not vice versa. Leaving at midnight, we steered pretty much due south under a wonderful canopy of stars, and by midmorning the light brown flat-topped island of Gozo came into view. We sailed past Gozo and arrived in the port adjoining the Grand Harbour of Valletta on mainland Malta in the early evening. After travelling for seven months and about 4000 nautical miles, I had at last reached my ultimate destination.

I had shown that it would have been quite possible for the ancient mariners to have sailed in a small boat from northern Europe to the central Mediterranean with no great feats of navigation and no lengthy voyages at sea. I may have been better equipped than my megalithic counterparts, but our boats were more or less the same length (7 metres) and we probably sailed at the same speed (4 knots an hour). I had an auxiliary engine, but they could count on more manpower. I had to make a secure anchorage or reach a port in bad weather; they could pull their light boats upon any open beach.

And it had been well worth the effort. Malta, for megalith-hunters, is a veritable Mecca. There are twenty-three classified ruins built between 3600 and 2500 BC, and possibly a score more which may have been destroyed over the centuries.[1] The best known are Ggantija on the island of Gozo and Tarxien, Hagar Qim and Mnajdra on mainland Malta – all very sacred places with special energy. The underground temple known as the Hypogeum of Hal Saflieni is also deeply intriguing, combining extreme complexity and sophistication.

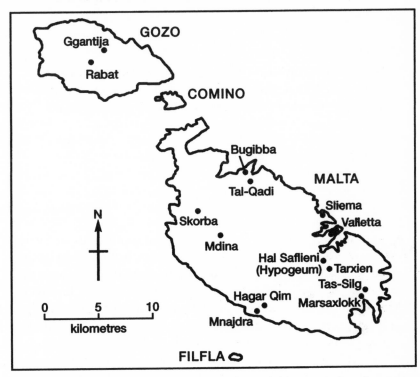

Map of Malta and Gozo, with the principal megalithic sites and modern towns

The Maltese megaliths have rightly been called 'the best-kept secret in Mediterranean archaeology'.[2] They show that a thousand years before the building of the pyramids in Egypt, a spectacular megalithic civilization centred on the worship of the Great Goddess was flourishing in Malta.

The earliest stone temple in the world

In the centre of the beautiful island of Gozo, a short trip from mainland Malta, stands Ggantija on the edge of Xaghra town. Built around 3600 to 3000 BC, it became the template of all the subsequent Maltese megalithic temples. They have a semicircular forecourt and are made of a series of kidney-shaped apses on either side of a well-built passage leading to an altar niche. The architecture is one of curves, with no straight lines, like the Great Goddess herself.

The complex contains two temples standing side by side. Its flowing curves embrace an inner space of five apsidal rooms interconnected by axial passageways. The walls consist of massive, perfectly interlocking stones of rough, hard coralline limestone, while smoother and softer globigerina limestone was used for flanking the passageways. The original façade of Ggantija may have been as high as 16 metres. At present it has an outer wall of Cyclopean blocks, some of which are 5 metres high and weigh 15 tonnes or more. If we bear in mind that the importance of a building is as much the empty space within its structure as its walls and roof, Ggantija's shape evokes the cosmic womb of the Great Goddess.

Colin Renfrew has called the façade of this magnificent temple 'perhaps the earliest architecturally conceived exterior in the world'.[3] It shows that from the earliest times the Maltese were consummate builders, the master masons of prehistory. Like their counterparts in northern Europe, they felt compelled, soon after settling down, to build great stone monuments above and below the ground, uniting heaven and earth. Aware of their own physical mortality, they tried to defy time by creating permanent temples in space.

On a hill overlooking the Ggantija complex to the west is the so-called Xaghra Stone Circle, often called the Brochtorff Circle after the man who excavated and painted it in watercolours in 1828–9. At that stage, it had two monumental pillars more than 4 metres high forming the entrance on the east side, as well as a 'Giant's Tower' which is still standing. Some years later a local farmer quarried many of the stones to build a farmhouse nearby and flattened the site to make way for an orchard and vineyard. It was only rediscovered in the 1960s, and excavated anew in 1987. It soon became clear that the 'circle' is not a typical ring as found in northern Europe, for its interlocking standing stones form a boundary wall built to protect a large underground burial chamber cut out of a series of natural caves.

The extraordinary complex is thought to be contemporary with the earliest so-called 'Zebbug phase' of Maltese prehistory (4100–3800 BC) named after the site where the earliest underground tanks have been found.

The recent excavation at the Xaghra Stone Circle has revealed a stone shaft leading to two circular chambers which contained more

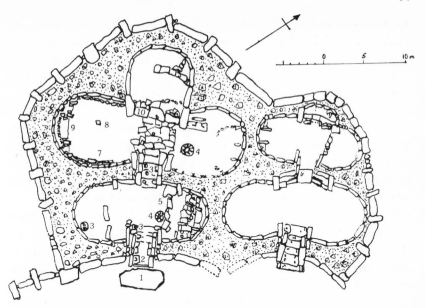

1. Threshold; 2. Purification block; 3. Libation holes; 4. Fireplace; 5. Decorated blocks; 7. Public Triangle; 8. Stone pedestal; 9. Niche altars; 10. Main altar.

Ground plan of the Ggantija temples, Gozo

than sixty individuals with their personal ornaments. These included bone amulets that looked roughly like humans, and axe-shaped stone pendants imported from overseas, some from as far away as the Alps. A large quantity of red ochre was splashed in one chamber. In addition, hundred of thousands of bone fragments have been found on the site, belonging to more than 1000 individuals, which show that they were part of an unusually healthy population with good teeth. Two articulated skeletons complete with their skulls have also been discovered.

Burial rituals seem to have taken place in a central area a few steps below the ground. A small statue group of two obese draped figures (one holding a smaller version of herself and the other a hollow cup) was found there, as well as the pieces of a broken statue of a similarly corpulent lady which once stood a metre high. A dozen terracotta figurines with enormous buttocks and thighs and small torsos and limbs have also been unearthed. They are all clearly fertility symbols of the Great Goddess.

A more mysterious discovery was a bundle of figurines with human heads supported by triangular bodies; one is attached to a two-limbed animal body, while another has a pig's head.[4] These were no doubt hand-held by shamans or priests during rituals and ceremonies which were held underground.

Of time and teeth

Who were these people who built the temple and chamber at Xaghra? This is the great mystery surrounding the origins of Maltese temples and tombs. Why did they suddenly appear 'ready made', without any obvious archaeological background? It is as if the islanders went from building huts to cathedrals in a space of 500 years. The Maltese islands were cut off from the mainland at the end of the Ice Age around 10,000 BC, due to the rise in sea level resulting from the melting of the ice caps. If the orthodox chronology of prehistory is right, there were no inhabitants in the archipelago in the Palaeolithic Age and the islands were first populated by Neolithic agriculturalists. Known as the Erastene people, they allegedly travelled 80 nautical miles across the sea – as I had done – from Sicily around 5200 BC.[5] This is still the official view as expressed to me by Mark A. Mifsud, assistant curator of the National Archaeology Museum in Malta's capital Valletta.

The principal evidence for this view is that they made a new kind of pottery known as Impressed Ware, which was very similar to that of the Stentinello culture in southeastern Sicily. On the other hand, rather than being the work of a new set of settlers from the north, the pottery could well have been made by the existing inhabitants, who had simply come under the influence of their Sicilian neighbours through their trading connections across the sea. Since there are no outstanding megalithic remains on Sicily, any settlers clearly did not bring their building techniques with them. Could it therefore be that the megalithic civilization of Malta was an entirely home-grown affair?

Although it has been assumed that Malta was settled at the beginning of the fifth millennium BC, a fiasco surrounding the dating of some ancient teeth has made this much more uncertain. Several human teeth, known as taurodonts because they look like the teeth of bulls, without roots, have been found in the Cervus layer (containing red deer) at Ghar Dalam (the Cave of Darkness) on the south coast of Malta. The layer dates back before 8000 BC to the Pleistocene, a geological period contemporaneous with the archaeological Palaeolithic period. It is known that Palaeolithic man had such molars and when these teeth were examined by the British

Natural History Museum in the 1950s the scientific tests confirmed that they were contemporaneous with the red deer of the Ice Age. Yet on the basis of a conversation with the chemist, the archaeologist David Trump asserted in his archaeological guide – now a standard work – that the tests showed that the teeth were not early and had possibly been inserted in the layer at a later date. It simply confirmed for Trump the view first expressed by the British doyen of Maltese archaeology, J.D. Evans, that the first settlers came by boat from Sicily in the later Neolithic era from Sicily.

The research of the Maltese paediatrician Dr Anton Mifsud and his co-workers, followed up by Graham Hancock, has shown, however, that several taurodent teeth found in the first part of the twentieth century could well point to the early habitation of Malta in the Palaeolithic era. In the meantime, the relevant page recording the tests in the so-called *Green Book* at the Natural History Museum in London has gone missing, and except for one molar, the teeth themselves have been lost. When confronted with these findings in 2000, Trump declared that he was open to the possibility of there being earlier inhabitants but the issue for the time being rested 'in limbo'.[6] For the present, the archaeological authorities in Malta are refusing to have the remaining tooth tested by more modern and reliable techniques. Why? Are they concerned that their cherished beliefs will be undermined?

Anton Mifsud has argued that the megalithic complexes on Malta were carrying on a tradition which had started among hunter-gatherers in the so-called Magdalenian Period (15,000–10,000 BC) in the Palaeolithic era when Malta was connected to the European continent.[7] However, no stone buildings have as yet been discovered predating 5000 BC in Malta, and as elsewhere in Europe, the era of megalithic building began only after the nomadic hunter-gatherers settled down to become agriculturalists.

Early inhabitants

About 7000 years ago, the inhabitants of Malta seem to have lived in natural caves and in small, scattered villages. The beautiful pottery found at Ghar Dalam, dated to between 5200 and 4500 BC, has bold diagonal designs and dynamic zigzags like waves, suggesting the water symbolism of a seafaring people. The only early village which has been extensively explored is at Skorba (dating from 4400 to 4100 BC) in the northwest of the island. It shows that the inhabitants lived in small oval huts made from mud bricks and wattle-and-daub built on low stone foundations.

Among the ceramics discovered were two spoon-like cups and a large round-bellied pot with moon handles. The most intriguing find however was a shrine in one of the huts which contained fragments of small female terracotta figurines with exaggerated breasts and genitalia. They were clearly associated with the cult of the Great Goddess, the fertile Mother, who as we have seen was worshipped throughout Europe during the early megalithic period. Concerned with the continued fertility of the land on which they relied for their survival, these people understandably celebrated a fecund Goddess as the personification of the earth which gives forth all life. The society was almost certainly matrilineal, tracing descent from one generation to the next through the mother.

The Maltese megalith builders lived in small scattered communities in a spirit of peaceful cooperation and sharing. There were probably about 10,000 of them.[8] The land was sufficiently fertile and life easy enough for them to dedicate much of their time to building beautiful temples and to engage in complex religious ceremonies. Renfrew has suggested that there may have been six competing communities, each with its own agricultural territory and temple complex, led by a chief.[9] There is, however, absolutely no evidence for the existence of leaders at this stage, whether male or female. Trump moreover has correctly observed that 'no hint' of conflict exists between the groups nor of any cultural or religious divergence between them.[10] Indeed, there are no signs of armed conflict in ancient Malta during Neolithic times and no weapons have been detected in Neolithic burials.[11]

Plato's island

If Malta's megalithic civilization was a home-grown affair, we are left with the problem, as Anton Mifsud and his collaborators put it, that 'Malta is presently too small in size to have sustained the earliest architectural civilisation; its *civilisation territory* is missing'.[12]

They came up with an intriguing solution to the puzzle: Malta is a remnant of the lost island of Atlantis, first mentioned by Plato in *Timaeus*. They argue that the sudden dropping of the earth's crust along the Pantelleria rift resulted in a deluge which wiped out Malta's great megalithic civilization, and reduced the islands to their present size around 2200 BC. It is a fascinating and well-argued hypothesis, but one which in the end I was unable to support.

In my view, the siting and ending of Atlantis in Malta does not fit in with Plato's own chronology, which points to a date around 9000 BC. Moreover, it overlooks a much more obvious fact: the knowledge to build in stone could have been brought across the sea in boats as it was in other parts of Europe, along with seeds of barley and wheat and specimens of sheep, goats, cattle and pigs. As I had shown in my own voyage, Malta is only a day's sail – about 80 nautical miles – away from Sicily and Africa. For an ancient mariner, the crossing would have involved no sophisticated navigation – just a fair wind.

The official view of the Maltese archaeological establishment, as expressed to me by Mark Mifsud, the assistant curator of the National Archaeology Museum, is that there was no influence from other Mediterranean Neolithic communities apart from Sicily. Certainly Stentinello pottery from around Syracuse in Sicily has been found on the island of Malta. But as an island nation, the Stone Age dwellers on Malta were undoubtedly competent and experienced navigators and had long-established trading links with their neighbours.

It is known that Pantelleria and the Lipari Islands provided obsidian from the earliest times. Prestige objects such as green axe-shaped pendants for necklaces were imported. At the temple of Hagar Qim alone, twenty-six instruments made from flint have been found; as the stone doesn't exist on Malta, they clearly indicate long-distance trading connections.

The influence of Egypt was also felt. Four Egyptian stelae carved in Maltese limestone were discovered in 1829 in the foundations of Villa Bichi. Another statue in local limestone, found on Gozo in 1713, depicted an Egyptian priest holding the figures of Horus, the son of Osiris and Isis, and Maat, the goddess of truth.

As we have seen, there can be no doubt that Malta, along with North Africa and the rest of the Mediterranean, venerated a fertility goddess.[13] Indeed, rather than being cut off from the rest of the world, the temples on the island, strategically placed in the middle of the Mediterranean and between Africa and Europe, may well have attracted pilgrims for worship and healing much as Lourdes or Santiago de Compostela do today.[14]

The ancient Maltese, as now, were undoubtedly capable seafarers. I was fascinated to discover that there are engravings on slabs at the Tarxien temples which show a number of different Neolithic boats. Some, which look like upturned combs, recall the engravings I had seen in Galicia. One in particular has an upturned prow and stern like the Egyptian boats. I was struck by its similarity to the four-man

Maltese *dghajsas*, which are still raced in the Grand Harbour at Valletta. These colourful boats, painted with an *oculi* on their bows, have double ends with a flattish bottom amidships, a tholepin for each oar and no rudder. They follow a very ancient design and resemble the Portuguese *saveiros*.[15]

I can see no reason why a civilization cannot suddenly 'take off' in a short span of time once the technological knowledge is acquired from overseas. For example, 100 years ago Kinshasa on the River Congo was scattered with mud huts; now skyscrapers and the glare of city lights blot out the stars. Computers hum in air-conditioned offices where drums once communicated in the jungle. If the knowledge of building and technology can change a society in Africa so radically a century after the arrival of a few people with new skills, why could it not within 1700 years on Malta, following the first secure dating for humans residing there?

My own view is that Malta was probably inhabited from the Palaeolithic era. Its seafaring people no doubt developed their own indigenous culture, but after becoming settled agriculturalists around 5000 BC, they were exposed to the influences of megalithic cultures in other parts of the Mediterranean, particularly North Africa, Sardinia, Sicily and southern Italy. No doubt their contact with them not only enabled them to acquire new techniques, but excited their passion to build great stone monuments for their already established cult of the Great Goddess. Once they had built their first temples based on the trefoil plan seen at Ggantija on Gozo, they kept the curved apsidal shape as their basic form. At the same time, they developed their own distinctive architectural style. As I had seen on my long voyage, the designs of megalithic peoples tend to be conservative once they are established.

Dolmen hunting

This view of overseas influence is confirmed by the presence of dolmens on Malta, and their complete absence in Sicily. The affable Anton Mifsud, who in addition to his medical practice is President of the Prehistoric Society of Malta, took Elizabeth and me on a tour of the main sites with his delightful partner Geraldine Camilleri.

None were far from the sea, and our first port of call was Borg In-Nadur overlooking Marsaxlokk Bay in the southeast of mainland Malta. 'It used to be called the Temple of Hercules', Anton informed me.

It had been neglected in the past; one of the megaliths had even been poorly carved into a human face in recent times. But the setting, on the spur of a hill overlooking the sea, was magnificent and the tranquil atmosphere at the end of a hot day was delightful. I immediately recognized a collapsed dolmen forming part of the outer wall. The shape of twin apses could also be discerned amongst the scattered stones. A megalithic wall, some 55 metres long, had once run here in a south–north direction. As Geraldine observed, the energy seemed very strong under the capstone of the dolmen, between the apses and on a mound which looked like a tumulus overlooking the site.

'No bodies have been found in the temples in Malta,' Anton said. 'We cannot be sure whether any burials took place here. Trump suggested that there could be a hypogeum underground, but no excavations have yet been carried out. Until recently, the site was abandoned and used by a local farmer for his sheep!'

He mentioned that the nearby megalithic temple of Tas-Silg had remained a sacred place, successively used for worship by Punic, Roman, Byzantine, Arab and Christian believers.

We next travelled to see the two adjoining dolmens at Tal-Qadi towards the north coast, on a slope above a plain facing west. They too formed part of a massive wall. It was late afternoon when we reached it, and the warm stones were lit by a golden light from the setting sun. Wasps had made their nests in the craggy coralline stones. We crouched under one of the massive capstones of the dolmens to enter the site from an adjoining lane. Nearby was a quarry from which the megaliths had been taken.

The dolmens were impressive enough – the lozenge-shaped capstones were more than 5 metres across. But the most extraordinary aspect of Tal-Qadi is the fragment of a stone which has been discovered there, now in the Archaeology Museum in Valletta. Measuring 29 centimetres by 24, it has radial lines fanning out from an observation point which divide the fragment into five segments. Four have stars engraved on it while a lunar crescent decorates the fifth. Its enigmatic inscription has been boldly deciphered by an expert in Sanskrit as:

Called up is the large and mighty female planet
which is visible from
The earth, counted from the outside, the seventh planet.
The increasing moon, a symbol of power,
some event is taking place.

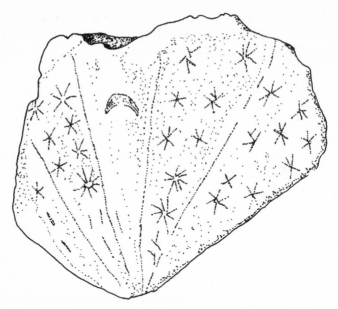

Stone depicting stars and a crescent moon from an observation point, Tal-Qadi temple, Malta

> The sun and nine planets, our solar system.
> The large mighty female planet has arrived, the fourth planet
> in our solar system, counted from the outside.[16]

From an astrological point of view, this translation seems suspect. According to the Chaldean system adopted by the ancient Mesopotamians and Egyptians, the seventh planet 'from the outside', including the sun, is the moon and the fourth 'planet' is the sun. The mention of the sun and nine planets, however, implies that the ancient Maltese knew about the recently discovered planets Uranus, Neptune and Pluto which are invisible to the naked eye. In which case, the fourth planet 'from the outside' would be Saturn and the seventh planet, excluding the sun, Venus.[17]

Chris Micallef, the archaeo-astronomer who has made a detailed study of the astronomical alignments of the Maltese temples, claims that the Tal-Qadi stone is a lunar calendar which would be entirely befitting for a people who worshipped the Great Goddess. Geraldine had other ideas: 'My meditation teacher sees the stone as a cosmic gateway. Psychically, it is linked with the sun, Orion, Mars and the Pleiades.'

As we spoke, the near full moon was rising in the sky and Mars, shimmering with a light-reddish tinge, was the closest to the earth it had been for more than a thousand years.'It is a time of transmutation and opening of awareness,' Geraldine said quietly, looking at the fiery planet in the star-filled sky.

To my mind, there can be no doubt that the ancient Maltese megalith builders were careful observers of the movements of the planets and the stars and marked the daily and yearly cycles of the sun and moon.

The most extraordinary siting of a dolmen on Malta is at the seaside resort of Bugibba. It is situated in the garden next to the swimming pool of the Dolmen Hotel on the edge of St Paul's Bay. There is a trilithon of dressed stone forming what must have been a ceremonial entrance to a temple. An altar block with three fishes carved in low relief has been found on the site. But on the western side there is a collapsed dolmen, with one side of the large capstone standing. I climbed in under it and shared the sacred space with a motionless lizard and singing cicadas. As the sun began to set behind the pine trees and the weary sun-worshippers returned from their sacred pool, I meditated on the nature of these Maltese dolmens.

Because the dolmens are incorporated into the structure of the temples and no bodies have been found under them, it has been argued that they were created 'spontaneously' by the local inhabitants.[18] Yet there are many dolmens which stand alone, usually on flat land, and because no bodies have been found in their vicinity it does not follow that they were never used for funerary purposes. They are, moreover, so similar in design to the ones in North Africa and Sardinia that, given the known maritime connections, I can see no reason why their creators should not have been impressed by the design of their fellow builders overseas and made it their own. It seems much more likely that it was a case of cultural influence rather than indigenous specialization.

There are some sixteen dolmens in Malta and Gozo, most of them in a ruinous condition. Nearly all of them are oriented in the southeast quadrant.[19] There are also half a dozen standing menhirs scattered across the countryside, but many have been lost and it is now difficult to see if they mark ley lines or are pointers for astronomical alignments. It is the temples and underground chambers which offer the supreme artistic expression of the megalithic civilization of the Maltese islands.

CHAPTER TWENTY-TWO

Light in the Darkness

To sleep within the Goddess's womb was to die and to come to life anew.

MARIJA GIMBUTAS

I could not have left Malta without visiting its most mysterious ancient wonder: the underground labyrinth known as the Hypogeum at Hal Saflieni. Constructed and used from 3600 to 2500 BC, it sits 10 metres below the streets in the Paola suburb of the capital. It is now a World Heritage Site, and justly so, for it is an artistic masterpiece of prehistory. Making use of natural caves in the area, it was cut into a limestone hill with only stone mallets and horn or antler picks and then smoothed by imported flint tools.

But it has been closed to the public for many years for restoration: green slime, the result of the breath and sweat of intrusive visitors, had begun to deface the walls. I was fortunate enough to get special permission to see it.

You enter this megalithic marvel from a nondescript door in a quiet street, then descend into a vast labyrinth on three levels. It has thirty-three 'rooms', sunken wells and galleries, including the so-called Snake Pit and Oracle Room. Some of the rooms and passages are rough-hewn, while others are smooth and carefully carved. The central chamber – the Holy of Holies – has carved pillars resembling trilithons, niches, windows and even a corbelled roof. Some of the rooms have clover-leaf lobes resembling the temples built above ground at Ggantija on Gozo. It was, as my guide, the assistant curator Mark Mifsud, suggested: 'architecture inside out'.

The overall shape is curvilinear, suggestive of the shape of the Great

Goddess herself. Although there had been some natural caves on the site, the rooms were cut with flint and bone tools into the solid rock, illuminated by candles, torches or possibly a system of mirrors bringing light from above. Clearly, the builders would have had to be well organized to complete the task, no doubt working in the slack part of the agricultural year. Nevertheless, the complexity of the building did not imply, as Mark Mifsud maintained, a 'hierarchy of power'. As we have seen, all the evidence of the early megalithic builders suggests that they lived in egalitarian and communal societies. While there may have been a priesthood of some kind who helped organize rituals and plan the construction of the temples, there is, as David Trump has observed, 'no hint of secular leaders' in megalithic Malta.[1]

Some of the walls are washed with red ochre, suggestive of menstrual blood, and decorated with spirals in black magnetite. The Oracle Room has an arched dome decorated in red ochre with a swirling pattern resembling a scroll with discs of different sizes. Some have interpreted the discs, which look like the cup-and-ring markings typical of rock art in Northern Europe, as representing planets and stars. But they also look like fruit, and since they flow from single stems, the whole tableau may represent the Tree of Life. With its roots deep in the earth and its branches reaching for the heavens, it has throughout the world symbolized the growth of cosmic energy and the spiritual path towards enlightenment.

The gallery adjoining the Oracle Room also amplifies sound up to a hundred times, especially the lower tones. A whispered invocation reverberates around the passages and rooms of the underground temple. It has not only been called the oldest sounding device in the world, but musicians have recently described it as having perfect acoustics. As such, it would have enhanced the rituals intended to induce visions or trances.

Along one passage there are seven steps and seven niches. The number is highly significant for seven is not only a sacred number, but the number of the levels of consciousness in the Cabbala and the number of planetary spheres in ancient astrology. It is amazing to think that the Maltese temple builders may have been part of this esoteric tradition.

The case of vanishing skulls

There would seem to be a history of neglect and carelessness in Malta's archaeological establishment. When this extraordinary under-

ground labyrinth in Valletta's suburbs was discovered at the beginning
of the twentieth century by builders digging water cisterns, a metre-
high deposit of 'dank, dark mud' was discovered. When excavated
soon after its discovery by Sir Themistocles Zammit, the godfather of
Maltese archaeology, it was reported to contain the jumbled bones of
some 33,000 persons, sherds of broken pottery, flint implements and
some animal bones. Only one complete skeleton was recorded. Even
if we accept that this was an exaggeration and there were only about
7000 human remains, only a dozen skulls were found, all of them
strangely elongated (a condition known as dolichocephalic). The
great Egyptian architect Imhotep is depicted with a similar skull; such
people were clearly venerated by the ancient Maltese and Egyptians
for having special powers. Now only six skulls remain. The official
explanation of Malta's Archaeology Museum is that they have simply
been 'lost'.

Another intriguing mystery associated with the Hypogeum is that
the British archaeologist Trump in his authoritative guide pointed
visitors to a faint but discernible shape of a bison bull outlined in
black on a wall. For Anton Mifsud and his fellow researchers this
would seem to support the idea of a much earlier date than the
official one of 4000 years. However, this is not necessarily so for, as we
have seen, bulls appear on the walls of chambers in Carnac dated to
the fourth millennium BC and are associated with the cult of the
Mother Goddess. Nevertheless, the mystery is that the outline of the
bull has recently disappeared – due to the excessive number of visitors
in the past, or deliberately erased? There is no definitive answer as yet.

In keeping with their Atlantis hypothesis, Anton Mifsud and his
colleagues have argued that the metre-high deposit of mud and bones
in the Hypogeum were washed there from a nearby necropolis by the
deluge which also destroyed Plato's mythical island. While they may
well have been deposited by a flood – which would explain their
disordered state – I remain unconvinced that it marked the ending of
an Atlantean civilization on Malta in 2200 BC.

The Dreaming Goddess

What has been recovered from among the deposits in the Hypogeum
and placed on show in Malta's Archaeology Museum are some
exquisite small figurines of curvaceous women with massive hips
and breasts, often disparagingly called 'fat ladies'. Some recline on a
couch, like the 12-centimetre-long terracotta 'Sleeping Lady'. Others

stand freely. Many are without heads or have sockets for removable heads; one headless woman lies on her stomach. Some are taken from other graves. They were clearly meant as votive offerings for the Great Goddess, fountain of all abundance and life. I could imagine priestesses of the cult sleeping in the niches of the Hypogeum in order to communicate with the dead in their dreams or trances.

The careful placing of these fertility symbols in temples, graves and caves was significant. The archaeologist Marija Gimbutas made a special study of the Goddess figures throughout Europe from around 7000 to 4000 BC, and argued that they were central to the early megalithic religion. As she observed: 'To sleep within the Goddess's womb was to die and to come to life anew.'[2]

Fragments of many pots have also been found in the Hypogeum. For Neolithic humans the pot was much more than a useful utensil for cooking and carrying food and water. Made and decorated usually by women, it had a symbolic meaning as a vessel of transformation, representing the womb, the house, the tomb, the earth, and even the Great Goddess herself. Making pots also brought together the two feminine and fertile elements of earth and water in a very symbolic way.[3]

I spent a long time observing the finely lit 'Venus' figurines in their perpetual slumber in Malta's Archaeology Museum. Looking at the famous little 'Sleeping Lady', with one hand pillowing her head and a skirt billowing over her massive hips, I wondered whether she was dreaming the world, or whether the dream world dreamed her.

I recalled the Sleeping Beauty hills along which the moon danced at Callanish in Scotland as the beginning of my long voyage. It was some 4000 thousand miles away and seemed an age since I was there, but I could see that it was part of a pan-European civilization centred on worship of the Great Goddess. As in Callanish, the people of Malta worshipped the Goddess in her three ages, as Maiden, Mother and Old Woman, and in her threefold aspect as Fertility, Death and Rebirth.

And the memory has not been lost. When a friend of my daughter became pregnant she travelled to Malta to lie in a temple of the Goddess to bring about a good birth for her child.

Despite the presence of the Goddess figurines, the Hypogeum has usually been called a collective burial chamber. Colin Renfrew called it a 'great charnel house' because of the bones found within it.[4] Even in exhibits at Malta's Archaeology Museum it is still called a 'prehistoric rock-cut tomb'. Yet it seems unlikely that it would have been so carefully carved and decorated if it were solely meant for that purpose.

As we have seen only one complete skeleton was discovered when it was first opened up. Given its womb-like nature and red ochre walls, it feels much more like an underground temple for special initiation rites to experience the passage from life to death and rebirth. It could also have been used as a place for initiates to engage in shamanistic trances and to experience astral travel before the death of the physical body. Sir Themistocles Zammit was much closer to the mark when he recognized the Hypogeum as a place intended for worship, for what he called the 'sorceries of a primitive religion'.[5] For me, the Hypogeum was undoubtedly a temple offering the supreme expression of the advanced sacred science and spiritual vision of the Stone Age.

Tarxien temples

The exquisite figurines from the Hypogeum are not the only images of the Goddess to be found in Malta. A colossal female statue, originally almost 3 metres high, once graced the Tarxien temples only a few hundred metres away. Dating as far back as 3600 BC, it is the earliest colossal statue in the world. But it has been cut off at the waist – accidently or deliberately, no one knows. All that remains is the lower torso, with massive pear-shaped legs and small feet covered by a wide pleated skirt down to below the knees. The broken statue, now in the Archaeology Museum, was almost certainly a fertility symbol of the Great Goddess cult. A fragmentary carved limestone slab near the original location of the statue in the temple showing two phalluses in a niche supports this interpretation. I was delighted to find the roughly inscribed sketches of boats on slabs opposite the gargantuan statue near the main entrance to the temple.

In the soft and mellifluous Maltese language, which is a mixture of Phoenician and Arabic with an overlay of Italian and English, Tarxien is pronounced 'tar-shen'. The colossal statue is only one of its marvels. The Tarxien temples are unique, for nothing has been discovered from the period that approaches their consummate artistry.

The monument consists of four distinct parts. The earliest, separated from the rest of the temple complex, was built during the Ggantija phase and has a similar five-apsed plan. The other three are protected by a common outer wall.

The middle section was the last to be built: its long axis with its three pairs of apses was boldly wedged between the other two.

Although this spoilt the symmetry of the whole, the ruins suggest that its builders had worked out the principles of the vertical arch and the dome.

A raised threshold before the inner niche of the south temple is beautifully carved with an elaborate system of spirals; they have become so well known that they adorn the sides of stone flower boxes in the streets of the capital. I was particularly impressed by the graceful and naturalistic relief carvings in a nearby chapel of goats, sheep and a pig. Below the main altar, a flint knife and a mass of horns and bones have been found, suggesting that the animals might have been sacrificed as part of the temple rituals. Many of the niches were crammed with horns, skulls and half-burnt bones of oxen, sheep, goats and pigs. But the spirits of the animals were clearly honoured; in one room, there is a relief carved on a slab with a sow suckling thirteen piglets below a powerful bull. They were clearly intended by the artist as symbols of fertility and strength.

That is not all. There are some whirling spirals, full of cosmic energy, which immediately reminded me of the ones I had seen in Kilmartin valley in southwestern Scotland, at Newgrange in Ireland and on the island of Gavrinis in the Golfe du Morbihan. Such spirals also decorate pottery found in the temple complex, the craftsmanship of which is comparable to that of classical Greece.

Were there giants in those days?

Clearly the megalithic builders of Malta were not 'primitive' as earlier generations of archaeologists called them, but were an outstandingly resourceful and creative people.[6] The supreme artistry and architectural skills of the megalithic civilization in Malta were so great that some have wondered whether it was indeed the work of 'giants'.

During one of the amiable conversations I had with the paediatrician Anton Mifsud, he confided in me an extraordinary discovery he had made on Gozo. A local workman told him that he had found a 'giant' some years ago while excavating the foundations of a building complex but he had hidden the bones so that he would not be stopped by the authorities from continuing his work. From the evidence, it seems that between 4000 and 6000 years ago a man, 2.64 metres tall, was buried upright in the soil. He had a boss on his skull. Significantly, as in the Hypogeum, some of the bones of the 'giant's' skeleton were painted in red ochre.[7] The method of burial suggests that he was held in particular veneration by his community.

Anton was given a heel bone of the skeleton. His medical training helped him confirm that it must have belonged to an exceptionally tall person. His tale reminded me of a well-known local story on Gozo, which recounts that the first settlers were the children of a giantess.

The story goes like this. The giantess lived very happily in a wood with her son and daughter. One day, some strangers came in a boat, landed and snatched her children away. She only found out after she took them some food at midday. Looking out to sea in her distress, she saw the boat sailing away and realized what had happened. She dived into the water after them. Being a giantess, she soon caught up with the boat even though it was by now far away from land. But as she held the sides of the boat to pull herself into it, one of the seafarers cut off both her hands with an axe and she fell back into the sea and drowned. The boat sailed on and eventually reached the Maltese islands, where the daughter of the giantess married on Gozo, and the son in Mosta, a town on mainland Malta, thereby begetting the first dynasties.

This story, of great antiquity, was first written down by the Jesuit priest Manwel Magri, who excavated the Hypogeum at the beginning of the twentieth century. It suggests that the first settlers came from a fertile land over the sea, that they were skilled seafarers and that they traced their descent in a matrilineal way. The whole story is rich in water symbolism. The fact that the swimming giantess was disempowered by cutting off her hands and then killed may point to the overthrow of the Great Goddess cult, associated with water, the earth and the moon, by a warrior people who worshipped the sun.[8] The transition from a matrifocal society to a patriarchal one seems to have taken place throughout Europe at the beginning of the Bronze Age, although elements of the Goddess cult continued underground, in woods and on mountain tops.

Running into the sea

Not far northwest from the southern temples on an exposed limestone plateau between the Buskett Gardens and the sea, there are some intriguing features locally thought to be cart ruts. Their age remains a mystery; it is only known that they were in place 3000 years ago, when datable Punic tombs were cut through by a number of them.[9] There are so many crossing over each other that the area has been called 'Clapham Junction' after the main train junction in south London.

They appear to be made by humans, and not naturally occurring faults. Some have argued that they were the tracks of sledges transporting stones from a quarry for the nearby temples; others, that they were made by two parallel poles pulled by cows to transport agricultural produce.

Yet it would take a great span of time to create them in the hard limestone, certainly longer than the estimated five years it takes to build a temple. Moreover, they do not seem to go anywhere and are in restricted areas in different parts of the island, notably at San Pawl Tat-Targa on the outskirts of Naxxar. Some even zigzag rather than run in a straight line; others run for more than a kilometre. Similar ruts have been found in Sicily.

The barren limestone escarpments on which the ruts were scored reminded me of the stony fields of the Aran Islands off western Ireland. But it seems unlikely that the megalith builders were obliged, like the northern islanders, to gather sand and seaweed from the shore to create soil fertile enough for their crops. Unlike the the rich waters of the Atlantic Ocean, the semi-desert of the Mediterranean does not produce seaweed in abundance. Moreover, the small island population would not have had the energy to engage in such back-breaking toil, and build the monumental temples above and below ground at the same time.

My own feeling is that the ruts are partly natural and partly man-made. The ancient Maltese may well have developed ruts already eroded into special patterns, possibly for astrological reasons, to draw down to the earth the energies of the planets and the stars.

Some of the ruts run into the sea, and divers off Marfa Point near Sliema have recently discovered ruts on a gigantic scale as well as a stone channel with a bridge underwater. They may have sunk underwater during a sudden land subsistence which, according to Anton Mifsud and his colleagues, occurred around 2200 BC, at the end of the megalith building period. Alternatively, they may have subsided more gradually into the sea, since the land in Malta is tilting down in the east and lifting the cliffs in the west due to the clash of tectonic plates.

No doubt there are more ruins waiting to be discovered which might throw light on these deeply intriguing ruts. Perhaps it is underwater too that evidence lies for the background to Malta's temples and chambers.[10]

Architects and astronomers

Five kilometres east of the cart ruts at Buskett Gardens, the paired temples of Hagar Qim (pronounced 'hajariim') and Mnajdra (pronounced 'munaidra') lie on a barren cliff facing Africa. It was once a fertile and wooded land, but now only tough coarse grass, thistles, drought-resistant carob trees, prickly pears and cacti grow on the rugged, tortured limestone. It is situated on the edge of a promontory facing the deep blue sea and the distant wave-tossed islet of Filfla.

When I visited the site, the whole area was strewn with cartridges and roughly built shooting hides, some made from dressed stones that had no doubt been taken from the temples. The rich game of the megalithic era had long gone; now local hunters with their telescopic rifles bring down the swifts and swallows on their migration from Africa to northern Europe. Where fertile land was once farmed in common, boundary walls now divide up the barren rock.

But the beautiful symmetry of Hagar Qim rises above it all. Colossal dressed stones form its entrance which leads into a large, carefully designed enclosure. There are two other outlying temples. The complex stands on soft globigerina limestone that flakes in huge slabs and is therefore easily quarried and dressed. The megaliths are not placed in the soil as in northwestern Europe, but stand on a platform of horizontal megaliths with hollowed-out grooves. To provide water, six large reservoirs were dug and covered with huge blocks of stone in the limestone plateau above.

The façade of the main temple reproduces the dimensions of the lower part of a model found at Tarxien. Another terracotta model of a temple from Hagar Qim demonstrates that the temple builders were not only master masons, but had architects who made abstract designs.[11] It also has a small section of corbelling which suggests that the Maltese had developed the technique a thousand years before the builders of the *tholoi* in Mycenae.

Hagar Qim has produced seven marvellous statuettes of ample proportions. These include the naturalistic and headless beauty with large breasts known as the 'Venus of Malta', which is now in the Archaeology Museum. In keeping with their fertility symbolism, a shrine placed on the outer wall of the façade contains figures which appear to represent male and female organs.

A kilometre away southwest down the escarpment on a low cliff overlooking the sea stands the temples of Mnajdra. Built around 3500 BC, they rise out of rough terrain scattered with abandoned fig trees, prickly pears and wild vines. Made mostly of hard coralline limestone, the complex looks much more rugged than its sister Hagar Qim, although some dressed and polished slabs of globigerina limestone were brought down. It's a heavenly place on a summer's evening when fragrant whiffs of aniseed and thyme are carried on the warm sea breeze.

The complex consists of three temples. The lower, on the left of the forecourt (Mnajdra 1), is circular with standing stones and lintels surrounded by a thick outer wall. The adjoining temple in the middle (Mnajdra 2) has two kidney-shaped chambers, the inner smaller than the outer. A smaller, earlier temple of trefoil shape (Mnajdra 3) stands on the right.

The complex has even better signs of corbelling than Hagar Qim. But I was most intrigued to discover that the unit of measurement used in the distances between the foci, the main axis and the perimeters of the main temples was the same 'megalithic yard' defined by Alexander Thom after his study of British and Breton megaliths.[12] It implies that the cultures of northwestern Europe and the central Mediterranean not only worked in a similar way, but may possibly have been in touch with each other.

Almost all Maltese temples face southwards, that is south of east or south of west, which could be to align them with the Southern Cross-Centaurus star group like the much later sanctuaries on

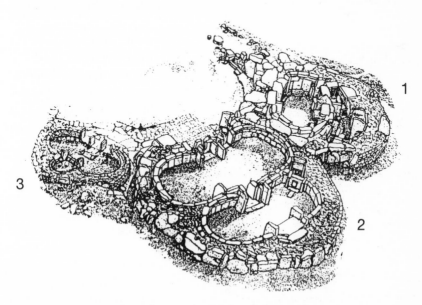

Mnajdra temples, Malta, facing south

Menorca.[13] Mnajdra 1 (dated to the early Tarxien phase, 3000 to 2500 BC) lies, however, on an east-west axis, perfectly aligned with the rising sun on the equinoxes. Taking into account the precession of the equinoxes and the obliquity of the ecliptic, the archaeo-astronomer Chris Micallef has calculated that in the year 2875 BC the sun exactly faced the main passage of the temple.[14] At the same time, the temple was aligned and still is toward Mars, followed by Saturn, Venus and Mercury. Just as the rising of Sirius was used to mark the New Year in Egypt, so the megalith builders in Malta could have used the alignment with Mars to indicate the beginning of the yearly cycle. Throughout the Maltese temple period the Pleiades, used all over the world to mark the passage of time and the seasons of the year, rose close to due east and could also have been a target for the Mnajdra astronomers.[15]

The higher middle temple Mnajdra 2, (with pottery fragments from the Ggantija phase of building, dated to circa 3450 BC) was moreover orientated to the rising sun on the summer and winter solstice like those in Britain so far to the north. Those who built it were clearly advanced architects and astronomers. Paul Micallef, Chris's uncle, has shown that when the sun on the summer solstice rises above the local horizon, its rays cast an image shaped like a flag for a few seconds on a great stone slab to the left of the temple entrance. The opposite occurs on the winter solstice when the sun illuminates a slab on the right of the entrance.[16] It would have been even more impressive when the temple was covered over. As at Maes Howe, Newgrange and Gavrinis, the rays of Father Sun would penetrate deep into Mother Earth.

The complex would thus have worked as a 'calendar in stone', with a pendulum sweeping to the left, to the right and then back again throughout the year. There are further subdivisions marked by slit images for the cross-quarter days, and the days in between.

The sun's rays on the solstice are now 2 centimetres from the edge of the large slabs at the back of the temple, but if we take into account the obliquity of the ecliptic due to the slight movement in the earth's axis, the rays would be spot on in the year 3700 BC or 10,205 BC.[17] I would accept the former date, which is supported by carbon-dating of artefacts found within the temple.

As at Callanish in the Outer Hebrides, Chris Micallef maintains that there are alignments on the major and minor standstills of the moon, which follow a cycle of 18.6 years, confirming the astronomical understanding of the builders and worshippers of the temple. He believes, however, that the main alignment was probably towards the first full moon during the equinox period, which takes place every year at a different time.

The complex horizontal system of pitted marks on the two pillars that flank the entrance to the inner chamber of the smallest and oldest temple, Mnajdra 3, could be recorded observations of celestial bodies. The total number of holes on each stone roughly equals the number of days in a half-year. Michael Hoskin has argued that the drilled holes 'seem clearly to be tallies, and tallies of lasting importance and of religious significance'. As a cautious archaeologist, he is 'reasonably' convinced that they were counts of days between heliacal rising of stars, beginning with the Pleiades on 6 April and ending with ß Centaurus on the 2 or 3 October.[18]

The heliacal risings of stars – their reappearance in the dawn sky following a period of absence while lost in the glare of the sun – were considered important makers in the yearly cycle by the ancients. It is well known that Egyptians marked the beginning of their year in mid-July by the heliacal rising of Sirius, which coincided with the annual flooding of the Nile. And Hesiod, writing down a long oral tradition in his poem *Works and Days* in the eighth century BC, observed that the farmer's year is ended in late October when 'the Pleiades and the Hyades and the might of Orion set'.

Like the stone circles of Britain, the Mnajdra complex thus served as an astronomical observatory to make solar and lunar predictions in order to determine the cycles of the agricultural year.

The age of bronze and war

Gazing out from Mnajdra to the south, across a narrow gap, I could easily make out the sparkling white rock of Filfla rising out of a turquoise, white-capped sea. The isle it is cleft-shaped, evoking the bull's horns used as a male symbol in the cult of the Great Goddess. For generations, the island has been a target for artillery practice (like the old head of the Sphinx), and because of the wasted ammunition I was unable to land there to search for the megalithic ruins and ruts which it is supposed to hold.

Such antics stand in stark contrast to the Maltese megalithic civilization which, as elsewhere in early megalithic Europe, was a peaceful one. None of the temples were fortified and no weapons of war have been found in or around them. But the extraordinary surge of architectural creativity and peaceful cooperation of the Maltese temple builders came to a sudden end in the middle of the third millennium. It was so abrupt that J.D. Evans states that the megalith builders vanished 'as if by magic'.[19] Reasons put forward have been deforestation (as on Easter Island in the Pacific), repeated droughts (leading to crop failure and famine) or floods (as in the Atlantis hypothesis). The most likely explanation, however, is the invasion of a patriarchal, warrior people who replaced the Great Goddess with a sun god. Like the seafarers who cut off the hands of the giantess in the Gozo story, they no doubt truncated the great statue of the Goddess at Tarxien.

It seems that at least three waves of people from the European littoral of the Mediterranean invaded the islands, bringing copper and then bronze weapons. As a sign of the newly turbulent times, they built fortified settlements on flat hilltops.[20] One group – now known as the Tarxien Cemetery people – cremated their dead and deposited their ashes inside pots in the ruins of the Tarxien temples. Among the marauders were no doubt some of the so-called Sea Peoples I have discussed earlier, who after attacking Egypt without success, dispersed or returned to Sardinia, Sicily and southern Italy.

The Phoenicians followed, coming from the east in the eighth century BC. They converted the megalithic site at Tas-Silg overlooking Marsaxlokk Bay into a temple dedicated to their god Astarte, and they buried their dead in rock-cut underground tombs. After a Roman raid in 218 BC at the beginning of the second Punic War, the Maltese islands eventually became part of a Sicilian province. Cicero records that they were still used by pirates as a wintering base, thereby continuing a seafaring tradition of thousands of years.

As I stood on the cliff face of Malta, looking across the glittering sea to Filfa, I recalled how organized fanatics had recently come to pull down the 'pagan' stones at Mnajdra and covered them in graffiti. At the other end of Europe, Christian fundamentalists had tried to pull down standing stones in Cornwall while I was visiting the sites. It reminded me of the Lateran Council of the Roman Catholic Church which decreed in AD 452 that all the stones 'be cast down and concealed in such a place that their worshippers may not be able to find them'. Like the distant Bronze Age, ours was indeed a destructive and warlike age in which tolerance was on the retreat.

CHAPTER TWENTY-THREE

The Golden Age

We have invented nothing!

PICASSO

I had begun my voyage in the grey waters of the North Atlantic. Now I was surrounded by the sparkling blue of the central Mediterranean, not far from Africa. I had left the oldest settlement in Europe, up in Scotland, and had arrived in Malta where the first temples were built in the fifth millennium BC. My voyage had taken four summers, had lasted more than seven months, and had covered some 4000 nautical miles.

For most of the voyage, my spirit had been restless, but having reached my intended destination I was now taking my ease. Elizabeth had occasionally complained that I was too relentless, forever wishing to continue my voyage; sometimes, I even felt like Captain Ahab in pursuit of his legendary white whale Moby Dick. I could have stayed on in many an enchanted island or magical valley by the sea, but I knew that if I lingered on too long I would be undone. I had once gone to the mountains of North Wales for a winter and stayed there twenty-one years. So I had persevered and sailed on and completed my voyage. I was now at rest – but not for too long. As every seafarer knows from time immemorial, however comfortable the hearth, when a certain wind blows, down to the sea he must go.

I had travelled through some of the wildest and most beautiful landscapes and seascapes of Europe. It had proved an enthralling adventure of ideas into the heart of a great and ancient mystery, raising a host of intriguing questions about the nature of history and civilization and the character of our ancestors – and by implication ourselves.

After my long voyage, I was as awe-struck as ever by the enormous achievement of the megalith builders. I could see why they have seized the world's imagination. You cannot survey the settlement of Skara Brae, the mound at Newgrange, the alignments of Carnac, the rock art of Galicia, the dolmens of Antequara, the navetas of Menorca, the statue-menhirs of Corsica and the Venus of Malta without this overwhelming sense of awe. No wonder that when people stumbled across the ruins of the megaliths in the past, they felt they must have been built by giants. The megaliths were clearly not the work of primitive savages, but of a sophisticated, thoughtful and deeply religious civilization.

I had visited all the major megalithic sites along the Atlantic seaboard and the western and central Mediterranean. It had been total immersion, and now I wanted to put it all together. During my travels and research, I had become convinced that there was indeed a pan-European megalithic civilization. The picture was more complex in the south, as more influences were involved, but to me it seemed that European megaliths were the expression of a single culture and religion in which the dead were venerated, the fertility of the land enhanced and humans made whole by the raising of great stones to the sky. The similar design and method of building, the standard unit of measurement, the common astronomical alignments, the same pottery and stone implements and a shared belief in the Great Goddess could not have been mere coincidence.

On the evidence of their skeletons, it would appear that the megalith builders were interrelated and possibly descended from a common people. Similar skulls have been found in Iberian chambered tombs and in the long barrows and cairns of England and Scotland. There are certain genetic features, such as common hair colour, blood groups and other anatomical features, which certain groups in parts of western Britain and Ireland share with others in the western Mediterranean. There might also be a linguistic link from before the arrival of the Celts: the people in Atlantic Europe who pronounce 'th' as 't' are now only to be found in Portugal and Ireland, but they could well have retained the pronunciation from a language spoken in megalithic times.[1]

The maritime connection

My voyage had further confirmed that the megalithic civilization was not only pan-European, but one principally connected by the sea.

Man raised a sail before he rode a horse. The very early use of boats is attested by the discovery of an oar dating back to the eighth millennium BC in northern Europe. As I had seen in Brittany, Galicia, Andalusia and Malta, there are carvings of boats on megaliths from the fifth millennium which are remarkably similar to the ocean-going, skin-covered curraghs still in use on the west of Ireland today.

With interiors deeply forested and rife with dangerous animals, the seas and inland waterways would have been the national choice as primary routes of communications. The sea united rather than separated the scattered communities. Expanding trade provided considerable cross-fertilization and impetus to cultural growth. Seafarers took their knowledge with them, passing it from one society to the next. And as navigators, they would have had a natural interest in the stars and the movements of the sun and the moon, an interest they shared with the megalith builders as they carefully laid out their monuments in the landscape and aligned them with the heavens.

Non-sailors may find it difficult to believe that Neolithic people could be in contact from the North Atlantic to the Mediterranean, especially as there are fierce tides around the British Isles and Brittany, treacherous seas in the Bay of Biscay and strong currents off Portugal and through the Strait of Gibraltar. Yet having followed in the wake of the ancient mariners and through all the same obstacles, I remain convinced that they would have been quite capable of such long-distance navigation in their skin boats. Apart from four days' sailing across the Atlantic, two days from Menorca to Corsica and two from Sardinia to Malta, the journey could easily be made as a series of day trips. And the great advantage of a skin boat for the ancient mariner was that being lightweight and without a keel it could easily be beached and dragged up on to the shore at night or in bad weather. If a curragh from the Aran Islands can brave the open sea of the Atlantic today, it could easily sail down to the Mediterranean in the quieter conditions and calmer seas of megalithic times.

My voyage further confirmed that there were three important sea routes and axes of communication for the Neolithic sailors. The first was from Scotland via Ireland, Wales, England and Brittany to Galicia. The second was from Atlantic Spain and Portugal into the western Mediterranean. Maritime transport would have been much easier than crossing the Iberian Peninsula by land, and the Strait of Gibraltar is not an impermeable barrier between two seas. The third axis was in the Mediterranean basin with its conveniently placed islands. In megalithic times, Europe and Africa did not have separate cultures as they do today, and there would have been great crisscrossing from

north to south, east to west. The great sailing nations of antiquity –
the Phoenicians, Greeks and Romans – were merely following the
routes pioneered by the earlier megalith seafarers. And while all three
routes can be hazardous, I had found in my small sailing boat that
they are not impossible.

Colonizers from the east?

In her otherwise fascinating work on the Corsican megaliths, Dorothy
Carrington could still write in 1971: 'Archaeologists are now pretty
well agreed that the megalithic faith came to Western Europe from
the East. The movement must have been seaborne; the great megalithic
centres are on the coasts, the peninsulas and the islands. From the
Aegean or the Near East, it is supposed, shiploads of adventurers set
out to explore, exploit and colonise the barbarous West. They went in
search of living-space, trade, and increasingly metals . . .'[2]

She was drawing on the work of earlier generations of archaeologists who, brought up in a classical tradition, thought civilization
must have originated in Greece, Egypt and Mesopotamia and spread
out of the eastern Mediterranean and along the Atlantic seaboard to
northwestern Europe.

At the beginning of the twentieth century, the archaeologist
T. Eric Peet had argued that building with the 'rude, rough stones'
of the megalith monuments was brought to various countries by a
'single race' in an immense migration or series of migrations.[3]
Following his cue, V. Gordon Childe maintained not only that the
megalith culture had spread from the Middle East, but that boatloads
of 'megalithic saints' had spread the culture like the Irish monks in
the Middle Ages.[4] Glyn Daniel, doyen of British archaeologists after
the Second World War, similarly argued that the megalithic chambers
of Western Europe were translations of chamber tombs in the Eastern
Mediterranean. Using the established Greek and Egyptian chrono-
logies, he dated them from 2500 to 1000 BC.[5]

But as we have seen, the carbon-dating revolution of the early
1960s totally undermined the old diffusionist theory. It soon became
clear that the megaliths in Western Europe were much older than the
stone monuments of Egypt and Mesopotamia, let alone the tombs of
Mycenae and Minoan Crete. The old motto of the British school of
archaeologists, *Ex Oriens lux* – 'Out of the East comes light' – could
no longer hold water.

In the 1970s, opinion swung against the idea of mass migrations towards the view of local developments along the Atlantic seaboard. Colin Renfrew maintained that megalithic building began independently in Iberia, Brittany, Britain and Denmark.[6] At the same time, Euan MacKie argued that the most likely candidate for the source of the megalith builders was in southwestern Iberia and that it spread east and north from there.[7] Today, archaeologists and prehistorians are much less dogmatic and more cautious about their claims. Indeed, Alasdair Whittle wisely prefaced his 1996 book *Europe in the Neolithic* with the comment: 'Any book of this kind is really a prolonged conditional sentence, an extended hypothetical argument'.[8]

My own view is that the megalith civilization developed along the Atlantic seaboard roughly at the same time since the communities were already connected by the sea. The culture may have first appeared along the coasts of France and Iberia, where the oldest megalithic monuments are to be found, but rapidly spread out along long-established sea routes and trading networks, reaching as far north as Scotland and as far south and east as the Mediterranean islands. It was therefore an indigenous one, largely independent of external influences.

The spread of megalith building did not require large-scale movements of people or boatloads of missionaries landing on disparate shores. It was stimulated by changing social and natural environments. It developed wherever new farmers arrived in their boats and settled down on islands, along the coasts or up waterways. Inevitably ideas and experiences were exchanged along with goods and gifts between the communities, fostering the development of a common culture. Over time, while the megalithic communities kept in touch by sea and continued to share the same culture, regional variations gradually evolved, according to local tastes and conditions.

The megalithic civilization was not therefore spread by the search for land and wealth, as happened with the great seventeenth-century European era of exploration. In a sparsely populated Europe, there was no pressure of scarcity or competition for resources. Nor is there any evidence to suggest that there was a desire to colonize and exploit in the early phase of its development. It was a case of cultural influence, not conquest. Only in the Bronze Age did Europe enter a period of conflict and war from which it has never recovered.

A global civilization?

During my travels, I often mulled over the fact that the megaliths are not only to be found in Europe but throughout the world. There are some 50,000 in Western Europe but that is just the beginning. You will find countless others in North Africa, the Caucasus, Palestine, Israel, Arabia, Egypt, Ethiopia, Sudan, Madagascar, Iran, Baluchistan, Kashmir, India, Java, Borneo, China, Korea, Japan, Peru, Guatemala and Mexico. They are not only similar in design, especially the dolmens and stone circles, but they have similar astronomical alignments. They also share a common religious impulse, involving respect for ancestors. They reflect a belief in the correspondence between heaven and earth, between the macrocosm of the universe and the microcosm of humanity. And they express the universal desire for the immortality of the soul. Could it be therefore that the megaliths were inspired by an ancient world religion spread by the sea?

Impressed by the sudden appearance and advanced state of megalithic buildings, many believe, like the author Graham Hancock, that the knowledge must have come from a 'common source' in a lost civilization.[9] Such a view is supported by myths from many countries, especially China, India and Egypt, describing an advanced civilization which disappeared under the sea after a catastrophe.[10]

The fact that the megalithic culture in Europe developed along the Atlantic seaboard further raises the possibility that the builders came from the lost civilization of Atlantis – which was, as I've noted, first mentioned by Plato in *Timaeus*. The nineteenth-century American senator Ignatius Donnelly argued in *Atlantis: The Antediluvian World* (1882) that the Azores were the mountaintops of Atlantis and that their warlike citizens had established colonies in Ireland and Iberia during the Bronze Age. I am not, however, convinced by the available evidence that such a society existed in the Atlantic, or for that matter, in Malta. The megaliths were moreover first built during the Stone Age, thousands of years before men started working metal like the Atlanteans. Yet while the myth of Atlantis has not been proved, neither has it been disproved, and it must remain a mystery waiting to be solved.

Despite the similarities between the structure and purpose of the megaliths throughout the world, we now know, thanks to the methods of carbon-dating, thermoluminescence and dendrochronology, that they appeared at different times in different places. The megaliths of Europe, as we've seen, emerged in the fifth millennium BC, while those in North Africa appeared just before the Christian era and continued to be built into the first centuries AD. Megalithic chamber tombs in Korea and Japan date from the first millennium BC while the Mayan temples in Guatemala date from around 300 BC and the Toltec pyramids in Mexico were build in the 1500s. Again, the monolithic statues of Easter Island were going up from AD 700 to 1700. In Madagascar, megalithic chamber tombs were being made in the last few centuries.

In my view, the most likely explanation for the near universality of megaliths is that the drive to build in stone on a grand scale comes from the universal nature of the human mind and the common experience of the human condition. Just as there is an innate grammar (all languages follow similar rules and are therefore translatable), so there is a universal desire to raise stone buildings in the form of elemental shapes such as circles, rectangles and lines. Like the categories of time and space, they are fundamental to the structure of the human brain and form part of the framework we impose on the world in order to organize and understand it.

Above all, the megaliths express our concern with the most universal and fundamental aspects of life and death: burying the dead, honouring the ancestors and ensuring that life on earth continues. All humans share a similar predicament: we are all born to die, yet we yearn for immortality. We all seek permanence, yet we live in a world of change. We are all insignificant in face of the immensity of the universe, yet we want to be remembered for our own worth. It does not therefore surprise me that our ancestors throughout the world should want to make their mark before they died and be remembered by placing stones into the earth which reach for the heavens.

A Golden Age?

The more I travelled and researched during the voyage, the more I became convinced that the society of the megalith builders in Stone Age Europe produced a civilization which enjoyed a Golden Age of peace and creativity.

What is called the Golden Age is not a utopian fantasy, but a dim memory of a real historical period which lasted for nearly 3000 years. From about 5000 BC, when people first settled down and began to build the megaliths, to about 2000 BC, when Europe was invaded by warlike people with metal weapons, there was a long and settled time of real stability and comparative plenty.

This megalithic Golden Age was undoubtedly a period of

peace unparalleled in human history. As we have seen, none of the early megalithic sites were fortified or defended and no weapons of war have been found in their vicinity. No doubt there was a degree of rivalry between individuals and groups and inevitably some disputes would have occurred, but they did not break down into organized warfare. It was the very opposite of Thomas Hobbes's fantasy of the 'state of nature' in which there is a 'war of all against all' and life is 'solitary, poor, nasty, brutish, and short'. Stone Age humans were not savages – and not even 'noble savages' – but intelligent, sensitive, resourceful and caring.

The civilization of Old Europe, as Marija Gimbutas has pointed out, was originally 'matrifocal and probably matrilineal, agricultural and sedentary, egalitarian and peaceful'. In Central Europe, belligerent Indo-Europeans arrived from the Russian steppes in successive waves of infiltration from 4500 to 2500 BC, bringing their 'patriarchal, stratified, pastoral, mobile and war-oriented' culture.[11] But they did not initially superimpose their culture in the southern and western parts of Europe, where the main megalithic activity took place, until the end of the period.

In Western Europe it was the Beaker People who arrived around 2000 BC to bring that long-standing peace to an end. In the Mediterranean islands, it was the the so-called 'Sea People' or Shardana who came from the east. Only then were forts built and metal weapons manufactured on a large scale. The dagger, the Bronze Age symbol of war replaced the axe, the Stone Age symbol of peace. Since then, virtually every generation in Europe has experienced the horrors of war.

What kind of society?

As we've seen, agriculture was the economic base of the megalithic civilization. After settling down in one place, clearing the forests and planting seeds, the first farmers began a whole new way of life. The resulting increase in production not only led to a growth in population, but enabled them to have the leisure to study the movement of the stars, to build immense monuments and to engage in great collective ceremonies and rituals. And not surprisingly for an agricultural people their religion was centred on the cult of the Great Goddess, the taker and giver of all life.

According to the model of society adopted by most earlier archaeologists and prehistorians, change in megalithic times evolved along a predetermined path and was driven by conflict and competition over material sources.[12] In reality, they tended to project the 'savagery' and 'barbarism' of their own society on to the peoples of the remote past. During the imperial era, many anthropologists did the same with the remote people in the colonies in order to justify their rule and 'civilizing' mission. My own study of the megalith builders shows however that their development was by no means uniform and that social, moral and spiritual influences were just as important as economic factors. They continued the long tradition of cooperation, sharing and solidarity which they had developed as hunter-gatherers. Indeed, the way they buried their dead in communal tombs and aligned their monuments with the heavens clearly reflected their long-cherished spiritual ideals.

A growing body of evidence now suggests that the early society of the megalith builders was not only peaceful and cooperative but also egalitarian. Euan MacKie's argument that the megaliths were built in Western Europe because an incoming elite of priests from Iberia imposed their rule on existing communities seems increasingly fanciful. There is simply no reasonable grounds for believing that 'by mixing and hybridizing they formed the top level of a variety of local stratified societies, dominated by the priesthood'.[13] This seems yet again a case of modern archaeologists and historians projecting their own view of the inevitable hierarchy and domination in existing society on to societies in the remote past.

On the contrary, no convincing case can be made for the existence of organized castes or leaders before the Bronze Age. The collective burial of dead with few grave goods suggests that the society of the megalith builders had little stratification between members of the community. There may have been some differences between age and gender and between separate communities, but in general the society was noticeably egalitarian and communal. Indeed, as Alasdair Whittle has recently written, the ideals of 'co-operation, sharing, solidarity, mutuality, honour and esteem' were central to their way of life.[14] As we have seen, it is only after the arrival of the Beaker People and the Shardana around 2000 BC that individuals were buried with elaborate items and bronze weapons, suggesting warlike leaders and chiefs had at last emerged.

As might be expected from a people who worshipped the Great Goddess, it seems likely that the early society of the megalith builders was matrilineal, tracing descent from one generation to another through the mother. At the same time, it was not a matriarchy any more than it was a patriarchy. Stone Age society was a genuine 'anarchy', that is, an ordered society without coercive rulers and external government in which men and women were recognized as different but equal. There was no polarization between male and female; neither one dominated the other; all were considered of equal value.

A true civilization?

After the carbon-dating revolution which pushed back the antiquity of the megaliths by some 2000 years, Colin Renfrew wrote an influential book which took into account the new understanding, but he still entitled it *Before Civilization* (1973). More recently, Richard Rudgley has been more generous and written about the *Lost Civilisations of the Stone Age* (1998), yet he still calls it a 'Savage Civilisation'.[15]

Having studied megalithic societies in so many different countries in Europe and visited so many different sites during my voyage, there is no doubt in my mind that the culture of the megalith builders was a genuine civilization. If we understand 'civilization' to mean a settled culture with a sophisticated artistic sensibility, a rich symbolic language and a deep spiritual vision, then the society of the megalith builders was undoubtedly a civilization. If a civilization is defined by the ability to build large-scale stone architecture, to have a complex social life, to adapt to and shape the environment, to have foresight and planning, to practise sophisticated religious rites and ceremonies, to develop the advanced science of astronomy, mathematics and engineering and to enjoy the arts of pottery, carving and painting, then the culture of the Stone Age was undoubtedly a high civilization. The most eloquent and permanent expression of this civilization is the megalith monuments themselves. Indeed, in many ways Stone Age civilization in its first phase was even more 'civilized' than our own, for its members did not conduct organized warfare and kill on a massive scale but rather cherished each other and cared for the earth and the heavens.

The megalith builders had a different consciousness from ours and a different kind of knowledge. Compared with them, we may have gained in information, but we have lost much in wisdom. In their holistic approach, they made no separation between art and science, religion and philosophy, astronomy and astrology. In their sacred science, they did not separate reason from intuition, the head from the heart, the left and the right sides of the brain. They used their reason to work out the problems of transporting and erecting huge stones and building domes, but they also had the imagination to conceive and create great works of architecture, mathematics and engineering.

They traced the movements of the heavenly bodies and marked the great cycles of the year. They recognized the link between the microcosm of humanity and the macrocosm of the universe. They understood the energy lines in the body and in the land and the sea. They had ample time for ritual and celebration, myth and magic, dance and song. They cared equally for the dead and for the living.

The megalith builders seemed to have had a magical understanding of reality, which we have largely lost in our mechanical age. Like the shamans of old, they not only used ritual objects but engaged in chanting, dancing, drinking and drug-taking to heighten their visionary awareness. Their monuments, especially the stone circles, temples and tombs, were used for rituals and ceremonies which were part of a magico-religious system used to enhance the health and fertility of the land and sea, animals and humans. Some of their beliefs and practices continued in the so-called 'Old Religion' which Christianity tried to stamp out.

Ecological awareness

In all this, it would seem that the megalith builders had a profound ecological awareness and sensibility. The stones embody the ancient understanding that the earth, heavens and humanity form an interdependent and seamless whole. Like all early peoples, they believed that the universe was a living being. We do not know what word they used to described Mother Earth, but the ancient Greeks called it Gaia. The idea of Gaia as a self-regulating, self-sustaining living organism is not only one of the earliest insights of philosophy and religion but one that scientists are increasingly beginning to appreciate. The modern concept of Gaia, may well be a manifestation of the Great Goddess in a more 'scientific', acceptable guise.

The siting of their monuments shows that the megalith builders had a profound sense of the earth's energies and a deep appreciation of the landscape. They clearly understood the principles of geomancy which in China became known as the art and science of feng shui. As their concern with the astronomical alignments of their monuments demonstrates, they deeply appreciated the correspondence between heaven and earth: as above, so below.

Compared to our own exploitative and conquering ways, the megalith builders lived lightly on the earth as frugal and caring dwellers in the land. They only took what they needed and respected the spirits of the animals whose lives they sacrificed in order to live. They knew they were part of a complex web of nature which they violated at their peril. Megalithic art shows that they had a profound reverence for the universe, the earth and non-human life. They did not see themselves as Lords of Creation, but as fellow voyagers in the odyssey of life and death. They were the first settled ecologists and anarchists without being conscious of it.

At the same time, I believe that the intuitive ecological awareness which they had developed over hundreds of thousands of years as hunter-gatherers led to a profound sense of guilt when they settled down to become sedentary farmers. By abandoning the old nomadic way of life, were they not breaking with their ancestors? They probably felt guilty at cutting the skin of Mother Earth with their picks and ploughs and tunnelling into her entrails with their tools in search of minerals and stones. Was it not a symbolic rape of the Great Goddess herself, a violation of her sacred nature?

Aware of what they had done, they may well have raised the megaliths in expiation for their transgression of the old ways and for their attempted matricide. I suspect they may have even placed their stones on known energy lines to preserve the fertility of the earth just as an acupuncturist places needles in the meridians of the body to restore its health. And to show respect for the ancestors and to earn their forgiveness, they placed them in grand and imperishable monuments of stone.

Many megalithic monuments seem to fit into a pattern in a ritual landscape, stretching sometimes over hundreds of miles. It would not surprise me that the ley lines which appear to connect megalithic sites follow the ancient routes of the nomads before they settled down. The megalith builders no doubt raised their stones at ancient meeting places which were already considered sacred. Despite the ravages of time, many sites still retain their special atmosphere.

Lessons from the megalithic age

When Picasso saw the Palaeolithic art in the caves of Lascaux, he is reported to have said: 'We have invented nothing!' Perhaps he should have said: 'We have made no progress in culture, although we have invented organized war on a massive scale . . .'

After studying in depth the lost civilization of the Stone Age, I have been compelled to abandon my youthful faith in inevitable progress, the product of the optimism of the European Enlightenment of the eighteenth century. The popular view of progress, fostered by Darwinists and Marxists, is that evolution and history develop from the simple to the complex, from savagery to civilization. But it is simply human arrogance to think that our industrial civilization, for all its technological prowess, is the last word. Our times are dire indeed, with constant war and terrorism and the spiralling clash of two great world religions, Islam and Christianity, despite their common values.

I now adhere to a much older belief in the rise and fall of civilizations. I perceive a distinct decline from the Stone Age to the Bronze Age. Grain may have helped civilize humanity, but metal brought about their downfall. As Plato argued in *Phaedrus*, the invention of writing may also have led to a deterioration in our memory and wisdom. The confident view of the ancient Chinese, Indians and Greeks that we are progressively leaving behind the Golden Age of early humanity may well be true.

With the coming of the warlike Indo-Europeans and their patriarchal gods, some of the megalithic monuments, like Stonehenge, were oriented towards the sun, reflecting the new masculine, solar religion. Analytical and rational thinking replaced the earlier intuitive lunar thinking. Although some elements of Old Europe were fused into the new, the Great Goddess, with her symbols of water, snake and moon, retreated into the forests and the mountains, into tombs and caves, only to reemerge in disguised form in myths, legends, fairytales and the dreams of the unconscious. Our ancestors became alienated from their roots and lost their reverence for the earth. Christianity furthered the split between mind and body, humanity and the rest of nature. The New Religion declared human beings to be fallen and corrupt like nature itself, needing the coercive rule of Church and State in order to check their inborn savagery and to save their souls. The modern world was born.

Modern Western civilization has proved technologically innovative, but these developments have been made at an enormous cost to the human community and to the planet. Our civilization cannot avoid conflict and war between individuals, classes, nations and religions. It is characterized by dualistic thinking, linear time, social inequality and militaristic violence. It contains the seeds of its own destruction, which are growing at an alarming rate. But as the Great Goddess knows, from death can emerge new life. In the long run, our recent western materialistic and exploitative civilization may prove to be the aberration rather than the rule in human history.

Appreciating the energies of the stones and studying their place in a ritual landscape reminded me that we are all threads in nature's web. The example of the care the megalith builders took in placing and constructing their monuments – and the fact they have lasted so long – underlined for me the importance of becoming custodians of the land and sea and of planning and building with future generations in mind. From my long study and distant travels among the megalith builders, I have been most impressed by their respect for the dead, their love of life and their sense of the sacred.

We can learn much about human nature and social organization from Stone Age society. It demonstrates that humans are not fundamentally egoistic and violent creatures driven by a 'selfish gene' or a 'territorial imperative'. We are not inevitably consumed forever by an ineradicable lust for power and wealth but capable of peaceful and cooperative behaviour. We do not have to worship Gaia as a Great Goddess or commune with nature spirits but if we have genuine respect for nature, we will find it difficult to continue to exploit and destroy the earth and sea.

We can learn a great deal from the Golden Age of the megaliths in order to create a new civilization in the third millennium which like theirs is sustainable, creative, cooperative, convivial and above all in harmony with nature. It can teach us to recognize the sacredness of the earth and reverence for all being. As we launch ourselves into the future, we can take up the experience of our creative and peaceful ancestors which is an inherent part of our history and deep within our psyche. A Golden Age of peace and creativity in a united Europe has happened in the past – for almost 3000 years – and there is no reason why it cannot happen again. It is central to the evolution of our human nature and an integral part of our social experience and history.

Lessons from the stones

Visiting the megalithic sites during my voyage, I could not help feeling sometimes that I was sitting among piles of dead stones. Some have been deliberately smashed by iron bars, cracked by fires, pulled down with chains, bulldozed and even dynamited. Robbed, plundered, violated, trampled down, turned over and scattered, it is no wonder that their spirits have fled and their energy has died. Even when they are protected behind barbed wire, like Stonehenge, they seem to have lost much of their vitality. But they are not all like this and many sites, especially the more remote and neglected, remain vibrant with energy, living symbols of the infinite, gateways to another world. They still draw down energy from the heavens and help the mysterious vital force to circulate through the channels of the earth.

As a person is, so he sees. For some landowners, farmers and planners the stones are damn things in the way yet they move others to tears. For some they are rough, rude remnants left over from a barbarous age, while for others, myself included, they are sublime sculptures in a ritual landscape encoded with ancient wisdom.

In my experience, the stones tend to be mirrors to our own consciousness. As in alchemy, the experimenter inevitably influences the experiment and the dynamics of an individual or a group of individuals visiting a megalithic site will invariably affect the level of energy there. The stones can often magnify our existing feelings and moods. Many people report having good or bad 'vibes' at certain megalithic sites; in my experience, this is as much due to the state of their mind as to the sites themselves. That being said, the sites, as I have indicated in my travels, undoubtedly vary widely in energy levels. Some feel as if they are vibrating with energy, while others feel as if their vitality has drained away, usually as a result of human disturbance over the millennia.

If, as I believe, the stones were originally built to maintain the balance of the earth and to ensure its fertility, then to disturb or destroy them is to court personal disaster and to harm Gaia. On the other hand, if one cares for the stones and their landscapes, one helps to heal the wounds of the earth and in the process to heal oneself and one's society.

The same is true in archaeology as in alchemy. The archaeologists who believe that the stones are just dead matter will only discover dead matter. If they see their sole task as simply to unearth the megaliths and to record and classify what they find without any attempt to interpret their meaning, then they will engage in an ultimately meaningless activity. They might further their careers, but they will not deepen their understanding. If, on the other hand, they respect the stones and are sensitive to the builders' original intentions and beliefs, then they can gain much for themselves and the modern world. Archaeology is often little more than a superior form of grave robbing but at its best it can be a wonderful source of ancient wisdom with lessons highly relevant to our times.

My own voyage amongst the stones has been part of a lifelong search for understanding – of myself, of life and death, of the universe itself. The circles, spirals, mazes and lines which I encountered in so many different terrains and climes had a special significance for me. They all seemed to represent different aspects of the spiritual path towards enlightenment and immortality.

The circle, forever turning on itself, has always been a symbol of eternity and wholeness, of the endless recurrence of the sun and moon, the coming and going of the seasons, the cycle of life, death and rebirth. It can help one to find stillness at the hub of constant movement, to feel centred while everything turned around, to be both at the centre and circumference of the universe in a state of silent opening.

The spiral recurs throughout nature, from the double helix of DNA, the curving of a seashell to the climbing of a vine around a tree. It has always been a symbol of the spiritual path, a circuitous route yet gradually winding higher and higher towards the heavens.

The maze, enticing us to enter, promises a central revelation. Most of us grope our way through the labyrinth of the world towards the celestial home and many get lost on the way. But like the cup-and-ring marks, the megalithic mazes invariably have a straight line to the centre – the fast and dangerous way to enlightenment which is only possible for a few.

Like my distant ancestors, I was thirsty to drink from the cup of wisdom; I was eager to discover the central revelation; I wanted to go straight to the heart of things. I had not yet reached it, but I felt I was getting closer. I was still going round in circles (on land and at sea), but it was in ever-diminishing circles. The experiences of my voyage had confirmed for me at least that I was on the right track. Like a good navigator, I knew where I did not want to be. I knew that while carefully steering to avoid the rocks and shallows of negative feelings, I should be ready for the spontaneous and unexpected. I knew that the last true act of my reason is to recognize its own inadequacy and that at a certain point I must rely on intuition alone for guidance. I knew that on certain occasions I should be prepared to go with the flow of the universe wherever it might lead me. I knew that I should open myself up to the winds and currents of the Great Ocean of Being. All this knowledge was strengthened during my voyage in search of the sacred science of the megalith builders.

Lessons from the sea

And what of my journey in search of Europe's lost civilization? Had my voyage taught me anything new? To sail along the sea routes – the 'wake lines' – of the ancient mariners enabled me to understand their perceptions of the world as well as to clarify my own.

The sea has taught me, as it did my seafaring ancestors, to be calm and centred when all around is uncertain, to live in perpetual mobility and to think that nothing is finally achieved. It has made me respect a force of nature which can never be tamed and never fully comprehended. Above all, it has encouraged me to live in the present as if every moment was my last.

Clearly every voyage has a destination, but a good navigator will always have a secondary harbour in mind if the weather changes or something unexpected happens. This has taught me a most useful lesson for life: to have a goal but not to expect to keep it, to change plans according to changing circumstances, and always to have an alternative if things go wrong.

Sailing has also taught me the true value of cooperation and solidarity. It has shown me that all religions are one and that whatever our nationality and culture we share a common humanity. A good sailor is always ready to save a soul, whatever the flag of his boat or the language he speaks.

Going to sea is like experiencing a little death. At sea you quickly realize how vulnerable and fragile you are. If something goes wrong, you can easily die. But you have no one to blame but yourself. Constant care is therefore the price of freedom at sea. If you half look after your boat, it will look after you.

However much I tried to understand the sea, it always escaped my reason and imagination. The sea is vast and beyond comprehension; it does not begin or end; it is always changing, yet always the same. It is the very image of our sublunary world with its constant flux of life above deeper and more permanent forms. While the surface of the sea may be lashed by a storm, in the depths below it remains quiet and still. The sea, controlled by the moon, gives and takes like the Great Goddess herself. It has taught me that we are just footprints in the sand: we make our mark, but we are soon washed away.

Navigating by the stars under the great moving dome of the night sky reminds you of your own insignificance and the infinity of the universe. Seeing the sun rise and set every day on the blue horizon tells you how fleeting is this life and how eternal the world.

Sailing prepares you for the final voyage into the Great Unknown, for the return to the Nothingness from which we come. The end of a voyage is as important as its beginning. Just as it helps to be well equipped before setting out on a long journey, it is wise to be prepared for the final voyage in what the Egyptians called 'The Boat of a Million Years'. I felt certain that the ancient mariners whose wake I had followed for thousands of miles knew all this – and much more.

I wrote in my notebook a piece on 'Sailing on Land':

> I will be like a boat,
> Trusting the water which keeps it afloat.
> When the weight increases, it sinks deeper.
> When the going gets rough, it rises and falls.
> When it is calm, it rocks to the rhythm of the ocean.
> I will be like a boat,
> Floating on the waves of the universe.

My voyage from Scotland to Malta has taught me a great deal. It has confirmed my belief that the megaliths are the beguiling remnants of a highly advanced lost civilization of Europe, a seaborne civilization which enjoyed a Golden Age unparalleled in human history. And unlike the civilizations of Egypt and Greece, it was not based on slavery but on the voluntary labour of an equal and cooperative society.

Yet, while all this is clear, mysteries remain. Seven millennia after they were first built, the megaliths still stand as enigmatic question marks against the historical skyline, waiting to be rediscovered and reinterpreted by every generation. But they can no longer be dismissed as rough, rude stones. They are essential in any attempt to understand our past, our future potential and our ultimate place within the universe. And however well mapped and charted Europe may be, there are many more megalithic treasures waiting to be uncovered.

Long lost under the earth and in the fragmentary knowledge of earlier archaeologists and historians, it is only now that Europe's lost civilization of the Stone Age is being properly understood and appreciated. Light at last is beginning to shine into the dark cave of our ignorance and prejudice, which for far too long has obscured the sacred science and beauty of the great stones raised to the sky.

Notes

Introduction

1 Richard Oram, *Scottish Prehistory* (Edinburgh: Birlinn, 1997), p. 27
2 Anna Ritchie, 'Summer on Papay', *The Orcadian*, 2 February 1984. See also her *Scotland BC* (Edinburgh: HMSO, 1988)
3 E.G. Bowen, *Britain and the Western Seaways* (London: Thames & Hudson, 1972), pp. 36–8
4 Alastair Service and Jean Bradbery, *The Standing Stones of Europe: A guide to the great megalithic monuments* (London: Weidenfeld & Nicolson, 1996), p. 18

Chapter 1: Orcadian Light

1 V. Gordon Childe and D.V. Clarke, *Skara Brae* (Edinburgh: HMSO, 1983)
2 Euan W. MacKie, *Science and Society in Prehistoric Britain* (London: Elek, 1977). See also Colin Renfrew, *Investigations in Orkney* (London: Thames & Hudson, 1979)
3 David Clarke and Patrick Maguire, *Skara Brae* (Inglis Allen, Kirkcaldy: Historic Scotland, 2000), p. 27
4 Patrick Ashmore, *Maes Howe* (Edinburgh: Historic Scotland, 1995)
5 Oram, *Scottish Prehistory*, p. 335
6 Geoffrey Cornelius and Paul Devereux, *The Secret Language of the Stars and Planets: A visual key to celestial mysteries* (London: Pavilion, 1996), p. 127
7 Anna and Graham Ritchie, *The Ancient Monuments of Orkney* (Edinburgh: HMSO, 1986), p. 8
8 Janet and Colin Bord, *A Guide to the Ancient Sites in Britain* (London: Paladin, 1979), p. 168
9 Aubrey Burl, *A Guide to the Stone Circles of Britain, Ireland and Brittany* (London and New Haven: Yale University Press, 1995), p. 148

10 Alexander Thom, *Megalithic Sites in Britain* (Oxford: Oxford University Press, 1967); Burl, *A Guide to the Stone Circles*, p. 147

11 Keith Critchlow, 'The Cosmology of Stone Circles', *Earth Mysteries: A study in patterns*, ed. Keith Critchlow and Graham Challifour (London: RILKO, 1978), p. 26

12 Marija Gimbutas, *The Language of the Goddess: Unearthing the hidden symbols of western civilization* (London: HarperCollins, 1989), plate 23

13 Alexander Thom and A.S. Thom, *Megalithic Remains in Britain and Brittany* (Oxford: Oxford University Press, 1979), pp. 122–37; Burl, *A Guide to the Stone Circles*, p. 146

14 Peter Marshall, *The Philosopher's Stone: A quest for the secrets of alchemy* (London: Macmillan, 2001)

15 Clarke and Maguire, *Skara Brae*, p. 28

16 Bowen, *Britain and the Western Seaways*, pp. 9, 29–30

Chapter 2: The Long Journey

1 Albert J. Ammerman and L.L. Cavalli-Sforza, *The Neolithic Transition and the Genetics of Populations in Europe* (Princeton: Princeton University Press, 1984), pp. 133–4, 63

2 David Souden, *Stonehenge: Mysteries of the stones and landscape* (London: Collins & Brown, 1997), pp. 14–15

3 Colin Renfrew, *Archaeology and Language: The puzzle of Indo-European origins* (Harmondsworth: Penguin, 1989), pp. 31–2

4 Alasdair W.R. Whittle, *Europe in the Neolithic: The creation of new worlds* (Cambridge: Cambridge University Press, 1996), p. 359

5 Service and Bradbery, *The Standing Stones of Europe*, p. 17

Chapter 3: The Great Goddess

1 Patrick Ashmore, *Calanais: The standing stones* (Inverness: Urras nan Tursachan, 1995), p. 13; Gerald and Margaret Ponting, *The Stones around Callanish* (Callanish: G. and M. Ponting, 1984, revised 1993)

2 Ashmore, *Calanais*, pp. 30–1

3 Hellmuth M. Schulz, *Callanish* (Callanish: H.M. Schulz, 1983)

4 Oram, *Scottish Prehistory*, p. 44

5 Ian Armit, *The Archaeology of Skye and the Western Isles* (Edinburgh: Edinburgh University Press, 1996), p. 83

6 Alexander Thom, *Megalithic Sites in Britain*

7 Gerald and Margaret Ponting, *New Light on the Stones of Callanish* (Callanish: G. and M. Ponting, 1984), pp. 28–9, 52

8 Boyle T. Somerville, 'Astronomical Indications in the Megalithic Monument at Callanish', *Journal of the British Astronomical Association* (1912) 23

9 Gerard S. Hawkins with John B. White, *Stonehenge Decoded* (London: Souvenir Press, 1966). See the appendix 'Callanish, a Scottish Stonehenge'

10 Peter Marshall, *World Astrology: The astrologer's quest to understand the human character* (London: Macmillan, 2004)

11 G. and M. Ponting, *New Light on the Stones of Callanish*, pp. 46, 50–2

12 Ron and Margaret Curtis, *Callanish: The stones, moon and the sacred landscape* (Callanish: privately printed, 1994), pp. 8–9

13 Diodorus Siculus, *Works*, trans. C.H. Oldfather *et al.* (Loeb Classical Library, 1936–67) (London: Heinemann, 1967), vol. 5

14 Robert Graves, *The White Goddess: A historical grammar of poetic myth* (1948), ed. Grevel Lindop (London: Faber & Faber, 1999), p. 64. See also Sibylle von Cles-Reden, *The Realm of the Great Goddess: The story of the megalith builders* (London: Thames & Hudson, 1961)

15 Gimbutas, *The Language of the Goddess*, p. 152

16 Ibid., pp. 237, 324

17 Martin Martin, *A Description of the Western Isles of Scotland* (London, 1703)

18 Stuart Piggott, *The Druids* (Harmondsworth: Penguin, 1977); Oram, *Scottish Prehistory*, ch. 4

19 G. and M. Ponting, *New Light on the Stones of Callanish*, p. 30

20 Otta F. Swire, *The Outer Hebrides and their Legends* (Edinburgh and London: Oliver & Boyd, 1966)

21 W.C. Mackenzie, *Book of the Lews* (Paisley, 1919)

22 T.C. Lethbridge, *Legend of the Sons of God: A fantasy?* (London: Sidgwick & Jackson, 1973)

23 Lynne Wood, *Reflections of Airgid* (privately printed, 1981)

24 Swire, *The Outer Hebrides and their Legends*

Chapter 4: Moulds and Wheels

1 Rachel Butter, *Kilmartin: Scotland's richest prehistoric landscape* (Kilmartin: Kilmartin House Trust, 1999), p. 40

2 Walter Traill Dennison, *Orkney Folklore and Sea Legends* (Kirkwall: Orkney Press, 1995), pp. 6–7, 20–2

3 Tom Graves, *Needles of Stone* (London: Turnstone, 1978)

4 Burl, *A Guide to the Stone Circles*, p. 112

5 Gimbutas, *The Language of the Goddess*, p. 324

6 Butter, *Kilmartin*, p. 52

7 Ibid., p. 66

8 *Argyll: An inventory of ancient monuments* (Edinburgh: The Royal Commission on the Ancient and Historical Monuments of Scotland, 1988), vol. 6, no. 222

9 Gimbutas, *The Language of the Goddess*, pp. 321, 312

10 Ralph Bradley, *Rock Art and the Prehistory of Atlantic Europe: Signing the land* (London: Routledge, 1997), p. 50

11 Marshall, *The Philosopher's Stone*, p. 272

12 *Kilmartin: Prehistoric and early historic monuments* (Edinburgh: The Royal Commission on the Ancient and Historical Monuments of Scotland, 1999), extracted from *Argyll* (1988), vol. 6, p. 8

13 William Blake, 'Jerusalem', ch. 1, 11.16–20, in Peter Marshall, *William Blake: Visionary anarchist* (London: Freedom Press, 1988), p. 47

14 Colin Renfrew, *Before Civilization: The radiocarbon revolution and prehistoric Europe* (London: Jonathan Cape, 1973), p. 133

15 Francis Pryor, *Seahenge: A quest for life and death in Bronze Age Britain* (London: HarperCollins, 2002), p. 314

Chapter 5: The British Mediterranean

1 Bowen, *Britain and the Western Seaways*, p. 8

2 Paul Johnstone, *The Sea-craft of Prehistory* (London: Routledge, 1980), pp. 98–100

3 Bowen, *Britain and the Western Seaways*, p. 36; Richard Mac Cullagh, *The Irish Currach Folk* (Dublin: Wolfhound Press, 1992), ch. 19

4 Mac Cullagh, ibid., p. 23

5 Claire O'Kelly, *Passage-grave Art in the Boyne Valley* (Dublin: C. O'Kelly, 1978). See also Michael J. O'Kelly, *Newgrange: Archaeology, art and legend* (London: Thames & Hudson, 1982)

6 Christopher Knight and Robert Lomas, *Uriel's Machine: The ancient origins of science* (London: Arrow, 2000), p. 264

7 Marshall, *The Philosopher's Stone*, pp. 143–4

8 Martin Brennan, *The Stars and the Stones: Ancient art and astronomy in Ireland* (London: Thames & Hudson, 1983), pp. 72–86

9 Chris Castle, 'Stone Markings', *Earth Mysteries*, p. 41

10 Knight and Lomas, *Uriel's Machine*, pp. 330–1

11 George Eogan, *Knowth and the Passage-tombs of Ireland* (London: Thames & Hudson, 1986)

12 This discovery has been made by Dr Philip Stook of the University of Western Ontario, Canada

13 For more evidence that the ancients had discovered the telescope, see Robert Temple, *The Crystal Sun: Rediscovering a lost technology of the ancient world* (London: Century, 2000)

14 J.H. Brennan, *A Guide to Megalithic Ireland* (London: Aquarian Press, 1994)

15 Bob Quinn, *Atlantean: Ireland's North African and maritime heritage* (London: Quartet, 1986); Emmet J. Sweeney, *The Lost History of Ireland: An enquiry into the pre-Christian history of the Gaels* (Derry: Grianan, 1992)

16 Geoffrey of Monmouth, *The History of the Kings of Britain* (circa 1136), trans. Lewis Thorpe (Harmondsworth: Penguin, 1966)

17 Teresa Moorey, *Earth Mysteries* (London: Hodder & Stoughton, 1998), p. 51

18 Alexander Thom, *Megalithic Lunar Observatories* (Oxford: Oxford University Press, 1971), p. 12

19 Knight and Lomas, *Uriel's Machine*, pp. 251, 257, 264–5

20 Pryor, *Seahenge*, pp. 310–11

21 Julius Caesar, *The Conquest of Gaul*, trans. S. Handford (Harmondsworth: Penguin, 1964)

22 Tacitus, *Germania* (Harmondsworth: Penguin, 1948)

23 Burl, *A Guide to the Stone Circles*, p. 172

24 Glyn Daniel, *The Megalith Builders of Western Europe* (London: Hutchinson, 1963), p. 17

Chapter 6: The Proudest Singularity

1 Burl, *A Guide to the Stone Circles*, p. 87

2 Souden, *Stonehenge*, p. 34

3 Alexander, Archibald Stevenson and Alexander Strang Thom, 'Stonehenge', *Earth Mysteries*, p. 16

4 Souden, *Stonehenge*, p. 93

5 Pryor, *Seahenge*, p. 89

6 'Man who brought new technology to Stonehenge', *Guardian*, 11 February 2003

7 Sir Richard Colt Hoare, *The Ancient History of Wiltshire*, 2 vols (1812) (Wakefield: EP, 1976)

8 R.J. Harrison, *The Beaker Folk* (London: Thames & Hudson, 1980), p. 165

9 Sir Norman Lockyer, *Stonehenge and other British Stone Monuments Astronomically Considered* (1906), 2nd edn (London: Macmillan, 1909)

[10] A., A.S. and A.S. Thom, 'Stonehenge', *Earth Mysteries*, p. 17
[11] Robin Heath, *A Key to Stonehenge* (St Dogmaels: Bluestone Press, 1995). See also his *Sun, Moon and Stonehenge: Proof of a high culture in ancient Britain* (St Dogmaels: Bluestone Press, 2001)
[12] Aubrey Burl, *The Stonehenge People* (London: Dent, 1987)
[13] Hawkins, *Stonehenge Decoded*
[14] Fred Hoyle, *On Stonehenge* (London: Heinemann, 1977)
[15] Souden, *Stonehenge*, p. 89
[16] Ibid.

Chapter 7: Merry Meet

1 Burl, *A Guide to the Stone Circles*, p. 84. See also his *Prehistoric Avebury* (London and New Haven: Yale University Press, 1979)
2 Caroline Malone, *The Prehistoric Monuments of Avebury* (London: English Heritage, 2001), pp. 46–7
3 William Stukeley, *Abury Described* (London, 1763)
4 Malone, *The Prehistoric Monuments of Avebury*, p. 25
5 David Derbyshire, 'Secrets of the Stone Age Uncovered', *Daily Telegraph*, 20 February 2002
6 Moses B. Cotsworth, *Rational Almanack* (1900)
7 John Aubrey, *Monumenta Britannica* (1695) (London: Little, Brown, 1982)
8 Stukeley, *Abury Described*, p. 41
9 Paul Devereux, *Symbolic Landscape: The dreamtime earth and Avebury's open secrets* (Glastonbury: Gothic Image, 1997), p. 162
10 Michael Dames, *The Silbury Treasure: The Great Goddess rediscovered* (London: Thames & Hudson, 1976), pp. 54, 107
11 Service and Bradbery, *The Standing Stones of Europe*, pp. 241–2; Michael Dames, *The Avebury Cycle* (London: Thames & Hudson, 1996)
12 Craig Weatherhill, *Belerion: Ancient sites of Land's End* (Penzance: Alison Hodge, 1981), p. 6
13 British Library, Harley MS 1585, ff.12v., R. Graves, *The White Goddess*, p. 68
14 Smohalla in *Touch the Earth: A self-portrait of Indian existence*, ed. T.C. Mcluhan (London: Abacus, 1989), p. 56
15 Malone, *The Prehistoric Monuments of Avebury*, p. 6
16 Stukeley, *Abury Described*

Chapter 8: The Civilized West

1 John Edwin Wood, *Sun, Moon and Standing Stones* (Oxford: Oxford University Press, 1978), p. 130–3

2 Burl, *A Guide to the Stone Circles*, p. 58

3 T. C. Lethbridge, *A Step in the Dark* (London: Routledge & Kegan Paul, 1967)

4 Tom Graves, *Needles of Stone; Needles of Stone Revisited* (Glastonbury: Gothic Image, 1986)

5 Paul Devereux, *Shamanism and the Mystery Lines* (London: Quantum, 1992)

6 Graves, *Needles of Stone*

7 Kathy Jones, *The Ancient British Goddess* (London: Ariadne, 1991)

8 John Michell, *The Earth Spirit: Its ways, shrines and mysteries* (London: Thames & Hudson, 1975), pp. 13–17

9 Paul Broadhurst and Hamish Miller, *The Sun and the Serpent* (Launceston: Pendragon Press, 1998); *The Dance of the Dragon: An odyssey into earth energies and ancient religion* (Launceston: Pendragon Press, 2000)

10 Philip Heselton, *Ley Lines* (London: Hodder & Stoughton, 1999), p. 80

11 Pryor, *Seahenge*, pp. 257–9

12 Ian Cooke, *Mermaid to Merrymaid: Journey to the stones* (Penzance: Men-an-Tol Studio, 1987), p. 51

13 Gimbutas, *The Language of the Goddess*, p. 324

14 Burl, *A Guide to the Stone Circles*, p. 33

15 Cooke, *Mermaid to Merrymaid*, p. 128

16 Weatherhill, *Belerion*, p. 30

Chapter 9: A Place of Sadness

1 Jean Laurent Monnier, *La Préhistoire de Bretagne et d'Armorique* (Luçon: Éditions Jean-Paul Gisserot, 1991), p. 93; Aubrey Burl, *Megalithic Brittany* (London: Thames & Hudson, 1985), p. 50

2 Johnstone, *The Sea-craft of Prehistory*, p. 98

3 Ibid., p. 99

4 Burl, *Megalithic Brittany*, p. 62

5 Jacques Briard, *Les Mégalithes: Ésoterisme et realité* (Luçon: Éditions Jean-Paul Gisserot, 1997), p. 105

6 Jean Mornand, *Préhistoire et protohistoire de Presqu'île de Crozon* (Crozon: Etre Daou Vor, 1998), vol. 1

Chapter 10: The Pillar and the Axe

1 Monnier, *La Préhistoire de Bretagne et d'Armorique*, pp. 79–82

2 Jean-Pierre Mohen, *The Carnac Alignments: Neolithic temples* (Paris: Éditions du Patrimoine, 2000), p. 32

3 Ibid., p. 39

4 Bowen, *Britain and the Western Seaways*, p. 39

5 Gérard Bailloud, Christine Boujout, Serge Cassen and Charles-Tanguy Le Roux, *Carnac: Les premières architectures de pierre* (Paris: CNRS Éditions, 2001), p. 116

6 Jean L'Helgouac'h, *Locmariaquer* (Luçon: Éditions Jean-Paul Gisserot, 1994), p. 13

7 Service and Bradbery, *The Standing Stones of Europe*, p. 60

8 A. and A.S. Thom, *Megalithic Remains in Britain and Brittany*; Félix Gaillard, *L'Astronomie préhistorique* (Paris, 1895)

9 L'Helgouac'h, *Locmariaquer*, p. 15

10 Ibid., pp. 26–9

11 Burl, *A Guide to the Stone Circles*, pp. 254–6

12 Philippe Gouezin, *Le site mégalithique d'Er Lannic* (Monterblanc: Archeo Douar Mor, 1998)

13 Zacharie Le Rouzic, *Les cromlechs d'Er Lannic* (Vannes, 1930)

14 Burl, *A Guide to the Stone Circles*, p. 257

15 Charles-Tanguy Le Roux, *Gavrinis* (Luçon: Éditions Jean-Paul Gisserot, 1995), p. 4

16 Ibid., pp. 18–31; Bailloud *et al.*, *Carnac*, pp. 84–97; Mohen, *The Carnac Alignments*, p. 41

17 Bradley, *Rock Art and the Prehistory of Atlantic Europe*, p. 9

18 Elizabeth Shee Twohig, *The Megalithic Art of Western Europe* (Oxford: Oxford University Press, 1981), p. 139

19 Paul G. Bahn, *Prehistoric Art* (Cambridge: Cambridge University Press, 1998), p. 171

20 Ibid., p. 222

21 Marija Gimbutas, *The Goddesses and Gods of Old Europe, 6500–3500 BC: Myths and cult images* (London: Thames & Hudson, 1982)

22 Gimbutas, *The Language of the Goddess*, p. 91

23 Gimbutas, *The Goddesses and Gods of Old Europe*

24 Burl, *Megalithic Brittany*, p. 110

Chapter 11: The Large Stones

1 Mohen, *The Carnac Alignments*, p. 4

2 Ibid., pp. 14–15

3 Aubrey Burl, *From Carnac to Callanish: The prehistoric stone rows and avenues of Britain, Ireland and Brittany* (London and New Haven: Yale University Press, 1993), pp. 135–40

4 A. and A.S. Thom, *Megalithic Remains in Britain and Brittany*

5 Bailloud *et al.*, *Carnac*, p. 65; Burl, *A Guide to the Stone Circles*, p. 254

Chapter 12: The Bay of Biscay

1 Service and Bradbery, *The Standing Stones of Europe*, pp. 67–8; Glyn Daniel, *The Prehistoric Chamber Tombs of France* (London: Thames & Hudson, 1960), p. 117

2 P.-R. Giot, 'The Megaliths of France', *The Megalithic Monuments of Western Europe*, ed. Colin Renfrew (London: Thames & Hudson, 1983)

3 Burl, *Megalithic Brittany*, p. 116

Chapter 13: The Coast of Death

1 Ramón Fábregas Valcarce, *Megalitismo del Noreste de la Península Ibérica: Tipología y secuencia de los materiales líticos* (Madrid: UNED, 1991), pp. 286–90

2 Bradley, *Rock Art and the Prehistory of Atlantic Europe*, p. 207

3 J. J. Eiroa and J. Rey, *Guía de los petroglifos de Muros* (Santiago, 1984), p. 100

4 Ibid

5 Valcarce, *Megalitismo del Noreste de la Península Ibérica*, p. 313

6 F. Antonio de la Peña Santos, F. Javier Costas Goberna, José Rey Garcia, *El Arte rupestre en Campo Lameiro* (Xunta de Galicia), Prologue; R. Sobrino Buhigas, *Corpus petriglyphorum Gallaeciae* (Compostela, 1935)

7 Antonio *et al.*, *El Arte rupestre en Campo Lameiro*, p. 15

8 Ibid., p. 35

9 Bradley, *Rock Art and the Prehistory of Atlantic Europe*, pp. 207, 215

Chapter 14: The Portuguese Trades

1 Euan MacKie, *The Megalith Builders* (London: Phaidon, 1977), pp. 154–62

2 Valcarce, *Megalitismo del Noreste de la Península Ibérica*, pp. 519–23

3 Roger Collins, *Spain: An Oxford archaeological guide* (Oxford: Oxford University Press, 1998), pp. 4–5

4 Valcarce, *Megalitismo del Noreste de la Península Ibérica*, pp. 470–2

5 António Faustino de Carvalho, João Zilhão, Thierry Aubry, *Côa Valley: Rock art and prehistory* (Lisbon: Ministry of Culture, 1996), p. 43. See also V.O. and S.O. Jorge, 'Portuguese Rock Art: A general view', *Trabalhos de Antropologia e Etnologia* (1995), vol. 35 (4), pp. 323–48

6 A. Leroi-Gourhand, *Préhistoire de l'art occidental* (Paris: Mazenod, 1965); M. Lorblanchet, *Les grottes ornées de la préhistoire: nouveaux regards* (Paris: Éditions Errance, 1995)

7 Faustino de Carvalho *et al.*, *Côa Valley*, pp. 54–6

8 Johnstone, *The Sea-craft of Prehistory*, pp. 92–3, 98

9 T.C. Lethbridge, *Boats and Boatmen* (London: Thames & Hudson, 1952), pp. 116–19

10 Johnstone, *The Sea-craft of Prehistory*, p. 98

11 MacKie, *The Megalith Builders*, pp. 186–7

12 Michael Hoskin, *Tombs, Temples and their Orientations: A new perspective on Mediterranean prehistory* (Bognor Regis: Ocarina, 2001), p. 90

13 Service and Bradbery, *The Standing Stones of Europe*, p. 86

Chapter 15: Eastward Bound

1 Peter Marshall, *Around Africa: From the Pillars of Hercules to the Strait of Gibraltar* (London: Simon & Schuster, 1994)

2 José Manuel Garcia and Rui Cunha, *Sagres* (Vila do Bispo, 1990), p. 29

3 Ibid., p. 81

4 *Portugal das Origens a Epoca Romana* (Lisbon: Museu Nacional de Arqueologia e Etnologia, n.d.)

5 Adolf Schulten, *Tartessos, Beitrag zur ältesten Geschichte des Westens* (1922) (Hamburg, 1950)

6 Plato, *Timaeus*, trans. H.D.P. Lee (Harmondsworth: Penguin, 1965), sects. 24–5, p. 37

7 Johnstone, *The Sea-craft of Prehistory*, p. 94

8 Jürgen Spanuth, *Atlantis of the North* (London: Sidgwick & Jackson, 1979), p. 251

Chapter 16: Mediterranean Spain

1 Jean-Pierre Mohen, *Standing Stones: Stonehenge, Carnac and the world of the megaliths* (London: Thames & Hudson, 1999), p. 89
2 Hoskin, *Tombs, Temples and their Orientations*, pp. 210–11
3 Quinn, *Atlantean*, pp. 44–5, 48
4 Service and Bradbery, *The Standing Stones of Europe*, p. 86
5 Spanuth, *Atlantis of the North*, p. 114
6 Hoskin, *Tombs, Temples and their Orientations*, pp. 59–60
7 Los Millares Archaeological Museum

Chapter 17: Islands in the Sun

1 Luis Pericot-García, *The Balearic Islands*, trans. M. Brown (London: Thames & Hudson, 1973)
2 Gabriel Pons i Homar, *Itinerarios arqueológicos de Mallorca* (Palma: Consell de Mallorca, n.d.)
3 Luis Casasnovas Marqués, *Conocer Menorca: su arqueología* (Menorca: Nura, 1994), p. 14
4 Hoskin, *Tombs, Temples and their Orientations*, pp. 49–50
5 N.K. Sanders, *The Sea Peoples: Warriors of the ancient Mediterranean* (London: Thames & Hudson, 1985)
6 Marqués, *Conocer Menorca*, p. 15
7 J. Gual, *Figures de bronce a la prehistoria de Mallorca* (Palma: Consell de Cultura, 1993)
8 Marqués, *Conocer Menorca*, p. 63
9 Hoskin, *Tombs, Temples and their Orientations*, p. 42
10 *Archaeological Guide to Minorca* (Mahón: Consell Insular de Menorca, n.d.), p. 8
11 Hoskin, *Tombs, Temples and their Orientations*, pp. 42–4
12 Marqués, *Conocer Menorca*, p. 66

Chapter 18: The Granite Isle

1 Dorothy Carrington, *Granite Island: A portrait of Corsica* (1971) (Harmondsworth: Penguin, 1984), ch. 4
2 Prosper Mérimée, *Notes d'un voyage en Corse* (1840) (Paris: Adam Biro, 1989)
3 Joseph Cesari, *Corse des origines* (Paris: Imprimerie Nationale, 1994), p. 116

4 Ibid., p. 28

5 Giovanni Lilliu, *La Civiltà dei Sardi: Dal neolitico all'età dei nuraghi* (1967) (Turin, 1975); Cesari, *Corse des origines*, p. 60

6 Gabriel Camps, *Préhistoire d'une île* (Paris: Éd. Errance, 1988)

7 Hoskin, *Tombs, Temples and their Orientations*, p. 179

8 Roger Grosjean, *La Corse avant l'histoire* (1966) (Paris: Klincksieck, 1981)

9 Jean-Dominique Cesari and Lucien Acquaviva, *Filitosa*, trans. R. Evans (Albertacce: Éd. Société Archéologique du Centre Corse, 1987)

10 Ibid., p. 28; Carrington, *Granite Island*, p. 35

11 Grosjean, *La Corse avant l'histoire*

12 Cesari, *Corse des origines*, p. 107

13 Diodorus Siculus, *Works*, vol. 5, xiii, 1–14

14 Carrington, *Granite Island*, p. 39

Chapter 19: The Sky-Exposed Land

1 Margaret Guido, *Sardinia* (London: Thames & Hudson, 1963), p. 36

2 Lilliu, *La Civiltà dei Sardi*, p. 68

3 Giovanni Maria Demartis, *La Necropoli di Anghelu Ruju* (Sassari: Carlo Delfino, 1986)

4 Ercole Contu, *L'Altare Preistorico di Monte D'Accoddi* (Sassari: Carlo Delfino, 2000)

5 Service and Bradbery, *The Standing Stones of Europe*, p. 112

6 Angela Antona Ruju and Maria Luisa Ferrares Ceruti, *The Albucciu Nuraghe and Arzachena's Monuments* (Sassari: Carlo Delfino, 1992), p. 6

7 Ibid., pp. 23–8

8 Hoskin, *Tombs, Temples and their Orientations*, p. 182

9 Paolo Melis, *The Nuragic Civilization* (Sassari: Carlo Delfino, 2003), p. 6

10 Alberto Moravetti, *Le complexe nuragique de Palmavera* (Sassari: Carlo Delfino, 1992)

11 Ercole Contu, *The Nuraghe S. Antine* (Sassari: Carlo Delfino, 1988), p. 5

12 Giovanni Lilliu and Raimondo Zucca, *Su Nuraxi di Barumini* (Sassari: Carlo Delfino, 1999), p. 44

13 Lilliu, *La Civiltà dei Sardi*

14 Melis, *The Nuragic Civilization*, p. 33

15 Hoskin, *Tombs, Temples and their Orientations*, p. 186

16 Alberto Moravetti, *Serra Orrios e i Monumenti Archeologici di Dorgali* (Sassari: Carlo Delfino, 1998)

17 Melis, *The Nuragic Civilization*, p. 59

Chapter 20: Africa and Back

1 Herodotus, *The Histories*, trans. Robin Waterfield (Oxford: Oxford University Press, 1998), 4.42, p. 248

2 Abdelmajid Ennabli and Hédi Slim, *Carthage: A visit to the ruins* (Tunis: Cérès, 1992), p. 8

3 Serge Lancel, *Carthage* (Tunis: Cérès, 1992), pp. 238–45

4 Ennabli and Slim, *Carthage*, p. 36

5 Hoskin, *Tombs, Temples and their Orientations*, pp. 204–8

6 S. Tusa, *La Sicilia della Prehistoria* (Palermo, 1983), pp. 130–1

7 T. Eric Peet, *The Stone and Bronze Ages in Italy and Sicily* (Oxford: Clarendon Press, 1909), p. 510; Margaret Guido, *Sicily: An archaeological guide* (London: Faber & Faber, 1967), p. 23

8 Guido, *Sicily*, p. 24

9 Service and Bradbery, *The Standing Stones of Europe*, p. 79

10 Hoskin, *Tombs, Temples and their Orientations*, p. 196

Chapter 21: Temples of the Goddess

1 D.H. Trump, *Malta: An archaeological guide* (1972) (Valletta: Progress Press, 2000). See also his 'The Architecture of the Maltese Temples', *Facets of Maltese Prehistory*, ed. Anton Mifsud and Charles Savona Ventura (Malta: Prehistoric Society of Malta, 1999)

2 Hoskin, *Tombs, Temples and their Orientations*, p. 23

3 Renfrew, *Before Civilization*, p. 162

4 Anthony Bonanno, *Malta: An archaeological paradise* (Valletta: M.J. Publications, 2000), pp. 44–51

5 J.D. Evans, *Malta* (London: Thames & Hudson, 1959); *The Prehistoric Antiquities of the Maltese Islands: A survey* (University of London: Athlone Press, 1971)

6 Graham Hancock, *Underworld: Flooded kingdoms of the Ice Age* (London: Michael Joseph, 2002), p. 410

7 Anton and Simon Mifsud, *Dossier Malta: Evidence for the Magdalenian* (Mosta: Proprint, 1997)

8 Trump, 'The Architecture of the Maltese Temples', *Facets of Maltese Prehistory*, p. 92

9 Renfrew, *Before Civilization*, pp. 147–166

10 Trump, 'The Architecture of the Maltese Temples', *Facets of Maltese Prehistory*, p. 98

11 Joseph Magro Conti, 'Aggression and Defence in Prehistoric Malta', *Facets of Maltese Prehistory*, pp. 193–4

12 Anton Mifsud, Simon Mifsud, Chris Agius Sultana, Charles Savona Ventura, *Malta: Echoes of Plato's island*, 2nd edn (Malta: Prehistoric Society of Malta, 2001), p. 58

13 H. Vella, 'Fertility Aspects in Ancient North Africa', *Journal of Mediterranean Studies* (1993), vol. 3 (2), p. 220

14 Richard England, 'Megalithic Mandalas of the Middle Sea – The Neolithic Temples of Malta and their Builders', *Facets of Maltese Prehistory*, p. 146

15 Johnstone, *The Sea-craft of Prehistory*, p. 97

16 Kurt Schildman in Mifsud *et al.*, *Malta*, opposite frontispiece

17 Marshall, *World Astrology*, ch. 19

18 Daniel Sciberras, 'The Maltese Dolmens', *Facets of Maltese Prehistory*, p. 106

19 Emília Pasztor and Curt Roslund, 'Orientation of Maltese "Dolmens" ', *Journal of European Archaeology* (1997), vol. 5, pp. 183–9; Hoskin, *Tombs, Temples and their Orientations*, pp. 195–6

Chapter 22: Light in the Darkness

1 Trump, 'The Architecture of the Maltese Temples', *Facets of Maltese Prehistory*, p. 98

2 Marija Gimbutas, *The Civilization of the Goddess* (San Francisco: Harper, 1991), p. 286

3 Veronica Veen and Adrian van der Blom, *The First Maltese: Origins, character and symbolism of the Ghar Dalam culture* (Haarlem: Fia, 1992), pp. 11, 40

4 Renfrew, *Before Civilization*, p. 163

5 Sir Themistocles Zammit, *The Prehistoric Temples of Malta and Gozo*, ed. Karl Mayrhofer (Malta: Masterson, 1995), p. 115. See also Anton and Simon Mifsud, 'The Subterranean Sanctuary at Hal Saflieni', *Facets of Maltese Prehistory*, p. 160

6 Zammit, *The Prehistoric Temples of Malta and Gozo*, pp. 35, 110, 115; Evans, *Malta*, p. 168

7 A. and S. Mifsud, 'The Subterranean Sanctuary at Hal Saflieni', *Facets of Maltese Prehistory*, p. 162

8 Veen and van der Blom, *The First Maltese*, pp. 5–7

9 R. Parker, M. Rubinstein and D.H. Trump, *Malta's Ancient Temples and Ruts* (Tunbridge Wells: Institute for Cultural Research, 1988)

10 Mifsud *et al.*, *Malta*, pp. 42–3; Hancock, *Underworld*, pp. 331, 423–9, 441–2

11 Trump, 'The Architecture of the Maltese Temples', *Facets of Maltese Prehistory*, p. 96

12 Chris Micallef, 'Alignments along the Main Axes at Mnajdra Temples', *Xjendra: Journal of the Malta Chamber of Scientists* (December 2000), vol. 5(1/2), pp. 3–15

13 Hoskin, *Tombs, Temples and their Orientations*, p. 29

14 C. Micallef, 'Alignments along the Main Axes at Mnajdra Temples', p. 10

15 Hoskin, *Tombs, Temples and their Orientations*, p. 28

16 Paul I. Micallef, *Mnajdra Prehistoric Temple: A calendar in stone* (Malta: Union Print, 1990)

17 Ibid., p. 32

18 Hoskin, *Tombs, Temples and their Orientations*, pp. 31–6

19 Evans, *Malta*, p. 168

20 Conti, 'Aggression and Defence in Prehistoric Malta', *Facets of Maltese Prehistory*, pp. 198–9

Chapter 23: The Golden Age

1 MacKie, *The Megalith Builders*, p. 184

2 Carrington, *Granite Island*, p. 31

3 T. Eric Peet, *Rough Stone Monuments and their Builders* (London and New York: Harper, 1912), p. 152

4 V. Gordon Childe, *Prehistoric Communities of the British Isles* (London and Edinburgh: Chambers, 1940), p. 46

5 Glyn Daniel, *The Megalith Builders of Western Europe*, pp. 131–3

6 Renfrew, *Before Civilization*, pp. 14–19

7 MacKie, *The Megalith Builders*, p. 162

8 Whittle, *Europe in the Neolithic*, p. xv

9 Graham Hancock and Santha Faiia, *Heaven's Mirror: Quest for the lost civilization* (London: Michael Joseph, 1998), p. x; *Fingerprints of the Gods* (London: William Heinemann, 1995)

10 Marshall, *The Philosopher's Stone*, p. 460

11 Gimbutas, *The Goddesses and Gods of Old Europe, 6500–3500 BC*, Preface

12 Whittle, *Europe in the Neolithic*, p. 370

13 MacKie, *The Megalith Builders*, p. 184

14 Whittle, *Europe in the Neolithic*, p. 359

15 Richard Rudgley, *Lost Civilisations of the Stone Age* (London: Century, 1998), Introduction

Select Bibliography

General

Ammerman, Albert J. and L.L. Cavalli-Sforza, *The Neolithic Transition and the Genetics of Populations in Europe* (Princeton: Princeton University Press, 1984)

Bahn, Paul G., *Prehistoric Art* (Cambridge: Cambridge University Press, 1998)

Balfour, M., *Megalithic Mysteries: An illustrated guide to Europe's ancient sites* (London: Dragon's World, 1992)

Bender, Barbara and Robert Cailllard, *The Archaeology of Brittany, Normandy and the Channel Islands* (London: Faber & Faber, 1986)

Bradley, Ralph, *Rock Art and the Prehistory of Atlantic Europe: Signing the land* (London: Routledge, 1997)

Bradley, Richard, *The Significance of Monuments: On the shaping of human experience in Neolithic and Bronze Age Europe* (London: Routledge, 1998)

Burl, Aubrey, *From Carnac to Callanish: The prehistoric stone rows and avenues of Britain, Ireland and Brittany* (London and New Haven: Yale University Press, 1993)

Burl, Aubrey, *A Guide to the Stone Circles of Britain, Ireland and Brittany* (London and New Haven: Yale University Press, 1995)

Burl, Aubrey, *Prehistoric Astronomy and Ritual* (Princes Risborough: Shire, 1997)

Childe, V. Gordon, *The Dawn of European Civilization* (London: Thames & Hudson, 1957)

Cles-Reden, Sibylle von, *The Realm of the Great Goddess: The story of the megalith builders* (London: Thames & Hudson, 1961)

Cornelius, Geoffrey and Paul Devereux, *The Secret Language of the Stars and Planets: A visual key to celestial mysteries* (London: Pavilion, 1996)

Critchlow, Keith, *Order in Space* (London: Thames & Hudson, 1964)

Critchlow, Keith, *Time Stands Still: New light on megalithic science* (London: St Martin's Press, 1982)

Critchlow, Keith and Graham Challifour, eds., *Earth Mysteries: A study in patterns* (London: RILKO, 1978)

Cunliffe, Barry, *Facing the Ocean: The Atlantic and its peoples* (Oxford: Oxford University Press, 2001)

Daniel, Glyn, *The First Civilizations* (London: Thames & Hudson, 1968)

Daniel, Glyn, *The Megalith Builders of Western Europe* (London: Hutchinson, 1963)

Daniel, Glyn, *Megaliths in History* (London: Thames & Hudson, 1972)

Devereux, Paul, *Shamanism and the Mystery Lines* (London: Quantum, 1992)

Diodorus Siculus, *Works,* trans. C.H. Oldfather *et al.*, 12 vols. (Loeb Classical Library, 1936–67) (London: Heinemann, 1967)

Donnelly, Ignatius, *Atlantis: The antediluvian world* (1882) (London: Samson Low, Marston & Co., 1910)

Drury, Nevill, *Shamanism* (Shaftesbury: Element, 1996)

Edmonds, M. and B. Bender, *Ancestral Geographies of the Neolithic: Landscapes, monuments and memory* (London: Routledge, 1999)

Ennabli, Abdelmajid and Hédi Slim, *Carthage: A visit to the ruins* (Tunis: Cérès, 1992)

Fowles, John, *Islands* (London: Jonathan Cape, 1978)

Frankfort, H., H.A.T. Jacobsen and J.A. Wilson, *Before Philosophy: The intellectual adventure of ancient man* (London: Penguin, 1954)

Gaillard, Félix, *L'Astronomie préhistorique* (Paris, 1895)

Gimbutas, Marija, *The Goddesses and Gods of Old Europe, 6500–3500 BC: Myths and cult images* (London: Thames & Hudson, 1982)

Gimbutas, Marija, *The Language of the Goddess: Unearthing the hidden symbols of Western civilization* (London: HarperCollins, 1989)

Gimbutas, Marija, *The Civilization of the Goddess* (San Francisco: Harper, 1991)

Graves, Robert, *The White Goddess: A historical grammar of poetic myth* (1948), ed. Grevel Lindop (London: Faber & Faber, 1999)

Graves, Tom, *Needles of Stone* (London: Turnstone, 1978)

Graves, Tom, *Needles of Stone Revisited* (Glastonbury: Gothic Image, 1986)

Hadingham, Evan, *Circles and Standing Stones* (London: Heinemann, 1975)

Hadingham, Evan, *Early Man and the Cosmos: Explorations in archaeoastronomy* (London: Thames & Hudson, 1983)

Hancock, Graham, *Fingerprints of the Gods* (London: Heinemann, 1995)

Hancock, Graham, *Underworld: Flooded kingdoms of the Ice Age* (London: Michael Joseph, 2002)

Hancock, Graham and Santha Faiia, *Heaven's Mirror: Quest for the lost civilization* (London: Michael Joseph, 1998)

Harrison, R.J., *The Beaker Folk* (London: Thames & Hudson, 1980)

Heggie, Douglas C., *Megalithic Science: Ancient mathematics and astronomy in North-West Europe* (London: Thames & Hudson, 1984)

Herodotus, *The Histories*, trans. Robin Waterfield (Oxford: Oxford University Press, 1998)

Heselton, Philip, *Elements of Earth Mysteries* (Shaftsbury: Element, 1991)

Heselton, Philip, *Ley Lines* (London: Hodder & Stoughton, 1999)

Hitching, Francis, *Earth Magic* (London: Cassell, 1976)

Hodson, F.R., ed., *The Place of Astronomy in the Ancient World*, a joint symposium of the Royal Society and the British Academy (Oxford: Oxford University Press, 1974)

Hoskin, Michael, *Tombs, Temples and their Orientations: A new perspective on Mediterranean prehistory* (Bognor Regis: Ocarina, 2001)

Johnstone, Paul, *The Sea-craft of Prehistory* (London: Routledge, 1980)

Knight, Christopher and Robert Lomas, *Uriel's Machine: The ancient origins of science* (London: Arrow, 2000)

Lancel, Serge, *Carthage* (Tunis: Cérès, 1992)

Lawlor, Robert, *Sacred Geometry: Philosophy and practice* (London: Thames & Hudson, 1982)

Leroi-Gourhand, A., *Préhistoire de l'art occidental* (Paris: Mazenod, 1965)

Lethbridge, T.C., *Boats and Boatmen* (London: Thames & Hudson, 1952)

Lethbridge, T.C., *Legend of the Sons of God: A fantasy?* (London: Sidgwick & Jackson, 1973)

Lethbridge, T.C., *The Monkey's Tail* (London: Routledge & Kegan Paul, 1969)

Lethbridge, T.C., *A Step in the Dark* (London: Routledge & Kegan Paul, 1967)

Lorblanchet, M., *Les grottes orneés de la préhistoire: nouveaux regards* (Paris: Éditions Errance, 1995)

MacKie, Euan, *The Megalith Builders* (London: Phaidon, 1977)

Maringer, Johannes, *The Gods of Prehistoric Man* (London: Weidenfeld & Nicolson 1960)

Marshack, Alexander, *The Roots of Civilization* (London: Weidenfeld & Nicolson, 1972)

Marshall, Peter, *The Philospher's Stone: A quest for the secrets of alchemy* (London: Macmillan, 2001)

Marshall, Peter, *World Astrology: The astrologer's quest to understand the human character* (London: Macmillan, 2004)

Maspero, Gaston, *The Dawn of Civilization* (London: SPCK, 1894)

McGrail, Seán, *Ancient Boats in North-West Europe: The archaeology of water transport to AD 1500* (1987) (London and New York: Longman, 1998)

McGrail, Seán, *Boats of the World: From the Stone Age to medieval times* (Oxford: Oxford University Press, 2002)

Merrifield, Ralph, *The Archaeology of Ritual and Magic* (London: Batsford, 1987)

Michell, John, *The Dimensions of Paradise: The proportions and symbolic numbers of ancient cosmology* (New York: HarperCollins, 1988)

Michell, John, *The Earth Spirit: Its ways, shrines and mysteries* (London: Thames & Hudson, 1975)

Michell, John, *A Little History of Astro-archaeology* (London: Thames & Hudson, 1978)

Michell, John, *Megalithomania* (London: Thames & Hudson, 1984)

Mohen, Jean-Pierre, *Standing Stones: Stonehange, Carnac and the world of the megaliths* (London: Thames & Hudson, 1999)

Moorey, Teresa, *Earth Mysteries* (London: Hodder & Stoughton, 1998)

Norber-Schulz, Christian, *Architecture: Meaning and place* (London: Architectural Press, 1986)

Norber-Schulz, Christian, *Genius Loci: Towards a phenomenology of architecture* (London: Academy, 1980)

Peet, T. Eric, *Rough Stone Monuments and their Builders* (London and New York: Harper, 1912)

Pennick, Nigel, *Ancient Science of Geomancy: Man in harmony with the Earth* (London: Thames & Hudson, 1979)

Pennick, Nigel, *Lines on the Landscape* (London: Robert Hale, 1989)

Piggott, Stuart, *Ancient Europe: From the beginning of agriculture to classical antiquity* (1965) (Edinburgh: Edinburgh University Press, 1973)

Piggott, Stuart, ed., *The Dawn of Civilization* (London: Thames & Hudson, 1961)

Piggott, Stuart, *The Druids* (Harmondsworth: Penguin, 1977)

Purce, Jill, *The Mystic Spiral* (London: Thames & Hudson, 1975)

Rees, Lucy, *The Maze: From Hell to Hopi* (London: Bantam, 1992)

Renfrew, Colin, *Archaeology and Language: The puzzle of Indo-European origins* (Harmondsworth: Penguin, 1989)

Renfrew, Colin, *Before Civilization: The radiocarbon revolution and prehistoric Europe* (London: Jonathan Cape, 1973)

Renfrew, Colin, ed., *The Megalithic Monuments of Western Europe* (London: Thames & Hudson, 1983)

Roe, Derek, *Prehistory* (London: Paladin, 1970)

Rudgley, Richard, *Lost Civilisations of the Stone Age* (London: Century, 1998)

Sanders, N.K., *The Sea Peoples: Warriors of the ancient Mediterranean* (London: Thames & Hudson, 1985)

Scarre, C., *Exploring Prehistoric Europe* (New York: Oxford University Press, 1998)

Service, Alastair and Jean Bradbery, *The Standing Stones of Europe: A guide to the great megalithic monuments* (London: Weidenfeld & Nicolson, 1996)

Spanuth, Jürgen, *Atlantis of the North* (London: Sidgwick & Jackson, 1979)

Temple, Robert, *The Crystal Sun: Rediscovering a lost technology of the ancient world* (London: Century, 2000)

Thom, Alexander, *Megalithic Lunar Observatories* (Oxford: Oxford University Press, 1971)

Thom, Alexander and A.S., *Megalithic Remains in Britain and Brittany* (Oxford: Oxford University Press, 1979)

Thomas, Julian, *Understanding the Neolithic* (London: Routledge, 1999)

Trump, D.H., *The Prehistory of the Mediterranean* (Harmondsworth: Penguin, 1980)

Twohig, Elizabeth Shee, *The Megalithic Art of Western Europe* (Oxford: Oxford University Press, 1981)

Underwood, Guy, *The Patterns of the Past* (London: Abacus, 1972)

Whittle, Alasdair W.R., *Europe in the Neolithic: The creation of new worlds* (Cambridge: Cambridge University Press, 1996)

Wilson, Colin, *From Atlantis to the Sphinx: Recovering the lost wisdom of the ancient world* (London: Virgin, 1996)

Wood, John Edwin, *Sun, Moon and Standing Stones* (Oxford: Oxford University Press, 1978)

British Isles

Argyll: An inventory of ancient monuments (Edinburgh: The Royal Commission on the Ancient and Historical Monuments of Scotland, 1988)

Armit, Ian, *The Archaeology of Skye and the Western Isles* (Edinburgh: Edinburgh University Press, 1996)

Ashmore, Patrick, *Maes Howe* (Edinburgh: Historic Scotland, 1995)

Ashmore, Patrick, *Calanais: The standing stones* (Inverness: Urras nan Tursachan, 1995)

Atkinson, R.J.C., *Stonehenge and Neighbouring Monuments* (London: English Heritage, 1993)

Atkinson, R.J.C, *Stonehenge* (Harmondsworth: Pelican, 1960)

Barber, Chris and John Godfrey Williams, *The Ancient Stones of Wales* (Abergavenny: Blorenge, 1989)

Bord, Janet and Colin, *A Guide to the Ancient Sites in Britain* (London: Paladin, 1979)

Bottrell, W., *Traditions and Hearthside Stories of West Cornwall*, 3 vols (1870) (London: Frank Graham, 1970)

Bowen, E.G., *Britain and the Western Seaways* (London: Thames & Hudson, 1972)

Bowen, E.G., *Saints, Seaways and Settlements in the Celtic Lands* (Cardiff: University of Wales Press, 1977)

Bradley, Richard, *The Prehistoric Settlements of Britain* (London: Routledge & Kegan Paul, 1978)

Bradley, Richard, *The Social Foundations of Prehistoric Britain* (London: Longman, 1984)

Brennan, J.H., *A Guide to Megalithic Ireland* (London: Aquarian Press, 1994)

Brennan, Martin, *The Stars and the Stones: Ancient art and astronomy in Ireland* (London: Thames & Hudson, 1983)

Broadhurst, Paul and Hamish Miller, *The Dance of the Dragon: An odyssey into earth energies and ancient religion* (Launceston: Pendragon Press, 2000)

Broadhurst, Paul and Hamish Miller, *The Sun and the Serpent* (Launceston: Pendragon Press, 1998)

Burl, Aubrey, *Prehistoric Avebury* (London and New Haven: Yale University Press, 1979)

Burl, Aubrey, *Rites of the Gods* (London: Dent, 1981)

Burl, Aubrey, *The Stonehenge People* (London: Dent, 1987)

Butter, Rachel, *Kilmartin: Scotland's richest prehistoric landscape* (Kilmartin: Kilmartin House Trust, 1999)

Byng, Brian, *Dartmoor's Mysterious Megaliths* (Plympton: Baron Jay, n.d.)

Childe, V. Gordon, *Prehistoric Communities of the British Isles* (London and Edinburgh: Chambers, 1940)

Childe, V. Gordon, *Scotland before the Scots*, (London: Methuen, 1946)

Childe, V. Gordon and D.V. Clarke, *Skara Brae* (London: HMSO, 1983)

Clarke, David and Patrick Maguire, *Skara Brae* (Inglis Allen, Kirkcaldy: Historic Scotland, 2000)

Colt Hoare, Sir Richard, *The Ancient History of Wiltshire*, 2 vols (1812) (Wakefield: EP, 1976)

Cooke Ian, *Mermaid to Merrymaid: Journey to the stones* (Penzance: Men-an-Tol Studio, 1987)

Curtis, Ron and Margaret, *Callanish: The stones, moon and the sacred landscape* (Callanish: privately printed, 1994)

Dames, Michael, *The Avebury Cycle* (London: Thames & Hudson, 1996)

Dames, Michael, *The Silbury Treasure: The Great Goddess rediscovered* (London: Thames & Hudson, 1976)

Dennison, Walter Traill, *Orkney Folklore and Sea Legends* (Kirkwall: Orkney Press, 1995)

Devereux, Paul, *Symbolic Landscape: The dreamtime earth and Avebury's open secrets* (Glastonbury: Gothic Image, 1997)

Eogan, George, *Knowth and the Passage-tombs of Ireland* (London: Thames & Hudson, 1986)

Harbison, Peter, *Ancient Ireland* (Oxford: Oxford University Press, 1996)

Hawkins, Gerard S., *Beyond Stonehenge* (London: Hutchinson, 1973)

Hawkins, Gerard S. with John B. White, *Stonehenge Decoded* (London: Souvenir Press, 1966)

Heath, Robin, *A Key to Stonehenge* (St Dogmaels: Bluestone Press, 1995)

Heath, Robin, *Sun, Moon and Stonehenge: Proof of a high culture in ancient Britain* (St Dogmaels: Bluestone Press, 2001)

Hoyle, Fred, *On Stonehenge* (London: Heinemann, 1977)

Hoyle, Fred, 'Stonehenge: An eclipse predictor', *Nature* (1966), vol. 211, pp. 454–6

Kilmartin: Prehistoric and early historic monuments (Edinburgh: The Royal Commission on the Ancient and Historical Monuments of Scotland, 1999), extracted from *Argyll*, vol. 6

Jones, Kathy, *The Ancient British Goddess* (London: Ariadne, 1991)

Lockyer, Sir Norman, *Stonehenge and other British Stone Monuments Astronomically Considered* (1906), 2nd edn (London: Macmillan, 1909).

Mac Cullagh, Richard, *The Irish Currach Folk* (Dublin: Wolfhound Press, 1992)

Mackenzie, W.C., *Book of the Lews* (Paisley, 1919)

MacKie, Euan W., *Science and Society in Prehistoric Britain* (London: Elek, 1977)

Malone, Caroline, *The Prehistoric Monuments of Avebury* (London: English Heritage, 2001)

Martin, Martin, *A Description of the Western Isles of Scotland* (London, 1703)

Michell, John, *The Old Stones of Land's End* (London: Garnstone, 1974)

Michell, John, *The View over Atlantis* (1969) (London: Abacus, 1973)

O'Kelly, Claire, *Passage-grave Art in the Boyne Valley* (Dublin: C. O'Kelly, 1978)

O'Kelly, Michael J., *Newgrange: Archaeology, art and legend* (London: Thames & Hudson, 1982)

Oram, Richard, *Scottish Prehistory* (Edinburgh: Birlinn, 1997)

Payne, Robin, *Romance of the Stones: Cornwall's pagan past* (London: Alexander, 1999)

Piggott, Stuart, *Neolithic Cultures of the British Isles* (Cambridge: Cambridge University Press, 1954)

Pollard, Joshua, *Neolithic Britain* (Princes Risborough: Shire, 2002)

Ponting, Gerald and Margaret, *New Light on the Stones of Callanish* (Callanish: G. & M. Ponting, 1984)

Ponting, Gerald and Margaret, *The Stones around Callanish* (Callanish: G. and M. Ponting, 1984, revised 1993)

Pryor, Francis, *Seahenge: A quest for life and death in Bronze Age Britain* (London: HarperCollins, 2002)

Quinn, Bob, *Atlantean: Ireland's North African and maritime heritage* (London: Quartet, 1986)

Renfrew, Colin, ed., *British Prehistory: A new outline* (London: Duckworth, 1974)

Renfrew, Colin, *Investigations in Orkney* (London: Thames & Hudson, 1979)

Ritchie, Anna, *Scotland BC* (Edinburgh: HMSO, 1988)

Ritchie, Anna and Graham, *The Ancient Monuments of Orkney* (Edinburgh: HMSO, 1986)

Schulz, Hellmuth M., *Callanish* (Callanish: H. M. Schulz, 1983)

Somerville, Boyle T., 'Astronomical Indications in the Megalithic Monument at Callanish', *Journal of the British Astronomical Association* (1912), 23

Souden, David, *Stonehenge: Mysteries of the stones and landscape* (London: Collins & Brown, 1997)

Stukeley, William, *Abury Described* (London, 1763)

Stukeley, William, *Stonehenge* (London, 1740)

Stukeley, William, *Stonehenge, A Temple Restored to the British Druids; Abury, A Temple of the British Druids* (London: Taylor & Francis, 1984)

Sweeney, Emmet J., *The Lost History of Ireland: An enquiry into the pre-Christian history of the Gaels* (Derry: Grianan, 1992)

Swire, Otta F., *The Outer Hebrides and their Legends* (Edinburgh and London: Oliver & Boyd, 1966)

Thom, Alexander, *Megalithic Sites in Britain* (Oxford: Oxford University Press, 1967)

Thomas, Charles, P.A.S. Pool and Craig Weatherhill, *The Principal Antiquities of the Land's End District* (Penzance: Cornwall Archaeological Society, 1980)

Wainwright, Geoffrey, *The Henge Monuments: Ceremony and society in prehistoric Britain* (London: Thames & Hudson, 1990)

Watkins, Alfred, *The Old Straight Track* (1925) (London: Abacus, 1974)

Weatherhill, Craig, *Belerion: Ancient sites of Land's End* (Penzance: Alison Hodge, 1981)

Weatherhill, Craig, *Cornovia: Ancient sites of Cornwall and Scilly* (Tiverton: Cornwall Books, 1997)

Wood, Lynne, *Reflections of Airgid* (privately printed, 1981)

France

Bailloud, Gérard, Christine Boujout, Serge Cassen and Charles-Tanguy Le Roux, *Carnac: Les premières architectures de pierre* (Paris: CNRS Éditions, 2001)

Briard, Jacques, *Les Mégalithes: Ésoterisme et realité* (Luçon: Éditions Jean-Paul Gisserot, 1997)

Burl, Aubrey, *Guide des dolmens et menhirs bretons* (Paris: Éd. Errance, 1987)

Burl, Aubrey, *Megalithic Brittany* (London: Thames & Hudson, 1985)

Camps, Gabriel, *Préhistoire d'une île* (Paris: Éd. Errance, 1988)

Carrington, Dorothy, *Granite Island: A portrait of Corsica* (1971) (Harmondsworth: Penguin, 1984)

Cesari, Jean-Dominique and Lucien Acquaviva, *Filitosa*, trans. R. Evans (Albertacce: Éd. Société Archéologique du Centre Corse, 1987)

Cesari, Joseph, *Corse des origines* (Paris: Imprimerie Nationale, 1994)

Daniel, Glyn, *The Prehistoric Chamber Tombs of France* (London: Thames & Hudson, 1960)

De Lanfranchi, F. and M.-C. Weiss, *La Civilisation des Corses: Les origines* (Ajaccio: Cyrnos, 1973)

Giot, Pierre-Rolland, *Brittany* (London: Thames & Hudson, 1960)

Gouezin, Philippe, *Le site mégalithique d'Er Lannic* (Monterblanc: Archeo Douar Mor, 1998)

Grosjean, Roger, *Filitosa: Haut lieu de la Corse préhistorique* (Strasbourg and Corsica, 1975)

Grosjean, Roger, *Filitosa et son contexte archéologique* (Paris: Piot, 1961)

Grosjean, Roger, *La Corse avant l'histoire* (1966) (Paris: Klincksieck, 1981)

Le Roux, Charles-Tanguy, *Gavrinis* (Luçon: Éditions Jean-Paul Gisserot, 1995)

Le Rouzic, Zacharie, *Les cromlechs d'Er Lannic* (Vannes, 1930)

Le Rouzic, Zacharie, *Les monuments mégalithiques du Morbihan: causes de leur restoration* (Le Mans, 1939)

L'Helgouac'h, Jean, *Locmariaquer* (Luçon: Éditions Jean-Paul Gisserot, 1994)

Mérimée, Prosper, *Notes d'un voyage en Corse* (1840) (Paris: Adam Biro, 1989)

Merlet, R., *Exposé du système solsticial néolithique* (Rennes, 1974)

Mohen, Jean-Pierre, *The Carnac Alignments: Neolithic temples* (Paris: Éditions du Patrimoine, 2000)

Mohen, Jean-Pierre, *Standing Stones: Stonehenge, Carnac and the world of megaliths* (London: Thames & Hudson, 1999)

Monnier, Jean Laurent, *La Préhistoire de Bretagne et d'Armorique* (Luçon: Éditions Jean-Paul Gisserot, 1991)

Mornard, Jean, *Préhistoire et protohistoire de Presqu'île de Crozon* (Crozon: Etre Daou Vor, 1998)

Riskine, Anne-Elisabeth, *Carnac, l'armée de pierres* (Paris: Imprimerie Nationale, 1992)

Riskine, Anne-Elisabeth, *Carnac Museum of Prehistory* (Rennes: Éditions Ouest France, 1991)

Iberia

Almagro, M. and A. Arribas, *El Poblado y la necropolis megalítico de Los Millares* (Madrid, 1963)

Archaeological Guide to Minorca (Mahón: Consell Insular de Menorca, n.d.)

Collins, Roger, *Spain: An Oxford archaeological guide* (Oxford: Oxford University Press, 1998)

Eiroa, J.J. and J. Rey, *Guía de los petroglifos de Muros* (Santiago, 1984)

Faustino de Carvalho, António, João Zilhão and Thierry Aubry, *Côa Valley: Rock art and prehistory* (Lisbon: Ministry of Culture, 1996)

Gual, J., *Figures de bronce a la prehistoria de Mallorca* (Palma: Consell de Cultura, 1993)

Jorge, V.O. and S.O., 'Portuguese Rock Art: A general view', *Trabalhos de Antropologia e Etnologia* (1995), vol. 35 (4), pp. 323–48

Marqués, Luis Casasnovas, *Conocer Menorca: su arqueología* (Menorca: Nura, 1994)

Pericot-García, Luis, *The Balearic Islands*, trans. M. Brown (London: Thames & Hudson, 1973)

Pons i Homar, Gabriel, *Itinerarios arqueológicos de Mallorca* (Palma: Consell de Mallorca, n.d.)

Portugal das Origens a Epoca Romana (Lisbon: Museu Nacional de Arqueologia e Etnologia, n.d.)

Valcarce, Ramón Fábregas, *Megalitismo del Noreste de la Península Ibérica: Tipilogía y secuencia de los materiales líticos* (Madrid: UNED, 1991)

Italy

Brea, L.B, *Sicily before the Greeks* (London: Thames & Hudson, 1957)

Contu, Ercole, *L'Altare Preistorico di Monte D'Accoddi* (Sassari: Carlo Delfino, 2000)

Contu, Ercole, *The Nuraghe S. Antine* (Sassari: Carlo Delfino, 1988)

Demartis, Giovanni Maria, *La Necropoli di Anghelu Ruju* (Sassari: Carlo Delfino, 1986)

Guido, Margaret, *Sardinia* (London: Thames & Hudson, 1963)

Guido, Margaret, *Sicily: An archaeological guide* (London: Faber & Faber, 1967)

Lawrence, D.H., *Sea and Sardinia* (1923) (Harmondsworth: Penguin, 1974)

Lilliu, Giovanni, *La Civiltà dei Sardi: Dal neolitico all'età dei nuraghi* (1967) (Turin, 1975)

Lilliu, Giovanni and Raimondo Zucca, *Su Nuraxi di Barumini* (Sassari: Carlo Delfino, 1999)

Melis, Paolo, *The Nuragic Civilization* (Sassari: Carlo Delfino, 2003)

Moravetti, Alberto, *Le complexe nuragique de Palmavera* (Sassari: Carlo Delfino, 1992)

Moravetti, Alberto, *Serra Orrios e i Monumenti Archeologici di Dorgali* (Sassari: Carlo Delfino, 1998)

Peet, T. Eric, *The Stone and Bronze Ages in Italy and Sicily* (Oxford: Clarendon Press, 1909)

Ruju, Angela Antona and Maria Luisa Ferrares Ceruti, *The Albucciu Nuraghe and Arzachena's Monuments* (Sassari: Carlo Delfino, 1992)

Tusa, S., *La Sicilia della Prehistoria* (Palermo, 1983)

Malta

Bezzina, J. *The Ggantija Temples* (Valletta, n.d.)

Bonanno, Anthony, *Malta: An archaeological paradise* (Valletta: M.J. Publications, 2000)

Evans, J.D., *Malta* (London: Thames & Hudson, 1959)

Evans, J.D., *The Prehistoric Antiquities of the Maltese Islands: A survey* (London: Athlone, 1971)

Micallef, Chris, 'Alignments along the Main Axes at Mnajdra Temples', *Xjendra: Journal of the Malta Chamber of Scientists* (December 2000), vol. 5(1/2), pp. 3–15

Micallef, Paul I., *Mnajdra Prehistoric Temple: A calendar in stone* (Malta: Union Print, 1990)

Mifsud, Anton and Simon, *Dossier Malta: Evidence for the Magdalenian* (Mosta: Proprint, 1997)

Mifsud, Anton and Charles Savona Ventura, eds, *Facets of Maltese Prehistory* (Malta: Prehistoric Society of Malta, 1999)

Mifsud, Anton and Simon Mifsud, Chris Agius Sultana, Charles Savona Ventura, *Malta: Echoes of Plato's island*, 2nd edn (Malta: Prehistoric Society of Malta, 2001)

Parker, R., M. Rubinstein and D. H. Trump, *Malta's Ancient Temples and Ruts* (Tunbridge Wells: Institute for Cultural Research, 1988)

Trump, D.H., *Malta: An archaeological guide* (1972) (Valletta, 2000)

Veen, Veronica and Adrian van der Blom, *The First Maltese: Origins, character and symbolism of the Ghar Dalam culture* (Haarlem: Fia, 1992)

Zammit, Sir Themistocles, *The Prehistoric Temples of Malta and Gozo*, ed. Karl Mayrhofer (Malta: Masterson, 1995)

Index